# The Universal God

Also by James E. Will
and published by
Westminster John Knox Press

*A Christology of Peace*

# The Universal God

*Justice, Love, and Peace*
*in the Global Village*

# James E. Will

Westminster John Knox Press
Louisville, Kentucky

*Book design by Susan Jackson*

*Cover design by Bill Green*

*First edition*

Published by Westminster John Knox Press
Louisville, Kentucky

This book is printed on acid-free paper that meets the American National Standards Institute Z39.48 standard. ∞

PRINTED IN THE UNITED STATES OF AMERICA

94 95 96 97 98 99 00 01 02 03 — 10 9 8 7 6 5 4 3 2 1

**Library of Congress Cataloging-in-Publication Data**

Will, James E., date.
    The universal God : justice, love, and peace in the global village
James E. Will. — 1st ed.
       p.    cm.
    Includes bibliographical references and index.
    ISBN 0-664-25560-4
    1. God.  2. Hermeneutics—Religious aspects—Christianity.
3. Christianity and culture.  4. Christianity and other religions.
5. Christianity and justice.  6. Love—Religious aspects—
Christianity.  7. Peace—Religious aspects—Christianity.
I. Title
BT102.W55  1994
231—dc20                         94-523

# Contents

# Acknowledgments

Grateful acknowledgment is made to the following for the use of copyrighted material:

Continuum Publishing Company, from Hans-Georg Gadamer, *Truth and Method*, second revised edition, edited by Donald G. Marshall and Joel C. Weinsheimer, published by Crossroad, 1989.

The Free Press, a Division of Macmillan Publishing Company, from *Process and Reality*, corrected edition, by Alfred North Whitehead, edited by David Ray Griffin and Donald W. Sherburne. Copyright © 1978 by The Free Press, a Division of Macmillan Publishing Company. Copyright 1929 by Macmillan Publishing Company, renewed 1957 by Evelyn Whitehead.

Alfred A. Knopf, Inc., from *Body and Raiment*, by Eunice Tietjens, copyright 1919 by Alfred A. Knopf, Inc., and renewed 1947 by Floyd Head.

University of California Press, from *Religion and Nothingness*, by Keiji Nishitani, translated and edited by Jan van Bragt, copyright © 1982 Keiji Nishitani.

# Preface

Is there anyone anywhere able to complete alone an interdisciplinary, interreligious, and cross-cultural study? Completing this book has confirmed what I knew as I began: If there are such prodigies, I am not one of them.

I have been privileged, however, to participate in a joint doctoral program committed to interdisciplinary work relating the theological research of Garrett-Evangelical Theological Seminary to a range of academic disciplines in Northwestern University. Whatever competence I have in the "dialogical hermeneutics" I have sought to practice in this study has been developed largely in its student-faculty colloquia during the past fifteen years.

Thus in gratitude to many good colleagues, I dedicate this book to the Graduate Council of Garrett-Evangelical Theological Seminary, with the prayer that their efforts to relate Christian faith to a wide range of human experience and culture will continue to be blessed.

Neither this interdisciplinary, dialogical program nor this book would have been possible, however, without the institutional commitments and intellectual stimulation of the entire community of Garrett-Evangelical Theological Seminary, where I have been privileged to teach for thirty-three years. Early commitments to empower African American and women's ministries, more recently amplified with similar commitments to Asian and Hispanic ministries, with peace and justice for all peoples, have provided formative experiences that are at the root of this study.

Many persons have provided more particular assistance: Sarah Forth, Jeanne Matthews, and Weaver Santaniello have served at various times as research assistants. Many others, notably Hwa Young Chong, Sang Bok

Lee, and Wafiq Wahba, have made significant contributions in seminar and personal discussions. Professor Evan Hazard of Bemidji State University, while "visiting scientist in residence," made helpful suggestions, as did my colleague James Ashbrook, after critically reading earlier portions of the manuscript. George Lucas, Jr., now serving the National Endowment for the Humanities, as well as editor of the SUNY Press series in philosophy, did me the extraordinary service of bringing both his scholarly and editorial competencies to bear in a critical response to the entire manuscript. Jeffries Hamilton, my editor at Westminster John Knox Press, has always been helpful and encouraging. Linda Koops's help has ranged from secretarial service and computer instruction to editorial assistance. I am grateful to all.

I cut my dialogical teeth, so to speak, twenty-five years ago in the Christian-Marxist dialogue and remain grateful to Milan Machovec of Charles University and Josef Hromádka of the Comenius Theological Faculty and their colleagues in Prague for their courageous creativity in those turbulent years. Special opportunity for Jewish-Christian dialogue was afforded while studying and teaching at the Interfaith Academy of Peace in the Ecumenical Institute (Tantur) in Jerusalem in 1986, and I remain grateful for the leadership of Landrum Bolling and William Klassen at that time. My too-little experience in Muslim-Christian dialogue came largely through lecturing and participating in the symposia on "Religious Leaders and Middle East Peace" in 1988 and 1989, sponsored by the American-Arab Affairs Council. The outline of this book was conceived during a sabbatical appointment as guest professor in the University of Zimbabwe in southern Africa for six months in 1989, with its dialogical opportunity to learn something of African (especially Shona) culture and traditional religion. I remain grateful to Dr. Ambrose Moyo and his colleagues for this rare privilege.

To be given a place in so great a cloud of witnesses has enabled whatever witness this book carries to God's creative and redemptive love for the whole creation.

# Introduction

The central and, in a way, the only issue of this book is God: God as our existential ultimate concern and the ontological ultimate reality. The acknowledged context, however, is the ambiguities and uncertainties of an increasingly complex life-world. The polar dangers recognized from the outset are the religious "heaviness" of prereflective certainty and the academic "lightness" of pluralistic reflective options. The challenge, therefore, is to think, write, and pray as both a faithful believer and philosophical theologian in a religiously and culturally pluralistic world rapidly becoming a global village. The question is whether the pluralistic primal religious experiences of finite persons may be reconciled with the universality of our modern and postmodern mentalities. The movement toward an answer is considered a small contribution to an open-ended dialogical process.

The scope of such issues is so comprehensive that some fear any attempt to comprehend them portends a plunge into an incomprehensible abyss. Even those of us who persevere do so with both fear and fascination. The fascination is the lure to become more clear and concrete as we articulate what it means to believe that one God is the Creator and Redeemer of the whole world's vast array of cults and cultures. The fear is losing our focus in faith and simplicity of spirit because so complex a reality is beyond our limited powers to comprehend.

The difficulty of maintaining spiritual integrity while seeking a conceptual synthesis of complex experience was already well-expressed seventy years ago and has become increasingly true for those who venture down our world's cross-cultural and interreligious roads:

> I have too many selves to know the one.
> In too complex a schooling was I bred,

1

> Child of too many cities who have gone
> Down all bright cross-roads of the world's desires,
> And at too many altars bowed my head
> To light too many fires.[1]

If that could already be the struggle of a sensitive spirit whose Eurocentric life-world was just beginning to deconstruct after World War I, how much more is it true in our diverse and conflicted global life-world at the end of the twentieth century. Few can escape some sense of the immense difficulty of integrating the altars of our world into a meaningful perspective on the whole. Most of the readers, like the author, of this book may be Euro-Americans and remain Judeo-Christians, but we now know how culturally conditioned and religiously relative are the ways we have expressed our belief in the God who has "created heaven and earth." We recognize that the universal God, who may be conceived only onto-logically, if at all, became our symbolic *Abba* through a concrete salvation history centering in Jesus of Nazareth. Spiritual experience within this formative tradition has grounded and shaped our existence.[2] The christological dimensions of this concrete faith, however, must now be compre-hended within a theocentric model that articulates God's relation to the enlarging whole of our complex world. It is precisely the need to articu-late God's relation to the whole—no matter how complex and even con-flicted we find it to be—that requires resistance to the postmodern, deconstructionist eulogies of chaos and anarchy increasingly found in contemporary literature.

The emergence of a world-historical consciousness during the past few centuries, however, has radically ruptured the Western philosophical and theological traditions that once served to articulate the "universal."[3] Nev-ertheless, if we take our finitude seriously, we must take our particular histories seriously as well. Our ideas are formed, reformed, and trans-formed, perhaps at the limit but also always within the traditions that have formed us. We may seek to enlarge the traditional hermeneutic circle of whole and part within which we articulate any new synthesis, but our whole is never *the* whole. It remains partial and fragmentary. Thus, I want to make what Hans-Georg Gadamer somewhat misleadingly calls "hermeneutic universalism" more genuinely universal by opening it be-yond the Western tradition he interprets:

> Nevertheless, the tradition of metaphysics, and especially of its last great creation, Hegel's speculative dialectic, remains close to us. The task, the "infinite relation," remains. But my way of demonstrating it seeks to free itself from the embrace of the synthetic power of the Hegelian dialectic, even from the "logic" which developed from the dialectic of Plato, and to take its stand in the movement of dialogue, in which word and idea first become what they are.[4]

Is it possible, however, for us Euro-Americans to forge in a universal dialogue fresh ideas that entirely transcend Western systemic structures? If so, I have not found that way. The ideas articulated here may be recognized as falling into the "series of footnotes to Plato" that Alfred North Whitehead claimed to be the safest general characterization of the European philosophical tradition.[5] Indeed, they take their place as an extension of Whitehead's own footnotes to this seminal Western thinker. Like them, I also think that "the actualities constituting the process of the world are [best] conceived as exemplifying the ingression (or 'participation') of other things which constitute the potentialities of definiteness for any actual existence."[6] To understand the world as an internally related organic process, however, one does not have to seek the systemic closure found in either classical Neoplatonism or modern Hegelianism. It is possible to conceive this dialectic as open to ongoing dialogue, thus subsuming any attempt to understand the ontological dialectical process within an ongoing transcultural dialogical process.

The theological conceptual model developed in this discussion may be designated as "the universal relationality of God."[7] It has both continuity with and transcends the Western Christian tradition in which I participate. Though it has some roots in what is sometimes termed the "economic" form of the doctrine of the Trinity, it opens it toward the universal in new ways.

To experience God as relational is not new in religious experience. Many have testified to the compassion, grace, and love in their ultimate experience. Yet the implications of God as Love or loving remain strange to the spirituality and theology of many Western Christians. Many still falter with their traditional concept of the God in whom "there is no shadow caused by turning" before the possibility of conceiving a God who is actually responsive to every human form of self-actualization.[8]

To think of God as relational is also not entirely a new venture for Western Christians, as Trinitarian doctrine indicates. Yet, relational conceptions of God remain surprising, if not shocking, to many contemporary theists. They wonder how the infinite, omnipotent, omniscient, unchanging One may be conceived as related? relational? and thus in some ways relative?[9]

We shall attempt coherently to understand God as universally relational on the basis of comprehensive cultural, scientific, and religious experience. Thus the following chapters address the questions I find most relevant for understanding God's universal relationality: Can the ultimate creative Origin of all being be better understood as relational community rather than infinite substance or subject? Can we conceive the ultimate Logos that is the ground of all symbolic and conceptual meaning more coherently as transculturally related, and thus in some way relative, rather than as transcendentally wholly other and mysteriously one?

If so, then perhaps in our ecumenical and interreligious global village, our universal search for, and fragmentary experience of, various dimensions of redemption may be better interpreted as complementary and relative, rather than exclusive and even conflicting. If we can dialogically approximate universal symbols, shall we not have to understand them relationally because they are related to and relative to all?

Perhaps we can then even approach the multiple political theologies of our era, so variously contextualized by class, ethnicity, gender, and nationality, in a way that recognizes their universal interrelatedness without reducing them imperialistically or abstractly to one perspective or sentimentally to some eclectically reconciled mush. If we can learn to think in this way, will we not have to interpret the righteousness and justice of God as contextually conditioned by a universal relationality?

Religious persons may increasingly learn to articulate, and more importantly to live, a personal and communal spirituality in our diverse concrete communities that enables a universally loving praxis because it participates in the universal relationality of God. It may even prove possible to contribute to a genuinely universal peace in our dangerously conflicted world because we have moved toward a more adequate understanding of God's relation to each and all.

Such are the motives and questions that engender this philosophical theological discussion. The formulation of the questions may prove more important than the tentative form of my, or anyone else's, answers at this nascent stage of cross-cultural and interreligious dialogue. No one is ready to attempt philosophical or theological closure; any answers we provisionally articulate are relative to our limited contextual experience. Yet all who participate must vigorously contribute their carefully formed perspectives, for the issues are too momentous to be addressed with anything less than ultimate concern.[10] I look forward to my tentative formulations being complemented and corrected in an ongoing dialogical process.

Any method for thinking about so complex a set of issues must itself be complex. My method might best be called "dialogical hermeneutics." Hermeneutics because thinking about cross-cultural and interreligious issues requires clarity about our cultural and religious horizons. Increasing clarity about the traditions that have enculturated us enables a better definition of the margins where we meet the culturally and religiously other. Dialogical because the defining of margins may either harden into polemics or open into dialogue. Dialogical hermeneutics may appear redundant to philosophers who know that philosophical hermeneutics dare not become polemical. Unfortunately, not all have this understanding, and even some of us who do, fail sometimes to practice it. Dialogue, however, may be the only choice for those concerned to move traditional horizons toward the universal without losing the variety and richness of personal centeredness in diverse cultures and religions.

The dialogues developed here are less dramatic than Plato's prototype but more so than many forms of philosophical conversation. That is, they imitate neither Plato's dramatic genre where a cast of philosophical personae speak throughout in their own voice, nor the more usual philosophical genre where the author synthesizes all of the others so as to write only in his or her own voice. Whatever unity Platonic dialogues have derives from Plato's Socratic voice really structuring the whole. My philosophical and theological voice, of course, provides whatever conceptual unity the following discussions have. But I have sought not to insinuate any premature unity from only one perspective, whether derived from Plato's Athenian or Gadamer's more inclusively European culture, or my Christian faith. Any such implicit unity must be made to give way to genuine dialogue at the author's and reader's margins.

This method requires more quotation than good literary form usually allows. Cross-cultural, ideological, and interreligious margins are not yet harmonized and perhaps never shall be by any conceptual model. Thus no synthesis into one philosophical or theological voice can make the contribution now necessary. The move toward universality requires the medley of many voices. The price, however, is a book harder to read. I hope it is a price that readers of this discussion will find worth paying.

No stronger contrast to dialogical hermeneutics may be found than the "monological meditation" of Thomas Altizer in his recent *Genesis and Apocalypse*.[11] His all-too-Hegelian notion of the Absolute dialectically actualized in modern Western culture probably requires this monological genre for its articulation. Altizer seeks to express, so as to provide the possibility for his readers to make, an "absolutely solitary judgment."[12] Thus he forgoes "all scholarly citation."[13] Though he wants to understand his reader to be "everybody and everyone,"[14] his "everybody" must already be sufficiently Jewish or Christian to understand that "Israel *alone* is the site of the full advent of a wholly transcendent and eternal voice,"[15] and that "Israel and Israel *alone* is the site of the dawning realization of the forward or evolutionary movement of history."[16]

My margins also are defined by the Judeo-Christian tradition. No one has had a greater influence on the discussions that follow than Jesus; or if that seems too naively presumptuous, then my reception and interpretation of Jesus' gracious influence mediated through a long ecclesial and cultural history. I desire no other spiritual center than I have found in Jesus as the and my Christ, nor do I hope to become anything other than a better Trinitarian theologian. But that center, so far as I can see, requires the resolute effort begun here to open our cultural and theological horizons to the universal. For those centered in and by Christianity, that universal is the gracious Creator and Redeemer manifested in Jesus. But genuine movement toward realizing God as universal requires seeing her grace and truth under many other names.

Some margins of contemporary Christian theology, of course, continue to emerge within modern Euro-American culture. The objectification and alienation of personal and communal life in its scientific and technical rationality, as well as the divisive consequences of its modern hegemonic colonialism require the move toward some form of postmodernism. The discussion with Euro-American confreres found here intends the transformation of our tradition by opening it cross-culturally and interreligiously to a more universal sense of grace and truth. This cannot and does not mean total repudiation of Western cultural and religious traditions, for they obviously continue to have great scientific, technical, economic, and religious power. But it does require vigorous intracultural dialogue for the sake of cross-cultural openness to God's universality.

# 1

# The Spatiotemporal
# Relationality of Creation

## Religion's Cosmological Function

A crucial issue for contemporary faith is God's relation to our world, experienced by all as both cosmos and chaos. The traditional Western, but not only Western, concept is *God as Creator*. But the traditionally associated religious sensibility of our world as a providentially ordered "creation" has become deeply ambiguous, if not altogether lost, especially for many in the Eurocentric cultures where Judaism and Christianity have articulated it. The wasting away of traditions may be part of the narrative of every culture. But the struggle to sustain, revise, or revive this tradition has continued in Western culture since Plato sought to combine the mythopoeic understandings of the Greek gods with his philosophical cosmology,[1] and the authors of Job, interacting with their Middle Eastern wisdom tradition, sought to respond to Egyptian pessimism and Babylonian skepticism with a faith consecrated to a faithful Creator.[2] This long-continued struggle from Plato and the Judeo-Christian scriptures down to the contemporary controversy between fundamentalist "creationism" and Darwinian scientific evolution indicates the classic status of religious faith in God as the Creator of an essentially good world. It belongs to the "essence" of religion, at least in some of its most dynamic and universal forms.

The use of "essence" to understand religion must be put in quotation marks in any contemporary discussion, however, because historians of religion have largely abandoned any attempts at essential definitions of the variegated phenomena they research and analyze. Philosophers and philosophical theologians, however, cannot readily agree that the comprehension of religious phenomena may be left in the disjunctive form of

7

empirical facts. Provisional operational definitions of religion may be heuristically sufficient for the research programs of anthropologists, ethnologists, and historians, and indeed may provide necessary safeguards against any imperious, reductionistic interpretations of concrete religions by monological conceptual systems; but operational definitions do not finally enable the dialogical comprehension that is the heart of human knowing.

Religion has a cosmological function.[3] That is, it provides its believers with a system of significations that order their world into a meaningful "cosmos." Whether prereflexively held in primal experience and preliterate religion or reflected in the developed conceptual and doctrinal systems of Buddhism, Hinduism, Judaism, Christianity, or Islam, this sense of centered and ordered cosmos gives profound meaning to human life in this world. Various forms of positivism, dialectical materialism, evolutionism, or existentialism may dispute or provide alternatives to traditional religious cosmologies, especially in post-Enlightenment Western cultures, but even they thus provide their own kind of testimony to the importance of this cosmological orientation for human existence in this world. The traditional religions of preliterate societies may have little need for a conceptual development of their cosmological orientations because they are never in doubt, but once put in question by dialogical interaction with more secular developed societies, the cosmological problematic becomes also important for them.[4]

The most fundamental issue for almost all religious thought is: Who is God in whom we trust? The primary answer for many religious traditions is: God is the Creator of the heavens and the earth. The basic givenness of our world, the sheer facticity of its being there evokes ever and again the at-first religious and then philosophical issue of why there is something rather than nothing. Recent secular answers in Western culture have ranged from Jean-Paul Sartre's "nausea" before the arbitrary and meaningless thereness of *l'en-soi*,[5] through Bertrand Russell's passionate positivism in accepting his universe,[6] to Albert Einstein's affirmation that "cosmic religious feeling" was the strongest and noblest motive for his research.[7] Many millions of Judeo-Christians continue with Einstein to adore the Creator's wisdom that has filled the earth with riches: "O Lord, how manifold are thy works! In wisdom hast thou made them all; the earth is full of thy riches" (Ps. 104:24, KJV).

The experience of sheer facticity, whether in sensory particulars or primal symbolic forms, is, of course, always an abstraction from the richly textured whole of our total experience. My experience while beginning to write about these issues has ranged from the majestic eastern highlands of Zimbabwe to the more honky-tonk ambience of Chicago's Division Street. The "thatness" of our world is sometimes framed by experiences like the gorgeous colors of Msasa trees on southern African mountains in the spring, and at other times by the often artless graffiti in Chicago's subways. The majestic height of waterfalls in the sublimity of nature's beauty sometimes shapes our awe of being, while at other times our memories of nature's sublimity are shaded and reshaped by the in some ways similarly fascinating order of urban technology, despite the disorder of closely packed human passions.

The point is that we respond variously to the "whatness" of our life-world along a vast continuum of human experience. Most human beings throughout history, responding to the terror and sublimity of natural structures, have affirmed their world as a divine creation.[8] What is at first an expression of primal experience, then articulated as revealed truth in holy scriptures and sacred traditions, becomes finally the argued conclusion of philosophical theologians. It may be, and has been, variously articulated in the theisms of Judaism, Christianity, and Islam, and the pantheisms of Vedanta Hinduism, Mahayana Buddhism, classical Neoplatonism, and nineteenth-century European idealism; but all are human attempts to understand our life-world as caused or grounded, emanating or made, in relation to the ultimate or absolute Being many name God.[9]

The religious metaphor of creation, however, has not always been interpreted, nor is it now readily to be interpreted, with the conceptual model of a beneficent divine order as articulated in theism. Recalling the Babylonian creation myth in the *Enuma Elish* and the Greek mythology of *Prometheus* (the latter more latterly beloved by Karl Marx as he worked out his atheistic Hegelian philosophy in Berlin) remind us early and late that our experience of natural limit and fear of natural disorder have led some to fear or even hate the gods and finally to deny God. The recent attempt in neo-orthodox Christian theology to ingraft the traditional understanding of God as transcendent Creator and sovereign Lord onto the modern scientific understanding of the world as a spatiotemporal process has proven unsuccessful. Even Langdon Gilkey, who made a valiant attempt to do so, later had to conclude, "The union of these two world views, one modern and one ancient, proved more difficult than it promised to be; the secular elements warred against the biblical ones, and the result was the break-up on the intellectual level of neo-orthodox theology."[10]

It is just at this point that many, as I do, find their theological existence. We may not agree with Thomas Altizer's radical assertion, "To exist in our time is to exist in a chaos freed of every semblance of cosmological meaning or order."[11] But neither can we reconstruct a traditional theistic cosmology simply on hermeneutical foundations, because neither the biblical accounts nor the traditional doctrinal formulations are any longer scientifically tenable. The possible good consequence of suffering the ambiguities of this kind of theological existence arises from the felt necessity of opening ourselves to a wider range of common human experience and the conceptual models to interpret it. Like Sisyphus, we have the privilege of trying again, without succumbing to his (and Camus's) myth that all such creative efforts are necessarily futile.

## A Hermeneutical Perspective on a
## Cosmology of Spatiotemporal Relationality

The attempt to understand the universal relationality of God requires a cosmology of the spatiotemporal relationality of creation. This is in part a hermeneutical process for Judeo-Christian theologians because the biblical articulation of the metaphor of creation with the conceptual model of a beneficent divine order was affected from the beginning by Hebraic primal historical experience. All of the Abrahamic religions—Judaism, Christianity, and Islam—interpreted their creation mythology within a prophetically interpreted historical experience of human salvation.

The primal Hebraic experience of liberation and covenanted blessing within an ambiguous historical and natural process is what enabled their theological affirmation of the ultimate goodness of the Creator and creation. Their categorical affirmation of creation derived from their experience of a partial historical fulfillment of what may be called the "Abrahamic promise." Their attitude toward their ambiguous cosmos was shaped and reshaped by the fragmentarily fulfilled promise of an "already but not yet" future. That is, the Hebrew (*Habiru*) people interpreted their liberation from Egyptian slavery, the possibility of developing a relatively secure and orderly existence in Palestine, and the emergence of relative political stability through the Davidic royal house as fulfillment of divine promises in their history.

Gerhard von Rad has interpreted and evaluated the connection that Israel made between creation and saving history as a "great achievement."[12] It came to expression only late in their canonical literature, mainly in Second Isaiah, the Priestly document, and a few psalms, because it took time for their faith to articulate its implied cosmology in proper relation to the primal confessional formulae expressing their sense of saving history. This soteriological understanding of creation underlies the more familiar creation stories in the book of Genesis, where they are incorporated within an interpretation of history leading to the call of, and promise to, Abraham—a promise partially fulfilled in the ambiguous history of Israel. The fact that even God's creation of the cosmos is interpreted as a work within time was given special emphasis in the Priestly account in Genesis, where creation is presented as a temporal sequence, capable of being marked out in "days."

Von Rad finds that Israel's historical, soteriological understanding of creation differs from the similar Greek concept of "cosmos" because Israel's world was experienced much more as interacting "events" than as static or structured "being." As von Rad puts it:

> Israel did not see the world as an ordered organism in repose, for on the one hand she saw Jehovah as much more directly at work in all that goes on in the world, and on the other, man on his side recognized that he had a share in this, because he continually determined the reactions of the world about him by his actions, whether good or bad.[13]

Another dynamic dimension in Israel's theology of creation was provided by their interpretation of the chaos mythology they shared with Babylonian and Canaanite cultures, in which they interpreted the Creator as having to struggle against the powers of chaos, often symbolized as a great dragon or sea monster.[14] The conceptual consequence was a dynamic understanding of saving history requiring human work within a created but ambiguous cosmos.

Abraham Joshua Heschel, the distinguished philosopher of Judaism, made much the same point but with a stronger antimetaphysical twist:

> The Bible points to a way of understanding the world from the point of view of God. It does not deal with *being as being* but with *being as creation*. Its concern is not with ontology or *metaphysics* but with history and *meta-history*; its concern is with time rather than space.[15]

Similar to the neo-orthodox Christian theology of his period, Heschel was concerned to stress the differences between biblical religion and science or metaphysics. The philosophical concern to discern, analyze, and explain the essence of things or the principles of being is sharply contrasted with biblical religion. Like von Rad, he stresses that "biblical religion starts with events."[16] What he apparently fails to consider is that a philosophical understanding of the cosmos might join, or at least approximate, this biblical perspective in seeking to understand the cosmos as a spatiotemporal process of events. Time need not be conceptually disjoined from space, nor being played off against events. When Rabbi Heschel did consider "process," he was only concerned strongly to contrast it with "event":

> What is the difference between process and event? A process happens regularly, following a relatively permanent pattern; an event is extraordinary, irregular. A process may be continuous, steady, uniform; events happen suddenly, intermittently, occasionally.[17]

The qualifiers he uses in this characterization of process, however, should indicate to those who take this contrast too disjunctively that a process of events can be coherently conceived. Processes have a *"relatively* permanent pattern" and "*may* be" (not need be) continuous and uniform. Which is to say that processes may have a relatively variant pattern and may allow for relatively creative freedom.

The concern to interpret reality so as to allow for the creative freedom of God and humanity deeply motivates Heschel and many other religious people, and it moves many to make his kind of conceptual disjunctions. Heschel properly criticizes that way of conceiving cosmic order that excludes events grounded in free decision. Thus he argues, "Countless relations that determine our life in history are neither known nor predictable."[18] A metaphysics that interprets the spatiotemporal relationality of creation, however, would not restrict the truth of this assertion to history in contrast to nature. That is, the whole cosmos may be interpreted as having a historical, relational character, within which our analogous human history emerges and develops. In this perspective, the conceptual disjunctions he makes are no longer necessary.

This analysis of the relation of history to creation of an eminent Christian scholar of the Hebrew Scriptures and an equally eminent Jewish philosopher of religion shows the hermeneutical continuity of a relational cosmology with the Judeo-Christian tradition. Adherents of the biblical tradition, however, shall have to develop a more coherent cosmology of the spatiotemporal relationality of creation, whose relative order is an ever new synthesis of the interaction of finitely free events in relation with the universal and everlasting freedom and relationality of God. The relative order and disorder of such a relational process must be interpreted within the open-ended future, which many religious people refer to the gracious freedom of God as relativized and contextualized by the finite freedom of humanity.

## The Crisis of the Traditional Hermeneutics of Creation

The creation mythology and theology of the Abrahamic religions—Judaism, Christianity, and Islam—provide the continuing, though sometimes eroding, basis of most Euro-American, Middle Eastern, North African, and increasingly all of Africa's affirmation of the goodness of the created order. The limits and ambiguities of human experience, focused upon by other mythologies, contemporary existentialists, and a variety of atheists, are not unknown or ignored but continue to be eschatologically interpreted as requiring future resolution.

The erosion of this tradition is far more apparent in Judeo-Christian cultures, however, than in Islamic societies, at least to the inexpert eye of Christian theologians like me. Christians engaged in dialogue with contemporary Muslims report:

In the struggle to create modern societies, Muslims are not content to accept without criticism and alteration the Western ideologies. . . . In the totality of their lives, Muslims must first be faithful to God, because Islam is a total way of life. . . . The challenge of secularism is for Muslims more than a matter of social values and mores. It is a question of God's Lordship over the world. To the Muslim ear, Western ideologies seem to be saying that life can be lived without God. . . . Muslims are understandably cautious about accepting such Western ideas.[19]

The creation of modern societies in Judeo-Christian cultures, however, has spawned a secular ideology that precisely disputes God's Lordship over the world. Christians may not seek to instruct Muslims how they should understand their central tenet of "submission to the will of Allah," but they can share with them what wisdom may accrue from the struggle to understand God as Lord. Those struggles, in their cosmological dimension, derive from the necessity of relating our understanding of an eschatologically oriented creation to the scientific understanding of an evolutionary natural process. And they derive in their historical dimension largely from the excesses of the associated ideology of inevitable social progress. In my judgment, all religious people must come to terms with the scientifically demonstrated theory of evolution, while critically analyzing the ambiguities in the notion of social progress and forthrightly denying the notion of its inevitability.

The experience and reflection of Charles Darwin has been central to this discussion for more than a century. His arguments in *The Descent of Man* relate to both the natural and historical points above. Though Darwin recognized that human rationality and morality exceed that of all other species, he found the gulf between human beings and other animals not so great as many Christians and humanists had supposed. His biographer John Bowlby interprets why:

Having seen human life in the raw in South America, not only the rude existence of the Indians of Tierra del Fuego, but also the savagery of the colonizing whites, he thinks it easy to overrate both the mental powers and, especially, the moral dispositions of the human species. In a similar way, he thinks there is a marked tendency to underestimate the intelligence and socially co-operative behavior of other species.[20]

Biographer Bowlby also comments, "These are lessons, I believe, that a century later many have still to learn." I think he is correct, while I also share the misgivings and concern of Darwin's religiously devout wife, who wrote in a letter while reading the proofs of *The Descent of Man*: "I think it will be very interesting, but that I shall dislike it very much as again putting God further off."[21] But perhaps it shall prove possible, as we shall see, to learn Darwin's lessons while understanding God as very close.

## The Truth of Evolution

A cosmology of spatiotemporal relationality constituted by the finite freedom of internally related events within the universal relationality of God may, and I think must, include the notion of evolutionary change. The historical fulcrum of this religious and cultural struggle in Euro-America, and increasingly for much of the rest of the world affected by its science, was the Darwinian demonstration of biological evolution. The associated archaeological and paleontological evidence for the millennia-long processes of natural and cultural development cannot finally be denied by any creationist theology.[22] This, of course, does not imply that one must also accept a positivist view of science or a purely naturalistic view of the origins of being. An inductivist theory of science that reduces it to hard fact finding is clearly illusory, as practicing scientists know. The problem situation in any scientific research is always structured with meaning by its linguistic and conceptual context. Science is always an interpretive act, like all human knowledge.[23] Therefore, it cannot be ruled out a priori that scientists using the creationist paradigm may also make a contribution to our understanding of the origin and development of life.[24] But it is no longer possible to rule out the cumulative evidence supporting the evolutionary understanding of being as many creationists do.

Langdon Gilkey, in examining the "religious dimensions in science," makes the point that our capacity to make judgments relating theory to fact is "a surprise and a wonder":

> For here the destructive relativity that threatens all finite judgments, endlessly qualified by unknown conditions, is overcome and broken by the achievement of even probable truths. . . . Thus the undoubted fact of judgments is evidence of the experience of the conquest of ultimate relativity in which no finite truth could be possible at all. And this in turn indicates an apprehension that through our transient and relative experience of the fulfillment of these conditions, we have touched "what is" at some point.[25]

All cannot remain tentative in human knowing, else we could not even judge that this is the case. Even the skeptic knows that he knows. We cannot pretend that we do not know what we now know. The rational consciousness of human beings is grounded in the deep intuition that we have veridical knowledge even in judgments that are recognized to be proximate and relative. Such a basic faith in rationality guides all human science, philosophy, and theology. This religious dimension of contemporary rationality, I am convinced, requires and enables us to affirm the truth discerned in evolution: In the relativity of our interactive relational cosmos we have touched the ultimately religious truth of the universal relationality of God.

We touch this religious truth, however, only as we become finitely creative in interaction with the world God has created and is creating. The young Isaac Newton did not simply observe an apple fall in his mother's garden in 1665. Many before him had made this observation. Nor did he simply think that the apple was drawn to earth by gravity. Others had also thought this before him. What creatively struck Newton was the novel thought that the same force that reached to the top of the tree might reach to the moon to hold it in its orbit. Calculating the force from the earth to the moon, and comparing it to the known force of gravity at tree height, he found that the forces agreed. J. Bronowski, to whom I owe this recounting of Newton's story, then generalizes it to comprehend the creative progress of science as it has discerned the relational variety in unity of our cosmos:

> The progress of science is the discovery at each step of a new order which gives unity to what had long seemed unlike. Faraday did this when he closed the link between electricity and magnetism. Clerk Maxwell did it when he linked both with light. Einstein linked time with space, mass with energy, and the path of light past the sun with the flight of a bullet; and spent his dying years in trying to add to these likenesses another, which would find a single imaginative order between the equations of Clerk Maxwell and his own geometry of gravitation.[26]

Modern science from Newton to Darwin and beyond may be theologically interpreted as the fruit of our human creative interaction with a universe that is open to our comprehension because its variety in unity is an expression of the universal relationality of God with us. Alfred North Whitehead made a similar point in his study of the medieval foundations of modern science in his *Science and the Modern World*. A major point in the first of his Lowell Lectures was that modern science shares an "instinctive" faith in order, derived from faith in God, that grounds the mind-world correlation on which its whole enterprise rests: The human mind and the natural world ultimately reflect shared principles of organization; they cannot be utterly unlike and distinct if science is possible.

## The Inadequacy of Patristic and Medieval Conceptual Models

Whatever conflict we may experience between the religious doctrine of creation as expressed in the soteriologically interpreted cosmogonic myths of the Bible and contemporary scientific theories is not an essential contradiction. This conflict is primarily a consequence of the inadequate conceptual models developed by patristic and medieval Christian theologians in Greco-Roman culture to interpret the biblical mythology of the

Creator and creation. Patristic theology's attempt to interpret the origin of all being with the Paramenidean and Neoplatonic concept of *ousia* and the medieval interpretations of the Aristotelian concept of *substantia* left the church with a static interpretation of creation. The being of the Creator was understood as absolute Substance whose perfect eternal form could suffer no change, and creation was interpreted as a nontemporal act of the eternal Creator.[27] The physical structures and biological species of creation consequently were interpreted as eternal and unchanging. To think that creatures might affect the basic structure of God's design or alter the substantial forms that had brought order to primeval chaos was considered tantamount to denying God's eternal omniscience and omnipotence.[28] Created forms might be, and were thought to have been, corrupted because of the "fall" of creation, but no finite interaction of mere creatures could help move creation toward the eschatological fulfillment first discerned in the promise of Abrahamic religion.

By the time modern science, as it was articulated by Charles Darwin, confronted this doctrine in the nineteenth century, it had been adapted to the more functional and pragmatic perspectives of an industrializing Europe. William Paley was the most influential theologian when Darwin studied theology in Cambridge with an early intention to become an Anglican priest. Darwin read Paley's *Natural Theology*, which argued that just as men were designing watches to tell time and telescopes to extend their sight, so the eternal God had more magnificently designed the eye to see, just as he had designed all else for his eternal and perfect purposes.[29] God's omnipotence was now understood to be working through the laws of nature that God had ordained, but these natural laws were conceived as uniform and regular in the mechanistic mode of eighteenth-century sciences.[30] A clear continuity and congruence with the patristic and medieval understanding of the eternal and unchanging structures of creation was thus maintained in Paley's more scientific arguments from design.

Darwin learned these arguments from design well, but what they omitted from his later scientific point of view was the causally efficacious interaction of finite entities affecting the forms of creation. Darwin did not so much disprove the argument from design as to transmute it from a static model of eternal order to a temporal model of emerging order. Indeed, he sometimes wrote in ways that seem continuous with what he had learned from Paley:

> To my mind it accords better with what we know of the laws impressed on matter by the Creator, that the production and extinction of the past and present inhabitants of the world should have been due to secondary causes. . . . There is grandeur in this view of life, with its several pow-

ers, having been originally breathed by the Creator into a few forms or into one; and that, whilst this planet has gone cycling on according to the fixed laws of gravity, from so simple a beginning endless forms most beautiful and most wonderful have been, and are being, evolved.[31]

Yet Darwin was never quite sure, at this nascent stage of evolutionary thought, how to understand the relation of God as Creator to the process he was coming to understand scientifically.[32] This was in part because he interpreted the darker side of nature in the struggle for survival with analogies learned from Thomas Malthus and Adam Smith.

What is now clear, however, is that when Darwin began the definitive demonstration of the correlation of changes in the environment to the adaptive changes in biological species, he effectively began the destruction of the classical conceptual model for creation theology. The forms of creation could no longer be understood as eternal and perfect but now must be conceived as the ongoing and open-ended result of an interacting spatiotemporal process. My basic theological contention is that this conceptual model, despite theology's long struggle with it, is more analogous to the biblical model of creation interpreted by the Abrahamic eschatological promise than is the static Greco-Roman model worked out when Christendom was primarily interested in stability. This new theological interpretation, however, requires a relational understanding of God's creativity that understands it as enabling and responding to the finite creativity of other entities in our universe. It is with this relational understanding, rather than with a traditional but less biblical theism, that Christianity should participate in the cosmological dimensions of our world's growing interreligious dialogue. God understood as the universally relational Creator of, and in, our spatiotemporally related universe will provide new openings for interreligious and cross-cultural dialogue, especially with Asian religions.

## The Fallacy of Inevitable Progress

Unfortunately, other cultural developments associated with cosmological evolutionary theories have emerged in recent Euro-American history to block such creative revision of Judeo-Christian theology and to inhibit such dialogue, especially in third world colonized cultures. The notion of emergent order in a relational universe has been rendered at least as problematic by the excesses of its proponents as by the rejection and resistance of its conservative opponents.[33] Nothing has made the notion of process more suspect than the ideology of progress covering the economic, political, and cultural aggression of Euro-American societies.

Darwinian evolutionary theory also provided the scientific fulcrum when European culture tipped toward its peculiarly modern form of historical optimism defined as inevitable progress—both in the social Darwinism of Herbert Spencer and the dialectical revolutionary ideology of Karl Marx. One of the fascinating ironies that I find instructive for contemporary culture is that these two philosophers are buried across from each other in London's Highgate cemetery. I think it high time that the destructive aspects of both of their ideologies also be buried through fundamental revisions of the paradigms inherited from both. The theological and cultural danger, however, is that the eschatological understanding that enabled the affirmation of the basic goodness of creation can also be swept away with the denouement of the excessive ideology of inevitable progress.

Those who early decided that historical evolution was a substitute for God as Creator turned to their own humanity as the leading edge of evolution with Victorian, Napoleonic, Hohenzollern, and other forms of imperious optimism; though a better metaphor in the light of these destructive imperialisms might be as the cutting edge of evolution. Evolutionary optimism drove their industrializing and colonizing energies in many creative—but alas, also destructive—ways. North America became the model of what European colonization and industrialization could achieve on a "virgin" continent.[34] The U.S.A. became for many, and continues to be for some, the realized dream of Europe, that now awaits the "awakening" of Africa and Asia for its realization there. The growth of technology, the success of industrialization, and the triumphs of colonial expansion, interpreted through the model of biological evolution, created an ideology of progress in eighteenth- and nineteenth-century Europe that could not, and should not, be sustained in our twentieth and twenty-first centuries.

The European time of troubles in the twentieth century, framed by its second "thirty years war" from 1914 to 1945, a worldwide economic depression, decolonizing wars of national liberation, the ecological consequences of industrialization, and seeding the earth with thirty thousand nuclear warheads during forty years of cold war has burst the ideological bubble of inevitable progress. We are well rid of its justifications of present evils for the sake of promised utopias, whether in their radically revolutionary Marxist, or manifest destiny colonialist, or trickle-down capitalist forms. The related danger, however, is the tipping of our cultural and theological fulcrum back to earlier static models to recover and justify some *status quo ante*.

The theological correction of any residual evolutionary optimism in our cultural context is necessary because it lacks any sufficient sense of the divine transcendence that had been so carefully formulated in classical theology. There was little sense of the proper limits on technological and industrial transformations of natural structures until the ecological consequences became so blatant as to require reluctant attention. There was minimal sense of the moral and social limits placed on personal and national ambitions until economic depressions and world wars required attention to universal human rights and their correlated duties. We have all too slowly learned the existential consequences of our self-definition as the leading edge of evolution while a growing anomie undermines the fabric of human relations in families, communities, nations, and world.

## The Creativity of God

The reexperience of limit through the experienced consequences of the violation of limits, however, does not necessarily lead to the reaccepting of limit in the transcendent Wisdom of the Creator. It can just as well lead to cultural decline and personal despair, and already has as some forms of Western existentialism and deconstructionism reveal. Existentialism may raise again, as Paul Tillich taught us,[35] the questions growing out of alienated being and demonic processes for religious revelation to answer; but it also has articulated alternative atheistic responses to the human anxiety, ontological nausea, and metaphysical rebellion in contemporary Western culture.

Thus we must articulate a conceptual model of the Creator's transcendence that more adequately expresses God's relation to a causally efficacious, interactive, spatiotemporal process. Hermeneutically, this may be a revisionist interpretation of the Abrahamic orientation that primally related the biblical understanding of the Creator to historical process and eschatological promise. Cosmologically, it shall require a more radical revision of the classical tradition so that the Creator's internal relation to, and consequent relativity within, the spatiotemporal process may be coherently interpreted. Theologically, it must contribute to an understanding of the universal relationality of God that undergirds and guides participation in interreligious dialogue across barriers of class, ethnicity, gender, and race.

The crucial category that needs careful articulation is creativity. The traditional doctrine of *creatio ex nihilo* sought to understand God's creativity as absolute. God's creativity was conceived as unconditioned, that is, unaffected by any relation. To interpret humanity's sense of creatureliness before a Creator so conceived requires the denial of creativity in finite persons. Whatever creativity a finite being exercises, if any, is the effect of God's creativity upon and in him or her. To receive revelation from such a God must be interpreted as absolute truth, and to be sent into one's world to share truth so conceived may not be accomplished dialogically. It may be done graciously, but such grace is always tinged and tainted by some form of imperious condescension, perhaps best symbolized in the blessing

of an ecclesial hierarch. Yet even the charismatic witness of any lay believer understood through this conceptual model is finally also tinged
with this imperious form. Even the excellent metaphor of the Asian ecumenical theologian D. T. Niles that evangelism is "one beggar telling
another where to find bread" implies that bread may not be universally
found through the creativity exercised in many cults and cultures.

The crucial revision of the paradigm of absolute creativity attributed
exclusively to God requires reinterpretation of creativity as a universal
activity efficacious in all events, which does not deny or even reduce the
ultimate creativity of God. There is increasing recognition that the philosophical development that Alfred North Whitehead carried on in public,
to paraphrase Hegel's ironic remark about Schelling, has provided Euro-
American philosophical theologians with the most important impulses
and categories for this necessary revision.[36] Whitehead's project finally
was to articulate a *relativistic cosmology*, which "brings the aesthetic, moral
and religious interests into relation with those concepts of the world
which have their origin in natural science."[37]

Whitehead, as a mathematician and mathematical physicist, began his
reflections with the data of this most hard (that is, mathematically precise)
of all contemporary sciences. Mathematical physics seeks to understand
the unity of the world, which appears so variously in our perceptions,
thoughts, and feelings, through the abstractions of a mathematics that is
supposedly independent of such feelings. Whitehead's problem with this
scientific "prejudice" (in Gadamer's sense) arose because as a philosopher,
he could see no rational basis for according a privileged position to the
abstract paradigms of mathematical physicists over the insights of poets
and theologians. Thus he concluded that our sense of living in an infinite
whole, that is, a universe, is not given in the experience of anyone, including the physicist in his laboratory. Concrete experience is always fragmentary, and our conceptions of unity, order, and wholeness are constructs of
thought that integrate our fragmentary experience and allow it to be
objectively communicated.[38] This could have left him, and those like him
who think in this relativistic way, with only a subjective unity constructed
from a fragmentary experience by a transcendent ego. But then a serious
question becomes persistent: Shall we be able on this relativistic basis to
comprehend and live together in a transindividual world, to say nothing
of a transcultural and interreligious one? Or is there an ontological coherence in the *known* that enables us to live and to communicate in a cosmos
that is more than an epistemological construct in the thought of the
*knower*?

Whitehead saw that these are the questions that religious experience
and thought addresses. Religion enhances both self-experience and
world-experience. Religion is both, in Whitehead's terms, "what the indi-

vidual does with his own solitariness" and "world-loyalty."[39] Religious experience and thought abstracts from the immediate needs of the body and finally even its social community for the sake of a more inclusive world consciousness, and it issues in not only an intellectual system of reference but a profound sense of world-relatedness and world-loyalty. This religious augmentation of world consciousness increasingly discloses what is held in common among more and more human beings, which Whitehead then sought to understand as a series and nexus of occasions in a common cosmos.

I find Whitehead's interpretation of religion, though stated in a quite different idiom, congruent with the experience and vision of the earliest Christian communities: "For [God] has made known to us in all wisdom and insight the mystery of his will, according to his purpose which he set forth in Christ as a plan for the fullness of time, to unite all things in him, things in heaven and things on earth" (Eph. 1:9–10). The question we face is how this religious vision, engendered in the concrete particularity of personal existence and articulated in one of the religious traditions of our world, may actually contribute nonimperiously to the cosmic unity it intends?

### Whitehead's Understanding of Creativity

Whitehead's reinterpretation of creativity as an ultimate category in a relativistic cosmology provides the most adequate answer to this fundamental question that I now know. Whitehead affirms our finitude while overcoming conceptually the egoism of finitude that religion at its best overcomes existentially. He requires humility before fact while demonstrating that "there are no brute, self-contained matters of fact, capable of being understood apart from interpretation as an element in a system."[40] By relating religion to the conceptual generality of systemic thought, he is able to defuse the insistent particularity of religious emotion and enable its proper work of "stretching individual interest beyond its self-defeating particularity." Whitehead's way of doing this was to fuse "religion and science into one rational scheme of thought"[41] in a modern cosmology.

The crucial religious category, as we have already seen, is *creativity* as it interprets the meaning of Creator, creation, and creature. Creativity in Whitehead's philosophy is also the ultimate category to understand why there are actual entities, why new actual entities arise, and why they are related to each other.[42] He interprets creativity as "the universal of universals characterizing ultimate matter of fact." Creativity is the ultimate metaphysical principle by which the universe as disjunctively many, "creatively advances" to conjunction or concrescence in the novel one. Each one, which Whitehead calls "actual entity" or "actual occasion," is the creative production of novel togetherness. Whitehead's ultimate understanding of the "nature of things" is that the many creatively enter into complex unity, which is summarized in the famous sentence, "The many become one, and are increased by one."[43]

These statements already make obvious that the two other ultimate categories for Whitehead are "one" and "many." Wherever and however we experience any aspect of reality, we must interpret it in both disjunctive and conjunctive terms. There are no particulars that formal logic may deal with as only externally related aggregates. There are no atomic facts discussed in any empirical science that are not constituted by their internal relation to the many. But neither is there an absolute universal as postulated by transcendental idealism that can be what it is apart from internal relation to the disjunctive many. Reality is constituted by the creative, reciprocal relation between the one and the many, whether "one" is understood as God, person, or electron.

The similarity and difference of Whitehead's understanding of creativity to the Christian tradition is illumined by the Swiss philosophical theologian Reto Luzius Fetz in his comparison of Whitehead to Thomas Aquinas. He compares Whitehead's ultimate categories to the scholastic transcendentals that were also understood to pertain to any and all existents and to explain what every existent is.[44] Whitehead's "creativity," like Aristotle's and Thomas's "being," may only be known in its concrete appearance in actual entities. But unlike Thomas, Whitehead postulates creativity as a *new* transcendental because it pertains both to God and to temporal creatures, and not to God alone. Whitehead interprets creativity as internal and intrinsic in every actual entity. Each is self-creating. Whereas for Aquinas only God was *causa sui* (cause of oneself), for Whitehead every actual entity is self-caused. God's primordial nature is the "creature of creativity" in this sense of being creatively self-caused.[45] But all other creatures are analogous as they participate in creativity. They too are creatively self-caused.

The Christian tradition, classically expressed in Thomas Aquinas, reserved the concepts of *creare* (creation) and *creatio* (creativity) only for God. Their univocal meaning pertains only to God, and there are no analogous terms pertaining to other beings. Thomas even denied that secondary causes instituted by God can ever be genuinely creative. Creation is only a radical calling into being that bridges the gap between nothing and something. This is the classical concept of *creatio ex nihilo* (creation out of nothing).[46] Whitehead denied the classical limiting of creativity to the solitary act of God. All beings are creative, and the creativity of each is conditioned by internal relations to the creativity of the many others. In this sense, Whitehead can affirm, "Each task of creation is a social effort, employing the whole universe."[47] Even God's creativity must be seen as conditioned by the creativity exercised by all other actual entities in the cosmos.

It is clear that the major difference between classical theology and Whitehead's philosophy is the recognition and affirmation of freedom for each individual being/actual entity. There is no efficient causality in Whitehead's conception of the universe that is exercised by any preceding other or Other, nor is there any formal or final/teleological causality exercised even by God, that can reduce the creature's free and creative self-causality to nothing. Another way of expressing the same principle is to say that novelty is actualized in creation by both the creativity of God and all others. Both Thomas Aquinas and Whitehead affirm creativity as the principle of novelty. Novelty for Aquinas, however, was only the newness of existing in contrast to being nothing, while for Whitehead it is the novelty of the self-actualization of new forms of definiteness that heretofore were only pure potentials. That is, novelty is the spatiotemporal actualization by the finite freedom of an actual entity of what had been a pure potential in the primordial nature of God.

## The Relativity of God's Creativity in an Evolutionary Universe

It is the difference in the conception of novelty that brings us back to the necessity of conceiving the cosmic process as evolutionary. Or in Whitehead's terms, of conceiving the spatiotemporal process as a "creative advance" in which "the many become one and are increased by one." Thomas's metaphysics presupposed Aristotle's physics, in which nature does not produce anything genuinely new but only reproduces what is already actual in genera and species. Thus creation was considered formally complete. Creation, of course, continues even for Thomas, else all would fall back into nothingness, but Thomas equates continuous creation with conservation. Whitehead repudiated this conception of a "static morphological universe," substituting the evolutionary concept of the "universe as a creative advance into novelty."[48] Thus novelty is not simply the creation of existence by God's sovereign power but the co-creation of something genuinely new by processes immanent in the world.

This reconception of creativity to coherently account for the emergence of novelty in the cosmos through the finitely free interaction of actual entities in the spatiotemporal process now returns us to our basic issue of the relativity of God's creativity. Has God's creativity been so reduced in this revised, neoclassical metaphysics that religious believers may no longer conceive God as Creator? Perhaps it is needless to point

out that many conservative theists think so. Carl F. H. Henry articulates
the criticism of conservative Christians with great force:

> The God of the Bible is absolutely sovereign and omniscient. He at
> least has the advantage of knowing who he really is, since change and
> process do not apply to the Godhead. The living, self-revealing God is
> eternally self-sufficient, the voluntary creator of the universe and sover-
> eign monarch of all. . . . All other gods, including the God of process
> theology, are either lame or walk backward.[49]

In the light of such challenges, we must see how Whitehead understands the creativity of God as Creator. We have already noted that as a
mathematical physicist and philosopher of science, Whitehead began with
an analysis of natural process. He was not primarily a theologian. Indeed,
for several decades he understood his own religious position to be agnos-
tic, returning to a form of theism, better called panentheism, only after
experiencing the tragedy of World War I. The fact that he came to affirm
the rational necessity of God as Creator from a more naturalistic perspective adds credence in the minds of many to his theological conclusions.
His rejection of any conception of God as a *deus ex machina*, arbitrarily
and incoherently introduced into our understanding of the cosmos, is
widely approved. The reigning mechanistic model of mathematical physics in the eighteenth and nineteenth centuries was epitomized in Laplace's
celebrated response to Napoleon that "he had no need for that [God]
hypothesis." Whitehead was part of the subsequent development of science that transformed and replaced Laplace's mechanistic materialism
with a conceptual model of the interactive relation of energy events in a
four-dimensional spatiotemporal process.

This new philosophy of nature convinced Whitehead of the necessity
of reintroducing the concept of God into cosmology. Toward the end of
his discussion of *Science and the Modern World*, Whitehead comes to the
concept of God by noting, "Aristotle found it necessary to complete his
metaphysics by the introduction of a Prime-Mover—God."[50] With this
comment Whitehead intended to associate his philosophical motive with
Aristotle's, whom he described as the last European metaphysician of
first-rate importance to come to the conception of God "dispassionately."
Whitehead claimed that he too had come to his God concept only to
complete a coherent metaphysical model for contemporary science.
Whitehead was also convinced that Aristotle's concept of God was inadequate for religious purposes, but his criticism of it was primarily directed
to the erroneous physics and associated erroneous cosmology on which it
was based.

Aristotle's conception of God as Prime Mover now had to be replaced
with the concept of God as the "Principle of Concretion."[51] But this dare

not be a *deus ex machina*. Whitehead insisted: "God is not to be treated as an exception to all metaphysical principles, invoked to save their collapse. He is their chief exemplification."[52] Thus not even God can be conceived in the traditional way as an "unchanging subject of change" but must also be conceived as a becoming actual entity. God's "being" also "becomes." We shall return to the relation of being and becoming in God when we interpret God as Trinitarian in chapter 5.

Whitehead found it metaphysically necessary to affirm that there was one unique, everlasting, actual entity who was "the principle of concretion" for all other actual entities. Why? Because it was necessary to account metaphysically for the emergence of novelty in the world. There must be an actual ground for possibilities that have not yet been realized in the temporal process. God for Whitehead is the nontemporal actual entity who completely "envisages" all possibilities and whose appetition for their actualization makes them relevant to the temporal world.

The temporal actualization of new possibility also requires a "principle of limitation" for the particular form of definiteness that is actualized. "Some particular *how* is necessary, and some particularization in the *what* of matter of fact is necessary."[53] Thus the "principle of concretion" is also the "principle of limitation." It is God who provides the "initial aim" for the concrescence (growing together) of the antecedent data from preceding entities and a new possibility into a novel, particular form of definiteness. God's initial aim provides the impetus for the finitely free subjective aim to synthesize the energies received from the many in its past into a unique unity. Without God's initiative, entities in our cosmos would continually reiterate their previous forms before degenerating into chaos.

Whitehead's way of conceiving God as the principle of limitation and concretion remained subject to experience and contextual interpretation in a way that is important for cross-cultural and interreligious dialogue in a scientific age. Whitehead was convinced that "the general principle of empiricism depends upon the doctrine that there is a principle of concretion which is not discoverable by abstract reason." What we may come to know concretely about God's everlasting appetition may be discovered only in experience. Our knowledge of God's will comes only through our experience of the persuasive power of God's ongoing initial aims in human history. Relating this perspective to religious experience and theology, Whitehead observed:

In respect to the interpretation of these experiences, mankind have differed profoundly. He has been named respectively, Jehovah, Allah, Brahma, Father in Heaven, Order of Heaven, First Cause, Supreme Being, Chance. Each name corresponds to a system of thought derived from the experiences of those who have used it.[54]

Whitehead's own system of thought came to comprehend God's creative functions as "the principle of concretion" and the "principle of limitation" in the concept of God's "primordial nature." In this dimension, God "is the unconditioned actuality of conceptual feeling at the base of things; so that, by reason of this primordial actuality, there is an order in the relevance of eternal objects [his final way of designating pure possibilities] to the process of creation."[55] But Whitehead's mature thought later came to see that "there is another side to the nature of God," which he conceived as God's "consequent nature." If God is the chief exemplification of the metaphysical principles for a world of becoming actual entities, constituted by their interactive internal relations, then Whitehead concluded there must be "a reaction of the world on God."

> The completion of God's nature into a fullness of physical feeling is derived from the objectification of the world in God. . . . Thus, analogously to all actual entities, the nature of God is dipolar. He has a primordial nature and a consequent nature. The consequent nature of God is conscious; and it is the realization of the actual world in the unity of his nature, and through the transformation of his wisdom. The primordial nature is conceptual, the consequent nature is the weaving of God's physical feelings upon his primordial concepts.[56]

It is especially Whitehead's understanding that God is not only primordial immanent activity at the base of a process of interrelated events, but God is also affected by the creative self-actualization of these events, that is crucial for our understanding of the universal relationality of God. Only so may God be interpreted as fully related to and interactive with the world. God's guidance of our world through the provision of initial aims may and must then be understood contextually. The relevance of God's creativity is then relative to the various contrasting, and even conflicting, cultural and religious histories that have resulted from the various trajectories of the long processes actualized by the subjective aims of finitely free creatures. God's universal relationality is constituted by God's "weaving" our various experiences and resulting systems of thought into God's own becoming, while transforming them by God's primordial wisdom so that we might be led toward reconciliation without destroying our finite freedom. Only so may our pluralistic world be a cosmos without destroying or devaluing its diversity.

## The Uniqueness of God as Creator
## in a Relational Cosmology

It is clear that this understanding of relativity in God's universal relationality fundamentally revises the understanding of God as sovereign monarch, so important to conservative theologians like Carl F. H. Henry. Whitehead himself stressed the difference because "the doctrine of an aboriginal, eminently real, transcendent creator, at whose fiat the world came into being, and whose imposed will it obeys, is the fallacy which has infused tragedy into the history of Christianity and Mohametanism."[57] Though basically agreeing with Whitehead's judgment, a theology that also understands itself hermeneutically as conditioned by its history of faith must be concerned to discern and conserve its tradition's relative truth, no matter how tragic the historical consequences of its distortion or exaggeration may have been. The issue for Abrahamic faith is the uniqueness of God as Creator. In what way may a universally relational God be understood as transcending Whitehead's formal requirement that God be conceived as the chief exemplification of all metaphysical principles, without thereby becoming a *deus ex machina* invoked to save their collapse?

The first clue to answering this crucial theological question may be found in Whitehead's thought itself. Whitehead conceived God as an Actual Entity analogous to all other actual entities but with certain crucial differences. God's primordial nature is exceptional because it is "unconditioned, atemporal and possible only once."[58] Perhaps more importantly, God was conceived as unique because temporal actual entities are "originated by physical experience," while "God is to be conceived as originated by conceptual experience." Why? I think part of the reason is religious experience. One can therefore think, as Whitehead does, in terms of "the *perfection* of God's subjective aim, derived from the completeness of his primordial nature."[59] One may then religiously affirm the Wisdom of God as the limit of this world's folly and sin, the logos for its growth in wisdom, and the lure for its transformation. And in more classical language, humanity may yet "press on toward the goal for the prize of the upward call of God in Christ Jesus" (Phil. 3:14).

More conservative philosophical theologians, noting the exceptions that Whitehead had to make in his metaphysical principles to conceive God, charge him with incoherence. The implication they emphasize is that no metaphysical system constructed by finite intelligence provides an adequate basis for understanding our God-relation. Even a metaphysician of Whitehead's scope and power, they contend, was reduced to incoherence when trying to bring God into his system. Thus the way is left open for dependence upon God's special revelation through Moses, Jesus, Mohammed, and many other and lesser religious and cult founders. Donald Bloesch, a self-consciously Reformed (Calvinist) theologian, "retorts" to process theology:

> The God of the Bible is not a passionless absolute, but absolute love and holiness. He is God in action, not a God who grows. . . . The

process God is not a God who is sovereign over the world, but a God who can only influence the world by the magnetic attraction of his beauty and love. No wonder that Whitehead describes God as "the poet of the world" rather than its creator.[60]

James Mannoia, a philosopher with a conservative theology, argues more metaphysically to demonstrate the incoherence in Whitehead's panentheistic view of God's interaction with the world. He focuses upon the relation of God's consequent nature to the primordial nature and the relation of both to the world. May God be coherently conceived, in Whitehead's way, as experiencing the world as past because entities really become and perish, and then mediating that past with new possibilities to the world through initial aims for the future? Mannoia objects on two grounds:

> But this version of the divine mediation view reduces Whitehead's entire system to a kind of panentheism, where the whole world is nothing more than an aspect or extension of God's own experience. That not only makes the system inadequate to express most Christian theologies, but it also reveals a fatal internal incoherence. Such a mode of divine interaction with the world cannot, as Eslick puts it, "be subject to the categoreal descriptions of *Process and Reality*." Eslick's point is that if the basis for God's privileged interaction with the world is his everlastingness, which in turn derives from His unique eternal incompletion, then this seems inconsistent with Whitehead's claim that God is not an exception to the metaphysic but its chief exemplification.[61]

### The Coherence of Panentheism

The criticisms of theologians like Bloesch and philosophers like Mannoia focus issues crucial to the reconception of God in terms of universal relationality. Is the revision of theism into panentheism a "reduction" that must be repudiated in order to adequately articulate God's power as Creator? Is the inadequacy of this reduction apparent in the incoherence of even Whitehead's metaphysics? It is clear, despite Mannoia, that philosophical theologians who have elaborated Whitehead's intuitions and preliminary formulations accept "panentheism" and evaluate it as gain rather than loss. They reject both the traditional theism that conceives God as solely independent and noninclusive of the world, and traditional pantheism that views God as identical with the cosmos. Charles Hartshorne affirms a more dialectical view that mediates these two polarized interpretations of God's relation to the world: " 'Panentheism' is an appropriate term for the view that deity is in some real aspect distinguishable from and independent of any and all relative items, and yet, taken as an actual whole, includes all relative items."[62]

The "actual whole" in Hartshorne's terminology is God as "Actual Entity" as conceived by Whitehead. The inclusion of all relative items is in that pole of God's becoming that Whitehead termed "consequent." The independent pole, distinguishable from what is included relatively, is God's "primordial nature." To conceive God as dipolar in Whitehead's way allows religious persons to conceive God pantheistically as both universal and even absolute in some dimensions, while being internally related, relative, and relevant to the world in other dimensions.

But can such panentheism be conceived coherently? Does the religious motive that affirms the atemporal, perfect envisagement of all possibility in God's primordial nature and the everlasting, unending concrescence of God's consequent nature make a naturalistic metaphysics like Whitehead's incoherent? Can we affirm the eternal Wisdom of God as the good limit to the hubris in humanity's seeing itself as the leading edge of evolution, while continuing to see our finite selves as limited co-creators of an emerging world process? May we continue to relate psychological, social, economic, and political processes to our understanding of spirituality, as we shall attempt in succeeding chapters? Can we continue to insist that criteria for moral action be conditioned by pragmatic sensitivity as to how they actually work in the course of events? Must we begin to realize that our fuller knowledge of God requires our dialogical openness to God's relation with others in quite different cultures and religious traditions? Or is all of this premised on an incoherent attempt to postulate God's internal relation to the spatiotemporal processes of what we believe is a good cosmos because it is ultimately God's creation, yet dare to think we may help co-create?

It is clear that religious persons who conceive God as the Creator of an essentially good cosmos, however we may see it as incomplete and distorted, must affirm God as at least in some ways infinite, universal, wise, and effectively powerful. Whitehead metaphysically accommodated this theological conception by interpreting God as the "mirror image of all the others (actual entities) in order to account for the power of possibilities."[63] Whereas all finite actual entities begin from the physical pole of energies received from previous actual occasions, the dynamics are reversed in God, who alone begins from the mental pole, conceived as God's primordial nature. Finite actual entities move toward unifying the energies received from others in their self-actualization, while God's becoming begins with a primordial unity everlastingly self-actualized. Human temporal becoming moves toward satisfaction; God begins with the satisfaction in which all possibilities are everlastingly unified in harmony and beauty. God's appetition, or "subjective aim," may then be conceived as the progressive actualization of these infinite possibilities, or "eternal objects," in the spatiotemporal process and God's consequent nature.

The whole is the everlasting concrescence of God but not conceived pantheistically as in some Eastern religions and Western absolute idealism. God is rather conceived pan*en*theistically as dependent upon and relative to the actualization of possibilities in the self-actualization of finitely free actual entities. This means that *relationality* is as essential in God as infinity and universality, and essentially qualifies God's power as *interactive*. That is, God has the infinite power both of acting and being acted upon. The rational coherence of this concept of God must therefore allow for the more ambiguous metaphorical and dialectical coherence of relationality.

Theism as a conceptual model cannot accommodate the ambiguity of relationality, and thus its proponents find Whitehead's panentheistic understanding of God incoherent. As Mannoia rightly says, "A theistic approach requires that God has a status and a way of relating to the world that are different from anything else in a system."[64] He especially objects as a theist to the ambiguity he finds in Whitehead's understanding of how the givenness of the past is mediated to the present. He notes that Whitehead affirms the finitude of all temporal actual entities: They become and perish; yet they remain as real potential and efficient cause for present actual occasions. Purely naturalistic metaphysics, he claims, sees the past as providing its own reason for being available to the present. Theistic metaphysics, on the other hand, appeals to God as providing that reason. Naturalistic metaphysics fails if actual entities really perish in the temporal process. How can something be dead but not gone? Whitehead, in Mannoia's judgment, chose the theistic alternative but at the cost of incoherence. He sees him as no longer talking about causal objectification in a spatiotemporal process: "If appeal is made to God to mediate all causal interaction, then God is an exception to the metaphysics and again incoherence is introduced; not to mention panentheism."[65]

When Whitehead affirms that "the world is felt in a union of immediacy" and that everlastingness in God means "combining creative advances with the retention of mutual immediacy,"[66] Mannoia thinks he has fallen into metaphysical incoherence. But in fact Whitehead had developed a dialectical understanding of the mediation of the past to the present, which Mannoia had left bifurcated into "natural" and "theistic." The past for Whitehead is "naturalistically" received and mediated through the prehensions of every present event, but it is uniquely received and mediated in God's everlasting concrescence, as God weaves all the values attained in the subjective satisfactions of every past entity ino the everlasting harmony made possible by God's primordial nature.

To mention and affirm panentheism, contra Mannoia, is just the point. Whitehead's metaphysical construct was completed only in the articulation of God's consequent nature. The coherence of the primordial and consequent, or mental and physical, poles of God's concrescence requires the everlastingness of the consequent pole. If God's being is an everlasting concrescence, then what is "causal objectification" in finite experience must be conceived as "causal subjectification" in God. This does not mean, to use Mannoia's language cited above, that the whole world is nothing more than an aspect of God's experience. This is to confuse panentheism with pantheism. The world is what it is through its own finitely free self-actualization in response to God's initial aims, and it becomes *also* an aspect of God's infinite and everlasting experience.

Our finitude requires us to abstract and eliminate from the past if we are to be able to synthesize in a new and limited unity the myriad energies that affect us. In eliminating, we objectify. But because God begins with the eternal unity of all possibilities, God can feel the entire subjective unity of all others. The whole world then is received, transformed, and mediated *in* God. God feels (Whitehead preferred "prehends") the entire concrescence of the actual entities in the consequent nature, relates them harmoniously to new possibilities in the primordial nature, and mediates them to the world as causal efficacy through initial aims, for the ongoing world process.

It is true that Whitehead developed his concept of God's consequent nature only late in the articulation of his metaphysics. He began, as we have seen, with a naturalistic metaphysics to interpret modern science's understanding of the spatiotemporal process. Thus he did not fully articulate the implications of the more theological dimensions of his thought. But once these were further elaborated by philosophical theologians, the coherence of his panentheistic vision became clear. I think we must agree with Marjorie Suchocki:

> This is not a violation of the metaphysics; it simply follows from the reversal of the polar dynamics. . . . Finite occasions end in definiteness, thus allowing the transmission of energy; God "begins" in the definiteness of the primordial vision, so that God's transitional creativity is copresent with God's concrescent creativity.[67]

The coherence of this vision becomes clearer, however, when we can differentiate its dialectical logic from the formal and transcendental logics more widely used in our scientific culture. Formal logic as the logic of external relations is a useful instrument especially for the sciences. Transcendental logic, developed by Kant and Husserl, responded to the inadequacy of the formal logic of objectivist science by articulating a logic of internal relations in the self-awareness of subjects. Dialectical logic, building upon but contrasted to the other two, is the logic of system as a structure of elements in relation, so that even the "transcendental" subject must be seen in relation to the whole. Errol Harris, who has instructed

me in making these distinctions, describes the dialectical logic of systems
in a way more influenced by Hegel but also akin to Whitehead:

> The principle of organization is one of unity making the system a co-
> herent whole, and at the same time a principle of differentiation deter-
> mining the disposal and mutual accommodation of the parts. Unity of
> differences is the hallmark of wholeness—unity by virtue of the in-
> termesh of diverse but mutually adjusted parts. A system is essentially a
> one of many.[68]

The interplay of unity and diversity in Whitehead's dialectical logic is
conceived, as it must be, as both a perpetual, temporal activity and yet as
prior to all temporality and process because the whole is already involved
in any succession or movement. Thus God's reversal of the polar dynamics, which God nevertheless experiences in its temporal form, fits exactly
the dialectical logic of diverse but mutually adjusted parts in a whole or
system. There is no incoherence. There would have been incoherence,
however, if Whitehead had tried to complete his dialectically panentheistic system with only the formal logic of the empirical sciences he first
interpreted as a mathematician and mathematical physicist.

## Conclusion

Our conclusion, then, is that God may be coherently reconceived as
the Creator of emergent order in a dynamic spatiotemporal process of
internally related, but finitely free, actual entities who must accept their
responsibility for limited co-creation of the values that they with God
must seek. It provides the theological foundation for the values of liberated self-actualization and reconciled communal interaction in our multi-
cultural and interreligious world, which we will seek to articulate in
succeeding chapters. The cosmological function of religion in our contemporary world may coherently relate our understanding of the spatiotemporal relationality of creation to the universal relationality of the
Creator in a way that invites, empowers, and informs the dialogical interaction of our world's cultures and religions.

# 2

# The Cross-Cultural
# Relationality of Meaning

## The Meaning of Meaning

To determine what one means by meaning is no mean task. So simple a
sentence in the language of only one culture may illustrate the difficulty.
The first use of "means" clearly points to a subjective purpose or intention, with an implied philosophical background of the free, conscious
subject characteristic of modern Euro-American cultures. The second use
as "meaning" means some kind of signification or significance, either
referring to an object in a commonly experienced world or relating to
another sign or symbol in the communicative system being used—neither
of which necessarily implies the "turn to the subject" of the first meaning.
The third is a value judgment, measuring in this case a degree of difficulty
on some continuum of experience, related to the widely used meaning of
"mean" as "that which is in the middle" or "occupying a middle or inter-
mediate place" (*Oxford Universal Dictionary*). To be "mean" in the sense of
inferior or of low degree is to fall below the middle as measured between
two polar contrasts. To be able to give meaning, on the other hand, is to
constitute some relational middle, logically or psychologically, that relates
one experience or symbol to another.

   This brief attempt at preliminary definition already reveals much of
the problematic of this chapter. It makes clear that how we understand
the subject-object structure of experience is crucial to the understanding
of the meaning of meaning. Is meaning determined by subjective intention? Or by the relation given or asserted between experiences and/or
their related signs and symbols? The emphasis on intention as the clue to
meaning is correlated with the turn to the subject in modern Western

culture in a way that is problematic for other more traditional or communal cultures, which do not experientially, religiously, or philosophically establish such clear ego boundaries between subject and object or subject and subject. Indeed, some Asian religions, especially Buddhism, find such firm ego boundaries to be precisely the problem that limits our discerning or intuiting meaning in relation either to our universe or to God.

## Agnosticism in the Meaning of God

The issue of meaning is especially difficult for those who think and speak about God. Indeed many have concluded that it is finally impossible and contend that our God-relation, if there is such, is "ineffable." They leave theology only with a *via negativa*, which allows meaningful statements only of what God is not. Those, on the other hand, who affirm the possibility of articulating what we mean by God, nevertheless recognize the difficulty for those who must express their meaning in symbolic, mythical, metaphorical, or analogical language.[1]

Though the philosophical discussion about religious meaning became more strident in Western culture as the formal logic of the empirical sciences became more dominant, the recognition of this problem by religious persons is in no wise new. The Hebrews three millennia ago forbade the utterance of the divine name, and when distressed by the suffering of national exile and oppression could testify, "Verily, thou art a God that hidest thyself" (Isa. 45:15, KJV).[2] When Augustine, the most formative theologian in the Western church, sought to articulate the Christian Trinitarian view of God, he qualified his whole discussion with the admission that it is "not because the phrases are adequate—they are only an alternative to silence."[3] Even Thomas Aquinas, who most carefully articulated the analogical nature of our God-language, could write, "This is what is ultimate in the human knowledge of God: to know that we do not know God."[4] But for him, as for many, this was surely a Socratic learned ignorance that does not deny the possibility of communicating religious meanings but, to my mind, only underlines how carefully dialectical we must be in attempting to do so.[5]

Modern Western culture under the growing hegemony of scientific reasoning, however, has had increasingly strong motifs of religious agnosticism. The kind of empiricism articulated two centuries ago by David Hume limited truth claims to "truths of reason" derived deductively and at best mathematically, or to testable "truths of fact" derived inductively from the five senses. Any other truth claims were meaningless, and books that contained them should be "cast into the flames."[6] The most severe recent form of this argument was in A. J. Ayer's logical positivism, which claimed that any sentence that is neither "analytic" in the sense of Hume's truths of reason or "empirically verifiable" in the sense of Hume's truths of fact, is not merely untrue but cognitively meaningless.[7]

Despite these attempts at semantic purification, modern human beings continue to have life-experiences that defy, yet demand, articulation. Some are experiences of great horror like the Jewish holocaust, as Elie Wiesel has written:

> The problem is that the essential will never be said or understood. Perhaps I should express my thought more clearly: it's not because I don't speak that you won't understand me; it's because you won't understand me that I don't speak. That's the problem, and we can do nothing about it; what certain people have lived, you will never live—happily for you, moreover.[8]

Peak religious experiences also leave us with the need to articulate the almost unspeakable sublimity at the depth or the height of our common world—its ultimate origin or transcendent telos (end). The issue of meaning in both cases is whether our finite, culturally relative rationalities and languages can hope to express the meaning of such experiences.

Even a rationalistic metaphysician like Whitehead, as he tried to articulate a modern cosmology, felt the limits of our rational capacity for so daunting a task: "How shallow, puny and imperfect are the efforts to sound the depths in the nature of things. In philosophical discussion, the merest hint of dogmatic certainty as to finality of statement is an exhibition of folly."[9] And in facing this limit, he recognized the religious nature of the hope that empowers our human attempts to discern and articulate meanings:

> This hope is not a metaphysical premise. It is the *faith* which forms the motive for the pursuit of all sciences alike, including metaphysics. . . . The preservation of such faith must depend on an ultimate moral intuition into the nature of intellectual action—that it should embody the adventure of hope. Such an intuition marks the point where metaphysics—and indeed every science—*gains assurance from religion and passes over into religion.*[10]

It is exactly this religious hope that empowers the kind of inquiry that now engages us.

## Idolatry in the Meaning of God

Religious persons, who know their limit and yet live, think, and communicate in hope, must be willing to participate in an ongoing dialogical process if we hope to articulate the meaning of religious faith for the whole of our common life-experience. That life-experience for too many has too often included the kind of horror that Elie Wiesel suffered and struggled to communicate, and that horror has been and is too often caused or magnified by the fear and hostility that one society has for another with its strange culture and religion.

The destruction of Tokyo and Hiroshima in 1945 led Kosuke Koyama to reflect critically on the "idolatry" in his own culture in a way that is instructive for many others:

> As I reflected on the destruction of Japan, I was led to evaluate critically my own nature-oriented culture, focusing on emperor worship and sun worship. Out of this critique arose the intriguing challenge of the Bible that "my help comes from the maker of heaven and earth," not just from "heaven and earth." . . . For a son of the East to dialogue historically, culturally and religiously with the tradition of Mount Sinai has been a strange and moving experience. . . . Wars are waged "in the name of God," that is with "theological" justification. Such justification is idolatry. . . . In the name of our own Solar Goddess we appointed ourselves to be the Righteous Nation that possessed the fullness of morality![11]

Koyama's motive for entering into cross-cultural and interreligious dialogue on the meaning of God should similarly move many of us in our own quite other cultural and religious contexts. How can those of us, for instance, who are part of the only society that has used nuclear weapons against an "enemy" nation be any less moved to reflect critically about our society's moral and religious justifications for perpetrating so unspeakable a horror? If the tribal theism of Shinto could justify the aggressive nationalism of Japan, is it not equally true that North American Judeo-Christian civil religion can and has functioned in similar ways? Could it not also be that resources for the healing of such tribal and national idolatries can be found not only in the tradition of Mount Sinai, as Koyama did, but also in the "compassionate fellow-feeling for all creatures" found in the "superbly aesthetic and communal life of Buddhism and Confucianism"?[12]

Kosuke Koyama suggests as much in his interpretation of Gautama Buddha's decision finally to preach in response to the persistent request of Brahma Sahampati:

> I am grateful to both Gotoma the Buddha and Jesus the Christ. Both of them communicated to us of their innermost mind. Silence must be placed towards Word. Silence placed toward Silence is ultimately meaningless. Word placed toward Silence is again ultimately meaningless.[13]

As we slowly learn in our increasingly complex life-world to be grateful to more than one religious revelatory source, however, how shall we give rational voice to such a renewal of hope in the depths of our spirits? How shall we escape the temptation to silence as we sense the complexity of the growing synthesis we are seeking to comprehend? How shall we dare to believe that whatever dialectical reconciliation we are beginning to discern in our own minds may be meaningfully communicated so as to contribute to the reconciliation our conflicted world so desperately needs? Can we also dare to come to "Word" after asking the Buddha's questions?

> Must I now preach what I so hardly won? Men sunk in sin and lusts would find it hard to plumb this doctrine,—upstream all the way. Abstruse, profound, most subtle, hard to grasp. Dear lusts will blind them that they shall not see,—in densest mists of ignorance befogged.[14]

We dare not, of course, only think of others as "sunk in sin and lusts." Such is the human condition, if not always in its more blatant forms, then in our inevitable overattachment to the cultural and religious tradition that has formed and nourished us. We are all sunk to some extent in our traditions and hold possessively to them to the same degree that they possess us. It is not that our traditions consist entirely of ignorance but that the dense mists arise from the insecurity that motivates our possessive lust for them. Is it possible for us both to stand in and stand out of our formative traditions so as to communicate meaningfully in our cross-cultural and interreligious contexts?

## A Hermeneutic for Creative and Free Participation in Traditions

It is just at this point that Hans-Georg Gadamer's already classic reflection about hermeneutics in our Western tradition should prove helpful. Toward the end of a lifetime of creative reflection about these issues, he concluded, correctly I think:

> It would become vacuous and undialectical, I think, if it [emancipatory reflection] tried to think the idea of a completed reflection, in which society would lift itself out of the continuing process of emancipation—the process of loosening itself from traditional ties and binding itself to newly constructed validities—so as to achieve an ultimate, free and rational self-possession.[15]

If no completed reflection is possible for our finite, historically conditioned spirits, then we must give ourselves to a dialectical and dialogical process within and beyond our traditions. This requires, however, a creative and critical participation in our own traditions that enables us to give up any attempts at their absolutization: "Tradition is not the vindication of what has come down from the past but the further creation of moral and spiritual life; it depends on being made conscious and freely carried on."[16] In our cross-cultural global village this further creation of moral and spiritual life must now be accomplished where diverse traditions meet.

Gadamer's conclusion about tradition is the more remarkable because it came from one who gave his scholarly life to elucidating the formative power of the Western tradition. He was convinced that "understanding . . . is participation in an event of tradition."[17] Hermeneutics is the "interplay of the movement of tradition and the movement of the interpreter."[18] But the interpreters are already conditioned by the tradition they are interpreting. No one may claim complete self-knowledge as he or she interacts with their formative tradition, for no one is ever a fully self-conscious transcendent ego:

> To be historical means that knowledge of oneself can never be complete. All self-knowledge arises from what is historically pre-given, what with Hegel we call "substance," because it underlies all subjective intentions and actions, and hence both prescribes and limits every possibility for understanding any tradition whatsoever in its historical alterity.[19]

It is this valuation of the formative power of tradition in relation to the finitely free creativity of the interpreter that leads Gadamer to his well-known definition of understanding as the "fusion of horizons." He follows Nietzsche and Husserl in using horizon to "characterize the way in which thought is tied to its finite determinacy, and the way one's range of vision is gradually expanded." The historical task of hermeneutics then is to investigate the past horizon from which any traditionary text speaks without denying its claim to be saying something true to a supposedly closed contemporary horizon of complete self-knowledge. We dare not, because ultimately we cannot, objectify tradition in this way. There can be no Robinson Crusoe-like dream of historical enlightenment within a closed horizon. The horizon of the past is always in motion and becomes aware of itself in historical consciousness. "Our own past and that other past toward which our historical consciousness is directed help to shape this moving horizon out of which human life always lives and which determines it as heritage and tradition."[20]

Our present horizon is continually in process of being formed as we test our "prejudices," which, surprisingly to many, is an essentially positive term for Gadamer. He finds the Enlightenment's attitude toward prejudice itself a prejudice.[21] We simply cannot form our present horizon without the attitudes, values, and commitments, which are the prejudgments we receive in any present from our past. Yet our modern historical consciousness differentiates us from and allows us partially to transcend our past as we test our prejudices. The understanding to which we come in any present, historically effected consciousness may thus be expressed as a "fusion of past and present horizons."[22]

## Participating in and Conceiving World History

The issue for us who must now learn to live cross-culturally and inter-religiously is whether the "past toward which our historical consciousness is directed" may increasingly become the universal past of all humanity in our whole universe. Besides Euro-American history, African history, Asian history, etc., can we hope to experience and coherently conceive world history? This question has traditionally received its Western answer from religious sources. What we called the Abrahamic tradition in chapter 1 has so formed Judaism, Christianity, and Islam that many religious persons affirm a goal for, and a plan in, history, and thus the unity of universal history. Reinhold Niebuhr articulated this perspective in a fresh way during the recent neo-orthodox period of American religion: "Historical religions are by their very nature prophetic-Messianic: They look forward at first to a point in history and finally toward an *eschaton* (end) which is also the end of history, where the full meaning of life and history will be disclosed and fulfilled." But he was equally aware of how this religious affirmation could be and has been corrupted in the cultures formed by historical religions. So he went on,

> Only gradually it is realized that man's efforts to deny and to escape his finiteness in imperial ambitions and power add an element of corruption to the fabric of history and that this corruption becomes a basic characteristic of history and a perennial problem from the standpoint of the fulfillment of human history and destiny.[23]

The historians who sought to articulate a unified world history during the era of European colonial hegemony, however, forsook all religious prejudices about a goal of history as the unifying factor in the interplay of historical forces they were studying. Gadamer found that historians of the caliber of Wilhelm von Humboldt and Leopold von Ranke thought "the whole continuity of universal history can be understood only from historical tradition itself."[24] But Gadamer recognizes that their attempt to construct universal history from an objective study of data alone is problematic because the historian is situated within history as a conditioned and finite link in a continuing, unended process. Despite their attempts to overcome a Hegelian philosophy of history by turning only to historical research, historians must assume some kind of continuity in history. Gadamer recognizes that the postulation of historical continuity is based on an "unconscious teleology":

> It is possible to see what Ranke considers an "event that is truly part of world history" and what the continuity of world history is really based on. It has no fixed goal that can be discovered outside itself. To this extent there is no necessity, knowable a priori, at work in history. But

the structure of historical continuity is still teleological, and *its criterion
is success*. . . . Whether or not something is successful not only determines the meaning of a single event and accounts for the fact that it
produces a lasting effect or passes unnoticed; success or failure causes a
whole series of actions and events to be meaningful or meaningless.
The ontological structure of history itself, then, is teleological, although without a telos.[25]

Unfortunately for the reputation of universal history, as we now see it,
Ranke's finite "fusion of horizons" occurred at the height of European
colonial success. The unity he saw in world history was not so formal and
independent of historical prejudice as postulated by his positivist philosophy of history. The associating of qualitatively different data indicates that
the unity in terms of which data were interpreted already functioned as a
criterion for selecting which of myriad data available were important
enough to be recorded and interpreted. The continuity experienced in
history was the continuity of their hegemonic Western civilization based
on the contemporary success of its science and technology.

This Western continuity also clearly had and has a religious
component.

It is also not by chance that Western civilization is characterized by
Christianity, which has its absolute temporal moment in the unique
redemptive event. Ranke recognized something of this when he viewed
the Christian religion as the restoration of man to "immediacy to God,"
which, in romantic fashion, he set at the primeval beginning of all
history.[26]

The possibility of immediacy to God, as the Lutheran Ranke understood
it, meant that the historian as historian is able to think like God and thus
see "the whole of historical humanity in its totality (since no time lies
before the Deity)" and find "it all equally valuable."[27] Yet no finite historian has this degree of self-transcendence. The criterion of success for the
continuity of history is and remains conditioned by historians' experience
of their own civilization's success. The concept of "universal history" as a
growing, unfinished whole was given its sometimes specious unity by
nineteenth-century Western historians through the emergence and success of Western civilization.

## The Insights of Heidegger and Gadamer

The philosopher Heidegger enabled contemporary Euro-Americans to
regain a perspective on their finitude and that of their civilization by
teaching us to recognize again the phenomenological relation of being to
time. Heidegger's philosophy constitutes the most successful recent at-

tempt to overcome the turn to the subject, which began with Descartes, continued with Kant and Husserl, and grounds the subjectivism of both the transcendental logic of absolute idealism and the understanding of subject-object relations in the formal logic of contemporary Western science. Illumined by Heidegger's phenomenology, we no longer understand ourselves in terms of the Cartesian "cogito" or Kantian "transcendental ego" but in the facticity of *dasein* (being there, existence). We have the possibility of understanding because there is a "there" (*da*), which constitutes the distinction between being and beings.

This turn away from the subject, however, is not to the object conceived as matter or stuff. We are able to understand because both subject and object share the particular mode of being that Heidegger calls "historicity." Gadamer appreciates the way Heidegger clarified the unresolved problem of metaphysics in Western civilization:

> In fact, however, renewing the question of being, the task that Heidegger set himself, meant that within the "positivism" of phenomenology he recognized *the unresolved problem of metaphysics*, concealed in its ultimate culmination: the concept of mind or *spirit* as conceived by speculative idealism. In grounding the "hermeneutics of facticity" he went beyond both the concept of mind developed by classical idealism and the thematic of transcendental consciousness purified by phenomenological reduction.[28]

The unresolved problem of metaphysics for religious persons who understand and accept the finitude of their historical conditionedness is how we may understand the metaphysical meaning of our God-relation. Is there a way to understand the relativity of our experience with the concept of *relationality* that enables a more coherent understanding of the God who is related to us all? We noted at the beginning of this discussion how crucial the way we understand subject-object relations is to our understanding of meaning and how the turn to the subject has made the communication of meaning more difficult cross-culturally, especially with Asian and traditional African cultures. Gadamer's analysis of why no completed reflection is possible for our finite, historically conditioned spirits has cleared the way for us to attempt a further illumination of these issues. If no completed reflection is possible for us as finite subjects, how may we reconceive our subjectivity so as to enter more dialectically and dialogically into the process of clarifying the metaphysical meaning of our universal God-relation? May we conceive God as a Reality that limits and exceeds the omnipotence of our reflection while remaining its rational ground, so that we do not undermine the religious hope that undergirds our rationality and escape the temptation to revert to religious silence? If so, then I think Gadamer is right, to quote him one last time on this issue:

Transposing ourselves consists neither in the empathy of one individual
for another nor in subordinating another person to our own standards;
rather it always involves rising to a higher universality that overcomes
not only our own particularity but also that of the other.[29]

Yet, not quite right: Particularity of person and culture must be more
included than overcome. Thus we must attempt to conceive the higher
universality in terms of *universal relationality*.

## The Horizon of African Religion and Culture

What does the attempt to rise to a higher universality look like if we
try to understand this issue by fusing our Western horizon with an African or Asian horizon? At our stage of cross-cultural and interreligious
communication, this is not a realistically realizable, though not a totally
impossible, task. When the African theologian John Mbiti discussed the
concepts of God in Africa, he provided an appendix of ten pages of different African terms for the Deity drawn from the religions of more than
270 different peoples or tribes.[30] Though he also recognizes the tremendous and rapid changes Africa is undergoing, Mbiti holds that the peculiar
strength of African religion lies in its integration with all the aspects and
contexts of Africans' human existence. Thus Mbiti expects many African
religious characteristics, including the multiple naming of God because of
God's omnipresent, concrete relation to many contexts, to persist through
these modern changes.[31]

One of the theological synonyms for God's universality that Mbiti
finds more fitting for African culture is omnipresence. The traditional
African way of experiencing and expressing God's contextual presence
appears in some ways analogous to the panentheistic interpretation of
religious experience, though Mbiti does not use this Western philosophical term. He rather speaks more concretely of "the localization and manifestations of God's omnipresence":

> In these and many other ways, African peoples acknowledge the omni-
> presence of God. He may be in the thunder, but he is not thunder; he
> may shoot like a waterfall, but he is not the waterfall; he may be associ-
> ated with the sky, but he is not identical with it.[32]

When Mbiti summarizes this rich variety of African religion, he
stresses that they have not delineated God with a clearly defined conceptual model:

> God evades or defies human comprehension; he cannot be grouped
> within the confines of the human mind. . . . It is perhaps for this reason
> that many African peoples have only a few phrases and words that

describe the fact of God's existence, and beyond that they readily admit that they do not know much about him.[33]

Thus, we would not expect African peoples to have the same temptation toward completed reflection as some Euro-Americans. Indeed, their shortcoming tends toward its opposite of inadequate theoretical reflection: Their world is alive but lacks the unity of an organism. Therefore, one does not often find the sublation of their concrete experience into abstract terms like "panentheism," or even their contextual experience of gods brought together into the understanding of one God that an African theologian like Mbiti seeks.

Another aspect of African religion has important implications for the theological understanding of universal relationality. Kinship relations in traditional African communities are affirmed more widely than the limited familial structures in Western societies. They provide the background from which many Africans address God as Father or Grandfather and some matrilineal societies refer to God as Mother.[34] The Shona and Ndebele people in Zimbabwe where I had the privilege to live sometimes speak of God as a triad of Father, Mother, and Son.[35] And many Africans add a rich variety of demigods related to natural, social, and political structures, and various spirits related to clans, families, or natural phenomena.[36]

Though this polytheistic mode of relating the Sacred to the multiple realities of their life-world may indicate inadequate theoretical reflection, I think it far more important as revealing that Africans experience and express God as universally related to the various dimensions of their life-world. The contrast with the classically Western monotheistic concept of God as absolute, unconditioned Subject or Substance infinitely transcending the world is strong—and I think important.

Mbiti finds a similar perspective in Africa's religious anthropology. Many African creation myths say that human beings were created as husband and wife, and many see the Deity as constituted by a family relationship in which God is parent and human beings are God's children.[37] When this original relation is broken, many forms of offerings, prayers, and sacrifices seek to restore it. This sense of relationship continues for Africans even beyond death. Mbiti found:

> Without exception, African peoples believe that death does not annihilate life and that the departed continue to exist in the hereafter. I have not found evidence in any of our sources where this belief is not held. But how long the departed continue to exist is not indicated in our sources. For some peoples, at least, this continuity of life lasts as long as the individual is remembered by those who knew him in his earthly life. According to this belief, the departed of up to four or five generations

back are still living as far as human beings are concerned. It is this
group of them that I have named "the living dead."[38]

The important point is that Africans experience and express the meaning
of life as relational. Human beings are created in and for relations,
grounded in their God-relation; and not even death can destroy life as
long as a living relation continues.

A Nigerian dramatist's summary view of the African sense of reality
supplements and supports the insights into relationality gained from
Mbiti's review of African religion. Zulu Sofola suggests that he writes his
dramas out of an awareness that "The African world is an integrated
cosmos with a unique fluidity that makes unbroken continuity possible."[39]
Sofola's statement might perhaps be freely translated into the language of
our discussion as "The African horizon sees the world as a process whose
fluid dialectic of change and continuity is sufficiently analogous to kinship
structures to be an integrated, relational cosmos."

Similar themes may be discerned in the reflections of a scholar of
African art in relation to religion. Engelbert Mveng of the Cameroun
contrasts his African ethos with some modes of Western theology:

> For us esthetics is not in the order of sensuousness linked with concu-
> piscence. The locus of esthetics are the laws of life and love. The beau-
> tiful is love incarnated, objectified, and personified. And for us love is
> always the victory of life over death. Thus the language of African art is
> eminently *religious*, not theological. It celebrates the human adventure
> under the gaze of God. But it does not judge God, or describe God, or
> unveil God, or profane God.[40]

Many elements of this statement are important to our discussion: The
refusal to link the esthetically sensual to concupiscence, as some Western
culture and religion has, denies the ontological dualism that underlies this
sometimes Western view. To see the beautiful in terms of love and life is
to affirm the relationality that gives and sustains life in the spatiotemporal
process. To focus on the adventure of life in relation to God, while mini-
mizing theistic forms of conceptualization, indicates the hesitancy (some
others would say failure) to construct a theoretical model that disjoins
God from the experienced life-world. A conceptual model adequate to
African religious and aesthetic experience must be able to interpret their
sense of God's omnipresent relation to the organic and communal structures of their world.

## The Horizon of Asian Religion and Culture

To turn to Asian culture(s) is to turn to an even more complex reality,
so that many see Asia as comprised of different cultures, separated by the

highest of the world's mountain ranges, vast expanses of water, and great differences of climate. Though its people may share a common genetic heritage, they have been long since differentiated into Chinese, Indian, Japanese, Korean, etc. Their religions show the same differentiation, with Taoism and Confucianism originating in China, Hinduism and Buddhism emerging in India, and Shintoism being native to Japan.

Yet Asian religion also has shown its transcultural, universal potentiality: Confucianism and Taoism have moved beyond China to become influential also in Japan and Korea; Hinduism is also found beyond India in Sri Lanka (Ceylon), the Malay peninsula, and the southwest Pacific islands; and Buddhism has spread most widely, almost wherever Hinduism is found, as well as to China, Japan, and Korea. Islam has also entered Asia from the Middle East, and Christianity from Euro-America. These two Abrahamic religions and Buddhism thus have become the most universal religions in our transcultural world, but in Asia Buddhism alone really approaches universality.

The Korean author Younghill Kang shows the transcultural spread of Asian religions as he articulates their beneficent affects on his poverty-stricken family in his autobiographical novel *The Grass Roof*:

> Our home was not exempt from this miserable dependence upon the elements, but my family did not seem to mind their helpless poverty, since most of them were indulging in the mystical doctrine of Buddhism, or in the classics of Confucius, who always advocated that a man should not be ashamed of coarse food, humble clothing, and modest dwelling, but should only be ashamed of not being cultivated in the perception of beauty. . . . My grandmother . . . was a true Oriental woman. The quietism of Buddha, the mysterious calm of Taoism, the ethical insight of Confucianism all helped to make her an unusually refined personality.[41]

F. S. C. Northrop has made one of the most sustained attempts by a Western scholar to understand and interpret the transcultural and interreligious unity of Asian culture. He strongly contrasts its mode of meaning-making to his and our Western form, where verbally designated connotative relations structured by grammatical syntax communicate theoretical meaning with minimal dependence upon immediate experience. In contrast, he writes, "the genius of the East is that it has discovered a type of knowledge and has concentrated its attention continuously, as the West has not, upon a portion of the nature of things which can be known only by being experienced."[42] He notes that the ideographic character of the Chinese and Japanese languages largely denotes what is immediately experienced, and its syntax structures its ideographic symbols in the way they are associated in immediate experience.

Thus he argues that "the Chinese language gains a superlative degree of fluidity, a capacity to convey the unique particularity, nuance, and precisely refined richness of the specific, individual experience which probably no other mature language in the world today achieves."[43] This mode of symbolic expression enables good poetry to convey rich, subtle, immediately felt aesthetic content; but because the rules of grammar are less definite, it limits the communication of syntactically precise, theoretically clear prose.

> This is the reason the Oriental, from one end of the East to the other, is continuously telling us that one can never understand what he is saying or writing by merely listening to or studying his spoken statements or published works alone and that one must in addition directly apprehend and experience, and then take time to contemplate, that to which they refer.[44]

If we give ourselves to this mode of immediate intuition, what shall we come to know? What does such an Asian claim mean? Can Western persons hope to fuse their traditional horizon with the horizon found in the great philosophical and religious classics of Asia to find in our immediate experience what has become primary in theirs? If so, what do Asians expect us to see?

### Asian Experience of the Undifferentiated Aesthetic Continuum

A part of the answer to these questions is found in the contrast of how we and they experience ethos and conceive ethics, which are grounded for Asians in aesthetic relationality. The three Confucian virtues of *chih* (knowledge, wisdom), *jen* (compassion, human-heartedness), and *yung* (courage, fortitude) are rooted in personal experiences filled with aesthetic content. *Jen* or compassion is the central virtue prerequisite to all of the others. It is first realized by human beings in the filial relations of their human families, but it more fundamentally denotes a factor in human nature as such.

In the teaching of Taoists like Mo-Ti, *jen* is even conceived universally and ontologically. That is in our terms, the reality of relational being expressed as *jen* is not only found in humanity but is to be found in the universe as a whole. From this standpoint, the *jen* found in human beings is also the *tao*, that is, the "way." It is an all-embracing mode of being that comprehends both human beings and nature.[45] But it cannot be epistemologically comprehended by focusing on any determinate sensory experience, as a Western empiricist might. It must be immediately apprehended in a mode that Professor Northrop designates as the "undifferentiated aesthetic continuum," which contrasts with our dominant Western modes of experience and thought. Northrop seeks to guard Westerners against misconstruing the experience that is so central to Asians:

> [We] must not confuse the immediately apprehended aesthetic contin-
> uum with the postulated external space of Western science and philoso-
> phy. . . . Between the aesthetically given self and the aesthetically given
> natural object there is oneness or identity, as well as difference, due to
> the fact that . . . [they] are not merely different from each other, but
> also differentiations of the one, all-embracing, immediately appre-
> hended aesthetic continuum.[46]

What is at issue here for Western interpretations of experience is the relation between such determinate sense data as colors, sounds, fragrances, and flavors and the all-embracing continuum or manifold in which we experience them. Or whether there is any such relation at all? For Asian experience, the manifold is as much the content of immediately experienced nature as are the differentiations within it. It is the experience of oneness given in this experience that is the basis for compassion/*jen* in all relations, and for human-heartedness in all human relations. It cannot be adequately known in the theoretical constructs of words and language but only through contemplation of its immediacy. The distinction between subject and object thus also cannot be adequately expressed through subject-predicate modes of syntax. It must be experienced within an all-embracing continuity. This is why aesthetic experience is finally the basis for the moral and religious life of Confucianists and Taoists.

Human beings, however, do not usually experience the aesthetic continuum as undifferentiated; it is usually at least partially differentiated. The differentiations in the form of our experience of persons and nature, however, are always temporal; they come and go. They are transitory and mortal; only the continuum abides. The richness of concrete human experience usually includes both the differentiation and the unity—except at the point of death. This is why, according to Lin Yutang, many Chinese become Buddhists when confronted with tragedy and especially death, even though they traditionally are Confucianist and Taoist when life is more successful. When one faces the loss of what is aesthetically and emotionally dear in the temporary relation with a beloved person, the cultivation of the undifferentiated aesthetic continuum for its own sake becomes important. Buddhism seeks to grasp this indeterminate immediacy as *nirvana*, which is not "nothing" as Westerners understand it, but the most emotionally and aesthetically rich experience one could have, as Buddhists understand it.

It is not that the time experienced in the transience of events and relations that become and perish—and that is experienced most poignantly at death—is nothing, but it is conceived differently than in most

Western culture and religion. It is best symbolized perhaps as the ripples on an otherwise placid and silent pool. The ripples are not without value as they are experienced in the differentiations of an aesthetically beautiful landscape or a beloved personality, but they are transitory. The tragedy of their transitoriness can be met only as we overcome our possessive desires to grasp and control these inevitably temporary and transient phenomena. Many Asians think it possible to experience this blessing, as they seek to reduce or remove the differentiations arising in objective sensory perception. This mode of experience removes or reduces the focus on the centered ego-self in relation with external objects, so that one may experience the immediacy of the unlimited, undifferentiated continuum.

## The Fusion of Asian and Western Horizons

William James studied similar forms of religious experience also by Western persons in *The Varieties of Religious Experience*. He quotes from J. A. Symonds's description and evaluation of his experience, with the comment that "probably more persons than we suspect could give parallels to it from their own experience":

> One reason why I disliked this kind of trance was that I could not find words to describe it to myself. I cannot even now find words to render it intelligible. It consisted in a gradual but swiftly progressive obliteration of space, time, sensation, and the multitudinous factors of experience which seem to qualify what we are pleased to call our Self. In proportion as these conditions of ordinary consciousness were subtracted, the sense of an underlying or essential consciousness acquired intensity. At last nothing remained but a pure, absolute, abstract Self. The universe became without form and void of content. But Self persisted, formidable in its vivid keenness.[47]

This is remarkably close to the Buddhist experience of nirvana, which Northrop describes as experience of the "undifferentiated aesthetic continuum." What marks it as Western is Symonds disliking it, while Buddhists would evaluate it as essential "enlightenment." What is even more Western is the criticism that James quotes from Crichton-Browne, who wrote of Symonds that his "highest nerve centres were in some degree enfeebled or damaged by these dreamy mental states which afflicted him so grievously"; to which James responds, "Symonds was, however, a perfect monster of many-sided cerebral efficiency, and his critic gives no objective grounds for his strange opinion, save that Symonds complained occasionally, as all susceptible and ambitious men complain, of lassitude and uncertainty as to his life's mission."[48] One might say that Crichton-Browne's objective grounds, in Gadamer's terms, were the prejudices of his Western tradition.

Another and more recent "perfect monster of many-sided cerebral effi-ciency" whose experience was similar to that of Symonds is Pierre Teilhard de Chardin. This author of fifteen books, several hundred arti-cles, and five volumes of published letters dealing with both modern sci-ence and revisionist theology often wrote of his "Cosmic Sense" or "sense of the universal." After reviewing Teilhard's whole corpus, a recent inter-preter of his "mysticism of knowing" describes Teilhard's experience with many interpolations from Teilhard's own works:

> He steps into "the deepest recesses of the blackness within" seeking the murmur of the "mysterious waters that rise from the innermost depths." Then with "terror and intoxicating emotion" he realizes that he is not just an observer of cosmic currents, his act of observation is also part of these currents. Influences from all the earth have poured into his consciousness, affected it, changed it, and will pass on. . . . His drives, his passions, and his aging proceed by rhythms he cannot con-trol. "My life is not my own." He urges that if we look beneath the superficial way that we ordinarily understand ourselves, we will begin to sense an Unknown One—one hardly emerged from consciousness and only half-awake. Seen beneath ourselves in half-shadow the features of this Unknown One seem to merge into the face of the world. Teilhard is stunned by "the vehemence and possessive force of the contact" be-tween his individual self and the universe: gripped "with religious hor-ror" he realizes that "what is emerging in us is the great cosmos."[49]

Because this cosmic consciousness interrupted his own personal con-sciousness, Teilhard, like Symonds, could sometimes complain of a "ner-vous weakness that paralyzes me in everything," when he could only "pray . . . until the current of activity reestablished itself."[50]

What marks Teilhard's experience as Western is precisely this emphasis on, and concern for, activity. This is a cosmic sense of a reality that actively moves toward expression. It is not quite Northrop's "undifferenti-ated aesthetic continuum," for it apprehends a cosmos that is moving toward differentiation—that is, a cosmos that is in process toward ever greater complexity. In the depths or heights of the consciousness that experiences reality in this way, there is the sense that one is participating in a cosmos and a humanity that is emerging. There is a creativity within that takes over and acts through one's person.

What is evident in Teilhard's sensitive reports of his religious experi-ences are both the traditional Western prejudices of a created order or ordering in the cosmos and the more recent scientific prejudice of an evolutionary process in the universe, which we examined and interpreted in chapter 1. We shall return to these issues later in this chapter, but what is important at this point is to note the similarity within difference of Teilhard's cosmic sense and that of the Asian cultures and religions we have been examining. Teilhard, like them, knew both the lassitude and exaltation, the agony and the ecstasy of participation in the cosmic universal. But unlike them, he could affirm that the cosmic universal is

> the more active the more personally vulnerable and fragile I feel. . . . God is all the more likely to act through us, the more aware we are of our own helplessness. . . . Now that the veil of my person is beginning to wear thin (because I feel so vulnerable), I have confidence that God will take over for me somehow.[51]

F. S. C. Northrop, however, does not admit any essential difference between East and West in their evaluation of activity. He argues that the "undifferentiated aesthetic continuum," as Asians experience it, provides a genuine basis for human freedom:

> Instead, as the Orient noted long ago, freedom has its basis in that part of the nature of man and things which is indeterminate and thus a potentiality for a determinateness that is not yet. As the Orient has seen, and as the Westerner, by the failure of his attempts to derive freedom from the behavior of determinate entities, has demonstrated, if all reality is determinate, then no meaning for human freedom can be found. This is precisely what the Oriental means when he asserts that if man gives expression only to the differentiated, specifically sensed, determinate portion of himself and of things, then he is caught in the remorseless wheel of fate. It is also what he has in mind when he affirms that it is only by recognizing the indeterminate, all-embracing field component of his nature and by giving expression to the creativity which it permits, that man attains freedom, while also gaining equanimity with respect to the coming and going of the transitory, differentiated portion of the self and all things.[52]

The Buddhist or Taoist may not refer to the creative activity of "God" at this point, as Teilhard did, but they both sense that the dynamic of their creative freedom rests on their participation in the ("as yet," as Teilhard would say) indeterminate cosmic universal.

There are Asians, however, who experience the agony and lassitude resulting from their fragmentary and largely unsuccessful attempts to participate in the "undifferentiated aesthetic continuum" much more than they experience any exaltation and ecstasy or consequent freedom. Kim Sung-dong's Korean novel *Mandala* interprets the terrible spiritual struggle of a despairing and depraved outcast Buddhist monk Chisan and his younger companion monk Pobun. Chisan contemplates suicide but holds back: "Everything in the world is boring, but I have to go on living, because it would be much more boring dead."[53] They struggle with their acute sense of alienation, even from the women with whom they break their monastic vow of chastity. They listen to Zen masters who try to teach them that "You see the ultimate truth only when language ceases to exist and when the mind vanishes. Only the wisest spiritual mentor can teach it to you"; but they conclude that "the masters everywhere simply kept repeating the cliches and the dead words left by other Zen masters in China a thousand years ago."[54] The despairing conclusion is

> O Buddha, our encounter was a fateful one. And a very unfortunate one in a sense. . . . I had the brazen hope that I would be like you some day. What a preposterous delusion that turned out to be. Hope is a fascination that corrupts and degenerates man fastest, and I joined the breed of mortals that are deprived of the ability to lead a normal life. I was a hallucinated being, who mistook a fake life for a true one.[55]

### Similarities and Differences

In comparing and contrasting these Western and Eastern modes of experiencing and expressing an immediate participation in the cosmic universal, we underline certain similarities and differences. They are similar in expressing the intuitive immediacy of participation in an all-embracing continuum or universal and the attendant reduction or obliteration of the ego boundaries of the differentiated, experiencing, rational self. The disjunction between the subject and the differentiated object is overcome while subjectivity is not entirely lost but in some ways is vividly enhanced. A oneness is experienced with nature or the cosmos, though some religious Westerners might more characteristically express it as an atonement (at-one-ment) with God. This intuition of oneness becomes existentially the more important as a human being experiences the transitory and vulnerable character of the self and all of its desires and attachments, especially in the contemplation and actual experience of death.

The differences within similarity are equally important. Westerners dislike their inability adequately to describe and theoretically interpret this experience, so that some judge it to be debilitating. The Western tradition enculturates persons to value discursive, systematic articulation of differentiated experience even as they may intuit their participation in the cosmic universal. A more fundamental difference is in the valuation of activity and the Western person's desire to be active. The Taoist affirmation of *wu-wei* (actionless activity) is interpreted by Northrop as being grounded in the indeterminate, all-embracing cosmic universal; it is this alone that enables creative, free activity. But he does not note that it is the desire for actualizing a "potentiality for a determinateness that is not yet" that is precisely a problem for the consciousness of many Asians he otherwise characterizes so well.

Teilhard found resolution for the finite limits of his Western desire for activity by intuiting his participation in the activity of the Creator God who is interpreted as creating the emergent determinate order of the spatiotemporal process. Teilhard's desire to be an active co-creator, despite the transience of his finitude, is affirmed within his experience of the cosmic universal: "God is all the more likely to act through us, the more aware we are of our own helplessness." This strongly contrasts with the Buddhist experience and evaluation of desire as vividly portrayed in Kim Sung-dong's novel, where even the desire for enlightenment stimulated by their tradition leads young monks to delusion, degeneration, and despair.

## The Meaning of Desire
## Motivating Human Activity

F. S. C. Northrop's focus on the undifferentiated aesthetic continuum leads him to minimize the crucial issue of desire and the dialectic of the desire for desirelessness in Asian, especially Buddhist, religion. Nirvana is not simply a positive aesthetic experience for Asians but gains much of its meaning because it is the experience that results when desire is eliminated.[56] This is what Kim Sung-dong's novel portrays so vividly, albeit negatively. Younghill Kang's characterization of the "miserable, helpless poverty" of his family in his autobiographical novel, which Northrop cites, only interests him, however, because the aesthetic cultivation inspired by Asian religion allowed them to live, nevertheless, with calm refinement. A critical review of Northrop's book defines this as his "major error":

> Mr. Northrop's major error, however, is his failure fully to appreciate Oriental quiescence and tranquility in relation to Western vitality. The Oriental is a mystic not merely because he is an aesthete, but in some measure because he considers life a grim battle. From the very beginning one of the major appeals of Buddhism was its offer of salvation to people who had conceived themselves as chained to caste and to a wheel of rebirth. The Buddha's Eightfold Path and the Four Noble Truths are a means to salvation which may be ecstasy on its positive side, but which is, on its negative side, an escape from craving and desiring, the course of suffering. . . . The mysticism of the East is therefore a symptom of a still more profound difference between East and West, a difference, namely, between a people who repudiate and a people who accept the claims of desire.[57]

Desirelessness, whether related to poverty or not—and it appears not to have been in Gautama's own life history—is certainly one of the basic concepts of Buddhism. The Four Noble Truths express the single proposition that the suffering of life can be ended only by halting the process of desiring that is its cause. Nirvana, the ultimate goal of the Buddhist, was originally a Sanskrit term meaning essentially "without desire."[58] Thus, this negative meaning must be seen as dialectically necessary to its positive aesthetic meaning, and it would seem that the widespread experience of helpless poverty would enhance for those who suffer it this negative dimension of nirvana's meaning.

Desiring must be characterized as "aesthetic" in terms of Northrop's polar analytic. But it differs from other aesthetic experience in that it issues in action: Sometimes in action to possess the desired object, which Buddhists insightfully criticize; other times in scientific, political, or artistic action to creatively actualize the possibility envisioned and desired. Diverse desires have diverse values. Thus a crucial issue for cross-cultural and interreligious dialogue, which a work like Northrop's left inadequately discussed, is how to interpret and resolve the conflict of desires and the very meaning of the experience of desire in East and West.

Northrop, like many others of his time, interpreted the problematic of desire in light of the crisis of Western culture during and following World War II. Just at the point where Western science and technology had gained unprecedented power to achieve its economic and political desires through its theoretical understanding of the inner structure of nature, that power seemed increasingly to be put at the service of humanity's lowest cravings. Northrop, like many others, examined our Western cultural history to judge where it went wrong and found in Eastern culture a principle of intuiting the undifferentiated substratum of experience that might heal the increasing arbitrariness of our destructive Western desires.[59]

Northrop and many others shared the Buddha's revulsion at the struggle of all against all and commended to the West the Buddha's answer to our individualistic, possessive desires: that we rid ourselves of the self that needs to be satisfied by the objects of its desires. The realism of the Buddha's analysis is not unknown, however, in Western culture. Many here also have experienced and expressed the tragic conflictual character of life. Only the rationalists of the eighteenth century and the liberals of the nineteenth, with their belief in inevitable progress, thought they knew better.[60] We already have criticized this perspective in chapter 1 with little need to turn to Eastern culture and religion to do so.

What Northrop failed to consider is the alternative answer found in the Abrahamic religions of Euro-America and the Middle East. We already have noted how this faith conditions the experience of the cosmic universal in the life and thought of Teilhard de Chardin. What is crucial here is the alternative understanding of creativity that is grounded in the Western tradition of God as Creator, which we also have analyzed and interpreted in chapter 1. Peter Munz has put this perspective well in his response to Professor Northrop, when he presents "another alternative" to the cravings and conflicts endemic to recent Western culture:

It is contained in the prophetic faith and in the notion of man as a fellow worker with God. It says that the world is a very terrible place but we must cooperate with God in order to improve it. It goes so far, in fact, as to identify the knowledge of God with such cooperation. Naturally, the God who is thus known is God the Creator. And the belief in God the Creator is the belief that the goodness which made the world has an intrinsic value and that one iota of it will outweigh, at every moment in time, all evil and all terror. It is necessary to understand that this belief is no flight from realism. It can be positively experienced that a moment of love can outweigh a moment of terror. Perhaps one does not know why this is so, but the fact remains, as a primary intuition of a certain state of affairs.[61]

This way of articulating the Abrahamic religious perspective is more adversarial, in a way too often found in the West, than is necessary or perhaps helpful. Munz powerfully expresses the alternative to Asian perspectives that we also have tried to articulate as the creativity of God. And he properly relates it to the central Christian experience in which our human terror of historical karma manifested in the terror of Jesus' cross is transformed by the creative love of God. That "perfect love casts out fear," as 1 John 4:18 puts it, is very near the center of Christian "aesthetic" experience. Thus, it is understandable why Munz concludes his response to Northrop with a rhetorical question, though he implies too monological an answer:

His [Northrop's] diagnosis of some Western troubles is no doubt correct. We need to understand more clearly than we have done so far the role of the aesthetic component. But I doubt whether the meeting of East and West can help. . . . It will help the West to detract attention from its basic intuition of God the Creator and of the irresistible moral drive and its intrinsic value. But would that be a good thing or a bad thing?[62]

The dialectical answer to this question should be that it may be either or both good *and* bad. These two traditions need not be adversarily disjoined so that to learn something of the meaning of our God-relation from the East requires the loss of the meaning discerned in the Abrahamic religions of our relation to our Creator. Such a consequence would be bad. But the fusion of these horizons may be very good indeed, even enhancing our experience and understanding of the meaning of both God's and humanity's creativity. We need not negate our Judeo-Christian or Islamic desire to serve or cooperate with God's creativity, even in some of the secular forms it has taken in our cultures, but we do have to limit its excesses as the leading or cutting edge of evolution if we are to be reconciled again with nature and be reconciled with a deeply divided humanity, many of whose divisions have resulted from the demonically possessive desires of the West's political and economic colonialisms.

## The Differentiated Aesthetic
## Continuum as Universal Relationality

The point of this analysis is to enhance our understanding of the cross-cultural relationality of meaning, especially at the point of our God-relation. As such, it is motivated by the desire or subjective intention to enable interreligious understanding. I mean to facilitate the communication of cross-cultural meaning. In terms of the definitions with which we began this chapter, such communication requires cross-cultural mediation both in the logical articulation of mediating concepts and the psychological discernment of mediating experiences. We turn first to articulate the mediating concepts.

The philosophical development of the Western tradition did not end with the empirical analysis of subject-object relations of David Hume and its attendant formal logic for understanding the aggregates of differentiated particular entities studied by the natural sciences. Awakened from his "dogmatic slumbers" by Hume, Kant revised our understanding of the external physical world from the independently existing cause of private experiences to the function of a priori categories in our common experience. Those who followed Kant's "Copernican revolution" in Western philosophy had to recognize that our human view of the world is a thought-structure. Some, like Hegel, then sought to understand the dialectical relation of these emerging and developing thought-structures to the "absolute substratum" or "in-and-for-itselfness" of the cosmos from which our human minds emerged and in which they continue to participate.

The physical sciences and the philosophy of science in the West have also continued their investigations of the structure of the physical world. At the turn of this century the theory of relativity also shifted the Western scientific understanding from a world-as-absolute-physical-entity to a world-picture as a structure of sensory experiences. Planck's quantum physics and Heisenberg's principle of indeterminacy brought Western science to recognize an inexpressible substratum of energy events or waves that underlies all of our phenomenological experience. Thus, Western science and philosophy through its own development has been brought far closer to the Eastern perspectives than seemed possible from the earlier Western perspective on subject-object relations classically articulated by Hume and continued in some Anglo-Saxon empirical traditions.[63]

To be sure, even modern Western science and philosophy appears to give a primacy to the conceptual over the intuited that seems excessive to

Asians. The Chinese scholar Kuang-Sae Lee notes this in contrasting Kant to Chinese philosophy:

> For Kant, moral feeling is a feeling "produced solely by reason" since reason "has an influence on the sensibility of the subject and effects a feeling which promotes the influence of the laws on the will." Understanding is to conceptually intuited objects what practical reason is to moral feelings. At this juncture, it is interesting to compare Kant's view of moral feeling with the Chinese notion of *jen*, which is a "natural, spontaneous" feeling of fellow-being-ness or wholeheartedness. This feeling "naturally" springs from the heart-mind of any reasonable man.[64]

This Asian perspective, however, misses how even Kant wanted to "deny knowledge in order to make room for faith,"[65] when the knowledge to be limited was the mechanistic subject-object structure of Newtonian science and the faith made room for was the rational being's moral experience of freedom and duty. Kant wrote something about "nature" far closer to the Chinese perspective than Lee recognizes: "Nature in her wise provision for us has indeed, in the constitution of our reason, been directed to moral interests."[66] For Kant too, though he expressed it in a quite different idiom, morality is naturally given in the heart-mind of any reasonable person. For Kant, too, moral feeling originates in the noumenal life of rational beings, and human experience is far richer than what is given in sense perception as interpreted by the eighteenth-century physical sciences. Unfortunately, however, much of Western sensibility and "common sense" has not yet caught up with even the Kantian revision of the Newtonian worldview.

### Whitehead's Mediating Concepts

It is again Alfred North Whitehead, in my mind, who provides the conceptual mediation needed for the cross-cultural communication of meaning. Whitehead critiqued the theoretic component of Western thought, as Northrop terms it, by showing it to be based on a highly abstract, derivative, and limited second-order experience, which he calls "experience in the mode of presentational immediacy." The more primal mode of experience is a vaguer but more rudimentary preconscious or subconscious feeling (Whitehead says "prehension") that the human mind shares with its body and the rest of the sentient world, which Whitehead terms "experience in the mode of causal efficacy."[67] The Cartesian clear and distinct ideas in the mode of presentational immediacy, upon which so much of Western theory has been based, are abstracted from the generic feelings (prehensions) that are the causally efficacious data in the concrescence of a subject. Whitehead's recovery of the experience of causal efficacy was intended to resolve the Western difficulty of crediting "immediate experience":

> All modern [Western] philosophy hinges around the difficulty of describing the world in terms of subject and predicate, substance and quality, particular and universal. The result always does violence to that immediate experience which we express in our actions, our hopes, our sympathies, our purposes, and which we enjoy in spite of our lack of phrases for its verbal analysis. We find ourselves in a buzzing world, amid a democracy of fellow creatures, whereas under some disguise or other, orthodox [Western] philosophy can only introduce us to solitary substances, each enjoying an illusory experience.[68]

When Whitehead, following William James, characterizes our basic experience as the prehension of a "buzzing" world, he is expressing more graphically than Northrop the *differentiated* character of experience. We experience the effects of diverse forms of definiteness that myriads of energy events (quanta) have upon the concrescence of the energy event that is our self in any given moment. But the experience is of a differentiated *continuum* because reality is not solitary substances, whether mental or physical, but an organism where each actual entity is constituted by its synthesis of other actual entities. Whitehead develops the Platonic alternative to the Aristotelian dictum that "a substance is not present in a subject," which underlies the subject-object dualism in much of Western philosophy and science, and which received its clearest (and worst) formulation in the Cartesian dualism between the *cogito* as mental substance and the world as extended substance that is best known through mathematical formulae. Whitehead characterizes his metaphysics as a philosophy of organism "mainly devoted to the task of making clear the notion of 'being present in another entity' "; and he affirms the proposition, "An actual entity is concrete because it is such a particular concrescence of the universe."[69]

Thus, the experience of a subject in the primal mode of causal efficacy is always that of a "differentiated universal" as a "particular concrescence of the universe." As we have seen in chapter 1, Whitehead completed his metaphysics with a revisionist theology. Here, though Whitehead developed what Northrop termed the "theoretic component," he argued that such theory allows nothing in the nature of proof, but "entirely depends upon the elucidation of . . . religious and moral intuitions." At this level of thought "the task of reason is to fathom the deeper depths of the many-sidedness of things."[70] He agrees that religions of the "Buddhistic type" have some truth but contends that they do not express the whole truth. We already have summarized Whitehead's vision of the being and

becoming of God. As the chief exemplification of the metaphysical principles that order and interpret our cosmos, God is the only complete concrescence of the whole universe. The finitude of all other actual entities
requires abstracting and eliminating ("negatively prehending") subjec-
tively centered forms of definiteness from the myriad energies that affect
us if they and we are to synthesize a new and limited unity. We as finite
subjects therefore objectify by abstracting from the subjective unity of
other actual entities. God alone prehends the complete concrescence of
all actual entities in God's "consequent nature." Thus, in God's physical
pole, God alone is the complete, concrete "differentiated universal."

But what of the Taoist and Buddhist experience of the "undifferentiated universal"? In Whitehead's terms, this is God's "mental pole" or
"primordial nature," defined as "the unlimited conceptual realization of
the absolute wealth of potentiality." As such, God is "the principle of
concretion" as the indeterminate ground and origin of creativity and novelty. Whitehead's notion here is remarkably close to what Northrop appears to think may only be found in Eastern perspectives as "the
indeterminate which is the potentiality for a determinateness that is not
yet."[71] But there is a fundamental difference, and it is at the point of the
validation of desire, which we already have found to be so crucial. Whitehead envisions the subjective form of God's conceptual feelings as including appetition for the determinate actualization of indeterminate
potentiality. Thus God is "the lure for feeling, the eternal urge of desire.
His particular relevance to each creative act, as it arises from its own
conditioned standpoint in the world, constitutes him the initial 'object of
desire' establishing the initial phase of each subjective aim."[72]

Western religious affirmations of desire, however, need not take the
form of "the irresistible moral drive" that Peter Munz affirmed in such
strong contrast to the East. In fact, Whitehead specifically repudiated
"God in the image of the personification of moral energy" for the sake of
affirming God in the image of Love.[73] God does not "combat productive
force with productive force," even if it is understood as moral drive, but,
like a poet of the world, leads it with tender patience by the vision of
truth, beauty, and goodness. This remains far closer to the Tao that,
"undifferentiated and yet complete, which existed before heaven and
earth," enables "acting without action."[74] That is, one acts on the basis of
one's empathic participation in the whole, which concretely takes the
form of sensitive, dialogical, mutual interaction. But this undifferentiated
whole must be seen as moving toward differentiation through such
activity.

This Whiteheadian understanding of a differentiated, relational, becoming universal may also be seen as a more precise conceptual model to
interpret the kinship metaphor so important in African culture and reli-

gion. We have already seen that a definitive theistic model does not fit the African experience as John Mbiti presents it. Africans experience and express the Divine in their religion and art as relational, communal, and universally related to all the dimensions of their life-world. Human beings are created in and for relations, grounded in their God-relation. The Western conceptual model that best interprets this African sense of relationality is the panentheistic model of God as a differentiated and relational universal. The dynamism of the African affirmation of loving relation in life and beyond death also fits the understanding that actionless activity is best interpreted as loving activity, which in acting and being acted upon everlastingly differentiates the panentheistic relational universal, which is the conceptual form most adequate to our experience of God.[75]

The hope that these concepts may be cognitively useful to mediate the cross-cultural meaning of our God-relation is strengthened by the contemporary Korean philosophical theologian Sang Il Kim. He analyzes the common interest that Eastern and Western philosophies have in understanding how the many are related to one by comparing Hua-yen Buddhism with Whitehead's philosophy. He notes that the Korean word *han*, which he understands to be the root for the Korean term for God, *Hanenim*, comprehends five major meanings: one, many, middle, same, and indeterminateness. He criticizes traditional Western philosophy for failing to synthesize the one and the many; and he criticizes Taoism and Buddhism for integrating the one and the many into the same by making them middle. The Korean philosophy of *han*, however, sees the one and the many as indeterminate so that they can appear in any form. He sees this Korean notion of indeterminacy as similar to Whitehead's understanding of creativity where the one and the many always concresce in new and creative forms.[76]

### Teilhard de Chardin's Mediating Experiences

These mediating concepts enable us to thematize the psychological discernment of mediating experiences, which is the second requirement for successfully mediating meaning cross-culturally. Just as Whitehead, the process metaphysician, articulated the necessary mediating concepts, so Teilhard de Chardin, as a process philosopher-poet, provides the most helpful Western expression of the associated experience. Teilhard's thought lacks the precision and coherence of Whitehead's but far exceeds it in poetic expressiveness, in a way similar to Northrop's evaluation of Chinese poetry.

On the one hand, Teilhard was deeply troubled by the division and conflict of our differentiated and pluralistic universe. "The multitude of beings," he wrote, "is an affliction hard to bear." In his *Writings in Times of War*, he grieved that "all around us, it would seem, there is nothing but incurable division and innate hostility," and he generalized that "the cosmos itself, taken in its totality, breaks down into a vast agglomeration of individual self-centered particles whose paths cross and obstruct one another."[77]

The pain of experiencing conflictual multiplicity was intensified for him because he had the mystic's sense and passion for the cosmic whole as strongly as any Buddhist or Taoist. He wondered how anyone could "ignore this fundamental vibration whose ring can be heard by every practiced ear at the basis, or rather at the summit, of every great emotion? Resonance to the All—the keynote of pure poetry and pure religion."[78]

His attraction to the cosmic All—no matter in how proper a reaction to the division and hostility he experienced in our universe, and never worse than during World War I—constituted for him as a Christian a "godless crisis." He describes imaginatively how he was

> possessed by a great yearning to go and find, far from men and far from toil the place where dwell the vast forces that cradle us and possess us, where my over-tense activity might indefinitely become ever more relaxed. [He relaxes and drifts] unresistingly to effortless enjoyment and Nirvana. [He approaches the Taoist sense that] Mighty nature is at work for us . . . any interference on our part would be wasted labor.[79]

But this "initiation into the cosmos" was not taken as enlightenment so much as it was felt to be a terrible temptation. Teilhard judged that his cosmic sense could either lead him to a sublime love for God or deviate into what he feared might become a banal and facile form of pantheism.

Teilhard later recognized his early attraction to rocks and iron to be a search for permanence beneath the evident transience of the world. Shaped in a European Catholic tradition of substance metaphysics with the Aristotelian notion of "prime matter," he could only conceive his cosmic passion for the All in terms of being drawn toward the "ultra-matter" at the base of all things. This tempted him toward a "pantheism of fusion": "If I was to be All, I must be fused with all."[80] It was this kind of pantheism that Teilhard judged to be banal and facile, and his temptation toward it to be a "godless crisis." But neither could he make his "cosmic sense" fit into the ontological dualism of traditional theistic theology or the epistemological dualism of traditional European philosophy. After reviewing all of Teilhard's works, Thomas King finds continuing ambiguity in his response to pantheism: "Teilhard was ambiguous in his use of the term 'pantheism.' Sometimes he would simply reject what it implies, at other times he would speak favorably of a 'Christian pantheism.' "[81]

It was only when Teilhard the scientist and paleontologist came to understand the theory of evolution that he could accept and interpret his cosmic sense as an entrance into a "spiritual or Christian pantheism." He now had a coherent, contemporary hermeneutic with which to interpret passages from his own scripture, like Colossians 1:17, Ephesians 1:10, and 1 Corinthians 15:28, to help thematize his mystical sense of the cosmic whole. Now he could accept his own and his world's transience, instability, and vulnerability because he found the passing of particular determinateness necessary to sharing in the commonality of all things, and as humanity, to the sharing in a common spirit. The stability he earlier sought at the base of things could now be coherently hoped for only in a final synthesis: "Contrary to the appearances still admitted by physics, the Great Stability is not at the bottom of the infra-elementary sphere, but at the top in the ultra-synthetic sphere."[82]

What Teilhard sought to articulate is far clearer, it seems to me, in Whitehead's concept of God's consequent nature; so Teilhard's resolution of the ambiguity he properly felt about pantheism is more adequately resolved in Whitehead's concept of panentheism. Whitehead provides a more definitively Christian revision of pantheism to interpret our cosmic sense of participation in the All, while enabling a continuing affirmation of the transcendence and creativity of God. Teilhard's preeminent value is his personal manifestation of a Christian form of spirituality that may open the West dialogically to the meaning of the cosmic sense of the East and the kinship metaphors of Africa. Teilhard had the advantage of participating directly in these religious cultures in his frequent paleontological expeditions in China and Africa. Fortunately, we no longer require an exotic vocation to enter into similar relational possibilities in our emerging global village.

Working as a paleontologist within Eastern cultures, Teilhard tried to understand the view that phenomena might be "regarded as an illusion (Maya) and their connections as a chain (Karma)." He weighed their argument in the following terms:

> We must persuade ourselves of the non-existence of all surrounding phenomena, destroy the Grand Illusion by asceticism or by mysticism, create night and silence within ourselves; then, at the opposite extreme of appearance, we shall penetrate to what can only be defined as a total negation—the ineffable Reality.[83]

He remained skeptical of this perspective, however, primarily because he thought the escape it sought from the phenomenal world to be premature. Humanity, he thought, shall achieve the unity they seek only through a process of growth. The notion of evolution clearly differentiated Teilhard's spirituality here from the Eastern forms he experienced and sought dialogically to understand. But what is even more deeply implicit is the difference in understanding the creativity of the Reality he and they both sought to understand—the creativity of God. Teilhard's way of putting this over and over again was to affirm the organic conceptual model in which "unity differentiates." Thomas King summarizes what Teilhard articulated in twelve different contexts as he again and again sought to correct the substantialist philosophy and materialistic science with which he had been enculturated:

> True unity does not fuse the elements it brings together, rather by mutual fertilization it renews them, or as Teilhard would often repeat, "*Unity differentiates.*" The living unity "super differentiates" the elements that it unites. This is again why the movement of life is the reverse of the movement of matter. Matter suggests a unity (one that is only apparent) in which all distinction is lost. But the living cell has a unity wherein the particular quality of each element—its form—is further intensified. The living organism does not dissolve the specific character of its elements, it needs this character, it accentuates it, and draws it into a more complex whole.[84]

## Conclusion

Whitehead's panentheistic metaphysics articulates, and Teilhard's spiritual (and scientific) experience expresses, an organic, evolutionary model for understanding the spatiotemporal process in which we creatively participate. There is cosmic unity, but that unity differentiates. The universal we prehend at the base of our experience as causal efficacy and seek to synthesize at the apex of our metaphysical conceptualizations in presentational immediacy is a *relational universal*. Because relational, it cannot be fully known in the completed reflection (Gadamer) of any one. It can only be increasingly known in the dialogical process that is passing into and bringing God's very being into fuller actualization. Our capacity to discern meanings in the sign-events of our commonly experienced cosmos or to communicate meanings in the syntactical relations of our various symbol systems is grounded in our participation in this relational universal, which is both the creative primordial ground and created consequent eschaton of our spatiotemporal process—God as conceived panentheistically in relation to our world.

No claim may now be made, however, that panentheism as articulated in the process theology of the West is a completed reflection adequate for communicating our universal God-relation cross-culturally and interreligiously. A number of reviews of F. S. C. Northrop's earlier masterful attempt to mediate the meanings discerned in East and West agreed with E. A. Burtt, who wrote:

His proposal inevitably reflects the characteristic slant of Western ways of thinking which are alien to the Eastern mind; what is needed is to confront it with equally comprehensive proposals expressing Eastern ways of thinking, and then for Eastern and Western thinkers to work out together a co-operative method by which such proposals can be systematically composed, pruned, and synthesized.[85]

We may hope that the alienation between Western and Eastern modes of experiencing and expressing meaning has been reduced in the intervening half-century since Professor Northrop did his work, not least by the increasing interest in and development of the work of Whitehead and Teilhard. There can be no doubt, however, that any adequate communication of meaning in our culturally and religiously differentiated world continues to require the kind of open, yet mutually critical, dialogical process to which he contributed so much. Without it there shall neither be the cultural reconciliation nor the religious peace that the worship and service of the universally relational God requires.

# 3

# The Interreligious
# Relationality of Redemption

## Introduction

Some may feel that our conclusions about God's relations to the world have been inordinately positive: God is the Creator of emergent order amongst the finitely free but internally related entities of our universe. And God is the divine relational Universal, who grounds our capacity both to discern meanings in our cosmos and communicate those meanings in the syntactical relations of our symbol systems. We know, however, that too neat a system of coherent abstractions is fit only for libraries; and then only for those where Job's suffering and Jesus' crucifixion are removed from its Bible, Shakespeare's *Hamlet* and Dostoevsky's *Brothers Karamazov* have no place in its literature, and news reports of the eruption of Mt. Pinatubo in the Philippines, the plight of the homeless and the starving in even our most affluent societies, and the danger of ecological and nuclear self-destruction of our "developed" world are eliminated from its reference files. Theology may no longer be written, therefore, as though the Jew's Shoah, the Soviet's gulag, the African's apartheid, and the Minjung's *han* are not part of our meaningful cosmos.

Our first intention has been to present an understanding of God's creativity and wisdom that enables a rational affirmation of humanity's religious faith that we, despite all, live in a basically good and meaningful cosmos. If we have enabled an interreligious articulation of this basic source of human joy, we now may and must turn to the sense(s) of alienation, evil, ignorance, sin, and suffering we also commonly experience, which undermine our joy and sometimes challenge our faith and hope. In Christian terms, we now turn to the themes of sin and redemption. But given the increasing interaction of the world's religions in our global village, we must recognize the problematic aspects of these traditional terms and seek to interpret them dialogically within the universal relationality of God.

## Dialogical Complexity as the Route Toward Universal Concreteness

Some hold that moving from cosmological interpretation to existential experience is a move toward clearer truth. Reinhold Niebuhr sometimes claimed that the Christian doctrine of sin was the only one capable of "empirical" proof.[1] But if this is in some sense so, we must also recall that there are no facts that may be dislodged from their contextual, interpretive structures. Even as he wrote this sentence, Niebuhr worked with a theoretical paradigm dependent on a worldview. All interpretations of moral and religious experience reflect the mediation and limitations of a tradition.[2] The Christian understanding of sin is not simply synonymous with the Hindu or Buddhist teaching about *avidya*, or the Muslim doctrine of *shirk*. Interreligious dialogue especially requires Mark Taylor's admonition to recognize the relativity of our finite social locations: "Own up to where you are, whoever you are and however complex your located self and group identities may be."[3]

Even able theologians of the previous generation came to interreligious dialogue late in their work, if at all. Paul Tillich's first encounter with Shintoism and Buddhism at age seventy-four, when visiting Japan five years before his death, led him to affirm, "No Western provincialism of which I am aware will be tolerated by me from now on in my thought and work."[4] In the last public lecture of his distinguished career, Tillich spoke of the need for a long, intense period of "interpenetration of systematic theology and religious historical studies," as he had begun during the two years of seminars he taught with Mircea Eliade.[5] The interdisciplinary studies he called for have been going on with increasing intensity for the past quarter century in the work of theologians such as Masao Abe, Wesley Ariarajah, John Cobb, Jr., Hap Kim Hao, Paul Knitter, John Mbiti, Lesslie Newbigin, Keiji Nishitani, Raimundo Panikkar, Pyun Sun Hwan, George Rupp, Huston Smith, Wilfred Cantwell Smith, C. S. Song, and Leonard Swidler, to name some from whom many have learned. It is not that any of these African, Asian, European, or North American theologians have become universal minds capable of completed reflection in Gadamer's terms, but that their located selves and group identities have become more complex, in Taylor's terms. Raimundo Panikkar, for instance, describes his own experience as a Roman Catholic theologian in interreligious dialogue: "I 'left' as a Christian; I 'found' myself a Hindu; and I 'returned' as a Buddhist, without having ceased to be a Christian."[6]

Conservative faithful in every religion, however, hesitate to enter such complexity for fear of losing the concrete meaning of their redemption. A recent (1991) debate in the Singapore meeting of the World Methodist Council, for instance, set what some feel and fear is a religiously imperialistic world evangelism against an interreligious mode of dialogical evangelism. The issue discussed was whether the Holy Spirit redemptively enters the world only through witness to Jesus Christ or whether God's Spirit is already redemptively present in other religions and cultures before Christians bring their faithful witness.[7]

This issue is philosophically analogous to the question of whether the meaning of any particular entity abstracted from its universal relations may be adequately known—even if that entity be Jesus the Christ. Or is any theological attempt to abstract the meaning of our God-relation another instance of what Whitehead called the "fallacy of misplaced concreteness"?[8] If every entity is internally related to an organic universe, we proceed toward concrete meaning only by interpreting an entity in the context of all its relations. This appears the more obvious for paradigmatic events, like the atonement of Jesus Christ or the enlightenment of Gautama Buddha, which have long since shown their universal salvific power. Whitehead expressed the theological implications of his concept of "misplaced concreteness" beyond its original context of Western science:

> In monistic philosophies, Spinoza's or absolute idealism, this ultimate is God, who is also equivalently termed "The Absolute." In such monistic schemes, the ultimate is illegitimately allowed a final "eminent" reality, beyond that ascribed to any of its accidents. In this general position the philosophy of organism seems to approximate more to some strains of Indian, or Chinese, thought, than to western Asiatic, or European, thought. One side makes process ultimate; the other side makes fact ultimate.[9]

The discussion in our first two chapters already has shown that a panentheistic understanding of God's universal relationality opens Christian theology to some strains of Indian or Chinese thought. From this dialogical perspective, the redemption Christians already know shall be more concretely known through interreligious dialogue. This need not, and must not, lead to some lifeless concept abstracted as the common element in all religions. But it can, and I think should, lead to Tillich's "dynamic typological" approach, which dialogically interprets the particular manifestations of the redemptively holy experienced in the world's religions.[10] Our discussion must continue from where Tillich's concluding sentence in his last lecture left many of us:

The universality of a religious statement does not lie in an all-embracing abstraction which would destroy religion as such, but it lies in the depths of every concrete religion. Above all it lies in the openness to spiritual freedom both from one's own foundation and for one's own foundation.[11]

## Mediating Universal Redemption
## Through the Western Tradition

We may find spiritual freedom from and for our own foundation only if we recognize that in some ways we remain where Tillich left off. The only possibility of moving toward a higher universality by those enculturated within Christian theology and Euro-American ideology is through that tradition. We may learn from Hegel's powerful but flawed attempt in the nineteenth century to open our Western tradition interreligiously toward the universal. But to stand on his shoulders, we must learn to use his "realist-nominalist-processive model," as defined by George Rupp below, more dialogically in the interreligious *kairos* in which we now live.

Some modern theologians have celebrated the "technocratic" pattern of Judeo-Christian culture as it displaces the "ontocratic" pattern of other religious cultures.[12] Postmodernists, on the other hand, have focused on the limitations of our tradition in its "individualism, anthropocentrism, patriarchy, mechanization, economism, consumerism, nationalism, and militarism."[13] Whether we focus upon the power or limits of Euro-American culture, however, our theology is in various ways formed, transformed, and perhaps deformed through it.

George Rupp provides a typology that learns from Hegel's classical nineteenth-century attempt to move through Western culture toward universality at the point of understanding the religious experience of redemption.[14] He correlates variables in Christology with varying interpretations of personal and social reality. His typology enables a more comprehensive analysis of the meaning of redemption than the traditional contrast between "atonement as a transaction of universal significance effected once and for all in the life and death of Christ," and the more liberal focus on the redemptive "significance of the historical Jesus."[15]

Rupp constructs his typology from two pairs of fundamentally contrasting ideas: The first derives from the medieval realist and nominalist controversy over the ontological status of universals, which he correlates with the growing priority of the individual over the corporate in Western culture since the eleventh century. The second is the contrast between the "transactional" and "processive," which is correlated with the sociocultural "tendency throughout the modern period to place less and less emphasis on the possibility of a transhistorical fulfillment for human destiny and to concentrate instead on life in space and time."[16]

The christological issues posed by this typology are first, whether God's redemptive action through Jesus has a *universal* effect in God, humanity, and/or the cosmos? or only in *individual* believers? And second, whether that effect is *mediated* through experience in space and time or accomplished *once and for all* without historical mediation?

Without reviewing all of the possibilities Rupp constructs from these variables, we take his point that only a *"consistently processive"* interpretation (in contrast to a "transactional") may combine both realist/universal and nominalist/personal meanings of redemption. Irenaeus, Lessing, and Schleiermacher are the historical progenitors of this realist-nominalist-processive correlation, but Darwinian science and Hegelian philosophy provided its definitive modern form: Darwinian evolutionary theory related human beings integrally to natural processes, and Hegelian philosophy incorporated the whole of nature into the history of spirit. We have considered Darwin's thought in chapter 1 in relation to Whitehead's metaphysical perspective on the "spatiotemporal relationality of creation." We now must look more closely at the philosophy most similar to Whitehead's—Hegel's—on the "universal relationality of redemption."[17]

George Rupp's summary of Hegel's thought is remarkably similar to the conclusion of our last chapter: "There is cosmic unity, but that unity differentiates":

> The movement of Hegel's thought follows a recurrent pattern. . . . The structure is typically threefold: from a relatively less differentiated unity there is movement first to increased particularization or differentiation and then to a re-established unity which in some sense preserves the greater individuation achieved in the process of differentiation.[18]

Hegel sought to demonstrate that there are no universals available to human knowledge in a purely transcendent and abstract form. He thus criticized the understanding of universals in Hindu philosophy and Western idealism as he came to his oft-quoted conclusion that "everything depends on grasping and expressing the ultimate truth not as Substance but Subject as well."[19] The meaning of this rather enigmatic assertion is that the Ultimate (or God for Christians) must be understood as self-differentiated process. Though he does not use the term "panentheism," Hegel understood the Absolute, or God, as a process that only can be known through God's relations with the evolving reality reflected in the system of human conceptions.

Hegelian philosophy thus postulated an extraordinary dignity for the spiritual existence of human beings in the reconciliation of their cosmos. Hegel's philosophy at this point was close to Christian theology: For the

Lutheran Hegel, the dying and rising of Christ had a crucial significance in human history. It was the historical point where human religious imagination grasped the unity of the human and the divine in a historical individual. When the infinite grief of Jesus' death was mediated historically in the spirit of his disciples, the abstract experience and conception of God as a totally other "Substance" died. The resurrection of Substance as Subject was also experienced by Jesus' disciples in that moment.

This was the atoning moment in human history for Hegel, where the alienation between God and human beings was and is being reconciled in Christian communities. The church for Hegel is a *koinonia* or *Gemeinschaft* of the Holy Spirit. The completion of the atoning process, prefigured for Christians in the Eucharist, requires the integration of fully differentiated, free individuals into a cosmic communal whole, and finally shall require the continuing transformation of church, society, and state. Hegel thus interpreted human freedom as emerging in Christian faith, deepened in the Protestant Reformation, expanded in the European Enlightenment, institutionalized in the rationalization of European society in his epoch, and open to further development.

Though Hegel's conceptual breadth and power must be recognized as Rupp and many others have, the claim that his philosophy provides the completed reflection that we with Gadamer have found inimical to interreligious and cross-cultural dialogue must be rejected. Even were we to become able to "think the very structure of reality," as Hegel's understanding of dialectical reconciliation implies, we are not Aristotle's *nous* or Plotinus's *logos*—that is "thought thinking thought." Even those who approximate the conceptual power of Hegel remain finite, contextually dependent human beings.[20]

There is no clearer example of the limit of Hegel's horizon than his Eurocentric interpretation of the history of human freedom:

> The Orientals do not know that spirit or man as such is in principle free. Because they do not know this, they also are not free. They know only that one is free. . . . This one is as a result a despot—not a free man, not a person at all. With the Greeks, consciousness of freedom first arose; and therefore they were free. But they along with the Romans knew only that some are free—not men as such. . . . The teutonic nations, under the influence of Christianity, were the first to attain the consciousness that man as man is free, that it is the freedom of spirit which constitutes its peculiar nature.[21]

Even if Hegel meant by "teutonic" something more pan-European than German, there is still an extraordinary hubris in this historical judgment. His limited understanding of Oriental history, and his entire ignorance and neglect of African history, allowed no such judgment as he dared to make. Even Christians who agree that Christ's atonement has had a salvific, reconciling effect on European peoples have little reason after the horrors of the twentieth century to believe that we have fully realized it or adequately understood it. Paul Tillich sometimes observed—and lamented—that Hegel's nineteenth century ended August 13, 1914; and after two world wars, a Shoah, a gulag, and a worldwide repudiation of European colonialism, we must recognize with greater clarity than Hegel the limits and the distortions of both Euro-American cult and culture.

Yet we are indebted to Hegel, as Gadamer and Rupp have recognized, for a conceptual model that enables us dialogically to seek and sometimes to recognize the dialectical relation of the particular to the universal. Rupp names it a "realist-nominalist-processive" model. We have named it heretofore "dialectical panentheism." It should be possible to use a more pluralistic, dialogical version of the Hegelian model to seek the universal relationality of redemption as we interact with non-Western cultural and religious traditions.[22]

### A World Kairos for
### Interreligious Dialogue

To be sure, modern Asia and Africa are rationalizing their societies in technical, economic, and even political modes that were first actualized in Euro-America. And the very rapid growth of Christianity in parts of Asia and even postcolonial Africa also reveals some correlation of this rationalization with Christian faith—as Hegel already discerned in the nineteenth century, and van Leeuwen celebrates in too triumphalistic a fashion in the twentieth.

This movement toward an interdependent world civilization, in my judgment, should rather be interpreted as a world *kairos* for interreligious dialogue.[23] We cannot uncritically celebrate the technocratic rationalization of our societies because it is evident that such technocracy has already created immense problems in Euro-American societies. Secularization has bred a growing anomie, even nihilism in many of our people. The neo-orthodox theological response of moving to a transactional understanding of a transcendent atonement, and the evangelical-fundamentalist hope for a transcendent eschaton to end our nuclear and ecologically threatened age, have addressed this growing despair but with little spiritual resource creatively to transform it. Our best, if not our only, hope is to turn dialogically to the religious resources of all humankind to understand the universal relationality of the redemption we all increasingly need.

Even the most universal of our religions, however, provide only a part of humanity that kind of spiritual community and comprehensive theological model required to interpret and shape life. The more universal, transcultural religions—especially Buddhism and Christianity, but also Islam—have moved toward the universal conceptually by articulating their theologies in more metaphysical modes that presumably transcend their cultures of origin. Buddhism is no longer specific to Indian culture, nor Islam to Arabic culture despite its attempt to forbid the translation of the Qur'an from Arabic. And Christians from the beginning were "no longer Jew or Greek"[24] as their theology emerged at the confluence of the Semitic and Hellenistic religious cultures—just as it is no longer specific to Euro-American culture. Yet it is becoming ever more clear that even the most comprehensive ontological formulations of the transcultural religions are contextually relative. They provide no completed reflection for even their most devoted adherents that is adequate to the increasingly complex personal and social, religious and ethical issues of our day. East has met West in myriad ways in our century, just as North began to meet South with colonializing energies in the previous two centuries. Up to now, it has been as much or more to humanity's bane as to our blessing. It is now, therefore, essential to our salvation that we meet each other religiously in a "genuine, sympathetic, essence-to-essence encounter."[25]

## Interpreting Redemption Both Philosophically and Theologically

Whether interreligious encounter is enabled by the kind of philosophical reflection we practice in this study is a moot but far from mute issue in the current discussion. Harvey Cox, though clearly aware of the contribution of philosophy,[26] weighs in, nevertheless, on the side of personal "testimony" as basic to dialogue: "I believe a certain careful and modest restoration of personal narrative—call it 'testimony' if you will—can help restore some of the life-giving particularity to the dialogue among religions."[27] He points out that his Buddhist, Hindu, and Muslim dialogue partners have expected him to speak of his faith in Jesus. Cox's understanding of Jesus motivates and guides his readiness for such dialogue; yet he stresses the importance of staying in relation with those Christians whose theology does not:

> I have often found it easier to converse with universally minded Buddhists or Hindus than with fellow Christians who not only dismiss such people as pagans but also want to dismiss me for not recognizing it. Still, I believe the critically important conversation among people of diverse faiths could founder and fail if we—the dialoguers—lose touch with our fellow believers who cluster on the particularistic side. We may not admit it, but we do need each other. They remind us that without the radical particularity of the original revelation, we would

have no faith to share. We remind them that without the universal dream they falsify the message and diminish the scope of the original vision.[28]

David Tracy's methodological reflection about interreligious dialogue leads him to the same insight. When dialogue becomes primarily a "passive response to more and more possibilities," it masks the ideology of the modern bourgeois mind in which "one tries to enjoy the pleasures of difference without ever committing oneself to any particular vision of resistance and hope."[29] Yet faithful interpretation of the canon and classics of Christianity leads Tracy to recognize that precisely Christianity's classical sources require the affirmation of God's universality:

> Any authentic speech on the reality of God which is really private or particularist is unworthy of that reality. Christianity, when true to its heritage, cannot but recognize that its fundamental faith, its most radical trust and loyalty, is to the all-pervasive reality of the God of love and power disclosed in Jesus Christ.[30]

Father Tracy thinks that theology must be articulated in three distinct but interrelated forms. He names them "fundamental, systematic, and practical,"[31] but his Catholic meaning of "fundamental" is what most mean by "philosophical." It is that mode of theology concerned to frame its discussion in ways that all reasonable persons can follow. Though committed to a particular religious tradition, its practitioners must "abstract themselves from all religious faith commitments for the legitimate purpose of critical analysis of all religious and theological claims."[32] Such critical reflection needs the discipline of philosophy, though the faithful may find their theological warrants in the canonical doctrines of creation and God's universal salvific will. Philosophical theology may and must remain open to the truths disclosed by the hermeneutical methods of systematic theology and realized in the transformative methods of praxis, but it will interpret these insights philosophically to make them dialogically available to public discourse and interreligious dialogue.

### Jewish Perspectives

A similar discussion goes on in the Jewish scholarly community. Kenneth Seeskin enters it as an interpreter of contemporary Judaism with his professional discipline of philosophy.[33] Though supporting a more universal philosophical perspective, he recognizes that particularism has become predominant in his Jewish community since Martin Buber and Franz Rosenzweig, and the establishment of the state of Israel. And he understands the reasons for its growing influence: the inadequacy of any ahistorical treatment of religious ideas, an earlier overemphasis on reason,

the danger of human autonomy undercutting religious law, the importance of personal relation with the God known through tradition, and the
horror of the Jewish holocaust.

Yet he interprets Jewish uniqueness as a dedication to ideas that transcend the peculiarities of their own context. Jewish particularity is legiti-
mated by the idea of a universal humanity, which is a direct consequence
of Jewish monotheism. Judaism also denies the possibility of any conflict
between God and moral reason; thus he concludes philosophically:

> The Creator has left a mark of His perfection on the soul of every being
> made in His image: respect for the law that God imposes on Himself
> and that we can impose on ourselves if we make the effort. . . . God's
> will is not alien. It is the paradigm by which we understand our own.
> He is in that sense the infinite possibility of my realization of myself as
> a person.[34]

Not all Jewish scholars, of course, agree with Seeskin's more or less
Kantian moves toward universality. Michael Wyschogrod, sometimes
characterized as the Jewish Karl Barth, argues that Jews read their scripture believing that "no spiritual essence can be extracted from the biblical
truth" and that the concreteness of the text should not be "dissipated in
sophisticated if not sophistical demythologizations, but connected with
the real world."[35] Jews, like Christians and many others, fear God's wrath
as they seek to fulfill God's law. Wyschogrod does not reject Seeskin's
focus on moral law as central to Judaism but emphasizes the impossibility
of living in perfect obedience. Thus Jews must also rely upon the grace of
God. Both Judaism and Christianity "emphasize works while realizing
that the mercy of God is nevertheless essential."[36] Jewish faith knows
God's mercy through their election and covenant. Other "children of
adoption"—such as Christians—whose traditions do not so intimately
mediate the grace of God, may require a greater guarantee of God's
mercy. This explains, in Wyschogrod's judgment, why Christians have
divinized Jesus. Jewish believers, however, have the privilege of living out
of the concreteness of their tradition.

The theological issue defined first of all for Jews by Seeskin and Wyschogrod enables us to focus exactly on the more universal issue of redemption. One of the philosophical universals not only Jews and
Christians use to mediate the particularities of faith is the common human experience of moral law. But it leads directly to more religious questions: May the ways our various traditions meet our religious needs after
moral failure be universalized? And may we be saved from being personally alienated by the universal morality our religion affirms? Wyschogrod
finds grace mediated through participation in the historical particularity
of his Jewish covenanted community. But is it possible philosophically to

universalize the idea of covenant without losing the concrete experience
of gracious relationality? That is, can we experience and conceive universal relationality in a way that does not lose the concreteness of covenanted
communal relations in the abstraction of the universal?

A basis for universalizing the idea of covenant may be found in the
particularity of the Jewish and Christian Bible:

> The covenant is a conception that extends for biblical religion from the
> divine creation of the world to its hoped for consummation by God.
> The covenants were not simply the means for securing the particularity
> of certain communities but also the means for expressing the universal-
> ity of God's sovereignty.[37]

The first eleven chapters of Genesis develop universal themes of creation
and rebellion, judgment and salvation, culminating in the covenant with
Noah sometimes termed the "cosmic covenant":

> The LORD said in his heart, "I will never again curse the ground because
> of humankind, for the inclination of the human heart is evil from youth;
> nor will I ever again destroy every living creature as I have done.
>
> As long as the earth endures,
>     seedtime and harvest, cold and heat,
> summer and winter, day and night,
>     shall not cease."
>
> (Gen. 8:21b–22, NRSV)

The more particular historical covenants with Abraham and Moses re-
counted later are similar in expressing a universally redemptive purpose:
"In you all the families of the earth shall be blessed" (Gen. 12:3b, NRSV).

These covenantal texts express the universality of the God-relation
precisely in terms of redemption. It is just where it is recognized that the
human heart is evil from youth that the faithfulness of God's creativity
through the structures of nature is discerned as salvific. Whatever may be
the form of divine judgment upon our human alienation, it is not to be
interpreted as coming through natural catastrophe. The relative order of
nature is interpreted in the Noahic covenant as an expression of God's
creative and redemptive purpose.

Much of the redemptive focus in the rest of the Hebrew scriptures may
be summarized as: (1) The interpreted narratives of God's establishing
and maintaining historical covenant relations with the people of Abraham, Moses, Joshua, and David. (2) The postexilic promise through Jeremiah of a "new covenant" when the law will be written on their hearts, so
as to heal the "covenant that they broke" (see Jer. 31:31–34). (3) The
prophetic vision so important to Christian faith of Isaiah-after-the-exile,
who interpreted the historical passion of God's suffering servant to be for
the sake of such covenanted renewal.[38]

*Christian Perspectives*
*on a Universal Covenant*

The Christian scriptures narrate the new covenant enacted through the life, death, and resurrection of Jesus. Christians throughout the Roman Empire interpreted the gracious relations they experienced through Jesus as transcending and reconciling the national, economic, and gender alienations then and still suffered by human beings:

> For in Christ Jesus you are all children of God through faith. As many of you as were baptized into Christ have clothed yourselves with Christ. There is no longer Jew or Greek, there is no longer slave or free, there is no longer male and female; for all of you are one in Christ Jesus. (Gal. 3:21–26, NRSV)

It is just at the point of our alienation and need for redemption that Christians experience God acting redemptively to restore universal relationality: "For he [Christ] is our peace; in his flesh he has made both groups into one and has broken down the dividing wall, that is, the hostility between us" (Eph. 2:14, NRSV).

The New Testament kerygma interprets God's universal redemptive activity with the concept of *Logos*, which joins the particularity of Jesus with the scope and significance of universal reason. The prologue of John's Gospel affirms that the divine Word or Wisdom was sent to the whole cosmos to redeem that which the same Logos had created; and Colossians and Ephesians affirm that the Logos Christians know in Jesus will "reconcile to himself all things" (Col. 1:20).[39] Richard Henry Drummond aptly, if abstractly, summarizes the theology of these scriptural texts: "In the relational mystery of God's cosmos, the destiny of all beings appears to be that of coming into relationship with all other beings in the spirit of love and the activity of service."[40]

I have earlier expressed the universality of the Christian experience of covenanted relations in the concrete struggles of contemporary Christians for peace:

> Only when we profoundly understand that there is one Creator at work through one Logos in the whole creation to bring it to communion through one Spirit will we be drawn into our finite communities without succumbing to the sinful dynamics of their alter-egoisms. Then we may elaborate our human ideas without absolutist ideologies, our national cultures without idolatrous civil cults, our human laws without destructive legalisms, our human economies without forgetfulness of nature's ecology, and our religious communities without divisively absolute claims.[41]

Now we are dealing more concretely with the last of the issues to which I then pointed: Can religious communities with all the concreteness of their particularity move redemptively toward universal relationality? Can they negotiate the narrow passage between the Scylla of absolutizing their particular concrete experience and the Charybdis of lapsing into abstract philosophical universality? Can they surrender all claims to absolute truth without reducing theology to a disempowering relativism?

To reconceive God within the concrete Christian tradition of covenant in universally relational terms is to understand God as actually responsive to every culturally differentiated form of human self-actualization. The primal but pluralistic religious discernments of finite persons in particular communities may both be affirmed and reconciled with our faith in the universality of God. Even theologians like George Lindbeck, who understands Christian theology in a more particularistic way as a "cultural linguistic system," may yet recognize that other religions actualize potentialities and explore realities "not within the direct purview of the people of Messianic witness, but that are nevertheless God-willed and God-approved anticipations of the coming kingdom."[42]

To understand God as actually responsive to every human form of self-actualization may be abstractly expressed in terms of panentheism. Christians, however, are moved toward this theology more by their concrete relation to Jesus the Christ. The redemptive God who meets us at the point of our finite alienation cannot be an abstract universal only defined through our speculative rationality. Forgiveness and restoration to communion and creativity come through a personal response to a particular manifestation of divine grace. A God projected by alienated persons cannot save them. The Christian's experience of redemption, therefore, leads to the affirmation that the grace of Jesus the Christ may be known universally in the Holy Spirit, who is continuous with the human person known in Palestine two thousand years ago.[43]

Knowing the pallor of abstractions, Paul Yorck von Wartenburg wrote to his friend, the philosopher Wilhelm Dilthey:

> I should consider it desirable for an attempt to be made to disregard all these categories, Pantheism, Monotheism, Theism, Panentheism. In themselves they have no religious value whatsoever, being only formal and of quantitative character. They reflect views of the world and not of God, and constitute only the outline of an intellectual attitude; and only a formal projection even for this.[44]

Though many think the form of our intellectual attitude is important, Martin Buber's response to Yorck is apt:

> It is not so decisive whether the existence of a Unity exalted over all is assumed in one's consideration, but the way in which this Unity is

viewed and experienced, and whether one stands to it in an exclusive relationship which shapes all other relations and thereby the whole order of life.[45]

It is precisely such lived redemptive relations that we seek through interreligious dialogue to understand both philosophically and theologically as the universal relationality of redemption.

## Muslim Redemption in a Universally Relational Perspective

Having articulated a universally relational perspective from Jewish and Christian standpoints, we turn now to that religion most closely associated with them—Islam. It is the third of what are often called "Abrahamic religions,"[46] which affirm out of their common Semitic heritage what Buber termed "the existence of a Unity exalted overall." The Qur'an is explicit about the congeniality of their relation: "Do not argue with the people of the Book [Jews and perhaps Christians], except in the best of terms . . . and say unto them: We believe in that which has been revealed to us and that which has been revealed to you. Our God and your God is one, and to him we are self-surrendered" (Sura 29:46).

Islam shares with Judaism a straightforward monotheism, while sharing with Christianity a clear affirmation of the divinely ordained mission of Jesus. The Qur'an teaches reverence for both Moses and Jesus as prophets and even speaks of Jesus as Messiah and a spirit from God who shall return as the instrument of God's judgment to establish the universal kingdom of God and the truth of Islam (Sura 4:157–58, 169).

Unfortunately, the Qur'an is little read or referred to by most Christians. Unlike the Hebrew scriptures, it constitutes neither an Old Testament nor an Apocrypha to be read in our liturgies or referred to in our sermons.[47] Thus few are in a position to recognize what is clear to faithful Muslims such as Gamal Badr: "It is obvious, therefore, that Islam's view of both Judaism and Christianity is not that of an alien faith. Islam views both religions as links in the one divine message revealed to mankind over time, culminating in Islam itself."[48] Seyyed Hossein Nasr notes that Islamic mystical literature often expresses "reverence for Christian piety and beauty of soul" even when Christian missionary activity, often identified by Muslims with colonialism, has fanned opposition to Christianity. Nasr represents a Muslim view of Christianity that sees it as an ally against "modern agnosticism, atheism, and secularism": "God has willed both religions to exist and to be ways of salvation for millions of human beings."[49]

We must come to understand Islam as a way of salvation for millions of our human brothers and sisters. The heart of the Muslim faith is that all of life's relationships depend on one's relation to God—Allah. A right relation to Allah yields a right relation to self and others. The relation to God, however, is unique, allowing no comparison or analogy with anything or anyone. The unforgivable sin for a Muslim is *shirk*, which may be translated as "polytheism" but which more literally connotes "sharing or association."⁵⁰ The point is that not even Muhammed or Jesus may be conceived as sharing God's deity. Muslims believe that sharing God's deity with anyone or anything leads to fanaticism and division. Only on the basis of *tawheed*, that is, belief in the absolute oneness and uniqueness of Allah, can humanity find a basis for its unity.

Human unity, when based on Islamic submission to the will of Allah, takes the form of ethical community. Human beings are understood to be unique because the breath of Allah has given them spiritual life. They have the dignity of being *khalifah*, that is, trustees of Allah on earth. Their finite freedom and its attendant responsibility are affirmed. Submission to Allah is not primarily fate but decision. The evidence of such submission is ethical behavior in the form of justice, kindness, and charity. Because all of life is related to the ethical will of one God, all aspects of life may and must be the worship of Allah. Purity of intention then seeks divine guidance within the parameters of Allah's will revealed through the prophets. The heart of the matter is that religious submission provides moral guidance for personal, social, and political life.

Yet it is as obvious to Muslims as to anyone else that human beings make wrong choices and forfeit their unique dignity. The Muslim scriptures contain narratives for interpreting human perversity similar to those found in the Hebrew and Christian scriptures. The Qur'anic version of the Adam and Eve story, however, does not imply any notion of original sin as the inheritance of sin. It rather symbolizes the universal ethical experience of moving through the cycles of freedom of choice, temptation, decision, error, realization of error, repentance, and forgiveness. Jamal Badawi emphasizes that the Qur'anic approach to sin and atonement "cultivates a sense of individual responsibility."⁵¹ Though Allah is "merciful and compassionate" as every Qur'anic Sura intones, forgiveness requires prior repentance. Human lapses are corrected only through *tawbah*, that is, repentance to Allah. This is understood as an ongoing process throughout one's whole life, moving through the ethical cycles of temptation, decision, error, realization, and repentance.

Responsible but errant human beings, however, require the *shari'ah* or divine law to guide them in this life process. Muslim law is divinely revealed for just such finitely free and sinful beings as we are. Muslims understand their law as neither "too sublime for ordinary human beings" nor "too exalted to be realized."⁵² It is realistically framed to provide the guidance and limit that are both necessary and possible for human beings. Thus, for instance, it does not insist on indissoluble monogamous marriage, thereby avoiding the sexual promiscuity Muslims point to in Judeo-Christian societies because the Christian marriage ethic is "too sublime for ordinary human beings."[53]

The fruit of a right relation with Allah through recurrent repentance in submission to his revealed will is spiritual "peace." Badawi testifies that "the Muslim's relationship with Allah is in essence a relationship of peace."[54] Nevertheless, the required religious and ethical behaviors of prayer, patience in adversity, care for the poor and weak, and justice in relationships will not issue in perfect peace in this world. One must expect and make allowances for continuing human error and evil in this life. Perfect peace and harmony may only be expected eschatologically in the paradise that Allah will give to the repentantly faithful. Muslims look forward eschatologically to a resurrection when "the Truth has come and falsehood has perished" (Sura 17:81). And they seek to sustain the process of *tawbah* until that day.

The Muslim eschatological view of history, coupled with the linear historical sequence of Judaism emerging through Moses, Christianity through Jesus, and Islam through Mohammed, raises the serious question of whether the *tawbah* that leads to saving submission to God also has been sustained through the earlier Abrahamic religions. This is the issue of supersession, which has caused so much conflict of Jews with Christians,[55] and Jews and Christians with Muslims. Some Muslims affirm *naskh*, meaning the abrogation of earlier revelations by a later one, but Islamic scholars like Nasr maintain the more common view that Jews and Christians "would be saved if they practiced their religion."[56]

Authentic dialogue between the faithful of the three Abrahamic religions, therefore, could yield mutual testimony and a measure of agreement concerning the redemption human beings may know if they come into right relation with the God whose moral will has been revealed through a line of prophets stretching from Abraham through Moses and Jesus to Mohammed. Some Muslims, like some Christians, may be counted on to stress the *khalifate* (priesthood) of all believers as they actively submit to the will of Allah. We may disagree as to the quality of the inspiration we have found in and through these prophets and even whether the category of "prophet" is adequate for understanding one or all of them. But at the same time we may agree with John Hick that these three religions are each and all authentic responses to the one God from "within different though related strands of the one human story."[57]

The Christian understanding of incarnation and the related Trinitarian understanding of God constitute the most difficult contrast, if not contradiction, with the Muslim view of *shirk*. The incarnation may be discussed in terms approximating the orthodox Christian tradition with Hindus and Buddhists (as we shall see) but not with Muslims. It is only the "heretical" Arian view of the Christ as a created being that approximates Islam's view of Jesus.

Dialogue with Muslims about redemption, therefore, is more fruitful in the area of anthropology. The issue of how finitely free persons are to understand their relation to God receives its starkest formulation in Muslim faith and theology. Though Christians may not be able fully to appropriate their theological answer, it provides important insights on the issue of human limit as the transcendent Wisdom of the Creator, discussed in chapter 1. Islam also provides important perspectives on the issue discussed in chapter 2, the religious crisis that may arise when a pantheistic sense and passion for the cosmic whole appears as a religious answer to the conflicted multiplicity we experience in this world. We shall return in our concluding section to an appreciation and appropriation of some of these Muslim insights. But they must be dialogically understood in relation to Asian testimonies to the cosmic whole that constitutes so much of their religious experience. We require to learn from both the Muslim type of redemption as communication of the divine will and the Hindu and Buddhist type that experiences redemption as participation in the relational Universal. We may attempt so comprehensive an interpretation, however, only after considering the non-Abrahamic Asian religions.

## Hindu Redemption in a Universally Relational Perspective

Any discussion of redemption in Asian religions must presuppose what was stressed in chapter 2: Understanding religious reality through conceptual theories is a Western perspective not easily transferred to the Asian life-world. Asians do not assume as readily as Euro-Americans that religion is amenable to logos, nor expressible in the syntax of any language. It is not only that many Hindus, guided by the *Bhagavad-Gita*, follow the way of *bhakti marga* (the way of devoted action), whether in the traditional form of the Vedic sacrifices or the neo-Hindu form of selfless service typified by Mahatma Gandhi. Even those who follow the way of *jnana marga* (the way of knowledge) liken such knowledge to the state of consciousness experienced in deep, dreamless sleep. Swami Nikhilananda interpreted the *Upanishads* in these terms:

> In the state of deep sleep the soul does not really become unconscious. The Consciousness belonging to Atman is not destroyed because this Consciousness is immortal. It appears, therefore, that in the relative world the nearest approach to the peace and desirelessness of Brahman is the experience of deep sleep.[58]

Raimundo Panikkar's subtitle for one of his essays expresses this difference between Euro-American and Asian mentalities as he contrasts "A Universal Theory of Religion or a Cosmic Confidence in Reality?"[59] He understands the Western mode of universal theorizing as having "no other way to reach peace of mind and heart—called more academically, intelligibility—than by reducing everything to one single pattern with the claim to universal validity."[60] Though the dialectical panentheism we seek to articulate conceives universality pluralistically and as dialectically relational, rather than one single pattern, Panikkar, nevertheless, would think no form of Being may be known exhaustively. Therefore, not even a relational theory can be universal. Not only because no one's contemplation is universal—a point we have also affirmed in Gadamer's terms that there can be no completed reflection. But also because truth expressed in verbal syntax cannot express all there is to Reality.[61]

Panikkar sometimes seems to mean only that all of our languages are culturally relative, and thus none are capable of articulating a universal theory. This point seems obvious and, if we dare say so, universally true. Panikkar even affirms exactly the relationality in this connection we have been seeking to articulate: "Any human affirmation, and thus any truth, is relative to its very own parameters, and that there can be no absolute truth, for *truth is essentially relational.*"[62]

Yet there seems to be a deeper meaning, not fully articulated but affirmed by Panikkar, which is more integral to traditional Hindu religious culture: Truth is not all there is to Reality because none of the finitely derived categories in any language are adequate to prehend or comprehend it. As the *Bhagavad-Gita* puts it: "Not to be cleft is This, not to be burned, nor to be wetted, nor likewise to be dried; everlasting is This, dwelling in all things, firm, motionless, ancient of days. Unknown is This called, unthinkable This, unalterable This."[63]

This is the *Brahman*, whom to know, love and/or practice is to be saved. As *Saguna Brahman*, in its conditional relative form, it is the immanent, inmost essence of things, but in its unconditional form as *Nirguna Brahman* it is the "negation of all attributes and relations . . . beyond time, space, and causality."[64] This is the traditional Hindu understanding of the reality that Indians less affected by Western Christianity than Panikkar experience as the basis of the cosmic confidence he contrasts with Western forms of universal theorizing.

Nikhilananda expresses the Vedanta form of Hinduism in a way that is accessible to Western minds, though in striking contrast with traditional forms of Judeo-Christian piety or theology:

Obviously, Nirguna Brahman cannot be worshipped, prayed to, or meditated upon. *No relationship whatsoever can be established with It.* Yet It

is not altogether detached; for It is the very foundation of relative existence. . . . It is the intangible Unity that pervades all relative existence
and gives a strong metaphysical foundation to fellowship, love, unself-
ishness, and other ethical disciplines. It compels us to show respect to
all in spite of their illusory masks. Though It cannot be an object of
formal devotion, yet It gives reality to the gods, being their inner substance, and thus binds all worshippers together in the common quest of
Truth.[65]

The contrast most relevant to our discussion is the assertion that with
Brahman or God no relationship can be established. But we might try
dialogically to mediate this contrast by interpreting it as denying only the
possibility of an *established* relationship, that is, an eternal, nonprocessive
relationship. When understood in this way, it is analogous to the traditional Christian and Muslim piety that understands its relationship with
God as developing only from God's free, prevenient initiative. The Trinitarian way of interpreting this analogy, as will become clearer in chapter
5, is that our God-relation is a participation in the relational process of
God's gracious communal being. We shall also return to this Trinitarian
issue yet in this chapter.

The Vedanta form of Hinduism is, of course, not the only, nor perhaps
even the preeminent, form of religion among Hindus. Their most popular and powerful form of devotion is given to Lord Krishna, the *avatar* of
Vishnu manifested in the *Bhagavad-Gita*. This form of devotion is much
closer to traditional Christian piety, as Harvey Cox notes: "Both traditions, for example, cherish the idea of a personal God who becomes incarnate in a particular figure, reveals who God is, and elicits a form of
participation in the life of God."[66] The Hindus call this form of participation in the divine life *bhakti*, best translated as "loving faith."

A crucial text in the *Gita* is Krishna's word to the troubled Arjuna:
"Surrendering all the laws, come for refuge to me alone. I will deliver
thee from all sins; grieve not."[67] The laws to which this text refers com-
prise all that religious traditions and customs require. One does not surrender them with an antinomian spirit, but rather one performs them in
loving faith: "Whatever be thy work, thine eating, thy sacrifice, thy morti-
fication, make thou it an offering to me."[68] Work done in this spirit of
devotion frees one from desire or attachment to the results of one's work;
thus one may work in peace.[69]

This peace is not to be confused with inaction, for an energetic form of
active holiness is to be practiced through loving faith in God. The best
known, continuingly influential exemplar of this active holiness in modern India is Mohandas Gandhi. Born into the Vaishnavite form of Hinduism, he developed an early disdain for Christianity because its
missionaries reviled Hinduism. While a student in England, Theosophists

introduced him to the *Bhagavad-Gita*, a religious classic of his own tradition he did not yet know. Tolstoy's *Gospels in Brief, What to Do* also im-
pressed him deeply at this time with its presentation of Jesus' ethic. These
Hindu and Christian influences served to convince Gandhi that service to
his community was the heart of religion: "I felt that God could be realized
only through service," he wrote.[70]

His response to Christianity on this point reveals both the profound
influence of Jesus on him and yet his rejection from a deeply Hindu basis
of the traditional Christian interpretation of Jesus:

> It was more than I could believe that Jesus was the only incarnate son of
> God, and that only he who believed in him would have everlasting life.
> If God could have sons, all of us were His sons. If Jesus was like God, or
> God Himself, then all men were like God and could be God himself.
> . . . His death on the cross was a great example to the world, but that
> there was anything like a mysterious or miraculous virtue in it my heart
> could not accept.[71]

The view of Christian salvation that Gandhi rejected was the doctrine of
the atonement Rupp names "transactional." He could not believe that
human salvation was accomplished once and for all in a transhistorical
event requiring no historical mediation. For Gandhi, and many others,
salvation is a process mediated through a history of human service.

A more vividly Hindu form of this view is Swami Vivekananda's interpretation of Jesus as one of the many incarnations of God. He held that
we may

> find God not only in Jesus of Nazareth but in all the Great Ones that
> have preceded him, in all that came after him, and all that are yet to
> come. . . . They are all manifestations of the same Infinite God. . . .
> They each and all suffer vicarious atonement for every one of us.[72]

Rammohan Roy preceded Gandhi as "the morning star of the Indian
renascence and the prophet of Indian nationalism."[73] He founded the
*Brahmo Samaj* in 1830 to seek renewal of Hindu culture through positive
response to Western Christianity and humanism. Like Gandhi, he was
active in educational and social reforms. And again like Gandhi, he ad-
mired and followed Jesus' ethics while rejecting the Christian doctrines of
incarnation and transactional atonement. Roy rejected the Incarnation
and the Trinity as too similar to the plurality of gods in Hinduism.[74] He
interpreted the unity of Jesus with God in the relational, ethical categories of "perfect concord, harmony, love, and obedience," rather like Kantian ethics and Ritschlian theology.[75] And the atonement was similarly
interpreted in a rational, moral sense.[76] Analogous views, according to
M. M. Thomas, were held by other prominent members of the *Brahmo*

*Samaj*: Keshub Chunder Sen, P. C. Mozoomdar, and Brahmobandhav Uphadhyaya.

The *Arya Samaj*, contrastingly, strongly resisted Western forms of Christian influence in India. The *Brahmo Samaj's* notion that the British *raj* (rule) was providentially returning Hindus to the essential theism of their own tradition was rejected. Ramakrishna, Vivekananda, Aurobindo, and Radhakrishnan rejected theism as a "lower level of truth."[77] They thus refused to interpret Jesus in the *Brahmo Samaj's* preferred theistic terms of "reformer, prophet and teacher," and rather interpreted him incarnationally as an *avatar* within the Vedanta Hindu categories of nondualistic "identity." Radhakrishnan said that Jesus recognized the divine within, freed himself from all imperfection, took refuge in God, and attained to divine status. Thus, they accepted the statement of the Johannine Jesus that he and God were one. Yet they did not consider Jesus' incarnation as unique, for it may be replicated "in the life of everyone who is on the way to the fulfillment of his destiny." Jesus is only "the ideal representation of the eternal reality within" us all.[78] The realization of unity or identity with that eternal reality is the meaning of salvation. Jesus as the Christ is thus depicted by the *Arya Samaj* as "the quintessential Hindu, the one who lives Hindu ideals as they ought to be lived and teaches the essence of Hindu truth as it ought to be taught."[79]

### Dialogical Learnings from Hinduism

What may we dialogically learn about human redemption from these strongly contrasting Hindu responses to Western Christianity? It may be found in trying to pose the question in Nikhilananda's clear terms: Is God's being and our being such that "no relationship whatsoever can be established"? That primal question may be articulated in many ways: Are human beings and other entities properly individuated in their finite freedom, so that their salvation is to be found in the restoration of just and loving relations? Or is the very notion of individuation as the premise for relationality grounded in illusion and ignorance? And is any attempt to realize individuation inordinate self-assertion that creates the *karma* that binds us to the everlasting struggle and suffering of this world? Can we participate relationally in this world as free and unique individuals and attain salvation as such? Or is such individuality the sin from which we require to be saved? Is our salvation finally a realization of identity with God? Or a restoration of right relation? Is the Jewish/Christian/Muslim form of theism, with its differentiation between God and humanity, a better conceptual model because it enables an interpretation of divine-human relations? Or is pantheism the better model because it leads us to negate and transcend our selfhood in the realization of identity? Finally, to put it in the terms most formative for our discussion: Is our salvation to be found in universal relationality? Or in ontological unity and identity?

The either-or form of these questions, however, need not be considered definitive. Individuation and relationality may be understood in a way that dialogically meets those who find salvation in cosmic confidence in a Reality known in ontological unity. The conceptual model of dialectical panentheism, with its realist-nominalist-processive understanding of redemption, enables a dialectical understanding of the relation of the particular to the universal that we may hope shall contribute to the salvation of us all.

Such an understanding of human-divine relations, however, must avoid any implication of Nikhilananda's rejected term "established." We may experience such a redeeming relation, but we cannot sustain or control it.[80] Our religious experience is also a process where every event becomes and perishes. We may find religious experience a basis of cosmic confidence for our becoming in the spatiotemporal process but not as a basis for any theological certainty in a fixed conceptual system.

The Hindu warning against desire and attachment, whose worst form may be fanatical religious absolutism, is relevant here. The history of all religion indicates that it can be either and both the best and the worst thing in life. Even modern Western forms of humanistic religion, with its self-justifying doctrine of inevitable progress, has led to many forms of historical horror, as the Indians know very well. Thus, we do well, as Martin Luther King Jr. and others have, to hear Gandhi's call to participate in this historical process through humble human service. We may hear that call through the prophetic voice of Moses or Mohammed or Jesus—as Gandhi also did. Or we may hear it through the *Bhagavad-Gita*. What is crucial is that we hear it in such a way that it grounds the self-actualization of our ultimate dignity in God while limiting and transforming all inordinate forms of self-assertion by realizing God's transcendence.

We may then "realize God" in Gandhi's terms and perhaps even understand that realization in the mystical Vedanta terms of unity or identity with Brahmā/God. But such unity or identity as human beings may have with God/Brahmā cannot be established, controlled, or sustained by religious or moral action. It is a spatiotemporal realization of God's primordial aim for an event that becomes and perishes. It may be received and sustained only in God's everlasting consequent nature, and this is something/ some One to whom we must be newly related in the subsequent self-actualization of each succeeding moment as long as we are in this world.

This may not be the unity of Brahman and Atman first envisioned by the ancient, aged "sitters" who created the *Upanishads*.[81] But it may contribute to the redemption of many in the contemporary life-world where Indian Hindus also live, serve, and die. The final test of our redemption in this world, however, is the *quality of our relations* with God and neighbor in the global village we are now creating, not in the conceptual formulations with which we seek to understand them.

## Buddhist Redemption in a
## Universally Relational Perspective

We may begin consideration of Buddhist understandings of redemption with the Buddha's famous simile of a raft:

> Then the Buddha said: O bhikkhus, even this view, which is so pure and so clear, if you cling to it, if you fondle it, if you treasure it, if you are attached to it, then you do not understand that the teaching is similar to a raft, which is for crossing over, and not for getting hold of.[82]

A dialogical perspective finds this simile useful for understanding not only Buddhism but all religions in dialogue with Buddhism.

What would the Buddha enable all to cross over? Not from a state of sin to redemption, in the usual Judeo-Christian or Muslim sense. "In fact there is no 'sin' in Buddhism as sin is understood in some religions," according to an authoritative interpreter.[83] The Buddha rather wants to help us cross over from the suffering inevitably involved in the spatiotemporal process we have been analyzing: birth, old age, decay, death, sorrow, lamentation, pain, grief, and distress, which he termed *dukkha*.

The Buddha was little interested in any metaphysical discussion that he thought of little practical use. Yet he focused on one metaphysical issue as having crucial practical meaning for the redemption he called *nirvana*: We must come to realize that we have no permanent or substantial ego/self/soul. What we experience and speak of as "I" is only a combination of ever-changing energies that arise and disappear in the spatiotemporal process. The Buddha, like Heraclitus, once likened personal life to a river:

> O Brahmana, it is just like a mountain river, flowing far and swift, taking everything along with it; there is no moment, no instant, no second when it stops flowing, but it goes on flowing and continuing. So Brahmana, is human life, like a mountain river.[84]

There is no Paramenedian "being," to put it in Western terms, behind or beyond this movement. It is only movement.

The Buddha taught that it is our craving to hold and possess any moment—like Goethe's Faust—or more paradoxically, to escape any moment into nonexistence—like Shakespeare's Hamlet—that is the source of our suffering (*dukkha*). Overcoming this craving delivers us from suffering and enables entrance into *nirvana*. Our Western prejudice tends to interpret *nirvana* as the extinction of the self or the negation of being. This, of course, is wrong because from a Buddhist point of view there is no being or self to negate. In a dialectical sense, the cessation of becoming is the realization of unconditioned reality for the Buddha: "O bhikkus, there is the unborn, ungrown, and unconditioned. Were there not the unborn, ungrown, and unconditioned, there would be no escape for the born, grown, and conditioned."[85] The Buddha taught that there is reality beyond duality and relativity, even though there is no unchanging, everlasting, absolute substance. But he also found the human mind unable to characterize that reality adequately with its conceptual categories; we may only realize it in calm insight and enlightenment.

It is this understanding of the process of existence (*samsara*) that leads some Buddhists polemically to criticize the Christian concepts of the soul and God, just as they earlier criticized the Hindu notions of Atman and Brahman. Gunapal Dharmasiri argues for the "empirical meaninglessness of the soul in its essence."[86] He contends that the Christian concept of soul as a substantial self is harmful existentially, morally, and religiously. Existentially, it leads to suffering. Morally, it leads to the "separateness which will make community impossible."[87] And since it is neither morally nor spiritually edifying, it cannot be a good analogy for "a morally and spiritually perfect God either."[88] His conclusion is that "from the point of view of salvation, such a conception would be regarded as positively harmful."[89]

### The Thought of Keiji Nishitani

Other Buddhists, however, are less polemical because they are more dialogical. Masao Abe, a Buddhist from the Kyoto School of Philosophy, thinks that both Christianity and Buddhism face a "transitional period of uncertainty":

> Both religions must fundamentally transform themselves such that their prevailing basic assumptions are drastically changed and a new paradigm or model of understanding can emerge. This might involve a revolutionary reinterpretation of the concept of God in Christianity and the concept of emptiness in Buddhism.[90]

This view has led Abe to active participation in dialogue with North American Jewish and Christian theologians.[91] Keiji Nishitani, his colleague in the Kyoto School, has been similarly engaged. But his interest is less theological and more philosophical, centering in the thought of Nietzsche, Sartre, and Heidegger (with whom he studied in Freiburg from 1936 to 1939). Nishitani's dialogue with the West is as much or more with its existential philosophy as its Christian theology.[92]

Despite Japan's growing openness to Western science and technology, Nishitani sees the uncertainty of Western culture articulated by its existential philosophers to be far more devastating than anything Asian cultures now face. Winston King summarizes his view of Western culture:

> Nishitani perceives the long-dominant Christian and Greek rationalist traditions as irretrievably undermined by their own inherent logic and by the modern scientific world view. They have been devoured by their own progeny, the consequences of their own intrinsic qualities. What is left? An underlying nihility, a spiritual vacuity, and a pervasive sense of meaninglessness. . . . Second, the West—and all those cultures affected by Western influences—present the spectacle of a massive superstructure of brilliant, scientific achievement strung precariously over a chasm of meaninglessness, and are apparently incapable of building themselves new foundations from within their own traditional resources. Hence they are in need of a more enduring foundation unassailable even by scientific and philosophical skepticism.[93]

The Kyoto School, since its inception a generation ago by Kitaro Nishida, has been concerned to "search for a harmonious integration of two philosophical worlds" and "to reformulate, in the categories of an alien Western philosophy, the philosophical insights of their own past."[94] Nishitani too, despite his negative assessment of Western culture, labors to bring the insights of Zen Buddhism into dialogue with Western experience and thought. Zen is that form of Mahayana Buddhism which developed from the philosophy of Nagarjuna (150–250 C.E.), called by some the Immanuel Kant of India,[95] whose seminal thought first influenced Vedanta Hinduism, and later the Buddhism of India, China, and Japan. Nagarjuna taught that "*Samsara* has no difference whatever from *Nirvana* and *Nirvana* has no difference whatever from *Samsara*."[96] That is, in more Western terms, salvation is to be sought and found fully within this spatiotemporal process. The speculative dimensions of Zen philosophy, therefore, have the religious intention of clearing the way for salvific enlightenment by analytically liberating humanity from false attachments that obstruct that way.

It is precisely this philosophical gift that Nishitani hopes to contribute to the Western life-world through Buddhism's dialogical interaction with Christianity. Since the philosophy of the Kyoto School is thoroughly religious, Nishitani's more philosophical reflection is finally also oriented to religious edification. He is convinced precisely as a philosopher that reality is revealed in religious manifestation, as may be seen in his affirmation that, "in religious Love or Compassion, the highest standpoint of all comes into view."[97]

It is not surprising that some of the most profound dialogue between Asian and Euro-American religious perspectives occurs with Japanese scholars, because their society has opened itself to Western culture, especially its science and technology, to a degree far beyond India or China.

Thus, the Japanese face on their home ground, so to speak, some of the same issues that have come to bedevil Western culture in the twentieth century. Despite this growing cultural analogy, however, it remains true that the philosophical and religious backgrounds are so different that analogous answers to similar issues are difficult to articulate. This is especially true of Nishitani's work, whose profundity demands a far more extensive discussion than can be developed here. We can only highlight some of the aspects most relevant to our concern to understand the inter-religious relationality of redemption.

Two perspectives shared with Western thinkers heighten Nishitani's accessibility to our thought: The first is not surprising, because his long study of European nihilism focuses him on exactly the same cultural question that Paul Tillich addressed in his theology of correlation. But the second is astonishing! Though there is no indication of any acquaintance with the thought of Alfred North Whitehead, close analogies with his thought run through the whole of Nishitani's work. It is not entirely hyperbolic to say that *Religion and Nothingness* could be understood as *Process and Reality* in an Asian idiom. There are, of course, crucial differences because Christianity is the background of Whitehead's thought while Buddhism is the background (and in many ways the foreground) of Nishitani's. Those differences shall constitute the dialogical nub of our discussion with Nishitani about the meaning of redemption for humanity in our scientific and technological age.

Nishitani's striking similarity to Whitehead may perhaps partially be understood because they both sought to reconcile religion and modern science for the sake of redeeming contemporary humanity.[98] Nishitani traces the emergence of pessimistic nihilism in Western culture to the displacement of its traditionally religious teleological worldview by the mechanistic model of Newtonian science. Euro-American Christians and Jews once teleologically understood their cosmic order as a witness to God's providential relation with them. But recent cultural history has disengaged their understanding of nature from the religious matrix in which it arose. Nishitani observes that, "as this intellectual process continued, the natural world assumed more and more the features of a world cold and dead, governed by laws of mechanical necessity, completely indifferent to the fact of man."[99] Thus the scientific understanding of the world cut through, and for many cut off, the personal relationship between God and human beings.

Nishitani, like Whitehead, emphasizes the negative power of the Cartesian understanding of the ego in the development of this modern worldview. His Buddhist sensitivities, however, enable him to see more clearly than many Westerners that Descartes's *cogito ergo sum* ("I think, therefore I am") allowed a narcissistic satisfaction with the self and an objectification of all else that is deeply problematic for religion. And especially problematic for Buddhists and Christians who know the consequences of "an ego that is self-centered on itself and clinging to itself."[100] This is the essence of the Buddhist notion of *avidya*, the "fundamental darkness," in Nishitani's terms, which his colleague Professor Abe further characterizes as "the thirst to be."[101]

This does not mean, however, that Nishitani would reverse Descartes, to derive the knowing subject from either preconscious matter, on the one hand, or God on the other. He agrees with Descartes that it is "absolutely inconceivable that the knower should be generated from or constituted by the known, since knowing always implies a transcendence over what is known."[102] He extends Descartes's method of doubt, however, also to doubt the self-evidence of the ego itself. The ego must be opened to the reality that comes into view when we face the limits of our self-existence. The "Great Doubt" of Zen Buddhism arises when we include the ego in the pain and transience of all things. The ego also becomes and perishes. And this great doubt has been illumined for Western persons, as Nishitani knows, by existentialist philosophers such as Kierkegaard, Nietzsche, and Heidegger.

It is exactly Zen Buddhism's understanding of human existence that focuses Buddhist insights on the universal relationality of redemption.[103] Nishitani agrees with many in the West that the idea of God and human beings as persons is "without doubt the highest conception yet to appear."[104] And he affirms that the Christian image of a personal God of love and justice has "elevated the human personality to remarkable heights."[105] But he argues that the ontological dualism of traditional Christian theism, joined with the epistemological and existential dualisms of the contemporary Western, Cartesian scientific worldview, have brought Judeo-Christian civilization to the brink of nuclear self-destruction and meaningless nihilism.

Contemporary persons can be redeemed in Nishitani's view only by going through this nihilism to "where the self is brought to utter 'nothingness' in a religious sense." That mode of being "is none other than Existenz as non-ego, the Existenz of the non-duality of self and other."[106] More simply—perhaps too simply—put, salvation is found in eliminating the Cartesian ego without ceasing to be a personal self. This ego must be overcome both existentially and theologically; that is, in both our self-experience and our God-relation:

> When something is self-sufficient merely in an immediate self-identity, the "self" of that self-sufficiency, even though it be the self of the one God who is *one* in himself and contains all things, still retains a residue of individual ego. True self-sufficiency must . . . be a self-sufficiency of

what we might call the "individual non-ego." It must be an "emptying" of self that makes all things to be.[107]

This insight into redemption is grounded in the Buddhist understanding of *sunyata* or emptiness. But this understanding may only be known experientially and existentially, not conceptually, for reasons we should by now have begun to understand. Nothing is not a form or a thing, not even a no-thing. Nishitani calls its realization a "conversion," which "does not come about as a conceptual conversion, but only as an existential conversion away from the mode of being of person-centered person."[108] *Sunyata* thus may not be adequately conceived as the negation of being; it may only be adequately realized as a self-attested living nothingness. We shall soon note that Masao Abe relates this Buddhist concept dialogically to the Christian notion of *kenosis* in God, Christ, and human beings. But we must yet remain with Nishitani's more philosophical characterization of *sunyata*, to realize how surprisingly close it is to the conceptual model of panentheism.

Keiji Nishitani articulates what he sometimes calls an "impersonally personal relationship," and at others a "transpersonal" that is "personally impersonal."[109] Though he claims support for this understanding in the theologies of Meister Eckhardt and Francis of Assisi, his basic arguments are philosophical. The self may not be understood as personal in the traditional sense because it becomes and perishes.[110] That is, it is a momentary concrescence. Though persons are active in their self-actualization, they are essentially passive in their internal dependence upon energies that they "prehend."[111] Given the reality of prehension, Nishitani holds that we must overcome the representationalism of Descartes and Kant that understands objects as only represented in a subject. Things "escape representation and appear in their own reality," according to Nishitani.[112] There is no thing-in-itself behind and beyond our prehensions. Nishitani is able to express all of this in our Western philosophical idiom.

Nishitani's more Buddhist mode for expressing much the same thing speaks of "nihility opening up at the ground of the subject" and "nihility looming up from the ground of all existing things, assaults us, and inserts itself into the ground of our existence."[113] But this should not put off our Western sensibilities. He is only saying in our terms that there is no distinction between the phenomenon and the thing-in-itself. When he writes so paradoxically that "a thing is truly an illusory appearance at the precise point that it is truly a thing in itself,"[114] he is making essentially the same point as Whitehead that we are internally related to reality by our prehension of energies that become and perish as actual entities. They are illusory only in the sense that they are not permanent substances. He too would have us overcome what Whitehead called the fallacy of misplaced concreteness.

What then is the structure of reality in which we realize impersonally personal relationships? Nishitani's answer may be astonishing for Christians. He speaks of this structure of reality as "circuminsessional," using the Latin term (the Greek is *perichoresis*) familiar to Christian scholars from the doctrine of the Trinity. Whitehead also affirmed the "metaphysical discovery" of the theologians who formulated this doctrine,[115] though he regretted the residual dualism in their thought that kept them from developing their insight into a general metaphysics.[116] Nishitani does generalize what Western theologians had restricted to the Trinity when he posits that "the being of things in themselves is essentially circuminsessional":

> The interpenetration of all things that comes about here is the most essential of all relationships, one that is closer to the ground of things than any relationship ever conceived on the fields of sensation and reason by science, myth, or philosophy. . . . Even the very tiniest thing, to the extent that it "is," displays in its act of being the whole web of circuminsessional interpenetration that links all things together.[117]

It should not detract from the brilliance of Nishitani's insight to object to his claim that it has only been developed on the field of *sunyata* and by no other philosophy.[118] The discussion of the previous chapters has made sufficiently clear that this same insight is at the heart of panentheistic metaphysics as derived from Whitehead.

### Comparing Nishitani and Whitehead

Both Nishitani and Whitehead affirm the structure of reality to be a unity that differentiates, to use the terms made familiar in chapter 2. Nishitani also uses these terms when he writes, "It is not an absolute unity abstracted from all multiplicity and differentiation in the world, but an absolute unity on the field where multiplicity and differentiation are absolutely radicalized."[119] There is an important difference, however, in how he and Whitehead conceive this differentiated circuminsessional unity, which may be traced to the difference between the Christian and Buddhist backgrounds of their philosophies.

For the Buddhist who has overcome all attachment in *sunyata*, this differentiation into suchness is an entirely new, spontaneous primal fact: "a world of *primal fact*, where such fact is bottomlessly on its own home-ground becoming manifest apart from all cause, reason, or end, without How or Why or Wherefore . . . and are encountered 'as oneself' in their 'suchness.' "[120] Because *sunyata* is not conceived dialectically, each entity is by itself the All and is experienced and conceived as an "absolute center." In Whiteheadian terms, the moment of satisfaction in the concretion of an entity is absolutized. That is, the unique synthesis of energies in the momentary suchness of the person is not experienced by the Buddhist as having any relation to an all-embracing Center. Nishitani says, "Each and everything becomes the center of all things and, in that sense, becomes an absolute center."[121] In almost a Cartesian sense, though only momentarily, the self is simply what it is at the center of all relations. There is no causal efficacy from God or anyone else. Nishitani writes of this as "the nihility that permits not a trace to be left behind at the base of all things from the very start."[122]

This Buddhist understanding of circuminsession is in startling contrast to the experienced causal efficacy of past spatiotemporal entities and the universal causal efficacy of God's initial aim in the Whiteheadian understanding of how "the many become one and are increased by one" in the cosmic process. Whitehead, like Nishitani, affirmed what might be called the moment of transcendent *ek-stasis* in completed concrescence, but he did not conclude that it left no trace in the spatiotemporal process. The objective immortality of all entities as "superjects" in the ongoing world process, and their subjective immortality in the consequent nature of God, allows for both the affirmation of aseity (but not absoluteness) in the moment of finite freedom and of relative dependence and efficacy in the spatiotemporal process.

The difference between Nishitani and Whitehead may be traced to Whitehead's Christian sense of a meaningful history. Nishitani is aware of this crucial difference, but he takes it up with Arnold Toynbee, not Whitehead, because Toynbee viewed the contrast between Buddhaic and Judaic thought as "determining the problems of the whole of humanity." Nishitani concedes that "a consciousness of history in the sense it is currently understood remains largely undeveloped within Buddhist teaching."[123] He also knows that it is the Jewish and Christian belief that the whole world process is ruled over by a personal Being that has made linear historical time meaningful for Western consciousness. But his response at this point is one of the few polemical points in his whole discussion:

> Human self-centeredness is a permanent fixture in religions of the West. Once negated, it reappears, as in the guise of God's chosen people. . . . Crudely put, what we have here is a *ressentiment* come forth in the guise of a self-centeredness that has passed through God so as to become religious.[124]

John Cobb, Jr., once commended Buddhism for having no such anti-Jewish teaching as can be found in some Christian theology, despite Buddhism's detachment from concrete historical involvement.[125] This is not quite accurate for Nishitani, however, because he polemically repudiates what he understands to be Judaic notions of covenant. His Buddhist perspective interprets the notion of a historical covenant with the idea of *karma*, which he defines as "freedom determined by causal necessity within the whole infinite nexus."[126] And he sees causal necessity as arising from *avidya*, expressed as greed and anger. It has shown its true face in the pessimistic nihilism of the West after the "death of God," where human will has become autotelic and autonomous in its infinite drive.[127] The infinite finitude of this self-centeredness, arising in the West originally from Judeo-Christian notions of covenant, now requires healing by realizing a "selfless self-centeredness" experienced as "circuminsessional interpenetration on the field of *sunyata*."[128]

### The Thought of Masao Abe

Masao Abe joins Nishitani on this point but more dialogically as he suggests that Western culture may move toward redemption by developing its faith in the *kenotic* God manifested in some Christian scripture, especially Philippians 2:5–8. He suggests that Christians should understand Christ as the Son of God precisely because he was essentially a self-emptying person.[129] And to receive the kenotic Christ as the manifestation of God implies the *kenosis* of God. Without the self-emptying of God, Abe holds, the self-emptying of the Son is inconceivable.[130] *Kenosis* is also seen by Abe as fundamental to the Christian belief in God's love. By virtue of God's love, God goes out of himself to give himself away to the other: "God's self-emptying must be understood not as partial but as total to the extent that God's infinite unrelatedness has no priority over relatedness with the other and that God's self-emptying is dynamically identical with God's abiding and infinite fullness."[131]

Abe is convinced that Christians will come savingly to understand the kenotic nature of their God only when their ego-self negates itself completely. Understanding the traditional Christian resistance to an impersonal pantheism, however, he argues like Nishitani that God so conceived is both personal and impersonal. Nishitani's notion of an "impersonally personal relation," in Abe's terms, means that God's impersonal kenosis fulfills God's personal love to save everything without exception, including the unjust and the sinful.[132] He finds support for his view in Jürgen Moltmann's Trinitarian theology of the cross, though he thinks Moltmann might yet learn from Buddhism's notion of *sunyata* to deepen his understanding of God as unconditional self-negating love.

Masao Abe understands Christianity and Buddhism to be similar in their primary concern for human salvation.[133] He brings Buddhism dialogically closer to Christianity by interpreting the true meaning of *sunyata* as the dynamic movement of emptying, not as the static state of emptiness. It should be understood as a verb, not as a noun, for it is the dynamic and creative function of emptying everything and making everything alive.[134] He recognizes like Nishitani, that the principal difference between Buddhists and Christians is the Buddhist understanding of *karma*, which blocks a positive understanding of free will and action. Abe defines *karma* as volitional action based on free will, which is morally qualified and determines the personal and social future.[135] He affirms the importance of acting morally so as to escape historical consequences like the holocaust. But as a Buddhist, Abe continues to regard all action, whether morally good or evil, as ultimately evil because it arises out of *avidya*, an unconscious, blind will to be.[136] *Avidya* is overcome and *karma* ceases through no volitional action whatsoever, not even moral action, but only by emptying our conception and its objects and abandoning our attachment and abiding.[137]

Abe thus appears clearer about how to lead Judeo-Christians toward emptiness than how to lead Buddhists toward greater dynamism although he affirms the importance of this latter transformation as well. His traditional conceptions of *avidya* and *karma* remain resolutely unrevised even as he interacts with Christians who evaluate the human will to live in its conscious and unconscious forms as essentially good, though often (or always for some) existentially distorted.[138] And despite the similarity to Christianity in stressing the *bodhisattva* perspective of *sunyata* as universal salvific love, Abe's understanding of divine and human compassion as absolute self-emptying to the point of undifferentiated identity appears to obscure the relational and ethical character of actual love in history.[139]

Nevertheless, there is much to ponder in Buddhism's profound emphasis on the relationality that characterizes all reality. We shall continue doing so, but now in relation with the other religions we have studied, as we seek to articulate our conclusions.

## Conclusion: The Interreligious Relationality of Redemption

What may we learn through the dialogical interaction of the world religions that enables a more genuinely universal understanding of redemption? The answer to so dynamic a question cannot be given as a universal abstracted from the saving particularity of these concrete religions but must be reflected with Tillich's dynamic typological approach. There are no abstract, transcendent universals, at least none that we may know and affirm as finite human beings. Whatever we may realize and understand of universal salvation is historically mediated. We think it possible for Christians to open themselves to the concrete testimony and theological reflection of other religions without giving up their faith in Jesus the Christ as the historical mediator of our redemption. This possibility is enhanced if we adopt the realist-nominalist-processive model for interpreting redemptive experience, as we have learned from George Rupp. That is, we may learn to interpret particular personal meanings in their relation to universal meanings with a metaphysics of process.

### In Relation with Islam

The Islamic understanding of redemption may be interpreted with this processive model: Muslims understand redemption as a continual dialectic between submission to God's law (*shari'a*) and the ever-recurring necessity for repentance (*tawbah*), through the cycles of temptation, decision, error, realization of error, repentance, and forgiveness. The law is God's salvific gift to call us to submission and to guide us through repentance when we recurringly fail. Through the revelation of the *shari'a*, God creates and sustains responsible moral beings. We should not aspire, however, to become anything more or other than the fallible and finite moral persons God wills to create. From this standpoint, the essence of sin is to seek to elevate ourselves or anyone else to the ontological level of God (*shirk*). Obedience to the law achieves no such elevation, for it is designed for just such fallible beings as we. Nor will the grace and power of the prophets who mediated the law enable such self-transcendence. They also remained human as they transmitted God's revelation to us. Islamic teaching thus affirms our dignity as responsible persons while strongly restricting any tendency to overstep our finite limits. Anticipating our failures, it also provides a way for restoration to our proper (submissive) relation to God.

Seen in this way, the Muslim belief in God's absolute uniqueness (*tawheed*) may be received even by Trinitarian Christians as contributing to universal salvation. It provides a spiritual bulwark against the absolutizing of anything finite, including the evolutionary understanding of human beings as the leading edge of cosmic progress in the modern West. Nothing has caused more havoc in human history than the various forms of the idolatry Islam so resolutely opposes. No universal religion denies the uniqueness of the divine Reality. Whether conceived as the Jewish *Yhwh*, the Christian *Abba*, the Muslim *Allah*, the Hindu *Brahman* or the Buddhist *Sunyata*, there is strong analogy to Islam's *tawheed*. No theologian would equate these conceptions, but from a realist-nominalist-processive perspective their analogous salvific function of denying idolatrous absolutization to any finite forms of being may be recognized and affirmed.

The Christian interpretation of Jesus' deity does not refer to the finite particularity of his Jewish, male, unmarried, etc. existence. It is rather the universal wisdom (*Logos/Sophia*) and universal love (*agape*) realized in him and expressed in his relationships that is worshiped. It is the circuminsessional interpenetration of the divine energies with Jesus' finite, human energies in the recurring personal syntheses of his life that Christians interpret as a revelation of the everlasting and universal relationality of God's Trinitarian being and becoming.[140] This is not a denial of that unique oneness of God's being that Muslim faith emphasizes; it is an affirmation of the gracious relationality of the one and only God.

Muslims also know Allah as merciful and compassionate. Christians extend this common salvific affirmation in their witness that God's mercy and compassion may be directly known in the life and death of Jesus through the Holy Spirit that universally expresses the gracious relationality manifested in him. Although we must recognize that the salvific form of Islam is communication of the divine will,[141] which should not be confused with the Christian form of the relational communication of the divine person, these are not mutually exclusive typologies. One may receive the power of the Islamic witness in this dynamic form while inviting them to receive other testimony in the dynamic form of gracious relationality.

### In Relation with Hinduism

It is noteworthy that dialogue analogous to the Abrahamic religions' struggle to interpret God's uniqueness also goes on within Hinduism, quite in contrast to preconceptions about the differences between theism and pantheism. This similarity may be recognized in the dialectic between the Vedanta's understanding of *Nirguna Brahman* as beyond all attributes and relations and the equally Hindu devotion given to the personal form of Krishna or the Gandhian realization of God in communal service. The same contrast is seen in the variant responses to Jesus by the *Brahmo Samaj* and the *Arya Samaj*. Jesus has been interpreted by Hindus both in the humanly relational terms of reformer, prophet, and teacher proper to a more dualistic theism, or in the ontological terms of identity as an *avatar* of *Saguna Brahman* proper to Vedanta pantheism.

This intra-Hindu dialogue suggests that the contrasts revealed in Hindu spirituality may also be mediated in the realist-nominalist-processive model of dialectical panentheism. This concept enables an interpretation of Brahman/God as both the all-embracing cosmic universal the Vedantists and the *Arya Samaj* affirm, and as internally (and in some dimensions externally) related to all the finitely free differentiations actualized in the spatiotemporal process. The more pantheistic understanding of Hinduism may thus be accommodated to the universal relationality of redemption in a panentheistic theology.

This requires, however, that we seek to understand the ultimate Brahman/God as both substance and subject (Hegel). The coherent model for the analogous revisions in the concept of God required by both the Abrahamic and Hindu religions is a self-differentiated process. God is substance, not as eternally actualized form, but as the primordial ground of all the forms that potentiate our spatiotemporal process and as the consequent unity of all that is actualized in that process. As primordial ground, God is pure, temporally undifferentiated potentiality, approximating the Hindu sense of *Nirguna Brahman*. (The Trinitarian modification of the Whiteheadian understanding of God's primordial nature we shall develop in chapter 5 does not destroy this analogy.) As the consequent unity of all that is actualized, God is the metaphysical foundation for finite community that finally binds all creation together, approximating the Hindu sense of *Saguna Brahman*. But these two poles of God's being are united in one Being; and the God who receives the whole dynamic of the creation into his/her being is a Subject whose being is in process from the primordial to the consequent dimensions of ultimate Substance.

Many Hindus, like many Christians, Jews, and Muslims, relate to God in loving faith as a subject. That their conception of Vishnu/Krishna is a lower level of truth, in the sense of being finitely limited, may be a proper warning by the Vedantists against absolutizing any of our theistic symbol systems through which we concretely relate to the divine Subject—whether as pietistic Christians, Vaishnavite Hindus, or Sufi Muslims.[142] In this sense, the Vedantists join and strengthen the Muslim rejection of *shirk*. We may not absolutize any of our symbol systems or conceptual models. The essential point remains, however, that such symbol systems do enable a redemptive relation to the God who is experienced both as Substance and Subject, Creator and Redeemer.

The dynamic typology appropriate to the Hindu experience of redemption may be designated participation in the relational Universal, with the emphasis falling more on the universal as transcending all the relational forms we experience as redemptive. We shall see that Buddhists similarly affirm participation in the relational Universal, but their emphasis is on the relational. The Hindu emphasis on the nonrelational transcendence of the cosmic Universal tends toward experiencing and construing redemption in the mystical terms of identity. To interpret human religious transcending in terms of identity with Brahman/God, however, is theologically dangerous—whether applied to intuitive knowledge, pious devotion, or moral service. These experiences may approximate the fullness of salvation to which they testify, but they also balance on the knife-edge of absolutizing the very particularity they seek to transcend.[143] Nevertheless, one may gratefully receive the power of their witness to saving participation in the universal while entering into dialogue over the danger we all face in our finite claims to fullness of identity with the universal.

### In Relation with Buddhism

The term "fullness" brings us to the contrast between the Hindu and Buddhist understandings of redemption, underscored by the Buddhist emphasis on emptiness (*sunyata*). The Buddha was as concerned to transcend the particularities of existence and enter into the unconditional universal beyond duality and relativity as any of his Hindu forebears. To be saved from suffering (*dukkha*) requires realization of the unconditional, but that unconditional universal is experienced and interpreted by Buddha as emptiness, not fullness. Or, as understood in Abe's and Nishitani's more dynamic process terms, it is a self-emptying that enables recognition of internal relations to all else, best interpreted as "co-dependent origination"—in Abe's more traditional Buddhist terms—or "circuminsessional interpenetration"—in Nishitani's revisionist philosophical terms. Redemption from this Buddhist standpoint is found in liberation from false attachments to our selves and the objects of our desires that block the realization of such relationality.

Zen Buddhism, as articulated dialogically by Nishitani and Abe, has been considered more extensively than any other theology because it comes closest to our conceptual model of dialectical panentheism. Though we have noted important differences, the emphasis has been on startling similarities. The most important similarity is circuminsessional interpenetration or co-dependent origination. The analogous Christian concept is the Trinitarian God as a perichoretic (Greek) or circuminsessional (Latin) community of mutual relationality and interdependence.

Participation in the self-emptying love of the Trinitarian God in Christian experience enlivens the whole creation to enter into communal relation.[144] The experience of salvific participation in the Trinitarian love of God in this world has led Christians to articulate the idea of the economic Trinity. The relational God is understood as acting creatively and redemptively to enable finite freedom and to transform its sinful distortion into just and loving community in the world. This doctrine has led some Christian theologians to develop a philosophical natural theology to show the incarnational and relational Trinitarian structure of all reality.[145] We shall return to this issue in chapter 5, but only continued dialogue will determine whether a Christian incarnational metaphysics of relationality may become more analogous to the Buddhist metaphysics of *sunyata*.

Masao Abe recognizes that the nub of the difference between Buddhists and Christians is the Buddhist affirmation of identity in *sunyata*, in contrast to the Christian affirmation of relation in God's love. This is the same issue recognized in the discussion with Hinduism, so perhaps it makes little difference on this point whether the divine universal is interpreted in terms of fullness or emptiness. Abe thinks that to stop at relation is still to stand outside of the full experience of salvation, so that we run the risk of objectifying it conceptually and absolutizing it existentially. To be liberated from such objectification, one must be "existentially identical with the self-manifestation of God."[146] The objectifiable transcendence of God must have disappeared. Christians, he believes, have experienced only an "immanent transcendence" in Jesus' crucifixion and resurrection understood as *kenosis*, but the full realization of the salvific meaning of this immanent transcendence awaits acceptance of the total *kenosis* of God.[147] Abe concedes, however, that the Achilles heel of the Buddhist experience of identity is its radical relativization of ethics. *Sunyata* is finally neither good nor evil, and there is no Buddhist analogue to the Christian notion of divine justice. Religion and ethics for Buddhists are discontinuous and find only a very dialectical relation in the realization of *sunyata*.[148]

We have developed a conceptual model of universal relationality that accepts the risk of objectifying our relation with God while guarding against its absolutization. Dialogical participation in a dialectical process, grounded in relation with, and the relations within, the Trinitarian God, allows for no such completed reflection. We may thus approximate the value that Abe calls "boundless openness," without negating all finite limits to affirm identity. The existential center of finite freedom we know in personal process remains, but recognition of its finite becoming opens it to relations with the potentially universal social process. Affirming the boundaries and limits of finite existence allows the ethics of love and justice to remain intrinsic in our relational experience of redemption in this world.

The issue posed especially by Buddhism for Abrahamic religions, which ground redemption on God's gracious action and human responsive action in history, is whether our understanding of that activity can escape the karmic consequences of an infinitized ego? Can we order our worship and praxis toward circuminsessional relationality without losing our sense of divine and human creativity in history? The obverse issue for Buddhism, posed especially by Judaism and Christianity, is whether Buddhists can reconceive *karma* so as to take responsibility for creative causal efficacy in history? Can they order their meditation toward a praxis that is more than a "life in which one whiles away one's time, accepting whatever may come," which Nishitani endorses because of his understanding of the absoluteness of concrescence.[149] Can both Christians and Buddhists increasingly enter into the experience of impersonally personal relations through circuminsessional relations in the universal relationality of God? Can all of humanity come to experience the universal relationality that enables and limits human creativity in history while celebrating the divine creativity of God—or the God beyond our humanly conceived God?

The religious experience of us all should be enhanced by learning from the dynamic type of redemption found in Buddhism. We have characterized it as participation in the relational universal, but with emphasis on the relational in contrast to the Hindu emphasis on the universal. By learning from Buddhists their kenotic experience of self-emptying—to give up any claim to personal permanence or universal fullness—we may enable the realization of impersonal personal relations with and within the universal relationality of God. In similar but more traditionally Christian terms, we may realize redemptive relations with God by sacramental participation in the Holy Spirit.

In whatever Buddhist, Christian, Hindu, Jewish, or Muslim terms native to us, may we increasingly find it so. Our world awaits, because it desperately needs, the interreligious relationality of such redemption.

# 4

## The Contextual
## Relationality of Justice

### Introduction

The struggles for and about justice have become so ideological and conflicted in our era that there are theological ethicists who contend that
"justice is a bad idea for Christians."[1] Liberationist and political theologies are inevitably, and sometimes so stridently, contextualized by nationality, gender, and class that some despair of finding any interrelation in
either their analyses or proposals for action. Indeed, some are convinced
that any attempt to move toward the universal relationality of justice
inevitably ends in some false universal as we infinitize our own egos or the
alter-egoism of our particular communities in demanding or protecting
our "rights." We faced this issue in chapter 3 in the dialogue between
Buddhism and Christianity, but now we shall make it the focus of our
reflection: Can human beings understand their participation in the Relational Universal—God—so that an ethic of universal but contextual
justice may be illumined and empowered?

Stanley Hauerwas develops the argument as to why justice is a bad idea
for Christians in a way that is remarkably, though seemingly unintention-
ally, similar to the Buddhist argument we have confronted from Nishitani
and Abe in the previous chapter. He strongly, and I think properly, criticizes the Kantian notion of a transcendental, autonomous ego.[2] His primary concern, however, as a Western Christian ethicist is that the ethics
of the Enlightenment have tended to infinitize the nation-state. Though
contrary to the intention of Kant's deontological ethics (a point that
Hauerwas does not discuss), when Kant's Enlightenment perspective is
translated into a more utilitarian mode it may contribute to a cultural

102

ethos that legitimates every felt personal need. When the pursuit of happiness becomes infinite, the nation-state has "the infinite duty to honor the infinite claim of every person to the pursuit of happiness," in the words Hauerwas cites from Lesslie Newbigin.[3] This analysis is analogous to the Buddhist notion of *avidya*. Noting this analogy is important because it raises important issue with the way in which Hauerwas and Newbigin infinitize their own religious community—the church—as though it were the only saving alternative to the nation-state.

The conceptual model of dialectical panentheism implies an understanding of universal justice as contextually relational. Justice may only be understood and actualized by finitely free social beings in concrete communities, which Christians find in their churches. But the church is theologically grounded in the universal Creator, who is known, but not only known, in the salvation history of Israel and Christianity. From this standpoint, Hauerwas's affirmation that there is no salvation outside the church is deeply problematic:

> If we say outside the church there is no salvation, we make a claim about the very nature of salvation—namely that salvation is God's work to restore all creation to the Lordship of Christ. . . . Such salvation is not meant to confirm what we already know or experience. It is meant to make us part of a story that could not be known apart from exemplification in the lives of people in a concrete community.[4]

We may very well agree that human salvation requires new forms of community, but this is something quite different from the position that the church is the only concrete community in which justice may be known.

Such affirmations about the church almost deserve the polemical Buddhist rejoinder of Professor Nishitani: "Human self-centeredness is a permanent fixture in religions of the West. Once negated, it reappears as in the guise of God's chosen people."[5] That this is too polemical a rejoinder, however, may be seen in the analogous response of one of Professor Hauerwas's own students, which he had the grace and good sense to publish as an appendix to his own discussion. David Toole's Christian sensitivity to the history, culture, and religion of Native Americans informs his claim that his teacher has "not done justice to the truth of the questions" he has discussed. In particular, Toole objects to what he calls the violent, exclusionary, and condescending language of Hauerwas and Newbigin, and advocates "humility in tension with truth" to us all.[6]

There is no universally rational, social, or political basis for realizing justice. The relational and thus relative understanding of human life articulated in this discussion supports the conclusion that all justice is contextually relative. Christians are well advised then to realize justice first in their communities as God's chosen people. But also to learn humility in tension with the truth in our churches requires seeking justice in and between all of humanity's concrete communities.

The concern for universal justice raises serious issue also with the notion that Christians or anyone else achieves a fully human identity through the narrative of only their own community. David Toole responds insightfully also to narrative theology by noting that "so much is excluded from the continuity of narrative. And I wonder of the motives which move so many of us to insist upon identity."[7] All of our narratives are only small, interacting, and interdependent parts of humanity's total story. There must be no premature closure of ongoing processes of identity formation by excluding what must be dialogically learned from the narratives of others. We realize true identity through the particularity of our churches only as we hold them open to the universal relationality of becoming human in, with, and under our universal Creator.

This insight may be expressed more traditionally, and thus perhaps more helpfully for many in the churches, in the christological terms of Leonardo Boff:

> It was said that only through the church can one arrive at Christ. In this way important elements of history and life that were not tied to the ecclesiastical structure were placed outside the reach of Christ's mystery. . . . No concrete historical reality can exhaust the riches of Christ.[8]

This understanding of Christ, as Boff realizes, requires a fully Trinitarian theology as the Christian conceptual model for the universal relationality of God. We shall return to this issue in chapter 5.

We now seek more particularly to understand how relative and relational beings may learn the virtue of justice. This may, and I think must, begin through participation *in* concrete just communities. Yet in our increasingly interdependent world, it is equally necessary to realize justice *between* our familial, ethnic, political, and religious communities.

To become universally just, we must increasingly become "syncretic selves" able to recognize the multiple spiritual centers of our world: "As Mircea Eliade saw so clearly, humans need to be somewhere, to have a symbolic dwelling, a spiritual center, a true home. But as he also knew, and as the Oglala Sioux Black Elk reportedly observed, 'anywhere is the center of the world.' "[9] Our world may have multiple centers either because of the truly universal relationality of God or because of the false infinitizing of particular narratives and perspectival horizons.[10] We may be saved from the alter-egoism of infinitizing our political or religious communities by better understanding the contextual relativity of their notions of justice in the light of the universal relationality of God.

## The Justification of Justice in Democratic Market Societies

The religious problem with the understanding of justice in Western societies is its presupposition of alienated individuation.[11] Religious communities, on the other hand, seek reunion or reconciliation on a continuum ranging from mystical participation to covenanted community. Theories of justice in democratic market societies usually presuppose the egocentric character of human nature, which presumably justifies the drive to accumulate as the force that drives the market.

Christians like M. Douglas Meeks who affirm God's justice in democratic market societies have a strong sense of tension between such a society and the Christian faith: "The crisis for the Christian church in North America is that it has become too absorbed into the market society in whose logic God's grace and God's justice cannot appear."[12] The justification of justice from this religious perspective requires the realization of God's justice in so antithetical a society. The obvious strategy is to create disciplined, countercultural churches and synagogues. It must be noted, however, that this strategy in itself does not meet the greater need for a universal manifestation of God's justice in our cross-cultural and interdependent world. The more comprehensive question we face is how the gracious relationality that may appear in renewed religious communities may recognize the universal relationality of God and revive the universal relationality of humanity?

No one in the North American milieu has articulated a theory of justice that has attracted more recent attention and sometimes support than John Rawls's *A Theory of Justice*.[13] Even those who criticize its content appreciate its scope:

> It is the most ambitious political project undertaken by a member of the school currently dominant in academic philosophy; and it offers not only a defense of, but also a new foundation for, a radical egalitarian interpretation of liberal democracy. *In method and substance it fits the tastes of the times.* Prof. Rawls believes that he can provide persuasive principles of justice that possess the simplicity and force of older contract teachings, that satisfy utilitarianism's concern for the greatest number without neglecting the individual, that contain all the moral nobility of Kant's principles, that will result in a richness of life akin to that proposed by Aristotle, and that can accomplish all this without falling into the quagmires of traditional philosophy.[14]

Allan Bloom concludes, however, that Rawls fits the tastes of the times so well because he understands so little of either the deep problems or the profound principles of the Western tradition of moral philosophy. If this is at all true for John Rawls, how much more must it be true of most who applaud him.[15] Perhaps the break in our historical consciousness Gadamer discerns has also severed many of the moral roots of Western culture. Without assessing Bloom's judgment about Rawls's philosophical competence, we may agree with his claim that "we are in no position to push ahead with new solutions of problems; for as this book demonstrates, we have forgotten what the problems are."[16]

There are those who think, however, that Rawls knows exactly what problems need solution. Essentially, they are how to balance "liberty and equality as the content of what is to be distributed."[17] The justice problem takes this peculiarly modern form because Western societies have used the utilitarian principle of maximizing the good of the whole to justify violating the liberty of minorities. Rawls then seeks to articulate deontological principles that will properly balance and protect both liberty and equality.

To create a deontological hedge against the majoritarian misuse of utilitarianism, Rawls develops a modified social contract theory, which begins hypothetically from what he calls the "original position."[18] This position, however, is strictly imaginary, in contrast to the original contract theorists—Hobbes, Locke, and Rousseau—for whom it was natural. It cannot be natural for Rawls because he has no metaphysics of nature, whether in the Platonic tradition of an essential harmony that we have interpreted in its Whiteheadian revision, or in the form of those such as Hobbes who found natural life to be nasty, brutish, and short. The original social contract theorists understood the natural position for contracting and maintaining civil societies as the threat of death in humanity's natural competitive state. Our self-interest, they taught, must be limited by positive law if our permanent vulnerability is to be mutually protected.

Rawls still bases his original position on self-interest but thinks it has become more rationally humane. In post-Enlightenment cultures and economically developed societies, our self-interest now takes the form of a life plan to seek happiness. He thus thinks it possible to induce enlightened persons to agree that the realization of their plan requires a set of principles all will continue to accept even when it is not in their apparent or short-term self-interest. Such principles may be successfully negotiated only from an "original position" behind a "veil of ignorance." Only when we cannot know our gender, talents, intelligence, class, race, or family tradition and inheritance will we be able to "nullify the effects of special contingencies which put men at odds and tempt them to exploit social and natural circumstances to their own advantage."[19] Rawls thus moves the modern foundation for a social contract from the negative fear of death to the positive hope for a fair chance at happiness.

To promote individual happiness by negotiating a social contract from an original position ignorant of the special contingencies that affect our happiness, Rawls thinks, should provide the philosophical framework for defining the principles of a just society. Rawls finds it easier to state the first principle on liberty: "Each person is to have an equal right to the most extensive basic liberty compatible with a similar liberty for others." The second principle on equality, however, proves more difficult, so that Rawls gives it several formulations. The first is: "Social and economic inequalities are to be arranged so that they are both (a) reasonably expected to be to everyone's advantage, and (b) attached to positions and offices open to all."[20] But since the formal liberty of all may be diminished by ignorance, poverty, and a general lack of means, so that liberty is not of equal "worth," Rawls modifies the equality principle to: "Social and economic inequalities are to be arranged so that they are both (a) to the greatest benefit of the least advantaged and (b) attached to offices and positions open to all under conditions of fair equality of opportunity."[21]

The revised equality principle intends to redress the bias of contingencies by providing resources for those born into less favorable social positions. Yet this stengthening of equality must remain subordinated to the first principle of liberty. Rawls insists upon what he calls their "lexical ordering," which is to say the first principle must remain first:

> The principles of justice are to be ranked in lexical order and therefore liberty can be restricted only for the sake of liberty. There are two cases: (a) a less extensive liberty must strengthen the total system of liberty shared by all, and (b) a less than equal liberty must be acceptable to those citizens with the lesser liberty.[22]

### Critique of Rawls's Theory of Justice

John Rawls's theory of justice clearly presupposes the context of economically developed, democratic market societies. He provides philosophical principles for what Gadamer might call the moral prejudices of such societies. These principles intend to reconcile the individual interests of reasonable persons with the social interests that establish the public good. His original position thus provides an *imaginary* foundation for the moral structure of civil society. The serious question is "whether it is substantial enough to support such a structure?"[23]—especially in a society where millions are without even the basic necessities of shelter and health care.

Why should self-interested persons bent only on fulfilling their life plans accept a less than equal liberty—in terms of Rawls's lexical order? Rawls himself says that dire social and economic conditions may undermine his order: "Until the basic wants of individuals can be fulfilled, the relative urgency of their interest in liberty cannot be firmly decided in advance."[24] He knows that his lexical order is only "the long run tendency of the general conception of justice consistently pursued under reasonably favorable conditions."[25] This is tantamount to saying that this is a contextual understanding of justice for the well-situated in democratic market societies. He assumes that at least in such societies, but perhaps only in them, the less fortunate will not pursue strategies that will restrict or reduce the possibilities of the more fortunate, or for that matter, that the more fortunate will not use their privilege and power to maximize their life plans at the cost of the poor and the marginalized.

Allan Bloom's critique of Rawls is most telling on this issue, even for those who may not fully share Bloom's concern especially to protect the possibilities of those considered superior:

> Rawls, while joining the modern natural-right thinkers in abandoning the attempt to establish a single, objective standard of the good valid for all men, and in admitting a countless variety of equally worthy and potentially conflicting life plans or visions of happiness, still contends, as did the premodern natural-right thinkers, that the goal of society is to promote happiness. Thus he is unable to found consensus on the knowledge of the good, as did the ancients, or an agreement about the bad, as did the moderns. He is able to tell us only that society cannot exist without a consensus, but *he does not give any motive for abiding by that consensus to the man who is willing to risk the breakdown of actual society in order to achieve his ideal society*—which is what any man who loves the good must do. Only the "veil of ignorance" in the "original position" makes consensus possible; but *once the scales fall from a man's eyes, he may very well find that his life plan does not accord with liberal democracy.*[26]

Profoundly religious persons do receive a compelling vision of the good in their religious experience. Rawls's contextual theory of justice, however, can accommodate only that tepid form of faith that does not challenge dominant forms of authority. Any form of religious manifestation, including the revelations in Moses and Jesus, must finally be subordinated in this theory to American civil religion's rationalization of life, liberty, and the pursuit of wealth/happiness.

This form of civil religion emerged in Euro-American culture as the Enlightenment's response to the devastating wars of religion that were fought during the Reformation and Counter-Reformation. Hobbes, Locke, Hume, Kant, and Rousseau all struggled with the consequences of civil conflict caused by powerful churches in Euro-American societies. Some conservative political commentators in contemporary North America continue to support their resolution of this sometimes disastrous struggle but now in the changed, more secular context where the dominance of the sovereign state goes almost unchallenged. George F. Will, for a revealing instance, supports a 1990 decision of the U.S. Supreme Court concerning the Native American Church:

> A central purpose of America's political arrangements is the subordination of religion to the political order, meaning the primacy of democ-

racy. The founders, like Locke before them, wished to tame and domesticate religious passions of the sort that convulsed Europe. They aimed to do so not by establishing religion, but by establishing a commercial republic—capitalism. They aimed to submerge people's turbulent energies in self-interested pursuit of material comforts. Hence religion is to be perfectly free as long as it is perfectly private—mere belief—but it must bend to the political will (law) as regards conduct.[27]

Given the contextual limits of Rawls's celebrated sense of North American justice and the civil religion of its Euro-American culture, the universal intent of both religion and ethics provides a necessary corrective.

## The Universalizing Intent of Religion and Ethics

Profound religious belief, contrary to George F. Will's or even the Supreme Court's opinion, cannot be submerged in the pursuit of material comforts, nor walled off from moral praxis into something perfectly private. The crucial issue here is the universal intention of religious and moral praxis. Immanuel Kant's moral philosophy remains instructive because he understood the crucial importance of universality to ethics. Philosophers of liberal democracy like Rawls want to retain Kant's principle of moral autonomy while substituting the pursuit of self-interest for Kant's universal rationality. Kant held that persons may be morally autonomous *only* by universalizing the maxim of their action, but certainly *not* by following their contingent and conditional desires.[28] Kant's categorical imperative, as the imperative of universality, required no veil of ignorance because moral persons by his definition obey the universal moral maxims no matter what their particular circumstances.

Kant and other Enlightenment thinkers substituted rational for religious universals because they had witnessed the devastation of Europe when Christians sought to universalize particular forms of their religion. Post-Enlightenment thinkers, however, have also had to recognize the grave difficulty, if not impossibility, of universal rationality. The human mind has no ready access to a universal a priori structure, as Kant thought. Nor do our cultures provide a universal structure of meaning. Our rationality remains as relational and relative, finite and contextual as our religion or anything else in human cultures.

We are left, then, with only the universalizing intent of both religion and reason. But it is an intent that alone seems to match the necessity for common principles to form the deontological but contextual ethos of particular communities, and the emerging necessity for universal principles if humanity is ever to achieve universal human community. We should realize by this point in our history that the universalizing intent of religion cannot be fully sublimated into reason, any more than the universalizing intent of reason can be wholly confined to the theology of any traditional religion. Thus it is necessary to affirm this universalizing intent in both its theological and philosophical modes.

Kant called it "good will," which he considered the only thing "in the world or even out of it, which can be taken as good without qualification."[29] Ronald Green, influenced by Kant, speaks of the same intention in religion as "the moral point of view":

> More important than these rules, however, is the fact that religions also seek to encourage their adherents to adopt "the moral point of view." Sometimes they take separate paths to this goal. Theistic religions commonly approach the matter very differently from mystical traditions. But despite these differences, the goal of impartiality—the ideal of transcending one's own immediate desires to make choices from a social point of view—is widely shared across religious cultures. Promoting this ideal is among the most important contributions religion makes to the moral life.[30]

Many influential theoreticians of religion, however, doubt that religion can ever so closely approximate the Kantian universal. Mark C. Taylor recently analyzed Durkheim's, Freud's, and Nietzsche's "modern" theories of religion, which they interpret as "the primitive" foundation of human psychic and social life.[31] Durkheim's sociological analysis of the sexual and violent passions released in the totemic festivals of Australian "Aborigines" and North American "Indians," Freud's psychoanalysis (which is also socioanthropological analysis) of the wish fulfillment, illusion, guilt, obsessional neurosis, and Oedipus complex he found in religion, and Nietzsche's philosophical analysis of the Dionysian energies revealed in Greek tragedy when released from the repressive moralism of bourgeois Europe, all point in these authors' minds to an archaic religious ground, which continues to frighten and fascinate modern Euro-American persons. Taylor summarizes their theoretical construct from his "postmodern" perspective:

> Primitivism is a psycho-social construction upon which modernism projects its deepest fears and most profound desires. Suffering the pain of fragmentation, differentiation, and isolation, the modern subject both longs and fears to return to the totality from which s/he came. When theory becomes practice—when tragedy leaves the stage and enters history, the longing for totality becomes totalitarian.[32]

Euro-American religion does indeed seek to address the painful fragmentation, differentiation, and isolation of modern democratic market societies. But neither its theology nor its praxis may be reduced to the irrational primitivism that is the repressed underside of these societies. To miss the logic and dismiss the praxis of authentic religion's universalizing intention to recover and restore community may, however, redirect some of its energies toward the more pathological destructiveness these theoreticians observed. The resurgence of militant fundamentalism in its various modern forms is witness to this danger. These modern theories may thus prove not only partial but potentially dangerous, as Taylor concludes: "Theory, as it has traditionally been understood, becomes as impossible as theology, as it has traditionally been understood. In the absence of end, things do not hang together. Analysis is interminable; there is no Final Solution."[33]

In the terms of our discussion, Taylor's conclusion means that no critical theory of religion, just as no theology, may present itself as a universally true, completed reflection. Neither should the sociocultural context of any theory be understood as universal. The individualistic, competitive, democratic market society that Rawls's theory presupposes is not, and in my judgment should not become, universal.

Though religion provides no absolute or completed reflection about the telos of human life, many religions envision the end of created and creative existence in terms of communal justice. A religiously based vision of communal justice, fortunately, also has strong motives for realizing the more personal forms of community so widely lost in the modern world. The sacred events, stories, and personalities of religion may not be reduced only to a philosophically conceived rational universal of justice. Religion also deals with the nonrational passions and needs for reconciliation and intimacy that we have tried to understand in our previous discussion of the universal relationality of redemption.

Religion may have no immediate access to our divine origin, nor unconditioned vision of our divine end, but profound religion does open our contextual visions of justice to the universality of divine justice. And religion may have to deal with the transmoral issues of guilt and condemnation that accompany so much of conscientious moral striving, but profound religion is not tempted by Kierkegaard's "teleological suspension of the ethical."[34] Religion must deal with the alienated individuation within our contextual structures that Kierkegaard knew so well, while moving in its own way toward both a more personal and universal justice that finds its ground and limit in the justice and mercy of God.

This universalizing intent of religion and ethics may also be articulated in terms more familiar to Christian theology. Leonardo Boff's way of doing so in his liberation theology deserves extensive quotation:

> The resurrected Jesus is present and active in a special way in those who in the vast orbit of history and life carry forward his cause. This is independent of their ideological colorings or adhesion to some religion or Christian belief. Wherever people seek the good, justice, humanitar-

ian love, solidarity, communion, and understanding between people, wherever they dedicate themselves to overcoming their own egoism, making this world more human and fraternal, and opening themselves to the normative transcendent for their lives, there we can say, with all certainty, that the resurrected one is present, because the cause for which he lived, suffered, was tried, and executed is being carried forward. . . . Christ did not come to found a new religion. He came to bring a new human being (cf. Eph. 2:15), one who is not defined by the established criteria of society (cf. Gal. 3:28) but by the option for the cause of love, which is the cause of Christ. . . . He touches all, especially those who by their lives struggle for what Jesus himself struggled and died for, even though they do not make explicit reference to him and to his universal salvific meaning.[35]

Such explicitly Christian terms are helpful for congregations opening themselves to the universal relationality of justice within their liturgies, prayers, and praxis. But they must not be misused to identify other people so committed as "anonymous Christians," which Boff, following Karl Rahner, unfortunately does.[36] The problem posed in such a phrase as "anonymous Christians," however, should enable the recognition of both the universalizing intent of profound religion and the difficulty of thematizing the universal in the particular vocabulary of any religion.

Thus, those of us who are at home with the concrete confessional expressions of the religious mind and heart also need to learn from the more philosophical articulations of justice. We must affirm and celebrate the universal intent of both and seek their dialectical interaction in our common enterprise. Only so may we become able to give more adequately universal expression to our religious understanding of the universal relationality of God's justice.

## A Philosophical Clarification of Phronesis

The philosophical ethicist Stephen Toulmin is as convinced as any theological ethicist that the use of reason in ethics is meaningful only in the ethos of a concrete community. Toulmin argues convincingly that modes of reasoning are meaningful only in relation to the larger activities of which they are a part and the ends these promote. The proper use of reason in ethics may be understood only by examining the practical situations in which ethical questions arise. Those situations always face us with the question of how our feelings and behavior require to be altered or supported if we are to live in community:

The only context in which the concept of "duty" is straightforwardly intelligible is one of communal life—it is, indeed, completely bound up with this very feature of communal life, that we learn to renounce our claims and alter our aims where they conflict with those of our fellows.[37]

The ethics of simpler communities as they seek "to correlate our feelings and behavior" are traditional and deontological, but as societies become more complex their deontological code is modified by teleology. Then ethics becomes the process of developing the moral code of a community by submitting its deontological structures to a teleological critique addressed to the motives and results of its social practices.

This socioethical process may be illustrated, as Toulmin does, by following G. M. Trevelyan's account of the Hanoverian monarchy in England. After stabilizing and unifying the country, the first necessity was to establish the rule of law. Only then could Jeremy Bentham's utilitarian program speed the social and legal reforms required in the nineteenth century. Bentham's teleological principle of "the greatest happiness of the greatest number" was contextually necessary to overcome the prevailing exaggerated respect for legal authority. Nevertheless, it should not be generalized as the principle of all value. The moral code that articulates the common good of a community may not be dissolved into a purely quantitative calculation of externally related units of personal happiness.[38]

To affirm a deontological ethic while excluding its teleological revision or amplification is equally problematic. To establish moral principles, rules, and laws to be applied to particular situations correlates all too closely with a hierarchical system maintaining a conservative and closed society.[39] A rational ethic serving the common good then must be a dialectical and dialogical process using both deontological reasoning based on tradition and teleological reasoning open to the change that process requires.

To realize that ethics may not be reduced either to universal, invariable, and certain principles or to contextual, variable, and relative decisions is to approach that understanding of the common good defined by Aristotle as *phronesis* or practical wisdom. In an Aristotelian perspective, ethics may not be entirely based on *theoria*, whether understood as science, metaphysics, or theology, nor on *techne*, understood as the application of their principles and rules. *Phronesis* is a classical moral strategy that may be more available to modern persons if interpreted in the contemporary terms of process philosophy and cultural hermeneutics. It may be understood as a particular form of "concrescence" in Whitehead's terms and of "concretization" in Gadamer's terms.

Gadamer says of the relation between hermeneutics and *phronesis*: "In the end it was the great theme of the concretization of the universal that I learned to think of as the basic experience of hermeneutics."[40] We already know that Gadamer does not understand concretization as a deduction from principles. For him, just as "interpretation aims at a concretization of understanding in a fusion of horizons, so practice aims at concretizing the universal in a particular good."[41]

Matthew Foster has developed the implications of Gadamer's hermeneutics for ethics. He mines Gadamer's insights into human historicity so as to restore confidence in the compatibility of historicity with the historical actualization of the common human good. Foster says Gadamer's premise is that "there is a wholeness to our existence, to the world, a conviction that universals and particulars not only should be joined, as conscience may dictate, but that reality permits them to be joined."[42] The problem met, however, is that there are so great a variety of traditions in our increasingly complex, pluralistic, cross-cultural, and interreligious world, with their various deontological principles, that none are readily recognized as universal. When all principles are thus relativized, we lose our basis for discerning the common good or placing our confidence in any claimed discernment of it.

Many still turn for guidance to the moral universals of one of the world's religions, and at the end of Foster's reflections as well as mine and many others, it remains so.[43] Yet even the most faithful realize, as Foster says, that "if we live by the stories and icons of one religious community, it seems we must do so in a mental chamber foreign to many around us and even to the rest of our own thinking."[44] Classical philosophical texts like Aristotle's *Nicomachean Ethics*, it must be added, also fail to provide sufficient guidance for modern *phronesis*. It may have been possible for Aristotle to practice *phronesis* within the limits of a Greek city-state by uniting *synesis* (understanding of another's discourse) with *gnome* (judgment) in a context of *syngnome* ("judging with," which is often misleadingly translated as "sympathy" or "empathy"). But such *syngnome* as a common sense of justice is exceedingly more difficult for those who must learn to live in what is already euphemistically called a global village.

When we remember that Aristotle's city-state included vast numbers of slaves with no participation in *syngnome*, just as modern societies include vast numbers of oppressed or marginalized poor and illiterate, our moral confidence in the adequacy of any *phronesis* is relativized. When we see with Marcus Raskin that even Toulmin's example of the successful amplification of England's deontological ethos by Bentham's utilitarian theory "worked only to the extent Great Britain's political leadership submerged its class conflicts at home by encouraging technological and geographic expansion, exodus, and colonization,"[45] we must reflect on how the factors of power and ideology form and deform any *syngnome*. Is there any possibility of a common sense of the common good?

## Habermas's Hermeneutics of Suspicion

A hermeneutics of suspicion must inform any *phronesis* based only in the hermeneutics of a particular cultural or religious tradition. Jürgen Habermas has brought home to many the danger of what he calls "systematically distorted communication":

> Language is also a medium of domination and social power; it serves to legitimate relations of organized force. Insofar as the legitimations do not articulate the power relations whose institutionalization they make possible, insofar as these relations merely manifest themselves in the legitimations, language is also ideological.[46]

Habermas fosters critical reflection to discern and correct such ideological distortion, thus protecting against the dogmatism of any tradition in defining the common good. All cultural and religious modes of thought must be tested sociologically for their sometimes hidden dependence upon economic and administrative power systems. The kind of purposive rationality (*techne*) developed in modern democratic capitalist societies, for instance, has reduced many who should participate in communicative action to the relative silence of mere clients, consumers, or producers.

Habermas's theory of an "ideal speech situation" seems to suffer from an idealism similar to Rawls's "original position behind a veil of ignorance."[47] But his concern to unmask any covert, coercive uses of power so that intersubjective communicative action may be based only upon the persuasive use of the best argument is persuasive. Communicative action requires equality and mutual reciprocity. Adequate *phronesis* may occur only in a "shared rational space where all participants, whatever their other particular differences, can meet to discuss any claim that is rationally redeemable."[48]

Habermas's recent critique of postmodern or poststructuralist thinkers—Derrida, Foucault, and Bataille—is useful in defending the possibility of such "shared rational space."[49] He supports their critiques of that understanding of rationality which presupposes an autonomous, transcendental, rational subject but faults their failure to consider the alternative of an intersubjective, linguistic, hermeneutical mode of rationality found in communicative action.

Human *phronesis* for the common good is possible on the basis of intersubjective relationality, shared knowledge, and reciprocal trust. Habermas's support for this possibility is informed by the inspiration that Hegel found in the harmonious exercise of reason in the early Christian communities and the Greek city-states. Habermas and Hegel both conclude, however, that these earlier models are irretrievable. But their agreement stops there. Hegel, in total contrast to Habermas, sought to restore rational harmony to modern societies through the sublation of civil society into the state on the model of the "absolute . . . unified only in the framework of monadical self-knowledge."[50] Habermas, rather, finds the proper alternative in the relationality and rationality of communicative action on a broader scale than either the religious congregation or the ethnic political community can provide.[51]

Habermas's project also rejoins Gadamer's and Whitehead's at exactly this point of understanding *phronesis*: "The issue could now again become one of meaning in history, not in terms of a single religious tradition alone (which is the task of theological hermeneutics) but in terms of the general human condition of living within cultures and their histories."[52] The moral task facing persons living within the particular histories of their various cultures, in Gadamer's terms, is the "concretizing of a universal in a particular good" or, in more Whiteheadian terms, the actualization of God's initial aim in the concrescence of persons internally related to particular social processes. Moral truth is thus recognized and accepted as "knit into our interpreting of the world."[53] The plurality and contextuality of these interpretations reveals our finite freedom, but the finitude of that freedom requires that our moral definitions of the common good be corrected and enriched in ever larger dialogues.

### The Relation of Habermas and Gadamer

The difference between Gadamer and Habermas is in the greater valence that Gadamer gives to historical finitude and thus a proper dependence on the authority of religious and cultural traditions. Habermas, on the other hand, gives greater weight to critical reason in order to break the dogmatism of any tradition. Gadamer fears, however, that a Habermasian hermeneutics that suspects all the traditional claims that constitute our effective history may end in claiming so culturally transcendent a perspective as to absolutize its own ideals.[54] The recent work of Habermas makes clear, however, that he would not absolutize any ideal speech situation. Neither Gadamer nor Habermas invokes transcendental reason in any form. Both seek that form of insight in which the whole is illumined by a part that understands itself as formed within and by the whole. Both thinkers appeal to a dialectical logic actualized in dialogue, rather than a transcendental logic actualized in a subject. Habermas gives greater weight to arguments based on critical social theory, while Gadamer gives greater authority to cultural, religious, and legal traditions, as both seek a more universal understanding of *phronesis* than Aristotle provided. They both seek to fuse the horizons between Aristotle's practical philosophy and our contemporary experience of cross-cultural and interreligious contingency and possibility.[55]

To affirm the possibility of a *universal phronesis*, however, turns philosophy toward the religious dimensions of philosophical reflection. Can a dialogue dedicated to this universal purpose ever end? Can a dialogical process open to the unlimited consideration of alternative answers ever contribute to praxis? Does not anything like Habermas's vision of the voiceless in our world becoming equal partners in a dialogue seeking universal *phronesis* anticipate, not just an ideal speech situation, but a religious eschaton or a utopian vision? The answers of both Gadamer and Habermas to such questions verge on the religious.

This is the more surprising with Habermas, who usually ignores the claims of religion. Yet he recognizes that he is "defending an outrageously strong claim in the present context of philosophical discussion: namely that there is a universal core of moral intuition in all times and in all societies."[56] Where Habermas uses the language of universality, Gadamer uses the language of infinity: "All human speaking is finite in such a way that there is laid up within it an infinity of meaning to be explicated and laid out."[57] The point of both is that we, even as finite human beings, already participate in the universal and infinite. Our finite freedom then is not an imprisonment in our historicity, but it is the basis for our participation in the universal community of being. Matthew Foster sums up the implication of Gadamer's philosophy in terms more religious than would be appropriate for Habermas but yet not far from the latter's claim for a "universal core of moral intuition":

> We fear, as well as wish, that the fate of truth and good lies in our hands, but in fact it does not: the acts by which we attempt to reach beyond our finitude are always exceeded by the power of being in the activity of language, which plays a game larger than we can devise.[58]

### The Relation of Ethos to Phronesis

This moral confidence in our philosophical ability to move dialogically with a universal *phronesis* toward a universal common good remains entirely abstract, however, until it is given content by either a cultural or religious ethos, or perhaps both. A good illustration is provided by returning to the more analytic and pragmatic discussion of Stephen Toulmin. As he reflected on the role of reason in English society, he saw its ethos as providing both "framework" and "limit" for evaluating its social practices. The illustration provided concerns the cross-cultural and interreligious question of marriage: "Is it really right to have only one wife, like the Christians, or would it be better to have anything up to four, according to the old Mohammedan practice?"[59] The limits of England's traditional ethos make such a question almost unintelligible for Toulmin because one cannot deal with possibilities as real alternatives when abstracted from their social context.

Ethical questions make sense only within the ethos of relative social "wholes" constituted by a culture and its religious base. What appears to be a personal question of "one wife or four?" must be asked in the more comprehensive terms, "Is Christian marriage or Muslim marriage the better practice?" That in turn becomes "Is the Christian or the Muslim *way of life* the better?" Toulmin holds that we can only compare "ways of life *as wholes*."[60] Therefore, the only intelligible form of this question is whether one will remain in English society or go to live in a Muslim society—though his English prejudice led him forty years ago to express the latter alternative as "an Arab tribesman in the desert."

Toulmin's analytic insight appears exactly right: One cannot intelligibly deal with issues of justice or the common good in abstract universals. *Phronesis* must be informed by ethos. A large part of any society's ethos derives from its religion. Gadamer, influenced by Hegel and Heidegger, understands *phronesis* as participation in infinite being, so that finite linguistical beings may be liberated to infinite dialogue. But he refuses to discuss more concrete questions. His *phronesis* remains empty because he refuses to participate in the finite and particular. He says in *Truth and Method* that he does not intend "to make prescriptions for the sciences or the conduct of life, but to try to correct false thinking about what they are."[61] Perhaps one of the reasons for Gadamer's vocational self-limitation paradoxically derives from the religious particularity of Gadamer's ethos—that is, his enculturation as a Lutheran Protestant Christian who knows well the danger of seeking to justify oneself by "works":

> He is not most worried about whether the conclusions of hermeneutics lead to the dilution of moral abstractions or accelerate the seeming slide into amorality of this age of takeover and plurality. Gadamer's anxiety is more like that of the Protestant—an anxiety about human arrogance, and most of all one's own arrogance—but here embodied in anxiety about the desire or need to observe certain absolute standards.[62]

These may be sufficient illustrations of the interaction of religion and philosophy to discern that the attempt to participate in a universal *phronesis* in order to articulate the universal common good brings philosophy to the margin of religion. The theological articulation of the world's religious traditions interacts with the philosopher's attempts to negotiate in and through the ethos of a concrete society as both seek the universal good of humanity. Religious persons would add "under God" or, in our philosophical theological terms, "under the universal relationality of God."

We have concluded heretofore that the universalizing intent of religion cannot be fully sublimated into reason, nor can the universalizing intent of reason be wholly confined within the theology of any religion. We must now further conclude that both must creatively interact if there is to be a human process of *phronesis* that concretizes the universal relationality of justice in the cross-cultural and interreligious ethos of what we hope may yet become a global village.

## Through Contextual Ethos
## Toward Universal Justice

The concept of "ethos" is so important to the understanding of social relationality that it requires careful interpretation if we are to understand the contextual relationality of universal justice. When Clifford Geertz began to use ethos in his cultural anthropology several decades ago, he thought it a kind of "prototheory" that was too vague and imprecise to be dignified as "theory." Yet he thought it important to use and develop because it moved the interpretation of religion and ethics—the normative dimensions of culture—from abstract principles to a "theory of value which looks toward the behavior of actual people in actual societies living in terms of actual cultures."[63] Crediting Max Weber as mentor, Geertz developed the study of culture as an interpretation of meaning:

> Believing with Max Weber, that man is an animal suspended in webs of significance he himself has spun, I take culture to be those webs, and the analysis of it to be therefore not an experimental science in search of law but an interpretative one in search of meaning.[64]

Max Weber had developed his important studies of religion's role in cultures with the premise that human history and culture could only be studied as "concrete genetic sets of relations," not in terms of "abstract general formulae."[65]

To seek meaning in concrete genetic sets of relations is a methodology for studying culture similar to the social presupposition of the hermeneutical perspective on *phronesis* we have developed. Just as Gadamer and Habermas were brought to religious perspectives on the infinite or universal through a relational hermeneutics seeking the common good, Geertz and especially Weber developed careful studies of religion as the most comprehensive set of relations affecting a culture's ethos. Geertz recognizes religion's general cultural power:

> Never merely metaphysics, religion is never merely ethics either. The source of its moral vitality is conceived to be in the fidelity with which it

expresses the fundamental nature of reality. The powerfully coercive "ought" is felt to grow out of a comprehensive factual "is," and in such a way religion grounds the most specific requirements of human action in the most general contexts of human existence.[66]

## The Contributions of Max Weber and Jacques Ellul

Max Weber provided specific illustration of the social power of religion in his cultural studies. His interpretation of the relation of religion to the ethos or spirit of capitalism enables a more adequate contextualization of the understanding of justice in modern capitalist societies than was possible in John Rawls's more abstract theory. When supplemented with later work like Jacques Ellul's, it provides a far thicker description of the social reality whose ethical meaning is being interpreted as well as a way to discern the moral roots from which it sprang and from which it is now largely severed. Weber found and helps us understand the origin of "sober bourgeois capitalism with its rational organization of free labor" in the religious context of "the rational ethics of an ascetic Protestantism."[67]

In contrast to Rawls, Weber recognized that self-interest was not the dominant motive in the ethos/spirit of early capitalism. Capitalism's original motive was religious, traced first to Luther's notion of vocation (*Beruf*) as the religious "fulfillment of duty in worldly affairs."[68] Despite Luther's transformation of the medieval meaning of vocation, his still medieval understanding of salvation remained too mystical and sacramental to satisfy some other reformers. Calvin's theology of the "absolute transcendality of God" with its correlate of the "disenchantment of the world"[69] continued to transform this medieval view. Since salvation is determined by the decision of the absolutely transcendent God, the believers' predestination to salvation cannot be known through religious experience. Only a life of diligent, obedient, self-denying work was considered to provide any assurance of a redemptive relation with God. From this perspective, salvation is not experienced through any form of mystical piety but only through doing God's will by ascetic action in the world. This religious commitment to disciplined work provided the religious context for the capitalistic ethos that Weber discerned in Geneva and Zurich in the sixteenth century.

European Pietism and Anglo-American Methodism joined the motifs that classical Lutheranism and Calvinism had kept separate. Though finding their assurance of salvation more in Lutheran forms of emotional piety, Methodists and Pietists turned from Luther's vague and traditional morality to the ascetic ethics of Puritanism. Thus the worldly asceticism of not only European Calvinism but also English Puritanism and American Methodism fostered frugality and industry. Their religious warnings against the temptations of the flesh were not aimed against the rational acquisition of wealth but against its self-indulgent consumption. Methodists often recalled, and sometimes even yet follow, John Wesley's well-known aphorism: "Earn all you can, save all you can, give all you can." Weber's analysis of the religious ethos fostered by these influential religious movements in Euro-America is clear about their economic consequence: "When the limitation of consumption is combined with the release of acquisitive activity, the inevitable practical result is obvious: accumulation of capital through ascetic compulsion to save."[70]

The same religious motifs also influenced the "good" laborers who worked for the original capitalist entrepreneurs. The industrialization of Euro-American societies required the division of labor that has characterized our productive processes ever since. In addition to its utilitarian necessity, it also provided the more constant, disciplined form of work that the Protestant ethic required. Thus, in Weber's judgment, early capitalism had a work force that was "available for economic exploitation for conscience' sake."[71] It was not necessary to motivate them by purely economic means, for they knew more powerful sanctions, for good and for ill, in their religious ethos.

The contemporary relevance of Weber's hermeneutical reflections on Euro-American culture is the recognition that what were originally religious motives were transformed into "purely mundane passions" once the capitalistic ethos was established. The condemnation of self-interest and self-indulgent consumption, found everywhere in the original capitalistic ethos engendered by Puritanism, Pietism, and Methodism, has now been transformed into "principles of justice" based on the self-interest originally prohibited. The most "general context of human existence," to remember Geertz's phrase, is no longer the relational universal of God's justice but the aggregate of individual self-interest, perhaps to be weighed and balanced on some utilitarian scale. The cultural basis for not only the concept of, but the concern for, the common good has thereby been lost in the ethos of modern capitalism.

The loss of the religious, relational basis for the common good paralleled the development of "the technical and economic conditions of machine production," which Weber thought might continue "until the last ton of fossilized coal is burnt." The technocratic consequence of persons being tied to machines led Weber to use a vivid metaphor that has become perhaps his most famous and oft-repeated thought. Responding to a paraphrase of Jesus' word that "my yoke is easy and my burden light," which a religious author had used to say that the care for the world's goods should lie on a saint's shoulders like a light cloak, Weber wrote: "But fate decreed that the cloak should become an *iron cage*."[72]

Jacques Ellul, philosopher of law, lay theologian, as well as once mayor of Bordeaux, developed Weber's analysis in the spirit of this powerful metaphor. Ellul articulated a "dialectical philosophy of the whole" to interpret the "phenomenology of the technical mind,"[73] which is analogous to the dialectical logic we have been using to interpret panentheism. He attributes the technocratic transition in the European ethos to the move from a Greek-influenced culture and science, which depreciated *techne* and understood *phronesis*, to a science where technique increasingly dominates every sphere of cultural life, while the practical wisdom of *phronesis* atrophies. Ellul's analysis of the "atomization" of European society through the industrialization of its economy thickens Weber's iron cage metaphor:

> The breakup of social groups engendered the enormous displacement of people at the beginning of the nineteenth century and resulted in the concentration of population demanded by modern technique. To uproot men from their surroundings, from the rural districts and from family and friends, in order to crowd them into cities too small for them; to squeeze thousands into unfit lodgings and unhealthy places of work; to create a whole new environment within the framework of a new human condition . . . —all this was possible only when the individual was completely isolated. It was conceivable only when he literally had no environment, no family, and was not part of a group able to resist economic pressure; when he had almost no way of life left.[74]

Many workers in contemporary Euro-American cities no longer suffer the kind of environment Ellul describes, though its atomistic consequences continue; but this tragic environment has now been extended to the working-class neighborhoods of almost every industrialized city in the developing world. Though Euro-American workers may have escaped the earliest form of the iron cage in industrialized cities, none of them or the rest of us have escaped the total technical environment that more and more resembles Weber's dark metaphor:

> Never before has the human race as a whole had to exert such efforts in its daily labors as it does today as a result of its absorption into the monstrous technical mechanism—an undifferentiated but complex mechanism which makes it impossible to turn a wheel without the sustained, persevering, and intensive labor of millions of workers, whether in white collars or in blue.[75]

The technical collaboration necessary to live in this complex mechanism, unfortunately, has not proven sufficient to reconstruct an ethos of community and a concern for the common good. Weber had already marked the "feeling of unprecedented inner loneliness of the single individual" in early Protestantism.[76] Philip Slater has extended this analysis to contemporary American culture's "pursuit of loneliness." The privacy that some originally sought with religious motives, because salvation was no longer mediated through sacramental community, is now driven by an individualistic ethos, technological progress, and social mobility to a form of alienation divorced from any religious matrix.[77]

The fruits of Weber's and Ellul's dark analyses of technocratic capitalism has been despair of any better future for some: "The answer to whether we can conceive of the future other than as a continuation of the darkness, cruelty, and disorder of the past seems to be no; and to the question of whether worse impends, yes."[78] Not all, of course, share Robert Heilbroner's dark sense of our human prospect. Some continue to hope for a technological progress that will finally make everything available to everyone. The most powerful present form of this technical vision of the good is the hope for an international economy built by transnational corporations with a free market for the transfer of capital, technology, and goods.

### The Influence of Marxism

Some who hold this form of hope today might be surprised to learn that Karl Marx was an ally in the last century. In contrast to Weber and Ellul, Marx defended the importance of *techne* and technology in human history:

> Technology discloses man's mode of dealing with Nature, the process of production by which he sustains his life and thereby also lays bare the mode of formation of his social relations, and of the mental conceptions that flow from them. Every history of religion even, that fails to take account of this material base is uncritical.[79]

The work of the young Marx, however, reveals that his concern for the alienation engendered by the technocratic ethos of capitalist society was entirely similar to that of Weber and Ellul.[80] It is now clear that his philosophical determination to transform capitalism was meant to overcome its workers' alienation. When he wrote his famous XIth Thesis on Feuerbach: "The philosophers have only interpreted the world in various ways; the point, however, is to change it," he had Hegel and Feuerbach in mind, but it could have been directed at Gadamer, Weber, or many other intellectuals.

Marx thought that *techne* in its modern form of machine production based on the hard sciences was fundamental to any conceivable transformation of history. It required, however, to be brought under the theoretical direction of that vanguard he named "Communist" in solidarity with the workers actually doing the work of industrialization. For three generations the movement Marx helped originate was one of the most dynamic in the effort to restore industrialized societies to communal wholeness, but finally it was one of the least successful. The "real socialism," as Brezhnev liked to call it in the Soviet Union of the 1960s and 1970s, had tragically exterminated or socially exiled most of its original theoreticians in the generation before, so that the real vanguard had become the technocratic *nomenklatura*. Since Gorbachev's *glasnost* and *perestroika*, and the dissolution of the Soviet Union, everyone realizes the failure of its so-called command economy and the horror of its gulag. Its failure reveals the danger of those who seek communal wholeness with a totalitarian political practice perhaps joined with too organic a metaphysical model.

Some of the earliest critics of this form of Marxism, however, were Marxists. Adam Schaff was still the acknowledged ideological leader on the Central Committee of the Communist Party in Poland when he wrote *Marxism and Human Individuality* in the early 1960s:

> In the atmosphere of the thirties there was no place in official Marxism for the problematic of the individual, the philosophy of humanity, and humanism. To enlighten that Marxism with the humanism of the young Marx was for the authors of the development of the labor movement of that time just as impossible and strange as was their policy in the light of the socialist humanism and the humanistic interpretation of Marxism. The traditional, strong, forced stereotype of Marxism, which was often on the border of mechanism, was in that atmosphere and in the context of certain requirements of actual politics not only sanctioned but even stiffened.[81]

What Schaff realized in Poland, Milan Machovec sought to actualize in Czechoslovakia through his leadership of the Marxist-Christian dialogue in Charles University, his presidency of the Society for Human Rights in Prague, and his support for "socialism with a human face" during the Prague Spring of 1968. He agreed as a Marxist with Christian confreres like the theologian Josef Hromádka that the human longing for communal wholeness had religious dimensions:

> In a certain sense there arises a new opportunity for religion, due to the "estranging" effects of progressing technique, automation, mechanization, one-sided specialization, institutionalism, demoralization, and the loss of the traditional values of life. There are millions of men who do not envisage any other way than religious integration of these corroding historical processes.[82]

It is exactly the role of religion in restoring communal wholeness in the corrosive ethos of modern societies that is our central concern. Even (former) Marxists now know that religion cannot be relegated to the epiphenomenal "superstructure" of a reality determined by humanity's productive relations, which gives *techne* complete predominance in human life. But neither may religion be divorced from political-economic issues. It surely must be understood "in intimate connection with the fundamental productive processes of life."[83] As religious persons know full well, the issues of life may not be reduced to the scientific, technical, economic, or political; but, as they sometimes forget, neither may a theological understanding lose its meaningful relation to these concrete issues that affect all of life.

### The Uses of Casuistry

Casuistry, one of the traditional ways of carefully articulating the relation between religion and the concrete ethical issues arising in its social ethos, is undergoing something of a revival. Stephen Toulmin, whose earlier work we examined with philosophical profit, now is seeking to develop *phronesis* in the more analytic form of casuistry.[84] Casuistry provides ethos with the more analytic framework that Geertz was looking for to make a prototheory more conceptually precise. Aristotle's conception of "ethos" was in the somewhat vague terms of the tone, quality, style, and mood of a people's life, which he related to the natural factors of age and the social factors of station and status.[85] Toulmin and his colleague Albert Jonsen now add the crucial factors of social structures and institutions, which also were important in the modern discussions of social ethos of Weber, Ellul, Marx, and Geertz.

Casuistry, as the study of cases, begins with ethos, just as English jurisprudence begins with common law. Casuistry must begin with some communal consensus about paradigmatic moral cases such as promise-keeping and immoral behavior such as cruelty. Analogous but more complex cases are identified, organized, and analyzed on the basis of their similarities to and differences from these paradigmatic cases. When new cases in unprecedented or ambiguous circumstances arise, analogical reasoning is used to make a relative and probable moral judgment on the basis of the moral precedent in an appropriate case.

The Jesuits gave European casuistry perhaps its most intricate development.[86] It was the almost universal form of the Roman Catholic Church that allowed the development of an economic casuistry that transcended the consensus of any national or ethnic ethos, despite the sometimes warranted suspicion that its universality was too Roman. This universality became important when the industrialization of Europe institutionalized new economic processes that transformed the ethos of all of its cultures and transcended older communal forms of moral consensus. Casuistry then enabled the adjustment of traditional Christian prohibitions against usury while continuing to provide moral guidance for Europe's increasingly transnational economic life. A moral basis with some communal consensus for allocating the profit of a growing industrial product to cover the cost of its capitalization could be more universally worked out without capitulating to the new form of power exercised by those who owned or controlled the capital.[87]

The limited success casuistry had in providing moral guidance for the earlier transnational industrialization of Europe raises the hope that it might so function in the more comprehensive transnational economic structures that are emerging in our global economy. Toulmin and Jonsen, however, give us little reason soon to hope for so great an achievement. Casuistry is possible only within institutional frameworks where standard situations arise that standard cases may help illumine. But, as Philip Turner points out in his review of their book, "widely shared institutional frameworks now seem to be missing or in a state of disarray."[88] Western forms of capitalistic economic institutions, like Western forms of scientific medicine, are becoming almost universal, but without even that semblance of institutionalized community and consensus that the Roman Catholic Church and tradition carried over from medieval to modern Europe. Jonsen and Toulmin have more hope for the development of casuisty in bioethics because the requisite medical institutions are developing more rapidly in that area.[89]

*Phronesis* then may deal with justice issues arising from the almost universal transformations of ethos in our world more concretely than Gadamer was willing to attempt, but it is as yet only seldom able to reach the analytic form of casuisty that Jonsen and Toulmin seek.

### The Uses of Theology

Human beings in the twentieth century are living through a profound and often tragic dialectic. On the one hand, older, particular forms of communal ethos engendered in large part by religion have been and are continually being destroyed; while, on the other hand, more inclusive forms of universal ethos are being engendered by cross-cultural and inter-religious dialogue that approach the vision of universal human community long held by our universal religions. How may theology best help religious persons and communities negotiate this difficult path through both destruction and creativity toward a more universal justice?

First, there must be continued resistance to the loss of communal ethics that is often concomitant with the loss of the older forms of communal ethos. Human ends may not be subordinated by an iron cage mentality to technical reason and morality. Not everything that becomes technically feasible is either socially necessary or morally acceptable, even if economically or militarily advantageous. Ellul observes that "documents such as the United Nations' Declaration of Human Rights mean nothing to a mankind surrounded by techniques."[90] To the degree this is true, it must be resisted; for human rights are the contemporary way of identifying "those values and obligations that give form and continuity to the possibility that humankind may become one covenantal community."[91]

The modern resurgence of subjective spirituality and divisive fundamentalism must be confronted both as an understandable reaction to the acids of modernity and a profound misunderstanding of the kind of community really needed for contemporary spirituality. Robert Heilbroner anticipated this religious response to an increasingly bleak human prospect twenty years ago:

> It is therefore possible that a postindustrial society would also turn in the direction of many preindustrial societies—toward the exploration of inner states of experience rather than the outer world of fact and material accomplishment. Tradition and ritual, the pillars of life in virtually all societies other than those of an industrial character, would probably once again assert their ancient claims as the guide and solace for life.[92]

Given the subject-object, fact-value, and tradition-progress dichotomies that modern persons have had to try to traverse, perhaps the turn to subjective spirituality and the absolutization of particular traditions is understandable, and maybe even necessary for some for a time. But it is not the kind of spirituality that allows religious persons to contribute to the universal ethos that is emerging and must be created. Religious persons need to relearn a *phronesis* that is grounded in the ethos of their contextual communities but seeks policies and practices politics committed to the universal common good.

Second, we may help move toward a more universal justice by focusing the felt need and cumulative fear rising from the iron cage experience that Weber, Ellul, and others have discerned and analyzed. This was the program of recent existentialist writers. With great literary force, Kierkegaard, the early Marx, Dostoevsky, Sartre, Camus, and many others focused the loneliness and suffering of many modern persons imprisoned in our industrial iron cage. The theologians Karl Barth in his early work and Paul Tillich in all of his work used this existentialist phenomenology to "shake the foundations" (Tillich) of alienated persons, to return them to participation in the holy, social being manifested in Jewish covenantal and Christian communal faith. Marcus Raskin's more philosophical analysis of how modern persons might be returned to a concern for the common good also supports this strategy:

> An organic understanding of the world, which crosses the boundaries of what is inside and what is outside (*res cogitans*, *res extensa*, and *in corpore*)

will occur when there is enough cumulative fear and felt need which forces this feeling on everyone.[93]

A third, more positive contribution is to focus the manifestations of gracious relationality that no iron cage or, in more recent parlance, iron curtain can entirely obscure or destroy. Karl Barth's mid-career theological adjustment to an exclusively revelational theology of pure grace is one of its recent neo-orthodox forms. Our more philosophical model recognizes God's gracious universal relationality wherever expressed in cosmos, culture, and religion. This philosophical theology joins the Christian tradition at the point of affirming sacramental participation in the power and pathos of God's Trinitarian relationality, actualized in the church as a foretaste of God's intention for the whole creation. This concretely Christian experience is opened toward the universal, however, through the conceptual model of dialectical panentheism, to help thematize a religious sense of universal community and to open our sense of social ethos to a concern for universal justice.

An increasing number of persons in our culture have lost whatever sense of security they have had from the promise of economic growth. Some are also recognizing the absurdity of allowing the market to dictate and dominate social values and relationships. There is even a new sense of politics emerging to replace the purely competitive dynamics of power politics:

> Martin Luther King Jr. had no power on his side except that of mobilizing the feelings and needs of people. . . . The women's movement and its projects of networking and consciousness-raising introduced a new dimension to politics which transcended traditional conceptions of power, causing men to have to invite women into the corridors of power, if not to their rightful seats. . . . Politics *is* the means by which people create relationships to live with others.[94]

The church in the German Democratic Republic provided a telling example of this new form of politics as it took up the issues of militarism, human rights, and ecology within its socialist society in the 1980s. They did not direct their politics "against socialism" or anything or anyone else but rather sought "the best for the whole." Nevertheless, their concern for the universal common good brought them into tension with the particularist interests of their Communist government:

> The peace question, because of its highly political character, necessarily became the touchstone and stress test of the new relationship between church and state. This was true from the point of view of the socialist state because the rejection of the "spirit and logic of deterrence" appears directed against an essential element of its defense strategy, and may be suspected of intending to weaken defense preparedness. It was

true from the standpoint of the church, because the church interprets its peace witness in the service of society as "not directed against socialism," but rather as "seeking the best for the whole." For peace is indivisible.[95]

A *phronesis* that seeks the best for the whole is exactly what the universal relationality of justice seeks through the ongoing transformation of our socioreligious ethos. The Berlin Wall that came down at the end of the decade in which this new politics was practiced by the East German churches may symbolize its efficacy for us all.

## The Contextual Relativity of Any Praxis of Universal Justice

A concrete religious concern for universal justice may be actualized only through active participation in particular communities working to form and transform the ethos of their society. The illustration from the German Democratic Republic at the end of the previous section is an equally good illustration of this point. The ideology and institutions of the German Democratic Republic under the Communist (Socialist Unity) party set the framework and sought to limit the *praxis* of the East German churches. After the transformation of that society in 1989, which was partially the consequence of their praxis, the now more obvious limits on their previous witness and work became the occasion for ridicule by some who shared too little of their struggle.[96] But such ridicule really reveals a failure to understand the contextual nature of praxis.

Even when understood, however, the value of *praxis* is contested. Liberation theology, especially in Latin America, made this term its own after it had been previously restricted for many decades almost entirely to Marxist use. Robert McAfee Brown noted that "the perennial interest in Marxism springs from that 'union of theory and practice' of which Marx himself was the first and greatest exemplar."[97] But it is exactly the *union* of theory and practice, rather than the more traditional application of theory to practice, that leads many to reject it as too radical. It may, indeed, appear too radical, as José Míguez-Bonino reveals, to philosophers and theologians accustomed to the formal or transcendental logic of our scientific, technological culture. Referring to Hugo Assmann and Gustavo Gutiérrez, as well as his own "doing theology in a revolutionary situation," he wrote:

> They are saying, in fact, that there is no truth outside *or* beyond the concrete historical events in which men are involved as agents. There is, therefore, no knowledge except in action itself, in the process of transforming the world through participation in history. As soon as

such a formulation is presented, objections will be raised that (1) biblical truth is reduced to ethical action, . . . (2) the vertical dimension is swallowed in the horizontal, and (3) this is the Marxist view of knowledge.[98]

From the standpoint of dialectical logic, however, *praxis* is radical only in the proper sense of recognizing the rootedness of all of our being and doing in the relationality of Being. Thus, the union of theory and practice is another way of expressing the union of the universal and particular, the ideal and real, or the spiritual and the natural that we have seen in the hermeneutic of Gadamer and Habermas, the cultural anthropology of Geertz and Weber, the casuistry of Toulmin and Jonsen, and the ethics of the common good in Raskin.

This understanding of praxis requires that religion and the human sciences not be divorced from the hard sciences and technology. The conceptual model of dialectical panentheism comprehends science and religion dialectically.[99] Whitehead's thought combined the aesthetic meditative form of Heidegger with the moral concern for social transformation espoused by Marx.[100] Some of Whitehead's more vivid prose reveals his similarity to Marx in his concern to move intellectuals beyond what he perceived to be their usual class-limited perspective:

> When we think of freedom, we are apt to confine ourselves to freedom of thought, freedom of the press, freedom for religious opinions. Then the limitations to freedom are conceived as wholly arising from the antagonisms of our fellow men. This is a thorough mistake. . . . The essence of freedom is the practicability of purpose. . . . The literary exposition of freedom deals mainly with the frills. . . . The literary world through all ages belonged mainly to the fortunate section of mankind whose basic wants have been amply satisfied. . . . Also the basic needs when they are habitually satisfied cease to dominate thought. Delicacies of taste displace the interest in fullness of stomach.[101]

Whitehead knew that even intellectuals dare not forgo a praxis that seeks to meet the basic needs of human life, as aided by the physical sciences and technological production.

### Whitehead's Contextual Relativity

Critical reflection on Whitehead's concretizing of universal justice within the particular exigencies of his late "Victorian age"[102] is, nevertheless, necessary.[103] While still in his native England he supported the reformist wing of the Liberal Party and, after its decline, the moderate wing of the Labor Party. Their political-economic praxis matched both his repudiation of the "liberal doctrine of an atomistic society"[104] and his developing metaphysics of social process. Randall Morris's analysis of Whitehead's social location uses Habermas's hermeneutics of suspicion to inquire whether there is evidence "that Whitehead's and Hartshorne's philosophical principles legitimate or rationalize the values and interests of modern liberals":

> If, as it appears, their metaphysics are generalizations of their social locations and if their philosophies function in turn to legitimate liberal democratic institutions—including a reformed capitalism and the social inequalities which that still entails—then a process political theology constructed from the perspective of process metaphysics could unconsciously legitimate this ideology.[105]

Morris concludes that a political ethic may not be derived directly from Whitehead's metaphysics, just as Gadamer and Habermas contended that no *phronesis* may be understood as derived from any *theoria*. *Phronesis* is a contextually relative concretion/concretization that always dialectically requires the ideology critique engendered by a hermeneutics of suspicion. Morris argues persuasively from this perspective that all first-world theologians, including process theologians, must be dialogically open to the liberation theologies of other societies. Otherwise, they may mask their ideology with a metaphysical theology. The provocative final thrust from Morris is "Process theologians can no longer allow a modern democratic liberal project to masquerade as the logical consequence of an objective metaphysical system."[106]

It is no masquerade, however, to recognize that an ethic influenced by Whitehead "will hold that human good is maximized when economic activity is made teleologically subservient to other forms of social life— precisely because Whiteheadian theory . . . calls for maximal socially constituted individuality."[107] If socially constituted individuality is to be maximized, it must transcend the enculturation of its original context by being religiously and philosophically opened to the social universal. When I first thought about this issue, I wrote a kind of first word that remains relevant:

> Religious consciousness may be that kind of cosmic egoism or alter-egoism which subordinates the real world to its own subjective needs or purposes; or it can be a genuine self-realization which embraces the real world and is correlated with a genuinely moral self-transcendence. . . . The crucial difference is whether one is really able to achieve a universal concern, perspective, and relation. Process theology provides the metaphysical constructs for articulating these universal dimensions. . . . Liberation theology fills these thought forms with the concrete dynamics of the economic and political activity of the oppressed poor. . . . When the universals of this conceptuality are not held together with

the concreteness of this suffering, this metaphysics can become the ideology of the comfortable who have achieved an aesthetic peace which has lost its truthful relation to the whole of reality.[108]

### The Value and Limit
### of Euro-American Culture

How may a *phronesis* from a privileged social location more authentically participate in a praxis seeking universal justice? It shall require to begin with a very careful assessment of *the value and the limit* of Euro-American culture and civilization, in the way Weber and Ellul have assessed its economic context—for it constitutes our inevitable prejudice. Especially at this time when the hegemony of Euro-American culture is being broken, it is important to recall its long historical evolution and spiritual development.

Europe has less ethnic homogeneity than many African and Asian cultures, and the U.S.A. even less, so whatever unity they possess is more social than racial. Sociocultural unity then "is not the foundation and starting point of European history, but the ultimate and unattained goal, towards which it has striven for more than a thousand years."[109] This heterogeneity has long fueled a profound striving for multiethnic, cross-cultural unity. The Roman Empire at the beginning of the European process toward unity, traced by Christopher Dawson, gave "the conquered peoples a share in her laws" and sought to make "the whole world into one city."[110] Too many Christians, then and since, have agreed with Prudentius's extravagant theological evaluation of the Roman attempt to impose unity:

> God wills the unity of mankind, since the religion of Christ demands a social foundation of peace and international amity. Hitherto, the whole earth from east to west has been rent asunder by continual strife. To curb this madness God has taught the nations to be obedient to the same laws and all to become Romans. . . . The Roman peace has prepared the road for the coming of Christ.[111]

There is in the Christian roots of European culture, for good and for ill, a wonderful and dangerous drive toward projecting whatever religious, cultural, or political unity is achieved toward universal dimensions.

The root of Europe's creative concern for universal peace and justice, we should now see with some distress, is too close to the root for the imperial hegemony many of its leaders have considered peace. Charles the Great (Charlemagne, Karl der Grosse), after reuniting Western Europe in the eighth century, claimed in a letter to Pope Leo III that he was "the representative of God who has to protect and govern *all* the members of God,"[112] Hegel was not much better in the nineteenth century with his more philosophical claim for the absolute right of a state that is "the carrier of the world spirit":

> The nation to which is ascribed a moment of the Idea in the form of a natural principle is entrusted with giving complete effect to it in the advance of the self-developing self-consciousness of the world mind. This nation is dominant in world history during this one epoch, and it is only once that it can make its hour strike. In contrast with its absolute right of being the vehicle of this present stage in the world mind's development, the minds of other nations are without rights, and they, along with those whose hour has struck already, count no longer in world history.[113]

The questions this history leaves with contemporary Euro-Americans are many: Was the Holy Roman Empire in medieval Europe ever really holy? Could Prussia in the nineteenth century, and the U.S.S.R. or the U.S.A. in the twentieth century, ever fully be the carriers of God's universal spirit of justice? The unequivocal answers must be no. Their justice was and is contextually relative.

Modern Western political thought from Machiavelli to Marx had two unifying characteristics: "A sense of existing in a new historical era" and "a predilection for active involvement in the world."[114] Tempered in some cases by humanistic wisdom, these philosophies, nevertheless, guided the hegemonic violence that Hegel rationalized. We may be coming to the end of this era. Though Dante Germino thinks F. S. C. Northrop's *Meeting of the East and West,* from which we learned much in chapter 2, was prematurely optimistic at the time it was written, he now concludes:

> From the interchange of cultural styles and norms between East and West it is not utopian to foresee the possible emergence of a postmodern age in which both the unity and diversity of mankind will receive their due recognition in the domain of political thought and life.[115]

To East and West should be added North and South, so that Africa and South America again may have the right (Hegel) in world history that European colonialism sought to deny them. Once we come to a more sober assessment of the contextual limits of our Euro-American civilization, we may be more ready for creative dialogue at its margins for the sake of a more universal *phronesis* and praxis of justice.

## A Creative Core at the Margin of the Other

One of the provisionally tragic, but ultimately hopeful, consequences of the end of colonialism is the number of refugees and new settlers from former colonies that have been resettled in Europe and the United States: 1.5 million "New Commonwealth" (a euphemism for "colored") citizens in Great Britain; 600,000 from Angola, Guinea, and Mozambique in Portugal; 10,000 Indonesians in Holland; 1.25 million from Algeria and Morocco in France:

> But now outsiders—native and foreign—have broken the mold of European life by the sheer force of their helpless and extravagant difference. They are part of a new mold. They are a social and political and certainly an economic fact of life, and they have made of Europe a more polyglot, more various sort of place. But Europe has yet to settle on an ethic, or even an appearance, appropriate to its new reality.[116]

Euro-American civilization must now seek its unattained cultural unity in an even more pluralistic context. What is true for Europe is even more true for the U.S.A. Extrapolating present trends, it is predicted that what are now called "minorities" will become the majority population of the U.S.A. before the middle of the next century. That is, a majority of the population of the U.S.A. will be people of color.

The most rapidly growing group in recent decades has been Asians. It began with a few Chinese in 1848 to work in the California gold mines. By 1880 there were 120,000 Chinese building railroads. The Japanese began to come only by the hundreds in the 1870s, but by the beginning of World War II there were 117,000 of them to be removed from their homes to "relocation centers." Beginning with Korea's opening to the West in 1883, Koreans became the most recent wave of Asian immigration. Thousands came to work Hawaiian sugar plantations in the first decade of this century; 28,000 came as war brides after the Korean war. Revision of the immigration laws in 1965 led to rapid increase, so that more than a million are expected by the year 2000.[117]

Jung Young Lee has reflected as a Korean American on the experience of "marginality" of those who exist between or in two cultures. The majority perspective tends to see the marginal person as "poised in psychological uncertainty between two (or more) social worlds," but Lee prefers a definition that fits an emerging pluralistic society that sees marginality in terms of "in-both" rather than "in-between":

> We are called to live in the margin where two or more worlds emerge. We are, by the very nature of our being at the margin to others, inclusive and open-ended to all centers, including our own. We are pluralistic, for we live in-both or in-all.[118]

What Jung Young Lee has discerned must increasingly become true for all in our pluralistic world. We all shall have to learn to live creatively at the margin of our cultures as we struggle to transform the dominant centers of our several societies. Lee foresees the emergence of a "creative core" at the margins of society that will work to transform the dominant center while continuing to recognize the contextual relativity of such work precisely because of its relation to that center.

Henry Young, who has experienced another margin as an African American, expresses a similar perspective. He argues on the basis of Whitehead's metaphysics for using conceptual models of organic and cultural pluralism to encourage creative dialogue at our margins:

> In eradicating the gulf between subjects and objects Whitehead paves the way for the present generation to rediscover a sense of intimacy with existence. The subject-subject mode of thinking suggests that all things in the world, including nature, are inextricably bound together. Whereas the subject-object approach establishes a monologue, the subject-subject approach rediscovers a creative dialogue.[119]

Learning to exist at the margins in cultural pluralism means that creative dialogue must characterize the creative core at both the sociocultural margins and the hermeneutical horizons of our existence. Many Euro-Americans find this difficult because the theory and form of our liberal, democratic, capitalistic culture has been too atomistic and contractual. So we shall have to learn from the more organic and functional models of community found in many other cultures of our world.

The contextual relativity of justice requires the kind of openness at our margins that opens us to the "other." Michael Harrington, influenced both by democratic socialism and Dorothy Day's Catholic Worker Movement, opened many Americans a generation ago to *The Other America* living in poverty at the margins of the most affluent economy in the world.[120] More than forty million Americans had fallen into an almost invisible subculture determined by vicious circles of poverty. Harrington's passion evoked an answering, though temporary, compassion. "We must perceive passionately," he wrote: "A fact can be rationalized and explained away; an indignity cannot."[121] His passion aroused sufficient compassion that the government responded with the so-called "war on poverty" of President Lyndon Johnson's administration.

Yet thirty years later, the poor are still with us. Based on governmental definitions of poverty, census data show that "in the 1980s progress against poverty stopped and some of the gains of the previous decade were reversed."[122] An economic recession seemed enough to convince many that the basis for justice was economic growth that must first benefit the dominant center. The result was that, though in 1978 only 8.7 percent of the Caucasian population were still in poverty, this percentage had grown in 1987 to 13.5 percent; the comparable statistics for African Americans were 30.6 percent to 33.1 percent, and for Hispanic Americans, 21.6 percent to 28.2 percent. Poverty has especially increased in American cities, by 7.6 million persons according to statistics reaching from 1979 to 1985.[123] One of the results is growing homelessness, whose terrible consequences can be measured in part by the 137 percent increase in deaths from freezing, from 427 in 1976 to more than 1,000 in 1985.

What is barely visible within an affluent society to many living near its dominant center becomes even less visible at its margins on a world scale. A book written on world hunger at the same time as Michael Harrington's by a more prestigious author had much less social effect. Though Barbara Ward's *The Rich Nations and the Poor Nations* went through at least eleven printings and received the endorsement of both Adlai Stevenson and Lyndon Johnson, no "war on poverty" at a transnational level was ever attempted. Ward's passion for the poor nations elicited little compassionate response:

> There is no human failure greater than to launch a profoundly important endeavor and then leave it half done. This is what the West has done with its colonial system. It shook all the societies in the world loose from their old moorings. But it seems indifferent whether or not they receive safe harbour in the end.[124]

Barbara Ward thought the lack of response to the world's poor was caused by the racism that turns margins into barriers and blocks the contextual *phronesis* of a creative core moving toward universal justice:

> But for three hundred years the white race has enjoyed a dominant position in the world. Its members were able to stamp their prejudices across the face of the globe because they were, in fact, on top. . . . And this belief that colored people are inferior has left its mark all over the world. Perhaps one realizes how deep the wounds are only when one has lived in ex-colonial lands.[125]

We may have to accept the reality of our enculturated prejudice, as Gadamer has taught us, but prejudice can become creative only as a moving horizon fused with other horizons, as Gadamer also has taught us. When prejudice is joined with the vested interests of economic and political power at the dominant center, it can block all creative response at the margins.

Another block to creative *phronesis* at the margins is the technocratic mindset at the center of Euro-American culture. A century and a half ago Alexis de Tocqueville said that nothing struck him "more forcibly than the general equality of condition among the people" in early nineteenth-century America. He thought it to be "the fundamental fact from which all others seem to be derived."[126] But looking to the future, he warned of the technocratic, nonrelational and thus immoral character of an emerging "manufacturing aristocracy":

The territorial aristocracy of former ages was either bound by law, or thought itself bound by usage, to come to the relief of its serving-men, and to succor their distresses. But the manufacturing aristocracy of our age first impoverishes and debases the men who serve it, and then abandons them to be supported by the charity of the public. . . . The friends of democracy should keep their eyes anxiously fixed in this direction; for if ever a permanent inequality of conditions and aristocracy again penetrate into the world, it may be predicted that this is the gate by which they will enter.[127]

This technocratic economic aristocracy a century and a half after de Tocqueville now occupies the dominant center, with the top 1 percent owning 90 percent of the wealth. Most economists who now interpret this economy, however, no longer relate economic issues to the context of world history as de Tocqueville did.[128] Why not? Because there is no *phronesis* that seeks to concretize the universal of justice through transformation of its contextual ethos. And there can be no *phronesis* where technocratic reason is abstracted from all relations to the margin of the other—the world's poor.

### Hearing and Heeding the Marginalized

What must be heard if we are to overcome such abstraction and give the kind of "preferential option" to the voices of the poor and marginalized that is required if a creative core is to emerge? We cannot review all that may and must be heard. But we can selectively illustrate:

The Christian Conference of Asia has sought to speak their word to us since the Ecumenical Study Conference for East Asia held at Lucknow, India, in December 1952:

The Asian revolution can be interpreted as the outcome of 450 years of European expansion and colonial domination. It is both a reaction against the West and an appropriation of many western features. Imperialism was all along resented by the people of Asia; yet during the centuries they acquired many new attitudes and techniques from their rulers. The growing struggle against western exploitation became associated increasingly with the desire that Asia secure the material and social advantages which the West so highly prized.[129]

Asian church leaders and scholars like Yap Kim Hao, the first Asian bishop of the Methodist Church in Malaysia and Singapore, later general secretary of the Christian Conference of Asia for twelve years, and now teaching at Trinity Theological College in Singapore, has tried to summarize the negative results of this revolution for many in the so-called third world:

The multinational corporations targeted themselves to be in countries which offer competitive wages for the unskilled labor. The poor countries were caught in the squeeze of either offering low wages or face no employment. Urban slums rose. . . . The rich local elites aligned with foreign interests to further industrialize and exploit the human labor in the country. The gap between the rich and the poor widened. The majority of the workers sank deeper into the hole of poverty and found it hard to extricate themselves.[130]

Widespread suffering has turned many Asian theologians, notably Korean Minjung theologians, to a higher evaluation of the experience carried in their people's (Minjung's) popular religiosity. The Korean theological ethicist Jong-Sun Noh of Yonsei University has written:

> The role of the people's religion (Minjung-chongkyo) should be recognized and valued in relation to their cries for the benefit of the people. . . . Popular religiosity could be carrying in-depth social biographical experiences of oppressed existence through generations. The people of the less established religions, in fact, know the will of God through their bodily experiences. In that sense, they are epistemologically privileged people of God. The God of justice is definitely working in and through the oppressed people's religion.[131]

It is dialogical openness to the suffering (*han*)[132] that continues to be caused by the technocratic transformation of Asian culture, that may enable the emergence of a more universal creative core for the "social revolution" that must accompany and correct the technological revolution our whole world is now undergoing.

There is a dualistic alternative based on the absolute transcendence of God also found in Korea, especially in its mammoth congregations,[133] which obscures the universal relationality of God. It has no place for the *phronesis* that emerges when the suffering of the marginalized becomes central in the contextualizing of God's universal justice. The senior minister of the Kuang Lim Methodist Church, for instance, lamented to me those who "waste their ministry" on human rights issues almost at the very same time that the director of the Human Rights Committee of the National Council of Churches in Korea, Rev. Kim Young-Ju, told me they were facing the worst human rights situation in their history, with the largest number of political prisoners (1,630 in mid-1991) they had ever had. Such prisoners are exactly the furthest margin of the other, struggling for social transformation and suffering political oppression, who must be included in the concerns of the creative core that emerges at the margin of marginality.

The contemporary emergence of such a creative core is increasingly being designated across our world as a *kairos*, the biblical term popularized by Paul Tillich to designate the momentous dangers and possibilities of post–World War I Europe. That *kairos* was aborted by the rise of fascism, World War II, and the cold war between the Soviet Union and the U.S.A. But this symbol has gained new currency as Christians in South Africa used it to designate the political crisis in their society in 1985–86, a time of a "national state of emergency" with thousands in detention in the last stages of the apartheid regime. At great personal and professional risk, 150 persons signed the *Kairos* document as the culmination of a long process of action and reflection. It received such wide resonance that a group of more than one hundred Christians in Central America created their own "Kairos Central America" in 1988. This was accompanied and followed by an international process of discussions and draftings that added Korea, Namibia, and the Philippines to South Africa and the Central American countries of El Salvador, Guatemala, and Nicaragua, to publish *The Road to Damascus: Kairos and Conversion* in 1989.[134]

The *Kairos* document in South Africa, after analyzing and condemning the apartheid "state theology" that already had been declared "heretical" ecumenically by the Lutheran World Federation and the World Alliance of Reformed Churches, interprets and supports a "prophetic theology." In our terms, it is the expression of a "creative core at the margin of the other":

> On the one hand we have the interests of those who benefit from the status quo and who are determined to maintain it at any cost, even at the cost of millions of lives. . . . They benefit from the system because it favors them and enables them to accumulate a great deal of wealth and to maintain an exceptionally high standard of living. . . . On the other hand we have those who do not benefit in any way from the system the way it is now. They are treated as mere labour units, paid starvation wages, separated from their families by migratory labor, moved about like cattle and dumped in homelands to starve.[135]

And the prophetic call of this creative core is to "establish a just government for the common good of all the people"—a call for universal contextual justice in South Africa.[136]

To become such a creative core in South Africa or anywhere else, of course, does not mean to sit on some neutral fence but rather to participate in the struggle to transform the culture's ethos. In religious terms, it is to participate in the struggle for God's justice, the contextual justice of the universally relational God.[137]

The *Kairos Central America* document describes a very similar suffering in a very different context:

> During the last ten years more than 200,000 persons out of a total of 25 million inhabitants of the region (about 1%) have died violently in Central America. In large part, these were poor people: labor union

members, Indians, peasants, guerilla fighters, cooperative members, and young people forcefully recruited to fight against their own brothers and sisters. All were victims of a policy of terror and counterinsurgency.

This war is not an accident, nor is it the result of the Central American's violent nature. It is the product of injustice. It is the struggle of the poor majorities in defense of their lives, against the privileged groups that have always kept economic, political, and military power for themselves.[138]

This reality is more difficult for North Americans to appropriate, however, because we are those on the other side of this margin, who have supported the oppressive Central American dominant elites. The Dutch and English who went to South Africa during the period of European colonial hegemony also were among those who came to the Americas. One of the cruelest margins in both of the Americas runs between the descendants of the Spanish, Portuguese, English, Dutch, French, and other colonizers on the one side and the indigenous and enslaved peoples who were and are their labor force. To become a creative core at this margin requires radical transformation of an ethos constituted by a half millennium of American colonialism.

It is no wonder that the third, more international *Kairos* document calls for a *phronesis* in the radical terms of conversion, which will lead to the praxis of universal justice. Its authors starkly underline the margins requiring transformation in the religious terms of idolatry, heresy, apostasy, hypocrisy, and blasphemy, to make more clear the religious depths of the conversion required.[139] Though such rhetoric is in danger of hardening the margins in the hearts and minds of some, its intention is to transform a creative core through openness to the marginalized other, which requires conversion by the grace of the universally relational God:

> We are bold enough to hope for something that fulfills and transcends all human expectations, namely, the Reign of God. We are even called to live with the hope that those who collaborate with the idols of death and those who persuade us today will be converted to the God of life.[140]

## Conclusion: The Contextual Relationality of Justice

The "God of life" discerned by those who see a *kairos* emerging in our universal history can only be conceived and worshiped as the universal, living God of all humanity. But human life is always and only engendered relationally in concrete communities. Such communities are always and necessarily contextually limited by their cultural and religious traditions, as well as by the needs, plans, anxieties, and self-interest of their members. Thus the reign of God is never fully transparent and realized in any of them, whatever the depth of the manifestation of God's grace in their history.

God's reign may become translucent and move toward realization, however, when a creative core emerges at social margins who continue to live from the manifestations of God's grace at the sacramental center of their communal histories. The necessity for Christians to live from the grace of Christ revealed at the center of their cult and culture gives point to the strong language of heresy and apostasy in the *Kairos* documents, but only if it also expresses a universal grace that meets people at their anxious and creative margins and assures them that opening to the other—whether in terms of class, race, gender, culture, or religion—is part of their opening to the gracious Holy Other, the universally relational God.

An essential part of the conceptual transformation that must emerge is the elimination of all premises for any domination over others. This is the principal reason why we have underlined the *contextual relativity* of God's universal justice at so many points in our discussion: John Rawls's principles of justice must be seen as contextually relative because they too uncritically presuppose the political economy and technocratic way of life that has become an iron cage for many within it and that wreaks such suffering upon most of the so-called developing world to which it is being extended. Even the philosophy favored in our whole discussion must be seen as contextually relative, because the thought of Whitehead and Hartshorne presupposes the social location of the relatively comfortable in this dominant system. The casuistry of Stephen Toulmin must also be seen as contextually relative when it presupposes the universality of the economic and medical institutions established by this dominant culture.

Even the ethos of the Christian churches must be seen as contextually relative, given its bond with Euro-American culture and a tendency to triumphalism stretching from the Roman/Byzantine empires, through the Holy Roman Empire, to the modern missionary movement's correlation with colonialism. Only a hermeneutics of suspicion that reveals and transforms the relationships of power and domination hidden in even relatively good modes of thought and praxis will allow the grace and truth they also carry to become transformative in the universal ethos that is emerging at the margins of our contemporary world.

Only a dialogical hermeneutics, prefigured by Gadamer whatever his limitations in praxis, and a communicative action, defined by Habermas whatever his underestimation of the traditional power of culture and religion, appears to point the way forward. They, of course, point that way in a contextually Western idiom. But their idiom opens those who follow it to the idioms of the other, so that a contextually conditioned universal justice may be sought through it. And then perhaps even the "universal common good," in the gracious phrase of Pope John XXIII,[141] might be sought by Christians as the universal telos of every contextual ethos in our multicultural and interreligious world. Douglas Meeks has expressed this goal of universal justice in the terms of biblical eschatology, which are native to those who come to our understanding of universal justice in the contextual relationality of Christianity:

> Searching for such a household of justice with peculiar shared meanings of social goods has always been a struggle of God's people. . . . The Torah is God's economy for Israel; the Gospel is the new economy for the New Israel. The God of Israel and of Jesus Christ seeks to create a household from whose livelihood no one will be excluded. Indeed, God's economy serves God's promise that the whole creation will have eschatologically the shape of such an inclusive access to life.[142]

This is why God's justice is a good idea for Christians and all others. Our capacity for the *phronesis* that concretizes God's universal justice must first be nourished in the cult and culture of our own communities. The transcendence of God's universals may only be known in contextual immanence. Christians will know them through the biblical Word and communal sacrament of their common life. But recognition of their universal transcendence may be facilitated by a more philosophical discourse that rationally reaches toward the universal, and by a critical discourse that reveals their community's contextual relativity while opening them to the universal relationality of God's justice. The response may often have to be that kind of *phronesis* that converts the prejudice of one's enculturation in a dominant system and leads to participation in the struggle to transform the ethos of that system.[143]

Perhaps one may finally put it this simply: Justice is an ethical universal ontologically grounded in the universal relationality of God. Finitely free human beings, however, learn the praxis of justice only in the concrete communities that form and nourish their spirits. Thus all justice is contextual, requiring critical dialogical reflection to discern its finite limits. When the relativity of our and every form of justice is recognized, we are saved from the despair of relativism by knowing that it is, nevertheless, a particular concretion of the real universal of God's justice, who lures and leads us toward a more adequately universal realization of it. To understand the just God as universally relational, and in this sense relative, thus leads not to relativism but to a transformative praxis at the margins of our relation with others—especially the poor and marginalized others in any dominant system. Only through such a dialogical praxis may we move toward universal justice, and only then, to complete the circle from where we began, is justice a good idea for Christians and all others in God's good creation.

# 5

# The Interpersonal
# Relationality of Love

## Introduction

Just as the social structures of human justice discerned by *phronesis* and actualized in praxis—no matter how contextually relative and limited—are particular concretions of the real universal of God's justice, so is human love—whatever its biological or social distortions—an interpersonal participation in the universal relationality of God's being and becoming. Yet many who have looked carefully and even therapeutically at human beings have as much difficulty discerning and affirming this about love as some discussed in the previous chapter had in affirming the universal reality of justice.

Sigmund Freud may stand for many in articulating a skeptical response to this religious belief, tinged with what Daniel Day Williams called "the aura of implausibility which surrounds the claims that love is real, that love transforms human life, that it is the key to the foundation of all things."[1] There are only a few who cannot share some of Freud's incredulity before the claim that human life is to be constituted by loving relations with all persons.

> But if he is a stranger to me and if he cannot attract me by any worth of his own or any significance that he may have already acquired for my emotional life, it will be hard for me to love him. Indeed, I should be wrong to do so, for my love is valued by all my own people as a sign of my preferring them, and it is an injustice to them if I put a stranger on a par with them.

And given the alienation that Freud, and not only Freud, found in human relations, this incredulity may become contradiction:

Not merely is this stranger in general unworthy of my love; I must honestly confess that he has more claim to my hostility and even my hatred. He seems not to have the least trace of love for me and shows me not the slightest consideration. If it will do him any good he has no hesitation in injuring me, nor does he ask himself whether the amount of advantage he gains bears any proportion to the extent of the harm he does me. Indeed, he need not even obtain an advantage; if he can satisfy any sort of desire by it, he thinks nothing of jeering at me, insulting me, slandering me, and showing his superior power; and the more secure he feels and the more helpless I am, the more certainly I can expect him to behave like this to me.[2]

Some might conclude from so vehement a response by so sagacious a psychoanalyst that post–World War I Vienna in what was left of the Roman Catholic Hapsburg Empire was not a very human context, especially for a Jew. But after twentieth-century horrors like the gulag, the Shoah, Hiroshima, Vietnam, South Africa, and El Salvador, many are tempted to enlarge and even universalize the generalization beyond the limits of any particular context. Alfred North Whitehead, who has influenced our whole discussion, may be counted among them. Writing at about the same time as Freud and prior to the continuing horrors named above, he wrote: "As society is now constituted a literal adherence to the moral precepts scattered throughout the Gospels would mean sudden death."[3] Whitehead's words, published in 1933, were prophetic for millions of Freud's Jewish neighbors not as fortunate as he in escaping Vienna to Whitehead's native England before Hitler's *anschluss* of Austria. Perhaps if more had had Freud's realistic assessment of the dangers posed by "neighbors," they too would have saved themselves.

But whatever our temporary safety, can we ultimately save ourselves, no matter how realistic or idealistic our perspective? Or does any "salvation" worth having finally depend upon our participation with our neighbors in the whole of creation as finitely free and limited co-creators? And if so, does it not ultimately depend upon the nature of that "whole" in which we participate and in some limited way might help co-create? Or better put, does it not ultimately depend upon the nature of that One who makes it whole, with whom we might be creatively related? We considered in chapter 1 a theological understanding of the Creator of emergent order in a dynamic spatiotemporal process, wherein God enables human beings to co-create liberated self-actualization and reconciled communal interaction.

We examined in chapter 2 our growing need and developing capacity to discern and communicate meanings across cultures, so that our communal interaction might move beyond what Freud called "our own people" toward becoming universal. And we discerned that our ability to communicate meaningfully in the syntax of our various symbol systems is grounded in the relationally universal God, who is both the creative, primordial ground and the created consequent eschaton of the spatiotemporal process in which we participate.

Given our terrible failures in such communication and the cross-cultural alienation that Freud prototypically felt so acutely, we probed in chapter 3 the theologies of the five major world religions to understand what might be the relational form of our redemption. And in the light of those interreligious understandings, we sought to illumine in chapter 4 how our participation in the universal relationality of God enables an ethic of universal but contextual justice.

Now we are at the very crux of this whole line of thought. God's being/becoming is either religiously experienced and theologically conceived as love in process, or all of what we have considered has little religious meaning. Freud's kind of incredulity may be met with the measure of agreement expressed by Daniel Day Williams: "Many distortions of religious devotion and ethical life come from a too simple view of what the love of God is, and from the use of love as escape from the risks of life, rather than as the will and power to accept them." At the same time, we must affirm as Williams does, that persons, "created in God's image, [are] created for participation in the infinite life of communion within the everlasting creativity of God."⁴ To experience and interpret human life as communion within the love of God is the very heart of the panentheistic, Trinitarian theology our whole discussion seeks to articulate. How then shall we interpret some of the dominant aspects of our culture that make this experience so opaque and this theology so problematic for so many?

## Reducing the Reductions of the Person in Scientific Culture

One of the crucial cultural issues that a theology of interpersonal love confronts is the reductive objectification of the person in modern scientific theories. The scientific need to become objective in its modern understanding of human life has so objectified the human mind and spirit as to make loving relations unintelligible for many persons. Freud is a typical instance, who insisted that his only intention was to "give recognition to the facts as we found them in the course of painstaking researches."⁵ The only worldview that he acknowledged as affecting his psychoanalytic theories was science in general, which he defined with philosophical naïveté: "A *Weltanschauung* based upon science has, apart from the emphasis it lays upon the real world, essentially negative characteristics, such as that it limits itself to truth, and rejects illusions."⁶ This worldview requires that human beings be investigated in as scientifically objective a way as possible, which Freud took to mean that psychology must be based on physiology, which in turn is modeled on the ideal science of physics.[7]

Thus Freud sought to ground his understanding of the human spirit in a biological psychology of instincts, though reluctantly admitting his inability fully to do so. "The theory of instincts," he wrote in his *New Introductory Lectures*, "is, as it were, our mythology."[8] Freud would like to have demonstrated scientifically that the human phenomena he was analyzing were the psychological concomitant of biological processes. Though at times self-critically aware of his inability to demonstrate their causal dependence upon physical processes, Freud nevertheless developed his "myth," or better metaphor, of an instinct as a hydraulic force in the psyche: "a certain sum of energy forcing its way in a certain direction."[9]

Freud interpreted love objectively as one of two biologically based instincts (the other being hunger), which constitute the entire dynamics of human life. Love in this reductive context meant only "the mental side of the sexual impulses."[10] Therefore, Freud preferred to use the term "libido" to speak of sexual energy: "In every way analogous to hunger, libido is the force by means of which the instinct, in this case the sexual instinct, as with hunger, the nutritional instinct, achieves expression."[11]

Freud joined this theory of instincts with his "scientific" belief that every person "automatically" seeks pleasure, understood as the release or relief of biological tension:

> In the psycho-analytical theory of the mind *we take it for granted* that the course of mental processes is automatically regulated by "the pleasure principle": that is to say, we believe that any given process originates in an unpleasant state of tension and thereupon determines for itself such a path that its ultimate issue coincides with a relaxation of the tension, i.e., with avoidance of "pain" or with production of pleasure.[12]

To reduce our understanding of the person to a function of automatic instinctual energies masks the reality of relational love. The finite spiritual freedom of the person to allow and enact relational love cannot be recognized and indeed must be denied within the logic of this reductionistic model.

Experience, however, affected Freud's logic, as it should affect the thought of all of us. The power of richer experience led him to alter his early theories. By 1920 when Freud published *Beyond the Pleasure Principle*, he had revised his idea of libido with the far richer philosophical concept of "eros," understood now as the force that brings disparate, atomistic matter together into relatively enduring, concrete form:

> With the discovery of narcissistic libido, and the extension of the libido concept to the individual cells, the sexual instinct became for us transformed into the Eros that endeavors to impel the separate parts of living matter to one another and to hold them together; what is commonly called the sexual instinct appears as that part of Eros that is turned toward the object.[13]

Freud now thought, however, that viewing eros as an ontological power creating organic unity also required affirming the polar contrast of a destructive "instinct" to be seen in sadism, masochism, and repetition-compulsion neuroses. Thus he revised his earlier pleasure principle to affirm a "desire for aggression . . . as part of instinctual endowment."[14]

The ontological dualism inherent in the mechanistic biology of his era led Freud to affirm a "death instinct." Because he believed that organic and psychic life arose in some inexplicable way from "lifeless matter," Freud concluded that the neurotic repetition-compulsion syndrome manifested a "conservative" instinct to return living organisms to their original inanimate state of being.[15] Our lives were thought to be entirely caught up in the dualism of these two conflicting ontological instincts.

Freud's continuing materialistic and mechanistic presuppositions deserve criticism as reductionistic. His human subject was so reduced to a function of instinctual energies as to deny the reality of the truly personal and thus the interpersonal relationality of love. To use biological and physiological categories so to objectify the human psyche and spirit is to make the understanding of interpersonal love impossible. Maurice Friedman says of him:

> Freud goes from the divided, sick person that he sees before him—a type of person that is very typical of our age—to a definition of human nature as such. Freud's picture of Man as id, ego, and superego is a *construct* of the human rather than an *image* of the human. It is a synthetic combination of analytical subcategories which systematically excludes from its view the wholeness and uniqueness of the person. . . . Freud has an "ego," but he has no true "I," no actual subject; for as soon as one tries to make the "I" into an object, it ceases to be "I." This Freud never seems to notice, perhaps because he believes that the ego is "lived" by impersonal, instinctual passion.[16]

Another way of saying much the same thing, in terms more familiar to our discussion, is that Freud's use of formal logic to interpret his materialistic paradigm blocked a wholistic understanding of persons in all their relations, which requires a more dialectical logic for its adequate articulation and understanding.

*Objectification of Persons
in Contemporary Neuroscience*

Contemporary empirical psychology in Freud's scientific mode remains undeterred by such philosophical responses, however, and seldom considers conferring with theology on such scientific issues. Freud could only suppose that what he termed the unconscious "id" was "somewhere in direct contact with somatic processes, and takes over from them instinctual needs and gives them mental expression"; but he had honestly to admit that "we cannot say in what substratum this contact is made."[17] Patricia Goldman-Rakic, professor of neuroscience in the Yale University School of Medicine, however, reveals the far greater confidence of today's theorists that they can objectively specify the "substratum" that eluded Freud:

> Until recently the fundamental processes involved in such higher mental functions defied description in the mechanistic terms of science. . . . Within the past two decades, however, neuroscientists have made great advances in understanding the relation between cognitive processes and the anatomic organization of the brain. As a consequence, even global mental attributes such as thought and intentionality can now be meaningfully studied in the laboratory.[18]

This generation's neuroscientists have grown far beyond what was available to Freud in Bruecke's Vienna laboratory to study the human brain as the most complex organism in the world. We now know that it is comprised of a trillion cells, 100 billion of which are neurons, with each neuron functioning like a "sophisticated computer."[19] Despite this daunting complexity, today's scientists are increasingly able to provide replicable empirical evidence for their theory that mental events can be correlated with patterns of nerve impulses in the brain. Recent advances in the pharmacologic treatment of schizophrenia, the correlation of visual phenomena with the firing of certain regions of neurons, the mapping of the brain systems for different forms of language competence, the use of positron emission tomographic (PET) imaging to study Alzheimer's disease, to list only some of the experimental work that has been reported, is impressive even (or perhaps especially) to the nonscientist.

No one rationally open to empirical persuasion can deny the increasingly demonstrated correlations between electrochemical nerve impulses in the brain and mental phenomena in the mind. But a careful, critical reading of these interpretive reports also reveals the high degree of faith and hope invested in a hypothetical scientific paradigm. When Antonio and Hanna Damasio, for instance, note how little is yet really understood about the correlation of "brain and language," they immediately affirm that their mode of research and interpretation will surely lead to complete understanding:

> Considering the profound complexity of language phenomena, some may wonder whether the neural machinery that allows it all to happen will ever be understood. Many questions remain to be answered about how the brain stores concepts. Mediation systems for parts of speech other than nouns, verbs, and functors, have been only partially explored. Even the structures that form words and sentences, which have been under study since the middle of the nineteenth century, are only sketchily understood. Nevertheless, given the recent strides that have been made, we believe these structures will eventually be mapped and understood. The question is not if but when.[20]

Thus they urge our understanding of human communication to continue on the path that they are pioneering.

Though the Damasios recognize that language is "a supremely efficient means of communication," their theoretical paradigm does not include the relational community within which such communication takes place. The only dimension of language beyond the neural activity of the brain that they recognize is a "collection of symbols in admissible combinations" that is correlated with "the embodiment in the brain of those symbols and the principles that determine their combination."[21] A clearer example of what Whitehead called the "fallacy of misplaced concreteness" could hardly be found. One cannot abstract the brain from the whole field of its internal and external relations. Language is not only symbols in syntactical structures embodied in the brain, but it is also a symbolic structure for the communication of meanings, which develop only in the relational processes of human communities. Even a fruitful scientific paradigm may not be so inflated by hope for its future fecundity as to obscure these communal dimensions of human experience.

Some neuroscientists, fortunately, are more philosophically aware. Francis Crick of the Salk Institute for Biological Studies and Christof Koch of the California Institute of Technology note in their discussion of "The Problem of Consciousness":

> In the past the mind (or soul) was often regarded, as it was by Descartes, as something immaterial separate from the brain but interacting with it in some way. . . . But most neuroscientists now believe that all aspects of mind, including its most puzzling attribute—consciousness or awareness—are likely to be explainable in a more materialistic way as the behaviour of large sets of interacting neurons. As William James, the father of American psychology, said a century ago, consciousness is not a thing but a process. Exactly what the process is, however, has yet to be discovered.[22]

Beyond characterizing subjective consciousness as the brain's "most puzzling attribute," Crick and Koch refrain from defining it because of "the dangers of premature definition." But this reticence is misleading, for they clearly imply that subjective consciousness is a function of the brain's electrical and metabolic activity.

Crick and Koch properly reject a Cartesian dualism between mind ("mental substance") and body ("extended substance"), with its fruitless search for the point of connection, perhaps in the pineal gland, as Descartes postulated. They join William James in rejecting any hypostasization of the self as a "thing" or substance. But they fail fully to reject Cartesian dualism and thus come to the dualistic conclusion that, if something is not immaterial, it must be material. William James would be astonished to find his carefully formulated conclusions about the process of the conscious self forced back into this dualistic, materialistic paradigm.

We can agree with Crick's and Koch's recognition that "radically new concepts may indeed be needed," as they remember "the modification of scientific thinking forced on us by quantum mechanics."[23] But they fail to recognize that radically new concepts already have emerged in the thought of Alfred North Whitehead and others, which enable "the new ways of thinking" they only postpone while continuing to follow their materialistic paradigm until "confronted with dilemmas" that require its reformulation.

The reports of experimental evidence are already filled with enough problems to constitute the dilemma they fail to recognize. After citing, for instance, the recent advances in the pharmacologic treatment of schizophrenia as illustrating "the power of the molecule-to-mind approach," Gerald Fischbach admits:

> The slow rate at which psychoactive drugs work presents a puzzle. Drug receptor interactions are immediate, yet symptoms of schizophrenia, depression, and other disorders do not resolve for several weeks. The first consequence of drug binding cannot be the sole explanation for their efficacy. This issue leads to a more general consideration of mechanisms by which the environment might affect the brain.[24]

Carla J. Shatz, professor of neurobiology at the University of California, Berkeley, speaks more specifically of the essential effect that environment has on the brain, but without the tendentious concept of "mechanisms" used by Fischbach. In writing of "The Developing Brain," she specifically rejects the mechanistic theory of fetal development that the brain wires itself in a manner analogous to the way a computer is wired. She recognizes, rather, that the brain *requires relational stimulation*:

Workers who have studied the development of the brain have found that to achieve the precision of the adult pattern, neural function is necessary; the brain must be stimulated in some fashion. Indeed, several observations during the past few decades have shown that babies who spent most of their first year of life lying in their cribs developed abnormally slowly. Some of these infants could not sit up at 21 months of age, and fewer than 15 percent could walk by about the age of three. Children must be stimulated—through touch, speech and images—to develop fully.[25]

In words more familiar to our discussion, the brain becomes what it is only through relational interaction.

Semir Zeki, professor of neurobiology at the University of London, brings even greater clarity to this scientific discussion because he knows that the interpretation of the data that he and other researchers experimentally develop is a "profoundly philosophical enterprise."[26] He virtually abandons the molecule-to-mind paradigm as he interprets the "difficulty" of the "binding problem" in understanding the visual image in mind and brain. The issue arises because the cells that respond to the same object in a field of view may be scattered throughout the region of the brain that neurobiologists designate as number VI. "Something must therefore bind together the signals from those cells so that they are treated as belonging to the same object and not separate ones." His conclusion is that perception and comprehension, visual knowledge and consciousness, must be simultaneous:

> The integration of visual information is a process in which perception and comprehension of the visual world occur simultaneously. . . . It is no longer possible to divide the process of seeing from that of understanding, nor is it possible to separate the acquisition of visual knowledge from consciousness. Indeed, consciousness is a property of the complex neural apparatus that the brain has developed to acquire knowledge.[27]

The recognition of the simultaneity and interdependence of mind and brain, or consciousness and neural apparatus, is so unusual for neurobiologists that Zeki does not recognize that it is as possible to say that the complex neural apparatus is a "property" of consciousness as it is to say that "consciousness is a property of the complex neural apparatus." That is, neither consciousness nor the neural apparatus may really be understood as simply a quality or attribute of the other, for both are ontologically actual and interdependently necessary in systemic interaction for the actualization of the other.

### The Dialogical Critique
### of James Ashbrook

To recognize and emphasize the dilemmas that emerge when neurobiologists interpret the relation between mind and brain with a materialistic paradigm is not to deny the value of their research but only to urge that this conceptual model no longer be used reductionistically but, rather, heuristically. The mechanistic view of the human person tends to support the alienation we experience in modern culture as we objectify, use, and abuse those, including ourselves, whom God has given us to love. Some of the dimensions of human persons may be discerned and interpreted with this scientific model, for human beings are in part body and brain. But, as Semir Zeki recognizes, and my faculty colleague James Ashbrook expresses so clearly:

> The cognitive revolution is returning "mind" to a substantial place in our understanding of ourselves and how we function. . . . No longer can we view ourselves . . . as passive objects, mechanical organisms, to be manipulated chemically with no attention to the experiential reality which is expressed in and through the physical.[28]

Ashbrook's interpretive strategy in dialogue with neurobiologists is to correlate neurobiological and phenomenological research metaphorically, so as to relate, rather than reduce, levels "as disparate as biochemical, cortical, cultural, and cosmic."[29] Because no conceptual model is adequate to provide analytic clarity for all of these levels, we cannot reduce them to any one set of explanations and must be at least tentatively satisfied with discerning their correlations metaphorically. Ashbrook uses split-brain research of the cerebral cortex's two hemispheres metaphorically to suggest that the scientific preference for more linear, rational explanations associated with the left hemisphere—like the molecule-to-mind paradigm—may atrophy the more relational and integrative input of the right hemisphere.[30] He further suggests that whether we use an analytic or integrative strategy is in part an emotional decision made in the limbic system, depending on whether we sense our situation as painful or pleasant.[31] Thus, the more alienated and threatening a cultural ethos becomes, the more we turn to analytic strategies.

Ashbrook's interpretive strategy recognizes the correlation of the neural activity of various regions of the brain with certain modes of emotional and rational consciousness. While denying the adequacy of any univocal, linear, monocausal explanations, the metaphorical likeness of analytical modes of thought to left brain activity and integrative modes of thought to right brain activity is discerned and affirmed.

James Ashbrook's work is helpful in "reducing the reduction" with which many contemporary psychologists and biologists objectify the human person. But the lack of a rational basis for the metaphorical is problematic for those who seek both analytic clarity and integration. Those influenced by the desire for analytic precision in our scientific culture will not readily accept that relational discernment may only take this metaphorical form. Ashbrook himself says with some resignation at one point: "Whether there is any correspondence between the way the brain works and the way the universe works is left to leaps of faith and paradigms of knowledge. Neurological correlates of consciousness cannot be specified easily."[32]

Will an ontology left only to "leaps of faith" be able to hold its own before the immense cultural power of the scientific "paradigm of knowledge" that continues so to objectify the person as to make the interpersonal relationality of love opaque and unintelligible? There is need for a more ontological discussion that continues to recognize that it must stretch whatever concepts are used "toward a generality foreign to their ordinary usage." Even carefully defined metaphysical terms "remain metaphors mutely appealing for an imaginative leap."[33] Religious leaps of faith are analogous to the imaginative leaps implicit in metaphysical reflection. No human categories directly derive from God's Logos or the eternal essences of classical Neoplatonic ontology but are as precise and coherent an interpretation of finite experience as are possible at a given point in human cultural history.

## Personalism's Flawed Ontology of the Personal

Any ontological attempt to articulate a more wholistic understanding of the person must remember that no "completed reflection" is possible for finite, historically conditioned minds. Carl Vaught's point that wholeness is not equivalent to completeness is helpful:

> Wholeness is not to be equated with completeness, and fragmentation is not a problem that can be dealt with at the exclusively reflective level. Human wholeness is finite, and it is finite precisely because it is human. But finitude must not be confused with fragmentation, and the finite character that wholeness exhibits should not force us to transform the quest for wholeness into a quest for complete comprehension.[34]

In terms more intrinsic to our conceptual model, the whole person we are seeking to understand is a finite, relative-because-related, incomplete-because-in-process, being-who-is-becoming. Such persons may discern and move toward wholeness only in dialogical communication and dialectical community. Dialectical here, as heretofore in our discussion, means that relation between part and whole where each part affects the whole, though the whole transcends and is more than the parts; and each part is affected by the whole, though not determined by it.

The wholeness of the person may never be realized apart from community, but no concern for complete systematic unity may reduce the person only to a function of community or any other absolutized conception of the whole. Vaught also puts this contra-Hegelian point clearly and concretely:

> Wholeness can never be found apart from the community, for the meaning of human existence is partly constituted by the human bonds that tie us together, first as members of an individual family, then as citizens of cities, states, and nations, and finally as members of the wider context that includes mankind as a whole. . . . On the other hand, the individual must not lose himself in the larger world, for to do so would be to lose the center of the fragmented self, and to abandon the hope that wholeness can be found in a fashion uniquely appropriate to oneself. . . . Though the quest for wholeness spreads outward toward the whole of humanity, and though it reaches down to the particularity of the individuals who undertake it, it also seeks a source of meaning that lies beyond the human realm.[35]

It was Hermann Lotze, one of Hegel's successors in the chair of philosophy in Berlin, who so focused on an ontological understanding of the person as to become the progenitor of a school of thought called "personalism" or "personal idealism."[36] Coming to a chair of philosophy in the University of Göttingen after initial training, research, and teaching as a medical doctor, Lotze shared the strong interest in empirical psychology that developed in the nineteenth century and continues in ours. But as a philosopher he insisted "there is an intrinsic unsoundness in the efforts to found a Metaphysic on a psychological analysis of our cognition."[37] In opposition to Kant, and on this point much like Hegel, he argued strongly for the precedence of ontology over epistemology:

> If then we are compelled to use as a basis some hypothesis respecting the connexion of physical and psychical phenomena, why are we to take the first hypothesis that comes to hand? Why not go back to the most general ideas that we necessarily form respecting all being and action, and so attempt to define the limits within which we can frame suppositions, sometimes trustworthy, and at other times at all events probable.[38]

Lotze was influential at the turn of the last century as he sought to provide an ontology comprehensive enough to interpret both the empirical data of natural science and the phenomena of intellect, purpose, and value focused upon by the philosophical idealists and theologians of his era. He thus helped overcome the conflict between religion and science by grounding a value-based idealistic metaphysics in empirically given reality.

The capstone of his metaphysics was the idea of self-existence derived from human introspective self-experience. Lotze argued that phenomena "have being when they are able to produce the appearance of a substance present in them":[39]

> It is in so far as something is an object to itself, relates itself to itself, distinguishes itself from something else, that by this act of its own it detaches itself from the Infinite. In so doing, however, it does not acquire but possesses, in the only manner to which we give any meaning in our thoughts, that self-dependence of True Being.[40]

And nowhere is this "self-dependence of true being" more clearly given than in our experience of ourselves as mind or ego:

> To the nature of Mind, of the Ego that apprehends itself, that is passive in feeling and active in willing, and that is one in remembrance in which it brings past experiences together, we can now point as to a similitude of that which is the nature of beings endowed with Realness; or we may believe that directly and without any similitude we find the thing itself, the nature of all Realness in this living self-existence.[41]

The human psyche or spirit, by showing itself to be an independent center of action and reaction, became for Lotze the paradigm for all other forms of experience that deserve to be considered ontologically real. Despite the importance of this corrective for the materialistic paradigm of modern science, Lotze's formulation was too dependent on the dualisms of Descartes and Kant. He thought of the subjective ego—Descartes's *cogito*—as the immediate experience of noumenal reality—Kant's *ding-an-sich*.

Though Lotze's thought gave precedence to ontology, G. T. Ladd of Yale considered him a "born psychologist."[42] Because trained as a physician, he recognized that the self depends upon a total system of environing being; yet he retained his philosophical conviction that the self-conscious experience of the ego is the clearest experience of noumenal reality we have. In disputing the mechanistic model of associational psychology, one of his characteristic arguments was analogous to Semir Zeki's discussion of the "binding problem," though Lotze, of course, did not have access to that level of brain research: "Any comparison of two ideas, which ends by our finding their contents like or unlike," Lotze wrote, " presupposes the absolutely indivisible unity of that which compares them."[43]

Lotze rejected the materialistic "molecule-to-mind" ontology because he found a total incongruity between the concept of matter in motion and the phenomena of conscious sensation, thought, valuing, and decision.

"However we may combine physical motions of nerve atoms with one another," he wrote in his *Outlines of Psychology*, "there never comes a point at which it would be comprehensible as a matter of course, that the motion last produced is bound to remain motion no longer, and must rather pass over into this process of sensation so totally different in kind."[44] Such incongruity led to the conclusion that the conscious mind and spirit is a unique and unitary reality:

> Even if exact observation should prove the activity of the soul to be still more closely bound up, than it is now proved to be, with the body and its agitations, still this dependence could in no way alter the essence of our conviction; and that essential conviction is that a world of atoms, and movement of atoms, can never develop from itself a trace of mental life; and that it forms, on the contrary, nothing more than a system of occasions, which win from another and unique basis the manifestation of an activity possible to that basis alone.[45]

### Personalists' Denial of Relationality

This Lotzean ontology became influential in North America when Borden Parker Bowne studied with Lotze in the University of Göttingen from 1873 to 1875 and returned to become professor of philosophy and dean of the graduate school in Boston University. He and his successors—Edgar Brightman and Peter Bertocci in philosophy and Albert Knudson and L. Harold DeWolf in theology—developed a school of thought for the next half century that continued to speak to these ontological issues.[46] They called it "personalism," which is apt because they attempted to derive all of their ontological categories from introspective self-experience. As Bowne put it, "Only personality is able to give concrete meaning to those ontological categories by which we seek to interpret being."[47]

The metaphysical primacy of the personal self in their thought was based on the psychological self-evidence of Cartesianism. Bowne, for instance, affirmed what other philosophers lamented as the "egocentric predicament": "We are in a personal world from the start, and the first, last, and only duty of philosophy is to interpret this world of personal life and relations."[48] Although accepting the Kantian distinction between phenomenal experience and noumenal reality at every other point, the American personalists rejected it for introspective self-experience. The noumenal or substantial self was understood as constituted by the very activities of consciousness. Conscious memory does not only disclose the continuity of the self, but it constitutes that very continuity. Bowne wrote: "The permanence and identity therefore are products of the agent's own activity. We become the same by making ourselves such."[49]

It became impossible, however, for personalists to persist in this Cartesian claim that the person was given in direct introspective experience. Brightman and Bertocci came to recognize that they had constructed an "ideal" concept of the person. Brightman wrote:

> No human being is fully personal; if he were he would always be conscious, always intellectually, emotionally, and purposively at his best, always alert and growing. Now and then a human person catches a glimpse of what he would be if he were truly personal. Most of the time, he is a mere shadow of a person, a fragmentary self, yet a fragment that contains a clue to what a person would be.[50]

They both accepted this ideal notion of the person and tried to correct it from a more phenomenological perspective.

Earlier personalists had used Kant's critical rationalism—that we may discern the essence of a thing by a rule or category of our thought—to interpret personal being. Brightman came to define "essence" in terms of "the experienced quality or *quale* of any datum or any aspect of any datum."[51] The essence of a thing thus is given in the phenomena represented in consciousness, and not as Bowne, following Kant, thought in the law governing its process. Brightman and Bertocci therefore could more fully incorporate phenomenological evidence for the limitations of the conscious subject:

> In the very *erlebnis* of momentary experience one is conscious of one's self, and his knowledge of himself grows as the nature of the self is unfolded in its activities. It is important to note that in this view the experience of ourselves always contains more than we can or do articulate; there is a penumbra we experience but of which our knowledge is not clear; we know *that* it is there and that it is *ours* but cannot say *what* it is.[52]

Their more phenomenological approach enabled a better understanding of the person in the complex context of all of his or her relationships—whether with brain or community. Nevertheless, this ontology even in its phenomenological mode remained too Cartesian and Kantian adequately to define this relational context. When Brightman near the end of his career gave his university lecture on "Persons and Values" to define what "has been central in philosophical research in Boston University since Borden Parker Bowne founded the department," he conceded:

> Nothing has been said about the chemical or biological causes of persons, nothing about the physical environment, nothing about psychological research in personality. Stress has been laid rather on the personal basis of all causal and value theory and research.[53]

Almost by the personalists' own admission, their approach was remiss at the crucial point of understanding the person in organic relation to the complex processes of physical nature and social history. The conscious subject in the context of all his/her relationships is too complex a reality to be understood as a self-evident datum directly open to introspection. The personal self is a center of being who may not be *reduced* to the structure and function of any physical or social process external to its subjective continuum, but it also is so completely and complexly *interrelated* with brain structure and functions and social structures and functions as to require a more dialectical, organic ontology to explicate its relationality.

Personalists resisted this more organic, relational ontology because they saw it as inevitably leading to a pantheistic dissolution of the person in some Absolute. Brightman resisted the idea of the subconscious as a part of the self because its acceptance would be a step "on the long road which includes the whole universe as belonging to myself and leads to absolutism."[54] However much one may deplore pantheism, or on the other hand, however much one rejects Freud's mythology, the phenomena Freud was studying—repression, hallucination, compulsion, fixation, and displacement—are interpreted better with the concept of a whole that includes both conscious and unconscious processes than that of a monadic subject complete in him/herself and dependent upon nothing beyond her/his own conscious activity. The regularly replicable correlations between energy events in the brain and phenomena in the conscious mind also require an interpretive paradigm of a whole constituted by interacting parts. Therefore the Cartesian ontological and Kantian epistemological dualisms that isolate the monadic self in personalistic ontology must be modified so that the person may be understood as constituted relationally.

## Whitehead's Organic-Relational Ontology of the Person

Alfred North Whitehead modified these Cartesian and Kantian dualisms as he developed his organic philosophy. "The organic philosophy interprets experience," he wrote, "as meaning the self-enjoyment of being one among many, and of being one arising out of the composition of many."[55] In the philosophy of organism, an actual entity is understood as composite. They are constituted relationally. In contrast to Descartes's and the personalists' concept of the monadic ego, there are no entities that need nothing but themselves in order to exist. Though "subjective experiencing is recognized as the primary metaphysical situation," the subjectivism that began with Descartes and continued to the personalists "requires balancing by an 'objectivist' principle as to the datum of experience."[56]

There are no Cartesian[57] private worlds of subjective qualities present in our egos only as sensations or phenomena. The world of each of us is constituted by our real experience of other actual entities, first of all in the form of primitive feelings that conform to their feelings. That is, we feel the feelings of other actual entities, from which we derive our sense of relation with causally efficacious environments. Though we may not immediately experience that we think *with* our brains, it is part of our experience that we see *with* our eyes, we taste *with* our palates, we touch *with* our hands, etc.[58] We do not experience seeing, tasting, touching, etc., as just mental phenomena, for our minds feel the feelings of our bodies. And since there is no reason to hold that the energies from beyond our skin transmitted through our nervous systems are metaphysically different, "the philosophy of organism attributes 'feeling' throughout the actual world."[59]

Whitehead defined a feeling (his preferred synonymous technical term is "prehension") as "a transition effecting a concrescence" and analyzed it into five factors:

> (i) the "subject" which feels, (ii) the "initial data" which are to be felt, (iii) the "elimination" in virtue of negative prehensions, (iv) the "objective datum" which is felt, (v) the "subjective form" which is *how* that subject feels that objective datum.[60]

The "subject" in this analysis is clearly not the "substantive soul" of classical theology, nor the dualistic "cogito" of Cartesian philosophy, nor the "monadic self" of the personalists. It is, rather, closely related to the "process" of William James, to which Crick and Koch briefly refer but fail to develop. Whitehead's subject is so clearly conceived as a relational subject in process that he suggests it must also be understood as a "superject."

Whitehead provided a teleological analysis of the relational process by which the subject becomes, which complements and corrects the causal analysis provided in the formal logic of metaphysical materialism:

> The subject/superject is the purpose of the process originating the feelings. The feelings are inseparable from the end at which they aim; and this end is the feeler. The feelings aim at the feeler, as their final cause. The feelings are what they are in order that their subject may be what it is. . . . The subject is responsible for being what it is in virtue of its feelings. It is also derivatively responsible for the consequences of its existence because they flow from its feelings.[61]

The subject is the telos of a process but not caused in the way that the molecule-to-mind paradigm of the neurobiologists posits. Their analytically reductive analysis uses the notion of efficient cause with a formal logic suitable only for externally related aggregates. A dialectical logic suitable for the understanding of relational wholes allows the subject to be rationally understood as "at work in the feeling, in order that it may be the subject with that feeling."[62] That is, the whole that becomes through its constituent parts already affects those parts.

Feelings enter into and constitute the subject as the subject guides their integration (Whitehead's preferred technical term is "concrescence") toward the unity defined by its subjective aim, that is, telos. The subject's subjective form cannot be abstracted from the pattern of the objective datum, but neither can it be reduced to that datum. A musical note, for instance, is an analyzable datum in terms of pitch, intensity, and quality. Hearing it is a feeling transmitted through the nerve routes of the auditor's body, but it would not be what it is if it did not have an auditor as its subject. Nor could the auditor become what she is apart from this feeling.[63] In the vector of the flow of energy there is a partial identification of the cause with the effect. This conceptual model enables an adequate understanding of the organic, internal relations between the objective datum, the body, the brain, and the subject.

Conscious awareness may not be understood as a phenomenological representation of a datum on the other side of an epistemological divide between subject and object. It is, in Whitehead's vivid terms, "the cumulation of the universe, and not a stage-play about it."[64] To be sure, consciousness emerges in the subjective form of a feeling, but such conscious feelings always recollect and synthesize physical feelings.

Consciousness, however, may not be reduced to just the synthesis of physical energies, for it requires the contrast provided by the pure potential of what Whitehead calls a "conceptual feeling." The vivid contrast in the feeling of pure and unrealized potential differentiates consciousness from the otherwise unconscious feeling of the physically given. Consciousness is constituted by the synthesis of contrasting data coming from the self's physical *and* mental poles.

Whitehead points out that "consciousness flickers; and even at its brightest, there is a small focal region of clear illumination, and a large penumbral region of experience which tells of intense experience in dim apprehension."[65] The region of clearest illumination is the contrast of what might be but is not. Our clearest consciousness entails a "feeling of absence" that is "produced by the definite exclusiveness of what is really present."[66] But this feeling of absence may not be hypostatized into a monadic ego dualistically abstracted from the givens of experience. The mental feeling of nonactual potential is an experience of polar contrast that requires the presence of the objectively given. Thus all ontological or epistemological dualisms between subject and object must give way to a recognition of the dialectical wholeness of the relational person.

Hermann Lotze was not far from this insight. He could recognize, though with a dualistic nuance, that "the governing soul, placed at a favoured point of the organism, collects the numberless impressions conveyed to it by a host of comrades essentially similar but lower in rank from the inferior significance of their own nature." [67] But his ontological dualism blocked his creatively developing this insight:

> Our spiritual nature is everywhere ashamed at finding itself in indissoluble connection with the world of sense—at the consciousness that while its own aims have intrinsic worth and are incommensurable with material processes, we are yet bound to the mechanical order of Nature.[68]

To be "ashamed" of finitude blocks the acceptance of personal relationality. Why have modern persons like Lotze become ashamed of what has always been obvious and often accepted? A major reason is that our modern sense of finitude derives from defining it in the demeaning scientific terms of mechanistic materialism. Brian Martine sees this clearly:

> Since the beginning of the modern age, we have thought of ourselves and our place in the world as governed by some set of laws larger than those that arise out of direct human experience. . . . But in the hands of the moderns, that structure takes on a strikingly different character in that the laws which constitute it are mindless. They stand there serenely divorced not only from this or that consciousness, but from consciousness itself.[69]

This materialistic paradigm deserves to be rejected because it makes human relationality unintelligible. But its rejection ironically led personalists to alternative ontologies that also denied personal relationality. Albert Knudson's philosophical and theological journey is illustrative. He found Bowne's philosophy so helpful in resolving his questions about scientific materialism that he spent an additional year studying with him. He evaluated that experience theologically in a book written a quarter century later as an enlightenment akin to a redemptive experience, and he remained so convinced after another quarter century that he repeated the whole passage in his last book:

> To the average mind nature is a barrier between the soul and God. It exists in lumpish externality to all thought, and makes difficult a rational and living appreciation of the Divine Presence. But all this is changed by a personalistic philosophy. . . . It would be difficult to describe the effect which Bowne's exposition of this truth had upon those who heard him. It proved to them a veritable gospel, a deliverance from intellectual bondage. Their spirit was released from the leaden weight of a crude realism or materialism or pantheism. What the doctrine of justification by faith meant to Luther's religious life, that did a personal-

istic metaphysic mean to their intellectual life. It wrought for them their intellectual redemption.[70]

Bowne's redemptive power in delivering Knudson from mechanistic materialism, however, blocked him from understanding the relational character of redemption and the interpersonal relationality of love. Reacting not only to Freud's psychoanalysis but also to John Dewey's and Alfred North Whitehead's philosophies, he insisted that experience could not be "broader than consciousness and inclusive of it, . . . [nor] prior to it and in its essential nature dependent upon it." On the basis of Bowne's monadic concept of the person, he argued that "a strictly impersonal or unconscious experience is a contradiction in terms,"[71] thus denying the organic relation of mind, body, and world mediated through unconscious feeling that a more wholistic ontology of the person needs.

Edgar Brightman provides insight into the internal contradiction of this line of thought in one sentence: "The body is that organ of the universe which creates a personality, although the spiritual and the intellectual life are proof that a personality has powers that a merely material body does not possess and could not explain."[72] But personalists interpreted the body ontologically as the activity of the Divine Person. Thus there should be no need to deny organic continuity between this "organ of the universe" and the "spiritual and intellectual" person, for there is no "merely material body."

Brian Martine, in dialogue with Hegel and Pierce rather than Knudson and Brightman, nevertheless has exactly the right prescription for those struggling with their issues:

> I believe that by concentrating upon the notion of relation itself—or, perhaps, upon what might be called "relatedness"—it is possible to overcome the most significant problems involved in the attempt to give an account of the individual. And if those problems can be overcome, the possibility will be laid open for a new description of the individual's relation to the universal, and ultimately for a metaphysical system which can do justice to the individual.[73]

We must recognize the palpable otherness of existing individuals. We know them through their causative force. The individuality they manifest is in some sense self-caused. It cannot be reduced to any external cause, as in the scientific paradigm, or to an internal mediation of universals, as in the Hegelian paradigm. All this the personalists knew well. But they needed to learn that there is no experience of sheer individuality. Individuals are both externally related in what Martine and Pierce call "dyadic relations" and internally related through general characteristics (Whitehead's technical term is "eternal objects") to more universal structures of being, which Martine following Pierce calls "thirdness" or triadic relations.

The vocabulary may be strange, but the insight is crucial: "Considered in terms of his Thirdness or universality," Martine writes, "the human individual, for example, is necessarily a part of a community. For the universals which he exhibits transcend his instancing of them, and form the fabric of the community."[74] I take this to be metaphorically true also of the community of brain and mind, where energy events in the brain are internally related to the conscious subject in mediating universals, which Whitehead defined as complex forms of definiteness. Neither, however, is reducible to the other in their dyadic, external relations. Likewise persons in families, congregations, and communities are internally related in larger wholes that habituate and socialize them. At the same time they remain externally related, because the human individual cannot be reduced to a function of any environing totality without being destroyed.[75]

Understanding human wholeness, thus, may not be confused with any attempt to articulate a complete ontological system. A "whole" person is both a social and an individuated self. The social dimensions of selfhood enable our becoming intelligent and intelligible within the physical and social universals in which we live, but the particularity of our individuation within finite cultural communities makes any and all of our interpretations perspectival and finite. Relational metaphysics, therefore, understands the role of the metaphorical in the ontological. As Martine puts it, "While logic need not bow to metaphor, it must come to accept it as something other than a bastard son. And a metaphor can never be complete in the way that a perfectly integrated logical system can be."[76]

Indeed, any attempt to understand our world as a whole is already a cosmic metaphor. "Since metaphors are open-ended and since the concept of the Whole is a metaphorical extension from finite contexts of cognition,"[77] as Carl Vaught recognizes, any and all attempts to complete an ontological system or to absolutize a conceptual model must falter. We must accept the imaginative and the metaphorical characteristics of our logical universals as we seek to articulate an ontology adequate to understand the interpersonal relationality of love.

## A Relational Understanding of Persons as Both Individual and Social

For love to be real and really understood, persons must experience and conceive themselves as both individual and social. In terms of relational ontology, this means persons must have both external relations that limit and affect but do not constitute them and internal relations that are constitutive of their very being. Some relations may be objectified because they are external. They may be experienced and understood in the scientific mode of subject-object relations, for such relations tell us only something of what we are. But other relations may not be objectified and abstracted from the concreteness (Whitehead would say "concretion") of our personal being, for they tell us who we are.

Martin Buber's brilliant characterization of the contrasts between "I-It" and "I-Thou" relations expresses this insight with force and clarity:

> The I of the primary word I-Thou is a different I from that of the primary word I-It. . . . The primary word I-Thou can only be spoken with the whole being. The primary word I-It can never be spoken with the whole being. . . . When Thou is spoken, the speaker has no thing; he has indeed nothing. But he takes his stand in relation. . . . As experience, the world belongs to the primary word I-It. The primary word I-Thou establishes the world of relation.[78]

Buber understood individuals to become persons through two primary ontological acts by which we distance ourselves from what we objectify as "It" and bind ourselves in relation to a "Thou" through "both will and grace."[79] Buber's insight that I-Thou relations are realized through both human will and divine grace shall require our later theological attention, but for now we continue in a more philosophical and psychological mode.

Buber's insight sharply contrasts with the Cartesian form of consciousness taught by personalism and many other modern philosophies. Many have also struggled to revise it. Freud and Jung opened the conscious, rational self to the dynamics of the subconscious. Husserl and subsequent phenomenologists interpreted the transcending self as existing in intentional relation with its field of consciousness, or life-world. Yet Jean-Paul Sartre showed the inadequacy of a purely phenomenological corrective to transform the alienating consequences of Cartesian subject-object dualism. The life-world of a phenomenologist like Sartre remained alienating and alienated in its very structure. And not only in its objectivity, for Sartre interpreted an object of consciousness as the more alienating when "given to me directly as a subject." For Sartre understood coming to awareness of the other-as-subject as strictly correlated with the self's objectification: "He is the object in the world which determines an internal flow of the universe, an internal hemorrhage. He is the subject who is revealed to me in that flight of myself toward objectivation."[80]

The existential distance from Sartre's phenomenology to Buber's relationality is illumined by examining the way Freud's colleague Ludwig Binswanger, under the influence of Buber, came to understand the relational self. His interpretation of "The Case of Ellen West," a schizophrenic suicide, examined just such alienation as Sartre so dramatically described:

> Ellen West's defiance and stubbornness exclude her from "the authentic I-Thou relationship of the being-with-one another" and leave her to a

world of interpersonal relations consisting of mere togetherness in which each seizes on the weak point of the other and tries to dominate him. . . . It is the lack of the *communio* of love and the *communicatio* of friendship, says Binswanger, that leads to extravagance—that basic element of schizophrenia that sets up an impossible ideal and progressively narrows the ground of its own existence in relation to this ideal.[81]

Binswanger was one among several psychoanalysts whose ontological interpretation of I-Thou relations precluded their ontological reduction to mere phenomena. Harry Stack Sullivan was another who concluded from his psychiatric practice that persons must be understood as participants in an interpersonal field. He substituted the concept of "dynamism" to revise Freud's instinctual mythology into a more relational understanding:

> The ultimate entity, the smallest useful abstraction, which can be employed in the study of the functional activity of the living organism is the dynamism itself, the relatively enduring pattern of energy transformations which recurrently characterize the organism in its duration as a living organism. . . . The dynamisms of interest to the psychiatrist are the relatively enduring patterns of energy transformation which recurrently characterize the interpersonal relations.[82]

Sullivan saw sociopersonal dynamisms as ontologically affecting the very being of the person: "It is possible to think of man as distinguished from plants and animals by the fact that human life—in a very real and not only a purely literary or imaginary sense—requires interchange with an environment which includes culture."[83] He therefore rejected Freud's naturalistic theory of personal development as inevitable stages of oedipal organization because he saw the basic human drive as growth and maturation. Sullivan interpreted interpersonal relations as so basic to growth as to be analogous to the organism's dependence upon constant exchange through its bordering membranes with elements in its physical environment.[84]

Such relationships, of course, are both wounding and healing. As a psychiatrist, Sullivan met many persons victimized by a history of negative relations. He found their self-systems to be injured in attempts to minimize anxiety by meeting the requirements of significant others. The other side of this coin, however, is that good relationships are personally enabling and therapeutically healing. A colleague wrote of Sullivan that "his respect for the individual's capacities to be something other than a compromise between circumstance and instinct conveyed itself to his patients."[85] His concept of the self-dynamism allowed for and communicated a greater possibility for genuine personal health. His colleagues later defined how good relations function therapeutically:

The patient comes to recognize the psychiatrist's striking difference from those who originally contributed to his constricted self-system. He finds himself in a situation in which hitherto disassociated impulses may be given the benefit of elaboration in consciousness, synthesis with the rest of the personality, foresight, and modification based on recognition of the presence of others. And as the patient begins to relate more appropriately to the psychiatrist, he learns to relate more appropriately to others.[86]

Though Sullivan was not influenced by Buber, there is obvious theoretical correlation between his interpersonal therapy and Buber's interpretation of I-Thou relations. The characterization of Buber's I-Thou relation as "a dialogue in which the other is accepted in his or her unique otherness and not reduced to a content of my experience" could function analogously as a description of Sullivan's therapeutic practice. Similarly, the characterization of Buber's I-It relation might describe the reductionistic analytic methods of Freud and others whom Sullivan theoretically opposed: "I-It is a monologue, the subject-object relation of knowing and using that does not allow the other to exist as a whole and unique person but abstracts, reduces, and categorizes.[87]

Yet there remains a significant difference between Sullivan's interpersonal field theory and Buber's relational understanding. Maurice Friedman put it this way: "Dialogue includes a reality of over-againstness and separateness quite foreign to Sullivan's definition of the self as entirely interpersonal."[88] Perhaps Sullivan's metaphorical use of naturalistic field theory to interpret the person's social dimensions leads him to miss the irreducible otherness of personal individuality. In any case, the concern of any of us to recognize the interpersonal dimensions of all of us must not be allowed to obscure the ontological particularity of each of us. A whole person must be, and therefore should be understood as, both a social and individuated self. Culture and even the structure of our consciousness are social creations, but they are so because of the mutual creativity of nonsolitary, unique, individual persons.

### Correcting Whitehead's
### Metaphysical Concept of the Person

Whitehead's comprehensive category for interpreting a person so conceived is "actual entity." The whole of his ontology is "concerned with the becoming, the being, and the *relatedness* of 'actual entities.'"[89] He understood an actual entity to be composed by its prehensions, that is, real experiences, of other actual entities. He thus revised the Aristotelian category of "qualities" inhering in "substances" to prehensions received in relations. An actual entity is no longer conceived as an enduring thing with inherent qualities but as an event whose qualities are constituted by its relations.

Whitehead's identification of actual entities with the most minute energy events known to quantum physicists, however, makes his category problematic for interpreting personal being. Whitehead interpreted all larger unities as societies of atomic energy events. From an electron through a molecule, rock, or animal to a person, everything is a "society" or society of societies for Whitehead.[90] Because as a physicist he understood our cosmic epoch to be basically constituted as a society of electromagnetic occasions, he thought it proper that physicists provide our basic concept of actual entities.

As a physicist-cum-metaphysician, however, Whitehead recognized that this cosmic electromagnetic society is pervaded by more special societies: "the regular trains of waves, individual electrons, protons, individual molecules, societies of molecules such as inorganic bodies, living cells, and societies of cells such as vegetable and animal bodies."[91] He interpreted a molecule as a subordinate society in a living cell, a living cell as a subordinate society in a living organ, and a living organ as a subordinate society in an animate organism.

An actual entity in a living cell is known to be "alive" when its reactions cannot be explained by any route of physical inheritance. Whitehead attributes such originality to the prehension of pure potentiality through the mental pole. The emergence of such novelty, however, requires the protection of stabler systems of inorganic molecules sustained by the inertia of inheritance through the physical pole. Thus Whitehead understood life to "lurk in the interstices of each living cell, and in the interstices of the brain"[92] protected by a stabler physical structure. This line of thought finally led him to the notion of the self or "presiding occasion" as an energy event "wandering from part to part of the brain, disassociated from the physical material atoms," whose movement is coordinated with the "peculiar richness of inheritance . . . enjoyed now by this and now by that part."[93]

Whitehead's metaphysics sought to interpret the novelty and creativity of the person as a sequence of living cells in the brain. It is just at this point, therefore, that he used his strongest language to repudiate the traditional philosophical and theological concept of the substantial soul:

> The doctrine of the enduring soul with its permanent characteristics is exactly the irrelevant answer to the problem which life presents. The problem is, How can there be originality? And the answer explains how the soul need be no more original than a stone.[94]

Whitehead knew, however, that his conclusions on the hierarchy of societies composing the order of nature in our cosmic epoch was "largely conjectural."[95] He denied any claim to dogmatic certitude in his interpretation of such complex issues. Thus those influenced by his ontology should also submit it to ongoing critical reflection: Do the atomic energy events of quantum physics provide the only or best paradigm for interpreting all actual entities? Are these hypothetical energy events at the edge of the microworld so foundational that everything else should be conceived as a society composed of them? Is Whitehead's self, conceived as a "presiding occasion" wandering in the interstices of its brain, still conceived in too dualistic and even Cartesian a way? Does this notion really fit our sense of organic relation with our whole body or our experience of unified consciousness and behavior? Is Whitehead's understanding of serial, personal order through a line of dominant physical prehensions—or in more usual terms, an unbroken sequence of memory—a sufficient explanation of enduring personal unity?

Such critical reflections led Reto Fetz to conclude:

> Whitehead's concepts of "society," of "social order," and of "social organization" stand for too many and too diverse things, so that precisely the most decisive distinctions get lost. What Whitehead denotes as the "social order" of the higher living beings can no longer be understood on the model of a society with its emphasis on multiplicity, but only on that of an organism focusing on unity.[96]

Fetz proposed understanding the self as an "encompassing unity" that arises in the ordering of the multiplicity of the millions upon millions (or trillions upon trillions) of the living cells of the brain and body. There is thus a more "decisive distinction" between personal and impersonal reality.

Though all reality is still understood as social in Whitehead's sense of immanence in prehension, personal reality has a higher unity and individuality. Impersonal reality, or things, may be adequately understood with a formal logic suitable for aggregates even though the "things" are societies, because they are constituted by energy events that essentially prehend and repeat the same formal pattern. But the person is constituted by an individuating form of novel unity and is sometimes able to integrate and guide its entire organism from this personal center of unified subjectivity. Fetz is convincing that "only the whole human being (or any higher form of living being), and not a 'presiding occasion' at the final focus of a strand of occasions (if indeed there be any such 'occasion'), can be viewed as such a subject."[97] I would add that this shows again that only a dialectical logic that can articulate the relation of part to whole is adequate to understand a reality that is both individual and social, unitary and multiple, and has both external and internal relations.

Whitehead's proper concern to interpret the whole of reality with a coherent set of nondualistic categories disposed him to understate the experienced diversity between the personal and the impersonal. Ian Barbour, a philosopher of science sympathetic with Whitehead's thought, nevertheless develops this critical point:

> Whitehead's use of such a very general conceptual scheme does not allow adequately for the diversity among levels of activity in the world. He has taken categories most appropriate for a "middle range" in the scale of being (biological organisms) and extended their use both "up" and "down" the scale. Consequently his concepts seem to be insufficiently "personal" to express the enduring unity of human selfhood, but too "personal" to be applicable in the inorganic realm.[98]

Edward Pols also has taken up this issue as a philosopher. Though agreeing largely with Whitehead's organic metaphysics, he focuses on Barbour's "diversity among levels of activity." Pols stresses the multileveled or hierarchic structure of nature. When he examines the hierarchic relation of molecule to cell, cell to organ, and organ to person, he recognizes that a hierarchical system has "levels some of which cannot exist (in a natural state) independently of the uppermost level of that system," and concludes, "then the 'real causality' operative at any of those levels must be ascribed to the 'real causality' of the uppermost level."[99] At the personal level, the real causality of the person as agent is able to unify, at least partially and temporarily, the multiple subsystems that constitute him/her as a spatiotemporal organism.[100]

Whitehead's too uniform and univocal understanding of our world's entities requires Fetz's metaphysical correction: "Whitehead's ideal of a uniform, coherent theory would be better secured through an analogical use of the concept of entity than through the reduction to a single genus of entities."[101] Whitehead himself modified his uniform and univocal concept of actual entities in his concept of God. At this decisive theological point he revised analogically his concept of an actual entity who could not also be an actual occasion, and he came to understand, as his metaphysical reflection became theological, that God had to be conceived as an everlasting actual entity originating in the mental pole.

If an adequate concept of God requires this analogical modification, it may also be necessary analogously to modify Whitehead's concept of the person. Since he did not, those who enter into his labors must try better to interpret the unity and relationality of the person. The whole person must be understood in the way Edward Pols does, as an emerging and maturing psychophysical unity, self-constituted in finite freedom by her/his acts grounded in the mental pole. We may also thus better understand the person's relational interaction as an individuated and social entity.[102]

With this relational understanding of persons as both individual and social, we may now return, as we indicated we would, to the theological implications of Buber's affirmation that human relationality ("I-Thou relations") is realized through *both* an act of human will and the gift of divine grace. We seek also to understand how some relations may be objectified into subject-object ("I-It") relations without damaging or destroying personhood—because they are or may become external relations—while "I-Thou" relations may not be abstracted from the concreteness of personal being because they are internal and constitutive, at least temporarily, of who we are. Though we shall continue to use and revise Whitehead's metaphysics, we turn now to the paradigm of God's Trinitarian being to understand our individuated and social being from Buber's and our standpoint of divine grace.

## Theological Trinitarianism as a Paradigm for Human Relationality

The dialogical reflection of this chapter began with those who scientifically objectified and reduced the relational person by using formal logic to interpret the human self and mind as though they were mere aggregates of externally related units. Both Lotze's personalistic and Whitehead's organic metaphysics addressed this issue helpfully, though the latter more so than the former. Personalism's Cartesian and Kantian conception of personal unity as precluding internal relations with its body and world was found inadequate, as was process philosophy's scientific reduction of the person only to a serial society of occasions in the interstices of the brain. Thus we require a more adequate conceptual model to interpret both the individuated and social wholeness of the person in the interpersonal relationality of love.

The ongoing discussion of Trinitarian theology arises from a tradition that has long considered analogous issues concerning the persons of the Trinity. Prior to Christianity's Trinitarian revision (and after as well for those who did not fully understand or accept it), God was conceived by almost all Christians as a transcendent, immutable, complete, and eternal whole. The heretical Arians were the most consistent of the patristic participants who held this view when they concluded that God, therefore, could not be internally related to the world process. They were even more heretically clear that the God so conceived could not become incarnate in a human being who suffered for the world's redemption. No one, not even Jesus, may be interpreted as internally related with so eternal and immutable a God.

The religious experience and canonical memory of gracious relations with Jesus, however, powerfully revised this God concept for many other Christians. So powerfully, indeed, that a council presided over by the reigning Roman emperor dared to affirm that this Jewish carpenter, convicted and executed by the same Roman Empire, was of one substance (*homoousios*) with God. The gracious and just relationality of Jesus—which reached from the anti-Roman zealot to the Roman centurion and tax-collector, and from the Hasidic Pharisee and Essene to the shunned leper and despised adulteress—had become so religiously ultimate that it opened Christian theology relationally to include Jesus as "God from God, light from light, true God from true God." The process of reinterpreting the holy and transcendent God as relational began by fusing a traditional theological horizon with the Jesus horizon of the Christian community in the concept of the Trinity. This process continues as we seek to fuse the traditional Trinitarian horizon with our contemporary psychological, sociological, and philosophical horizons to understand the interpersonal relationality of love.

The historical development of diverse Trinitarian models, however, has complicated such reflection: a modalistic model that extends in many variations from Sabellius through Augustine to Karl Barth and Karl Rahner in our century; and a communitarian model stemming from the Cappadocian theologians and extending to Joseph Bracken and Jürgen Moltmann today. The latter social model of God constituted by intersubjective, internal relations is the most useful for our reflection. Yet the misconception of "tritheism" when this model is interpreted with a formal logic, which sees all relations as external and all unities as mere aggregates, requires continuing interest in the stress on unity of the more modalistic models.

Modalistic Trinitarianism since Hegel has interpreted God as the absolute Subject who goes out from himself and yet remains himself. The God revealed in the gracious relationality of Jesus, though no longer interpreted with the patristic concept of substance, is now interpreted by Karl Barth as the absolute Subject who reveals himself in his Word. Moltmann objects to this "late triumph for Sabellian modalism" because it obscures the suffering and joy of the divine-human relations revealed in Jesus.[103] Yet Barth's theological intention in so conceiving God was not to obscure God's relatedness but to affirm God's unity and integrity. Eberhard Jüngel's more sympathetic interpretation makes this point:

> So long as the becoming in which God's being is, is understood as the becoming *proper* to God's being, the statement "God's being is in becoming" remains from the first guarded from the misunderstanding that God *would* first *become* that which he is, through his relationship to an other than himself.[104]

The crucial issue remains, however, how to conceive "the becoming proper to God's being," and analogously the becoming of human being, in a way that articulates both the integrity of personal wholeness and the love of interpersonal relationality.

Classical communitarian Trinitarianism articulated by the Cappadocians[105] did not even envision the problem of God's internal relation to "an *other* than himself." Jesus as the Son/Logos had been interpreted at Nicaea as *homoousios* with the Father/Creator, from whose substance he was "begotten." And the Council of Constantinople, under the influence of the Cappadocians, had extended this concept of consubstantiality to the Spirit.[106] God's internal relations as "immanent Trinity" were thus conceived as only of like with like. And the related conception of the Trinity's external relations as "economic Trinity" precluded the world's otherness affecting God's immanent or internal relations. God's activity *extra se* (outside or beyond God's self) was understood as unified and indivisible; therefore, God's external relations as economic Trinity could have no effect on the internal relations of the immanent Trinity. Although Cappadocian Trinitarian theology affirmed God's essential relationality, it becomes clear that they intended to modify traditional ideas of God's transcendence and immutability as little as possible.

It was and is theologically incoherent, however, to affirm the eternal Logos/Christ to be internally related with the Father while denying this for the fully human Jesus of the economic Trinity. The Council of Chalcedon had already repudiated any such division by affirming that Jesus Christ "is not parted or separated into two persons, but one and the same Son and only begotten God the Word, Lord Jesus Christ."[107] Dividing God's internal and external relations between the immanent and economic Trinities also is incoherent with the soteriological principle of the Cappadocian Gregory of Nazianzus himself, who affirmed: "That which God did not assume, he also did not redeem. If the Logos did not assume the human spirit, it was not redeemed."[108] The relational power and purpose of God's Logos revealed in the concrete historical relationality of Jesus, therefore, should not conceptually be parted or separated from the creativity, suffering, and struggle of the finite humanity that God fully assumed.[109] God is not an absolute Subject of whom Jesus is a mode for speaking the divine Word; God is a Trinitarian Community whose interactive love Jesus fully expressed.

The Cappadocians' concept of "mutual immanence" in the divine persons of the Trinity and Chalcedon's understanding of the direct immanence of God in Jesus constituted a creative advance in ancient metaphysics. Whitehead judged the Cappadocians to be "the only thinkers who in a fundamental metaphysical doctrine have improved upon Plato." He explained: "My point is that in the place of Plato's solution of secondary images and imitations, they demanded a direct doctrine of immanence." The concept of "mutual immanence" here is synonymous with his more usual "internal relations" that we have been using.

We share Whitehead's lament that this insight into mutual immanence/internal relations remained restricted in patristic theology to the immanent Trinity:

> Unfortunately, the theologians never made this advance into general metaphysics. . . . They made no effort to conceive the World in terms of the metaphysical categories by means of which they interpreted God, and they made no effort to conceive God in terms of the metaphysical categories which they applied to the World. For them God was eminently real, and the World was derivatively real. God was necessary to the World, but the World was not necessary to God. There was a gulf between them.[110]

Process theologians are misled, however, when they seek to universalize this Cappadocian insight while denigrating the traditional communitarian understanding of the Trinity in which it arose as "a mystification rather than a clarification of Christian belief." John Cobb, Jr., criticizes the formulation that his mentor valued so highly:

> Previously it had been rightly asserted that God was a single *hypostasis*. But now the word was used to designate the difference. This would have done no harm if it had been asserted that the Father was a *hypostasis* and the Son and Spirit were two modes of his activity in himself and toward the world. It would have done only moderate harm if Son and Spirit had been declared *hypostaseis* in which the one Father actualized himself. . . . But by using *hypostasis* both of the Father and of the Son and Spirit, serious confusion was introduced.[111]

It is paradoxical that what Whitehead thought was a locus of great metaphysical insight his followers find to be a source of great mystification. The paradox, however, is rooted in Whitehead himself, who developed his God concept in the modalistic form of one actual entity functioning through two natures. With no responsibility for, and little continuing interest in, the theological tradition, Whitehead first[112] articulated the direct immanence of God's "primordial nature" in the world process. He saw it as providing the initial aims necessary for entities to be actualized with a definite form in an otherwise random spatiotemporal energy field. He thus fused the Neoplatonic tradition with quantum physics to interpret God as the principle of concretion who grounded and guided the possibility of emergent order in a dynamic process of energy events.

Whitehead completed his metaphysics by articulating his concept of God's consequent nature as the direct immanence of the world process in God. This second nature is necessary to Whitehead's coherent understanding of God as the chief exemplification of an actual entity, all of which necessarily have both a mental and a physical pole.[113] Yet this concept of God as the everlasting Actual Entity with two natures provides only a modalistic interpretation of the Cappadocian insight Whitehead valued so highly. Schubert Ogden summarizes its essential modalism in his definition of God as "the strictly universal *individual* whose boundless love for all things is their sole primal source [primordial nature] as well as their only final end [consequent nature]."[114]

The difference between Whitehead as metaphysician and Ogden as theologian is the latter's greater obligation to interpret the Christian tradition. Ogden does discuss the Trinitarian doctrine more fully, but only to give it a modalistic interpretation. He uses the philosophical distinction between subject and object as synonymous with the difference between internal and external relations to interpret the traditional Trinitarian distinctions in God:

> There is hardly a greater difference than that between internal and external relatedness, and that is the difference between subject and object, which certainly applies to God, who in all his "operations" is the eminent individual who both loves and is loved by himself and all others. . . . For if it is nothing other or less than God's very self that is revealed to us as the ground and the object of our faith in him—and just this is the claim of Christian revelation—then God exists as God only by existing as the eminent subject and object of love in their primordial unity and difference, and hence as Father, Son, and Holy Spirit.[115]

The "hence" in Ogden's final clause, however, is problematic. It seems to me neither adequate to the Trinitarian tradition's originating insight into the mutual immanence of Jesus and God nor helpful in understanding internal and external relations. The early Christians, despite the later influence of Augustine's psychological analogies, were not only distinguishing between God as subject and as object when they affirmed God's Trinitarian relationality. They were affirming the internal relations of Jesus and God, interpreted interpersonally.

The difference between internal and external relations also may not be reduced only to God's, or anyone else's, self-experience as both subject and object. The transcendental logic used by Ogden, which reduces interpersonal relations to relations within a subject, must be replaced with a dialectical logic that interprets internal and external relations as interactions between persons understood as both parts and wholes. Henry Nelson Wieman was right when for his own quite different reasons he critiqued this Whiteheadian idea of a "cosmic" actual entity as "unable to experience love or justice" because these are not "experienced in one's own body . . . [but] are experienced in the relations between persons."[116]

*A Trinitarian Revision
of Process Metaphysics*

The Trinitarian revision of process metaphysics we propose continues to value the Whiteheadian cosmology to which we devoted chapter 1. But the revision now advocated was already adumbrated in chapter 2, where we probed opening this Western mode of thought to the more Eastern mode of experiencing an all-embracing universal. We explored the Eastern sense of reducing or relaxing the ego boundaries of the differentiated self while continuing to affirm the more Western understanding of personal will and activity. We came to the Trinitarian issue more directly in dialogue with Zen Buddhism's understanding of "circuminsessional interpenetration" in chapter 3, where we looked toward the analogous Christian concept of a communitarian Trinity that enlivens the whole creation to enter into communal relations. Redemptive participation in God experienced and understood as the Relational Universal, adumbrated through interreligious dialogue in chapter 3, should enable the practice of contextual justice. As this point was developed in chapter 4, it was found especially true of our relations with the others marginalized or foreign at the boundaries of our communities.

All of which leads to the heart of the matter: Can we reconceive the traditional Christian Trinity with a revised process metaphysics so as better to understand persons as finite centers of freedom and love? And can we thereby understand them interpersonally as empowered by internal, and bounded by external, relations, so that personal egoism and communal alter-egoism may be overcome, justice sought, and love realized?

Joseph Bracken revises Whitehead's modalistic God concept under the influence of Josiah Royce. Differentiating between modalistic and communitarian Trinitarian understandings as analogous to the differences between a community "mind" and a community "mentality," he wrote:

> The difference between a mind and a mentality might seem at first glance insignificant, but in point of fact it is a crucial distinction. For to ascribe a mind to a community is to regard it once again as a supraindividual person; a mentality, on the other hand, is simply the result of a process of interaction among persons, each with a mind of his/her own. Hence to say that a community has a mentality of its own which distinguishes it from other communities with different mentalities is implicitly to say that a community is a process, not a person. Yet, like a person, it has a character proper to itself, and out of this social character come by degrees language, customs, religions, etc.[117]

And on the basis of this differentiation, Bracken envisions the Trinity as a perfect community:

It seems altogether reasonable to suppose that the three divine persons, in virtue of their perfect understanding both of themselves as individuals and of their joint reality as one God, do achieve in fact total unanimity of mind and will, perfect accord in their relationships with their creatures, etc. They are, in other words, a perfect community, an ideal to which human beings in their relationships with one another may well aspire but which they will never attain.[118]

Some Christians may find that Bracken's clear articulation of an interpersonal model fails adequately to grasp God's unity. It does not fall into tritheism, however, because of Bracken's concept of person. He understands the "spiritual activities of knowing and loving" as able to relate every person intentionally to the whole of being. Human persons differ from God, however, in that their perspectival limits require submission to open dialogue if they are to contribute to the universal community of interpersonal relationality. The infinite knowledge of divine Persons, however, reduces their perspectival differentiation to an absolute minimum, so that the Trinity may be conceived as an interpersonal unity: "As distinct persons they possess separate consciousnesses, nevertheless they together form a single *shared* consciousness which is perfect in all respects and which thus corresponds exactly to their communitarian reality as one God."[119]

The same metaphor of communal mentality is used to understand the exercise of communal will by both God and human beings. Bracken's conception of similarity and difference, however, is not so much the metaphorical form of "is and is not," but of "is and is more":

While in human communities this interaction of individual agencies is often conflictual and filled with anxiety, within the Trinity, where the individual persons know and accept one another perfectly, there is absolutely no conflict but rather complete accord. Hence, even though each divine person has his own mind and will, they are of one mind and one will in everything they say and do, both with respect to one another and in their relationships with human beings and the whole of creation.[120]

Jürgen Moltmann develops a similar concept of the Trinity with less dependence upon philosophy and closer correlation with the theological tradition. With no apparent influence from Whitehead or Royce, his concept of the Trinity is almost exactly the same as Bracken's:

In their perichoresis and because of it, the trinitarian persons are not to be understood as three different individuals, who only subsequently enter into relationship with one another (which is the customary reproach, under the name of "tritheism"). But they are not either, three modes of being or three repetitions of the One God, as the modalistic interpretation suggests. The doctrine of the perichoresis links together in a brilliant way the threeness and the unity, without reducing the threeness to the unity or dissolving the unity in the threeness. . . . Interpreted perichoretically, the trinitarian persons form their own unity by themselves in the circulation of the divine life.[121]

Moltmann conceives the unity of the Trinity, not in the modalistic forms of one substance or one subject, but in the form of community. Moreover, the Christian God's (comm)unity is open and communicable to others, so it must be conceived as a process of both personal self-differentiation and social interaction. Moltmann uses at this point the same concept of the person as Bracken:

The Father, the Son, and the Spirit are by no means merely *distinguished* from one another by their character as Persons; they are just as much *united* with one another and in one another, since personal character and social character are only two aspects of the same thing.[122]

Moltmann's primary metaphor, however, is empathy rather than the knowing and willing developed by Bracken. He interprets John Damascene's view that God's eternal life is an exchange of energies in terms of "a process of most perfect and intense empathy." The Damascene's notion of *circumincessio* is understood in terms of an interactive process of love: "The 'circulation' of the eternal divine life becomes perfect through the fellowship and unity of the three different Persons in the eternal love."[123]

Moltmann understands the immanent Trinity's inner life as an eternal perichoresis of love, and the economic Trinity's work of creation and salvation as opening the circulatory movement of the divine relationships to take "the whole of creation into the life-stream of the triune God."[124] Though this is very close to the paradigm for understanding the interpersonal relationality of love we are seeking, some issues need further clarification before we can relate it coherently to our primary model of dialectical panentheism.

The first is whether "eternal" or "everlasting" more coherently characterize God's being? Moltmann regularly uses the notion of eternity:

At the centre of Christian theology stands the *eternal history* which the triune God experiences in himself. Every narrative needs *time*. For the narrative in which he praises the triune God, man needs his time too. That is more appropriate for the *eternal divine present* than the abstractions in which time is dissolved.[125]

Yet one must ask whether eternity understood as "eternal divine present" may be conceived in any other way than as dissolving time? This paradoxical assertion occurs in a paragraph whose major point is our human inability to sum up the concept of the Trinity—an appropriate context for so incoherent a proposition. Since there can be neither time nor history in an eternal present, an empathic, relational Trinity cannot be conceived in those terms but only in the more Whiteheadian terms of "everlasting process."

God's internal relations may be conceived with the Whiteheadian notion of God's primordial nature to approximate Moltmann's intuition of eternity in the circuminsession of perfect love. But God's internal and external relations with a spatiotemporal process, alienated through its anxious exercise of finite freedom, cannot be coherently conceived as "eternal." Whitehead's concept of "everlasting" in his characterization of God's consequent nature receiving the whole temporal process into itself is clearly more adequate. It can incorporate that notion of "eternal" that Robert Neville rightly sees as religiously powerful: "The eternity of the person's life consists in the fact that any part of that life, or the whole of it, exists eternally in the divine life."[126] But it will not dissolve all time into an eternal present.

In the second issue, on the other hand, Moltmann's theology suggests an important corrective to how process theologians have used Whitehead's concept of "primordial nature" to interpret the Son/Logos as only potential. John Cobb, Jr., interprets the Logos as "the ordered givenness of relevant potentiality" or "the order of unrealized potentiality making possible by its immanence the realization of novel order."[127] Cobb here reflects Whitehead's philosophical understanding of God's primordial nature as "the unlimited conceptual realization of the absolute wealth of potentiality," which as such is "deficiently actual" and "devoid of consciousness."[128] Moltmann, like Barth and Jüngel, rejects the notion that the Trinity becomes what it is through relationships outside of itself. Unlike process philosophy, their understanding of the Trinity does not move from potentiality to actuality entirely through its relation to the world.

Moltmann affirms that "the history of the world is God's passion," which relates coherently to Whitehead's notion of God's consequent nature; but he rejects the Whiteheadian notion that the history of the world is "the process of God's self-realization."[129] He rather affirms the traditional "eternal generation" of the Son. Despite the problematic eternal, the important point is that no person of the Trinity may be considered only potential until actualized in the creation: "The Son, like the Father, belongs to the eternal constitution of the triune God."[130] This is a necessary affirmation if God's being is to be understood as essentially relational. Expressed in Whiteheadian terms, God's primordial Logos everlastingly moves from potentiality to actuality in the essential relationality of God's being, as the ancient tradition of the immanent Trinity began to understand.[131]

The circuminsession of everlasting love in God's Trinitarian being may also fulfill John Cobb's notion of "potentiality" for novel order in a continuing creation, and redeemed and restored order in an alienated one. This potentiality, however, must now be understood as corresponding and responding to the everlastingly *actual* love in God. The eternal/everlasting actuality of the Son is the relational ground for the potentiality of creation and redemption. Moltmann's way of saying this is:

> The love of the Father which begets and brings forth the Son is therefore open for further response through creations which correspond to the Son, which enter into harmony with his responsive love and thereby fulfill the joy of the Father. Hence the love of the Father which brings forth the Son in eternity becomes creative love. It calls created beings into life, beings made in the image of the Son, who in fellowship with the Son return the Father's love.[132]

### Understanding Internal and External Relations

Though we may not hope to complete human reflection on these momentous themes, these clarifications of a Trinitarian model for understanding the interpersonal relationality of love may be tentatively sufficient to provide the paradigm we need. This paradigm illumines the complex issue of understanding the objectification of subject-object relations as sometimes acceptable in our technocratic culture but destructive when such relations are internal and constitutive. We are internally related as organic beings to processes constitutive of our personhood. In the first instance, these are our bodies. We do not so much *have* a body as we *are* our body. As we have seen, neuroscientists can teach us of our internal relations with the energy events in our brains. Freud and other psychoanalysts can teach us the dire consequence of disassociating sexual or nutritional dynamics from our person.

In the second instance, we are equally internally related to our engendering communities, though this requires the recognition that we are both individual and social selves. Family therapists can teach us how crucial to our well-being is the way we have been socialized in family systems. Social psychologists and cultural anthropologists may enlighten us as to how we have been habituated by language systems and enculturated in social structures.

We are quite literally constituted by our internal relations with our bodies and engendering communities. To objectify them is to alienate our selves, and to do so completely is to destroy our selves, at least in terms of our personal unity and identity.

Whitehead helps us understand internal relations in terms of prehensions that feel the feelings of other actual entities. In this sense all relations are internal but as Whitehead says, they are so with graded degrees of relevance. Because God's initial aim is basic to our personal self-actualization in each moment, our God-relation may never be objectified without personal alienation and self-destructive consequences. Though parts of our bodies may be objectified and even surgically alienated, it is always with great trauma and loss to the self. Since parental nurturing relations are crucial to our becoming, as the Hebrew Torah and other religious traditions know, we cannot live without honoring them as internal to our very being if our days are to be long in the land that God gives us.[133] Various forms of other social loyalties testify to the same reality, though with diminishing degrees of power. What is constitutive of our very beings must be realized in the form of "I-Thou" internal relations. To objectify such relations as "I-It" external relations is to court self-alienation and risk self-destruction.

Such self-integration or concrescence, however, is not eternal. We must integrate ourselves anew in each moment both as whole psychophysical individuals and as wholesome social selves in the communities in which we participate. Our concrescence is always a temporal occasion and thus a moment in a continuing process. Relations that are crucial and constitutive at one stage may become less so at a later stage. Relations that have been internal may, and perhaps should, become external. Earlier crucial relations that have been distorted and destructive may be objectified and recognized as such in therapeutic situations constituted by new internal relations. False or exaggerated loyalties and xenophobic fears may be altered or given up as we enter into more inclusive and universal communities. We may finally learn both to accept the finitude of our individuated and centered selves—because we cannot be the organic center of the whole of being; and to affirm the possibility of our universal relationality—because we may participate in the gracious relational being of the God who only is this Center.

To realize our participation in the universal relationality of God illumines Buber's insight that "I-Thou" relations are realized both through an act of human will and the gift of divine grace. In the essential relations of God's being as manifested in Jesus' relationality there is no alienation. To be drawn into and respond to the gracious relations of the immanent Trinity is to experience internal "I-Thou" relations that may never be objectified in the form of "I-It" relations. Buber wrote of this religious experience: "The extended lines of relations meet in the eternal Thou. Every particular Thou is a glimpse through to the eternal Thou, . . . the Thou that by its nature cannot become It."[134] Christians understand this experience of the eternal Thou as the everlasting circuminsession of gracious relationality in the Trinitarian God revealed in Jesus. Buber's "gift of grace," then, is to share in God's relational life; while the "act of will" is the integration of our personal self that is enabled, empowered, and affirmed in such gracious relations.

## Conclusion: The Interpersonal Relationality of Love

It may seem strange to many that so complex a discussion is necessary to illumine so universal a phenomenon as love. But our strangely complex modern cultures all too often alienate us from the most intimate, immediate, and in some ways simplest dimensions of our experience. Essentially, it should not be difficult for those created in God's image to realize ourselves as whole persons, but existentially it is, and for all too many the difficulties end in despair and tragedy. Our interpersonal relationality should be transparent to us, for we all know it as children if (and it is too big an "if" for too many) we have anything like normal nurturing parents. Yet all too few adults understand what it means, in terms attributed to Jesus, to enter into abundant life like little children. Carl Vaught is one who does understand and is able to articulate the life-experience of many:

> The larger world in which we exist allows us to develop what would otherwise remain implicit in our nature, and it gives us a rich domain of content to be transformed by our own actions. Yet in doing so, it tempts us to lose ourselves in what will always lie beyond our grasp, and it lures us away from the particular context out of which we come and to which we must finally return. To be sustained, but also to be destroyed; to have our own space, but to be separated from our own ground; to be allowed to grow and to develop, but to be lured away from our origins—these fundamental contradictions constitute the inherent ambiguity of the human situation.[135]

For the religious, the complex metaphysical discussion of contemporary scientific perspectives may seem utterly unnecessary. But only if we are not religiously concerned to include the scientists among us, and perhaps the scientist in us, in the universal relationality of love. On the other hand, the more secular among us, and perhaps in us, may have found the long and complex discussion of the Trinity irrelevant to their entering into loving relations. But only if they are not concerned to include millions of those formed by the Christian tradition, and perhaps they themselves in their own roots, in the universal community formed by loving relationality.

As for me as a Christian believer and theologian, the doctrine of the Trinitarian, relational God belongs to the internal roots of my very life. It is thus both my prayer and my work that a better understanding of the God "in whom we live, and move, and have our being" may enable a more adequate participation in the universal relationality of God's love. I do not think, however, that Christians should seek evangelistically to convert all to this Trinitarian belief. Our complex, interreligious world has long had too much religious imperialism, which I believe has brought great suffering into God's relational being. Rather, as we are enabled, Christians should relate to all others in the grace experienced by participating in God's Trinitarian relationality; recognize and rejoice in that grace wherever it is expressed in whatever religious or cultural context; and give witness to our Trinitarian theology for thematizing that grace only when the relational moment invites such witness.

Carl Vaught makes much the same point again in a more abstract, philosophical way: "There can be little doubt that the quest for wholeness moves toward a more inclusive unity, but it also moves backward to the origins from which it emerges. In both cases, it attempts to bring fulfillment to the human soul."[136] We must understand as we move dialectically out to others and back to our existential and religious origins that the only fulfillment we shall ever know is in community with our bodies, other persons, and God in a way that honors both the integrity and mutuality of all.

Having moved through many philosophical considerations, we may end with a theological affirmation from the thinker who helped us define the problematic at the beginning and who has never really been out of mind during the whole of our reflections. The hope at the end is that we are now in a better position to understand Daniel Day Williams when he wrote:

> We are created to find ourselves in belonging, and we really belong to that which makes us lovers. The only commitment which can sustain an absolute trust is that which accepts what we are in all the conditions of finitude, and yet offers participation in the infinitely creative life which takes our present loves beyond themselves into the service of God. . . . The truth in the Gospel which cuts into all our loves is that every love must be offered up to the creative transformation which God is bringing about in the whole creation.[137]

And perhaps we may even yet come to understand Jesus' dialogue with the Pharisees as a dialogue with us:

> "You shall love the Lord your God with all your heart, and with all your soul, and with all your mind." This is the greatest and first commandment. And a second is like it: "You shall love your neighbor as yourself." On these two commandments hang all the law and the prophets. (Matt. 22:37–40, NRSV)

For in our era, the law and the prophets of all of our cultures hang on universalizing our capacity to recognize all of our neighbors.

# 6

# The Universal
# Relationality of Peace

## Introduction

"Peace" is one of the most evocative symbols of the powerful motive that lures persons toward relational wholeness, societies toward contextual justice, and the world toward universal harmony. We now focus on understanding the drive toward universal peace within the universal relationality of God. St. Augustine wrote as the *Pax Romana* was being destroyed in the fifth century: "Whoever gives moderate attention to human affairs and to our common nature will recognize that even as there is no one who does not wish to be joyful, neither is there anyone who *does not wish to have peace*."[1] But how shall we understand the peace we want? The etymology of the word points toward its root religious meaning. Our English "peace" derives from Augustine's Latin *pax* by way of the French *paix*. Its root meaning is to make a "pact," perhaps contextually—and too often—meaning "to end hostilities," but with a more complete meaning approximating the biblical notion of "covenant." The covenantal understanding of peace expresses the richest meaning of the Hebrew *shalom*, the peace known in covenant relations with God and God's people. The Arabic cognate *salam* is similarly related to *Islam* as entering into peace through submission to God and God's law. *Santi* is the most commonly used Sanskrit term for peace, with connotations drawn from Hinduism of becoming quiet, tranquil, and blissful.[2] Every Hindu prayer ends with its invocation: "Om Santi, Santi, Santi—Peace, Peace, Peace." These etymological reflections underscore the close cultural correlation between a people's religion and their concern for, and understanding of, peace.

The president of the Asian Buddhist Conference for Peace underscored all religion's orientation to peace when he convened their confer-

ence in 1989 in the monastery in Ulan Bator, Mongolia, where he was
Khambo Lama:

> Lord Buddha said that there is no greater bliss than peace. There is not
> a single theologian who does not espouse this. Lord Buddha urged us to
> love all beings in the six realms like a mother who loves her only son.
> The Old Testament of the Bible teaches the love of one's neighbor as
> oneself. I believe that there is an identical lesson in Islam. Since the
> concepts of love in Christianity and loving-kindness in Buddhism are
> central to the respective religions there is enough reason for humanity
> to love one another.[3]

There may be enough reason; yet it is not so! Our spirits still echo
after 2,500 years the lament of the Hebrew prophet Jeremiah: "They have
treated the wound of my people carelessly, saying, 'Peace, peace,' when
there is no peace"(Jer. 6:14, NRSV).[4] As this is being written at the end of
1992, Hindu faithful have tragically disrupted the peace of India by destroying a centuries-old mosque built on what they believe to be the
birthplace of the god Rama. This is the most recent event in a continuing
controversy that has already cost the lives of Mahatma Gandhi in 1948
and more than a thousand persons in 1990–91 after the first attempt to
destroy this mosque.[5]

Equally tragic illustrations of religious conflict could be found in every
region of our world. Why? Is it because some religion is too facile an
idealism and the peace it teaches too vapid a value? Or perhaps religion
too often functions as an opiate to deaden life's pain and deflect us from
transforming the realities that cause it. Or is it, as I believe, that religion is
powerful in creating communities that often remain all too limited by
tribal, national, and class/caste boundaries? We may find some truth in
the answers suggested by the first two perspectives, and especially the
second, but it is the proposition suggested by the third that I find worthy
of careful reflection: The power of religion to create peace is short-
circuited, and the peace it creates is truncated and distorted when it is not
understood within the universal relationality of God.

A better understanding of the universal relationality of God, which
comprehends, transcends, and transforms our tribal, national, and class
relationships, may enable the awful power of religion to contribute to the
universal peace of humanity. My philosophical vehicle for this religious
reflection remains dialectical panentheism. At the end of Alfred North
Whitehead's long reflection on what helped "civilize" the peoples of
Western Europe, he struggled to elucidate his sense of peace. Though his
genre remained philosophical, a powerful paragraph reveals how close the
philosophical spirit may come to religious expression when seeking to
articulate the meaning of peace:

The experience of Peace is largely beyond the control of purpose. It comes as a gift. The deliberate aim at Peace very easily passes into its bastard substitute, Anaesthesia. In other words, in the place of a quality of "life and motion," there is substituted their destruction. Thus Peace is the removal of inhibition and not its introduction. It results in a wider sweep of conscious interest. It enlarges the field of attention. Thus Peace is self-control at its widest,—at the width where the "self" has been lost, and interest has been transferred to coordinations wider than personality. Here the real motive interests of the spirit are meant, and not the superficial play of discursive ideas. Peace is helped by such superficial width, and also promotes it. In fact it is largely for this reason that Peace is so essential for civilization. It is the barrier against narrowness. One of its fruits is the passion whose existence Hume denied, the love of mankind as such.[6]

The powerful motive interests of the religious spirit, as Whitehead recognized, continue to benefit from, and even require, the admittedly more "superficial play of discursive ideas" if the peace they have received as a gift of God's grace is ever to result in the universal love of mankind. For even genuine religion is often afflicted with a kind of tribal narrowness, whether class, ethnic, or national. Thus our first task is to understand, appreciate, and critique the provisional narrowness of primal religion.

## Benign Communalism and Malignant Narrowness in National Religion

Classicists who have studied the early forms of European tribal religion in Greece and Rome, and anthropologists who have focused on the tribal religions of "primitive" (preliterate or oral) cultures, have highlighted the communal and wholistic character of their religions. Their lack of differentiation between the sacred and secular makes it easier to discern both the power of religion to shape all of life's relations and its narrow relativity when relational concerns are limited to the needs and interests of only one's own tribe. The relation of tribal religion to the whole of life, and the tragic fact that tribal conflicts have been so obvious a part of that whole too much of the time, has led war to be "regarded as a religious activity, to be surrounded with prayer, ritual, sacrifice, and purification."[7]

Both the power and relativity of religion remain as societies become larger and more complex through a long history, but their interpretation becomes correspondingly more difficult. Gerald Larson provides a telling illustration of this complexity in the ceremony called "Beating Retreat" celebrated in New Delhi on India's Republic Day, January 26, which commemorates the inauguration of the postcolonial Republic of India. At its culmination at sunset, in the presence of the president, prime minister

and cabinet, the military bands of this largely Hindu and Muslim society
play the Christian hymn:

> Abide with me; fast falls the eventide;
> The darkness deepens; Lord, with me abide!
> When other helpers fail, and comforts flee,
> Help of the helpless, O abide with me.

Larson comments after experiencing this event in 1987: "Here was the
modern, secular nation-state of India with its largely Hindu and Muslim
population . . . nevertheless celebrating and remembering its emergence
into freedom after centuries of imperial domination with an old Christian
hymn."[8]

This astonishing illustration of contemporary cross-cultural and interreligious ritual is also interesting from a philosophical standpoint because
Alfred North Whitehead designated exactly this hymn as "the best ren-
dering of integral experience" he knew, since it expresses so clearly the
"permanences amid the inescapable flux." Perhaps it is for this reason, as
much as any lingering influence of colonial history, that a particular religious expression can function universally in a transcultural and interreligious setting. Whitehead's comment was:

> The best rendering of integral experience, expressing its general form
> divested of irrelevant details, is often to be found in the utterance of
> religious aspiration. One of the reasons for the thinness of so much
> modern metaphysics is its neglect of this wealth of expression of ulti-
> mate feeling.[9]

When Whitehead came to his own final interpretation of what he
considered humanity's ultimate feeling, he reverted to a discussion of the
metaphysical meaning of this hymn:

> In a previous chapter (Part II, Ch. X) attention has already been drawn
> to the sense of permanence dominating the invocation "Abide with
> me," and the sense of flux dominating the sequel "Fast falls the even-
> tide." Ideals fashion themselves round these two notions, permanence
> and flux. In the inescapable flux, there is something that abides; in the
> overwhelming permanence, there is an element that escapes into flux.
> Permanence can be snatched only out of flux; and the passing moment
> can find its adequate intensity only by its submission to permanence.
> Those who would disjoin the two elements can find no interpretation of
> patent facts.[10]

We too often disjoin relatively permanent traditions from the processes of change, increasing our difficulty of understanding contemporary
events. One "patent fact" that has become even more obvious in the last
decade of the twentieth century—in contrast to the secularity intended by
the government of modern India—is the continuing attempt of many, in

various ways, to protect the permanent meanings that they believe only a religion wedded to the cultural traditions of ancient ethnic structures may give. Orthodox Serbs and Catholic Croats are willing to destroy what little inclusive unity southern Slavs have had to this end, and both are even more willing at this writing to destroy what was the Muslim majority of Bosnia for the sake of a greater Serbia or Croatia. Muslim Azeris and Christian Armenians are involved in similarly murderous conflict in what was once the Soviet Union, as are the Jewish Israelis and predominantly Muslim Arabs in the Middle East, and the Protestant Scotch-Irish and the Roman Catholic Irish in Ireland. And the terrible list may be extended to the India of our illustration, where Sikhs and Muslims in the north seek autonomy from the Hindu majority, while Sri Lankan Buddhists and Tamil Hindus on the island off India's southern coast mix religious and ethnic motives in their deadly conflict.

We who are committed to the historical flux moving our world toward a planetary culture are often confused as to what attitude and action we should take toward the continuing and seemingly permanent nationalisms that remain so dynamic. Are they only to be deplored and resisted as a continuing source of the narrow loyalties that breed conflict and violence at their margins? But if so, how shall we interpret, and what shall we substitute for, their power to create community at their center?

It appears as true for establishing peace through social unities as it is for the religious redemptions discussed in chapter 3 that an abstract universal is almost powerless as a substitute for the concrete universals of particular communities. Unless one becomes able to serve his or her family and village, as Gandhi used to insist, there is little possibility of genuine service to any global village.[11] Ideological universals may provide critical criteria for interpreting reality, but the superficial play of discursive ideas is not powerful enough to transform it.

The power of religion to create ethnic and national communities must be appreciated if it is to be appropriated to help create a more universal planetary community.[12] The only universal we may ever hope to help co-create is a relational universal that builds upon the creative and redemptive relations that the universal God already and perhaps everlastingly has with the nations. Any attempt to substitute some abstract ideological universal for the concrete and contextual universals that God already has co-created with our actual brothers and sisters shall not succeed. Nationalism shall, and probably should, continue in the foreseeable future to play a role in the universal relationality of peace.

A review of some relevant aspects of the religious histories of India and Europe may elucidate this point. Large and complex societies with long histories provide microcosmic examples of what we now face on a macrocosmic world scale. While in Kottayam in 1974 and Bangalore in 1975 in meetings of the Christian Peace Conference, one of the greatest concerns of our Indian hosts was what they called "communalism." Given the religious strife in India then and since, punctuated by the assassinations of Prime Ministers Indira Gandhi and Rajiv Gandhi, their concern was more urgent and realistic than we could then realize. These murdered leaders with a relatively secular worldview sought to govern a society shaped by Hinduism, well characterized by John Ferguson as "a vastly extended and developed form of tribal religion."[13] Because it has been vastly extended and developed over a long history, Hinduism embraces a wide variety of beliefs, but because it nevertheless remains a national form of tribal religion, it demands a broad acceptance of the Hindu way of life. Mahatma Gandhi, though a faithful Hindu, paid with his life for advocating a political role for the Muslim minority in the new Indian Republic, which was felt by some Hindus more tribal than he to endanger their way of life.

There are regions and periods in Indian history, however, where the tribal character of Hinduism has been opened to more peaceful cross-cultural and interreligious relations. Kerala, the site of our 1974 conference on the southern tip of India, has long been a commercial crossroads, whose people have experienced many cross-cultural and interreligious influences. It is thus the only place in the world, so far as I know, where Hindus live in such numerical equivalence and equilibrium with Muslims and Christians; approximately 60 percent of Kerala's population are Hindus and 20 percent each are Christians and Muslims. Kerala's Christians claim their origin from the first-century apostolic mission of Thomas, and have been there as Syrian traders at least since the fourth century. Arabs, who controlled the Indian ocean trade before the Christian Portuguese, also came to Kerala in that capacity both before and after their submission to Islam.

On the basis of admittedly inadequate sources, Roland E. Miller concludes that interreligious harmony prevailed in Kerala from the eighth through the fifteenth centuries: "The Syrian Christians and Arab Muslims were predominantly traders, and they collaborated with the Hindu rajas and merchants to establish a flourishing trade with China, the Middle East, and Europe."[14] Whatever the degree of cooperation achieved in those centuries—even if only economic—it was brought to an end in the sixteenth century when the Portuguese took imperial control of its trade. Roland Miller interprets the tragedy of this development:

> With the coming of the fifteenth century, the age of harmony based on commerce moved to an age of rivalry based on economic and political domination; the period was also characterized by a militant religious flavor. The people who ushered in the new age were the Portuguese, agents of manifest destiny, and the partly unwitting destroyers of a precious interreligious harmony. . . . Within a century the patterns of

interreligious living were radically altered, and up to the twentieth century we have a history of rivalry, deteriorating relations—especially between Hindus and Muslims—and a great deal of tragic violence.[15]

These fifteenth-century events were only the beginning of the colonialist confrontation of Indian religious tribalism with a European Christian tribalism, whose "universal" pope dared to divide and bequeath the unexplored non-European worlds to Portugal and Spain for religious and commercial conquest.[16] King Manuel of Portugal gave the following Christian, albeit inhuman, instruction to Pedro Cabral before he set out in 1502 on the second Portuguese voyage to what is now Kerala:

> In order to persuade these people to accept the truth, the priests and friars were to put before them all natural and legal arguments, and employ ceremonies prescribed by Canon Law. And if these people were stubborn in their errors, and would in no wise accept the tenets of the true faith, denying the law of peace which should unite mankind for the preservation of the human race, and raising difficulties and obstacles to the exercise of trade and commerce, the means by which peace and love among men are established and maintained—for trade is the basis of all human policy—they should in this case be taught by fire and sword and all the horrors of war.[17]

We have examined in chapter 4 the Enlightenment's flawed attempt to curb the excesses of European religious fanaticism by subsuming religion under the canons of universal reason. Motilal Nehru, India's first prime minister after regaining independence from Portuguese colonialism continued by the British, attempted something similar there. A secular India was to transcend Hindu tribalism with a nonreligious rationality that respected religion in general and provided equality for all of its expressions. Communal differences were to be resolved in the interest of the good of the whole nation. Religious and cultural differences would remain, of course, but would be subsumed in, and moderated by, the growing national consciousness of simply being "Indian." The failure of this policy cost the lives of his daughter and grandson, who followed him in this high office. For many of their fellow citizens, both for good and for ill, the consciousness of being Indian correlates with the consciousness of being Hindu; and purely rational resources pale for many in contrast to the spiritual power of their traditional religion.

### European Religio-Nationalism

Euro-American cultures have been struggling to relearn this lesson of the relative permanence and spasmodic virulence of religio-nationalisms after struggling for the past two centuries to replace them with more

modern nationalistic ideologies. After Europe's second thirty years war of
1915–45, three hundred years after the first had ended with the Treaty of
Westphalia in 1648, Salo Baron sought to draw its lessons. It was no
accident that he was the greatest living scholar of the social and religious
history of the Jews, for his people had suffered the most from the virulence of continuing European religio-nationalisms. Among the sources of
his peoples' agony cited by Baron was the profession of faith formulated
by the Congress of German Christians in Nazi Germany in April 1933:

> God has created me a German; Germanism is a gift of God. God wills
> it that I fight for Germany. War service in no way injures the Christian
> conscience, but is obedience to God. . . . For a German the church is a
> community of believers, which is under the obligation to fight for a
> Christian Germany.[18]

Despite the great suffering of his people caused by religio-
nationalism, Baron still affirmed its value in his own faith. It is crucial
to note, however, that he carefully differentiated the *cultural* form of
religio-nationalism, which he supported, from its *political* form, which
has so often proven virulent and destructive in subsequent Middle Eastern and Euro-American histories. Commenting on the roots of "Jewish
ethnicism" in Deuteronomy, he wrote: "The Israelitic prophets and
priests may thus be designated the first exponents of a *religious and
cultural nationalism*, in which culture was equated with religion but in
which *all political aspirations were considered secondary*."[19] Although biblical Israel's cultural form of religio-nationalism was conditioned by military weakness in the face of Assyria, Babylonia, and Egypt, and was
rejected by a more royal theology, Baron nevertheless found it at the
heart of Jewish faith:

> With an enthusiasm often called disloyal but tested by subsequent his-
> tory as the main safeguard for Jewish survival, these immortal leaders
> viewed the victorious enemy as but a "rod of God's anger" and the
> downfall of their country as part of the divine guidance of history. . . .
> Of course, they did not object to their people's political self-determina-
> tion. But they found harsh words to castigate the abuses of power poli-
> tics and the monarchy, the social inequalities and the degradation of the
> poorer members of an essentially egalitarian community—all of which
> had appeared to advocates of the established order as but natural conse-
> quences of state rule and landownership.[20]

A more recent interpreter of religio-nationalism in the "history of
American civilization" fails to note Baron's careful distinction between the
cultural and political forms of biblical nationalism. Conor Cruise
O'Brien, who suffers the ravages of religio-nationalism in his native Ire-

land, simply asserts that the nationalism of Euro-American cultures began with the Bible:

> Nationalism, as a collective emotional force in our culture, makes its first appearance, with explosive impact, in the Hebrew Bible. And nationalism, at this stage, is altogether indistinguishable from religion; the two are one and the same thing. God chose a particular people and promised them a particular land.[21]

It is the repeated promise of "a particular land" in the books of Genesis and Exodus[22] that focuses O'Brien's interpretation, for its literal application to quite different societies by sixteenth- and seventeenth-century Christians has continued to affect even secularized forms of European and American nationalism ever since. It was primarily for this reason, after Europe suffered its first thirty years war, that the God who presumably inspired it was rejected or radically reinterpreted. The Enlightenment sought to reduce/exalt the biblical God to a remote First Cause who could no longer have anything to do with the concrete life of any nation.

Even enlightened thinkers, however, had to interpret the religious dimensions of the concrete dynamics of a people and their land. Baruch (Benedict) Spinoza, as an enlightened Jew, still affirmed in his *Tractatus* the identity of nationalism and true religion: "There is no doubt that devotion to country is the highest form of piety a man can show; for once the state is destroyed nothing good can survive."[23] David Ben-Gurion, the first prime minister of modern Israel, appealed to the rabbinate to revoke Spinoza's 1656 excommunication from Judaism after three centuries, perhaps especially because Spinoza also made a telling prediction concerning the future of his fellow Jews: "Did not the principles of their religion make them effeminate, I should be quite convinced that one day when opportunity arises—so mutable are human affairs—they will establish their state once more and that God will choose them afresh."[24]

Modern enlightened Israelis have ceased to be "effeminate," as especially every Palestinian knows, and the opportunity for Ben-Gurion and other Zionists did arise in 1948 and seemed to be secured in 1967. Many Jews of the dispersion, as Spinoza knew them, also are no longer willing to be what Salo Baron called a "permanent and universal minority."[25] This may be understandable and even acceptable in the enlightened perspective of *Realpolitik*. It is ironic, however, that it comes at a time when many are seeking to recover from virulent nationalisms—with the help of the Hebrew prophets—to learn to live as permanent and universal minorities in the universal relationality of God.

The nationalism that was only a small part of Spinoza's Jewish rationalism was larger and clearer in Rousseau's enlightened Christian philosophy. Just as Spinoza was steeped in a dissident form of Judaism, so

Rousseau was steeped in a secularized form of Calvinism. Jean-Jacques Rousseau was born and brought up in Geneva, where the Old Testament promises of the land had been interpreted literally with such powerful political effect—not only in Switzerland, but reaching to Hungary, Holland, Scotland, Puritan England, and New England—and from there into American "civil religion." But Calvinist Geneva was past and largely passé for Rousseau and his cohorts. O'Brien writes: "Rousseau's great achievement was to 'fix' the emotional loyalties formerly associated with religion and now displaced. He diverted these loyalties toward the nation and exalted it into an absolute, in the *Social Contract*, through the concept of The General Will."[26]

O'Brien illustrates the way in which the French nation assumed divine functions for many after the revolution by quoting Jules Michelet, its historian: "It is from you that I shall ask for help, my noble country: you must take the place of the God who escapes us, that you may fill within us the immeasurable abyss which extinct Christianity has left there."[27] Those of us who have lived long in the twentieth century have heard much the same sentiment in the political rhetoric of Charles de Gaulle, echoing in the mostly empty churches of secularized France. But not only there. Some of us have also heard its more explicit religio-nationalist echoes in quite full churches from Ronald Reagan and his cohorts of the Moral Majority in the United States of America.

The dangers posed by these modern but all too traditional nationalisms have led to several attempts to overcome their narrowness and heal their virulence by creating international structures during our century. We have suffered in this century the earlier failure of the League of Nations, and the more recent failure of the Communist International, while the fate of the United Nations hangs in the balance. Analysis of the recent Communist failure to achieve a genuine internationalism may help us move with and through the communal dynamics of religio-nationalism, while overcoming its malignant narrowness, so as to help co-create a more genuine internationalism and universally relational peace.

## The Failure of Imposed Internationalism

Marxism-Leninism, presuming the virtual extinction of religion in enlightened Europe, sought to create what must now be recognized as a failed form of internationalism. The early forms of this failure also had far-reaching consequences for the development of European theology. The failure of the European Social Democratic parties to overcome their own nationalisms during World War I led Karl Barth early in his ministry to rethink the basis for his theology, as well as his continuing commitment to socialism.[28] Barth was also deeply disappointed by the development of Leninist centralism in the Russian revolution, which at first he had greeted with enthusiasm while serving as the "red Pastor of Safenwil" in Switzerland.

Lenin had early appointed Stalin to be the party's expert on the "nationality problem," perhaps because Stalin/Dzhugashvili was a Georgian in a largely Russian party. As Stalin later developed Leninist centralism to monstrous proportions, he defined his policy for dealing with the nationality problem in his report to the Sixteenth Party Congress in 1930:

> We must let the national cultures develop and expand, revealing all their potential qualities, in order to create the necessary conditions for fusing them into one common culture with one common tongue. The flourishing of cultures, national in form and socialist in content, in the conditions of a proletarian dictatorship in one country, for the *purpose* of their fusion into one common socialist culture, common both in form and in content, with one common tongue, when the proletariat is victorious throughout the world and socialism becomes an everyday matter—in this lies the dialectical quality of the Leninist way of treating the question of national cultures.[29]

Stalin's style of "proletarian dictatorship" imposed for seventy years a kind of international peace on the more than one hundred ethnic groups comprising the Soviet Union, but with so heavy and terrible a hand that almost nothing of their transformation or fusion had occurred when the Soviet Union unraveled in 1990.

The same failure occurred in the dissident form of communism led by Josip Broz Tito in Yugoslavia, though it provided the southern Slavs with the longest period of peace they have known in centuries. The artificiality of its forced imposition has become clear, however, as Yugoslavia has disintegrated into conflicting nations again, and nowhere more tragically than in Bosnia. "Although a separate Bosnian republic was created [by Tito's government] precisely to prevent either Croatia or Serbia from dominating the postwar federation,"[30] according to Pedro Ramet, at this writing Croatia and Serbia are in the process of destroying Bosnia, and especially its Muslim population, for their own territorial and political aggrandizement.

The truth of Salo Baron's analysis and evaluation of Yugoslavia's disintegration at the beginning and end of the thirty years war from 1914 to 1945 has become obvious again forty-five years after he wrote it:

> Descended from the same Slavonic group, speaking the same language with minor dialectical deviations, the two peoples have considered themselves separate nationalities only because of an historic accident. The Croats had been converted to Roman Catholicism and hence adopted the Latin alphabet, while the Serbs followed the Church of

Constantinople and used the specific Slavonic script going under the name of their Greek apostle, St. Cyril. *We have all learned with dismay what tragic effects the overhasty attempts at merging both peoples into a new Yugoslav nationality had for the peace and security of that entire region.*[31]

Whether or not the religiocultural separation of the Serbs and Croats should be considered an accident, and I think it was not,[32] the Communist attempt to merge them into a more inclusive national consciousness on the basis of a common socialist ideology has again tragically failed.

One of the lessons of the failure of the nationalities policies of Communist societies is that any attempt *to impose* larger social unities is destined for failure. Nevertheless, Salo Baron's lament is salient:

> It was perhaps the greatest tragedy of our era that the two major genuinely international movements, Catholicism and communism (or what the Nazis chose to call the Black and Red Internationals), through their mutual hostility largely neutralized each other's efforts in combatting excessive nationalism.[33]

There is also a salient difference, however, between Catholicism and communism. The Roman Catholic Church, at least in its best moments, knew that excessive nationalism cannot be combated by imposing some more inclusive unity. As Europe's second thirty years war moved toward its culminating agony, Pope Pius XII's Christmas message of 1941 declared: "Within the limits of a new order founded on moral principles there is no place for open or secret oppression of the cultural and linguistic characteristics of national minorities, nor the hindrance or restriction of their economic resources, nor the limitation or abolition of their natural fertility."[34]

Nevertheless, the church in the West, stressing its catholic/universal character, has sought to relativize national distinctions in a way that the Eastern churches did not. The Eastern Orthodox tradition of autocephalous patriarchates, with the Ecumenical Patriarch of Constantinople being only first among equals, led to a closer symphony of Christianity with nationalism. The Russian Orthodox Church, therefore, is almost as Russian as it is Orthodox, and the same can be said for Bulgaria, Greece, Romania, Serbia, etc. Pedro Ramet has good evidence for his assertion that "the Serbian Orthodox Church is . . . probably more nationalistic than any other religious organization in Yugoslavia."[35] That comparison, of course, included the Roman Catholic Church of Croatia, which is also nationalistic enough.

The national form of church polity in Byzantium was strengthened by the *millet* system of the Ottoman Empire that vanquished it. Islamic understandings of religion and society led them to assign representative and administrative functions to the churches of the nations that comprised their empire. Leopold von Ranke's judgment that "in most periods of world history nations were held together by religious ties alone,"[36] seems particularly apt for the nations of Eastern Europe throughout their histories in the Byzantine and Muslim empires.

### Eastern European Experience
### Under Communism

It was especially tragic then that atheistic communism sought to impose its form of internationalism among peoples whose nationalism had been so deeply formed and carried by their religion. The kind of conflict to which it led between religio-nationalism—whether underground or officially tolerated—and ideologically imposed universalism could not be long endured. What Spas Raikin says of Bulgaria is largely true for the whole area: "Bulgarian nationalism was born, bred, nursed, and sustained for 1,100 years by the national Orthodox church."[37] When Patriarch Maxim was finally able to visit Bulgarians in the United States in 1978, after three decades of Communist rule, he called on Bulgarians, in the same way that other Patriarchs would have called upon their ethnic faithful, to "bow down with humility before the altar of Bulgarian sanctity, the heroes of spirit and self-sacrifices in the name of faith and church, of nationhood and Slavic brotherhood."[38]

The fervent Romanian nationalism fostered by the Communist regime of Ceauşescu in the 1970s and 1980s, in contrast to other Communist states, allowed the historic role of their church again to be publicly, though very carefully, acknowledged.[39] Now that the care of the Communist regime to manage this religio-nationalism has been overthrown, it has even greater, and sometimes more destructive, scope for its expression.

Poland's nationalism is unique among the states that were ruled by Communist parties because the Polish people are so predominantly Roman Catholic. The Polish church, however, is arguably the most national of the Roman Catholic churches in the world. They are the last, so far as I know, to have their own "Primate," the archbishop of Gniezno and Warsaw. Though not an Orthodox patriarch, he has sometimes functioned with more autocephaly than the Vatican preferred. Cardinal Wyszynski, the revered Primate through most of the Communist years, used the more Orthodox metaphor of body and soul to express the relation between his church and the nation. Wyszynski understood the church as a "Polish Church," not just the church in Poland:

> Since in the temporal order, the nation was the most perfect human community, it became a particularly appropriate subject for the embodiment of the universal church. Thus, with God's will, there came into

existence a truly authentic "Church on the Vistula"—the "Polish Church," and not just the Church in Poland. The church formed a locus for the creative convergence of religious and secular life and, in the course of common history, developed great social awareness, close communication with the community, and a unique ability of adaptation to the changing environment.[40]

Everyone knows the national power of the Polish church in the events that transformed Poland during the past decade.[41]

The lack of an Orthodox tradition in Hungary makes it the exception to this rule among former East European states. Leslie Laszlo says, "In today's Hungary nationalism has precious little to do with religion or the churches."[42] The fact that it was a Calvinistic minority that led Hungary's nationalistic struggle against the Catholic Hapsburgs undoubtedly has contributed to the more secular form of its contemporary nationalism. The continuing power of Calvinism in Hungarian nationalism remains clear, however, when one looks at Transylvania and sees the role played by that church's leaders, notably Bishop Tokes, in their struggle for autonomy in Romania.

*Dialectical Conclusions*
*Concerning Religio-Nationalism*

The conclusions I draw from this reflection on the complex relations of religion to nationalism and the failure of imposed forms of internationalism are at least three: The first is that religion has played and continues to play a dynamic and probably indispensable role in the creation of national cultures and societies. The logic of panentheistic theology also expects God's everlastingly repeated lure to loving and just relations, contextualized over a long history in the dynamics of a people, to create families, tribes, and nations. To recognize and celebrate the creation of such community belongs to the essential functions of religion. Thus some form of religio-nationalism constitutes the permanent memories and shall continue to constitute the social identity of most peoples. Any enlightened rejection of cultural forms of religio-nationalism is not only at our peril but to the peril of many who shall resist such enlightened resistance even to the death.

Euro-American peoples with a Judeo-Christian culture have a more difficult time understanding this point for cultures formed by other religions. Thus, we all too often misinterpret the role of Islam in Middle Eastern or Central Asian nations. A specialist in nationality issues in the central Asian republics of the former Soviet Union recently made this point about her work as a peace fellow in the U.S. Institute of Peace. Nancy Lubin wrote:

Islam has become a real catchword here in Washington for what is going on in Central Asia, and I think that kind of oversimplification can have a dangerous impact. Normally when we talk about the growth of Islam, it's as if it's a very threatening trend for us and I think that's misleading. There has definitely been a greater turn toward Islam as a religion, a culture, and a tradition. But it's not necessarily a political Islam, a fundamentalist Islam, or an anti-Western Islam. The more we look at Central Asia through the prism of Islam as a potential threat, the more we make it clear to new leaders that that's the way we define Central Asia, and the more we may encourage the growth of radical forces.[43]

The increasingly obvious perils of religio-nationalism, however, are the basis for the second conclusion: Beginning with European colonialism and continuing through the increasingly transnational character of contemporary corporations, commerce, and communication, we are well into an era where our permanent national identities may no longer rigidly delimit the communal boundaries that God is now calling us to co-create. We now resist this cross-cultural and interreligious flux toward a planetary society to our great spiritual peril, as well as at the peril of ecological, if not nuclear, disaster. The sovereign nation-state, therefore, is not the necessary or only form that continuing nationalism may take. Indeed, the terrible consequences of ignoring or misinterpreting the biblical-prophetic distinction between cultural and political religio-nationalism in modern European history should teach us that the modern nation-state is one of the most dangerous forms of nationalism.

The paroxysm of renewed religio-nationalisms that Europe is now suffering at the demise of the imposed supranationalism of communism, is occurring, as it were, on top of thousands of nuclear warheads, and under increasing ozone holes in our one and only planetary atmosphere. Thus we must find ways of mediating the permanent values of our religio-nationalisms in the process of creating the religious ethos of a universal human community. Though much of the contemporary supranational context is being created by technology and commerce, as mutually beneficial trade was once the basis for a period of peace in Kerala, it does not provide now, as it did not then, either the spiritual community or the value commitments necessary to create a sustainable universal ethos.

The necessity of creating a universal religious ethos leads directly to the third conclusion: We must reaffirm, and if necessary relearn, the wisdom of the Hebrew prophets in disjoining cultural from political religio-nationalism. The Calvinistic reformer's literal interpretation of the biblical promises of the land for the political benefit of particular peoples in sixteenth-century Europe tragically reunited the religiocultural and political nationalisms that Israel's prophets had wisely disjoined and some contemporary Israelis unwisely rejoin. The horror of the first thirty years war in the seventeenth century, spawned by this renewed religiopolitical nationalism, led the Enlightenment in the eighteenth century to remove the biblical God to a Deist heaven or agnostically banish "him" from any involvement in human affairs.

Euro-Americans were then left with absolutely sovereign nation-states whose unlimited political nationalisms, no longer "under God," might take idolatrous forms, and whose cultures could become demonic under the illusion that they were the leading edge of evolutionary progress.[44] Much of the rest of the world had to suffer their hegemony as sovereign European nations struggled for colonialist empire in Africa, the Americas, and Asia. The result was the second thirty years war of 1915–45, more horrible than the first. Its treaty of Westphalia worked out in San Francisco in 1945 has thus far given us little more than the oxymoron of the United Nations, which will only become what humanity now requires when we develop the religiocultural process to co-create the universally relational ethos necessary for its authentic political concretion.

The contemporary spiritual task of co-creating a universally relational religious ethos, which now responds to the *universal* relationality of God with the same spirit that religious nationalism had responded to the contextual *relationality* of the same God, brings us to the next part of our discussion: differentiating religio-national messianism from universal relationality.

## Transforming Religio-National Messianisms

Paul Tillich was one of the creative theologians formed during Euro-America's second thirty years war, after a century of European peace from 1815 to 1914. He sometimes remarked that the nineteenth century did not end in 1900 but in 1914 at the beginning of World War I, to indicate how fundamental was the social transition in European life marked by that terrible war. The end of that war also marked the beginning of his career as a professional theologian, at first in the University of Berlin. In terms made familiar to many who became his students, he considered those early years after the war a *kairos* pregnant with new possibilities for a theonomous age to heal the destructive gap between heteronomous religion and autonomous secular culture that had developed in Europe during the long struggle between the Enlightenment and the churches.

The failure of the Weimar Republic, the rise of Nazism, his removal to the United States as a German refugee, and finally World War II, led Tillich to conclude that "history took another path, and the question of religion and culture cannot be answered simply in those terms."[45] Indeed, his total experience of, and between, those two wars so reversed his sense of *kairos*, that he concluded Euro-Americans were now living through a period that could only be metaphorically described as "a void, an unfilled space, a vacuum."[46] Our second thirty years war had left even those of us who did not suffer its physical devastation spiritually in a cultural wasteland:

> Little is left in our present civilization which does not indicate to a sensitive mind the presence of this vacuum, this lack of ultimacy and substantial power in language and education, in politics and philosophy, in the development of personalities, and in the life of communities.[47]

Tillich put these meditations under the title "The Protestant Era" to indicate the religious era that was ending for Euro-Americans. The autonomy of scientific reason and the emptiness of technocratic culture had brought us to a sacred void that required a new beginning. The new beginning Tillich sought to make in the last years before his death was the study of non-European religions. Mircea Eliade remarks on the tremendous impact that Tillich's voyage to Japan had upon his life and thought: "For the first time he had immersed himself in a living and extremely varied religious milieu which was completely different from that of the Mediterranean and Judaeo-Christian traditions."[48]

Tillich's reflection on that experience and the seminars on the history of religions he taught with Eliade led him to conclude that "the inner aim of the history of religions is to become a Religion of the Concrete Spirit." But he cautioned, "we cannot identify this Religion of the Concrete Spirit with any actual religion, not even Christianity as a religion."[49] The last lecture he ever gave, from which these sentences come, was too brief to provide adequate definition of what he envisioned, but Tillich pointed toward the "possibility of understanding religious symbols in relation to the social matrix within which they have grown and into which we have to reintroduce them today."[50] The original social matrix for our religious symbols was tribal or national, while the new matrix into which they must now be reintroduced is transnational and universal. In Gadamer's terms, we must fuse their national horizons with our moving universal horizon. Tillich's concrete spirit then would be, in panentheistic terms, that moment of sociopersonal concretion where one "com-prehends" her or his internal relations to ever more inclusive prehensions of what God has been and is doing, both in one's own religiocultural history and in universal history as mediated through the symbols and narratives carried in the traditions of many religious communities.

Part of Tillich's sense of void and vacuum at the end of World War II arose from his judgment that neither of the superpowers then emerging as dominant had the cultural or religious resources to meet the challenges of a new era—just as his own Germany had proven not to have after World War I. He feared, with good reason, a repetition in the U.S.A and the U.S.S.R. of what had occurred in Germany after World War I, where even some able theologians had supported what became a demonic national religion. His brilliant friend Emmanuel Hirsch had published *Germany's Destiny* in 1920, articulating a relation between the Christian faith and the German *Volk* that finally led Hirsch to support Hitler's regime:

> Faith in God gives us two things that are crucial for our *Volk*. The one is . . . a clear sense of humanity and history, of *Volk* and State, which sharpens right and duty in our conscience so that we can do and suffer everything for our own *Volk* and our own State transcending our own person.[51]

Though Tillich never postulated the absolute separation between a wholly other God and a people, culture, or state, as Karl Barth had done to forestall the dangers of just such culture religion as Hirsch espoused, he also had discerned from the beginning the idolatrous tendency of Hirsch's kind of theology.

Hirsch finally went so far as to describe Hitler as "the voice of God to the German people," which Tillich found both then and later "incomprehensible and abhorrent."[52] Nevertheless, Hitler's voice had dominated the German people for more than a decade, perhaps because he had understood and exploited their spiritual weakness as defined in *Mein Kampf*:

> Like the woman, whose psychic state is determined less by grounds of abstract reason than by an indefinable emotional longing for a force which will complement her nature and who, consequently, would rather bow to a strong man than dominate a weakling, likewise the masses love a commander more than a petitioner and feel inwardly more satisfied by a doctrine, tolerating no other beside itself, than by the granting of liberalistic freedom with which, as a rule, they can do little, and are prone to feel that they have been abandoned.[53]

Ernest Koenker, studying the period Tillich lived through, concluded that "the erection of the National Socialist [Nazi] spiritual center can only be understood in its relation to the breakdown of the spiritual center which Christianity provided for the heart of Europe."[54] What Tillich first sensed as a spiritual *kairos* of new and creative possibilities turned out to be a void that national ideologues like Hitler could demonically fill for a time with such destructive consequences.

There is no guarantee that any attempt to fill the spiritual void at the heart of our emerging planetary culture, which thus far shares little more than the technocratic values of international commerce with which to construct its common good, will not result in some similar idolatry. We still have reason to fear that any attempts to make the universal relationality of God concrete in any particular spirituality and theology may only be an idolatrous extension of one or another of our religio-national messianisms. "Messianism" in this context means the idolatrous notion of a people that their destiny as God's elect is to bring the whole of history to fulfillment. American civil religion and Russian slavophilism have sufficient messianism of this kind to make anyone trained by Tillich (to say nothing of Barth) doubt whether any attempt by religious leaders in either of the superpowers to provide a universal spirituality could be anything other than idolatrous.

### North American Civil Religion

Conor O'Brien humorously illustrates this idolatrous danger by recounting a prayer with which the annual national prayer breakfast in Washington, D.C., was begun in 1985. The presiding Congressman prayed: "In the excitement of the presence of the President of the United States of America, help us to remember the presence of Your Son, Jesus Christ." And O'Brien comments: "I looked round at my neighbors, but none of them seemed to find anything incongruous about the idea that Reagan might upstage Jesus, unless the Father threw His weight into the balance."[55] Perhaps only someone from outside the United States could fully sense the incongruity. To the degree that is so, those of us who do theology in sermons or books within the United States need dialogue with "foreigners" like O'Brien who may help transform our insularity.

When Winthrop Hudson surveyed the "concepts of American identity and mission" in his *Nationalism and Religion in America* in 1970, he saw "a robust faith in a living God (judging, correcting, disciplining, guiding, and directing the American people) being slowly eroded and reduced to the pale affirmations of twentieth-century 'civil religion.' "[56] Perhaps some of the theological affirmations were becoming pale, but the nationalistic assertions clearly remained then and now all too robust.

The nationalism of American civil religion derives directly from the religio-nationalism developed in the Puritan revolutions, which Hans Kohn characterized as "the first example of modern nationalism" where a people was "roused and stirred to its innermost depths, feeling upon its shoulders the mission of history."[57] Puritan notions of God's election and providence guiding the chosen people toward messianic fulfillment were often reflected in the political rhetoric of President Ronald Reagan. His favorite religious metaphor for the United States was the "city on a hill," derived from the Bible but popularized by our Puritan ancestors. John Milton had written of Cromwell's England that it "should set up a standard for the recovery of lost truth and blow the first evangelic trumpet to the nations, holding up, as from a hill, the new lamp of *saving light to all* Christendom."[58] It was exactly this saving light to all (and not any longer only to all Christendom) that so dangerously inspired Reagan and many other Americans. It remained as robust for Reagan in the twentieth century as it had been for Cotton Mather, who preached to Puritan congregations in seventeenth-century New England that it was God's intention that the "scripture-pattern" they/we were establishing in America "shall in due time be accomplished *the whole world throughout.*"[59]

The point of this discussion, of course, is not a polemic against Puritanism. Charles J. Little, who became the president of the Methodist institution where I now teach, made much the same point to the General Missionary Committee of the Methodist Episcopal Church a century ago, when he rhetorically extended the western frontier of North America to include the whole world:

> For when our nation appeared among men, it was like the rising of the sun to thousands who had watched and waited for the morning. The burdened of the earth rejoiced and their gladness filled them with new strength, for they beheld a land where all men are brothers, where love was the light of the people and liberty clasped hands with law. . . .
>
> And beyond us on the west looms up the Day of Judgment. For yonder on our vast frontiers where gathered multitudes shall weave for America in the twentieth century either a garment of glory or a shroud; yonder across the blue Pacific where China stands sullen but slowly yielding to the light, where Japan is thrilling with new purpose and new experience; where India verges swiftly to some great surprise, there is our Day of Judgment.[60]

Little's rhetoric was primarily directed to the church, but his Methodist brother Sen. Albert Beveridge knew how to say much the same thing in a political idiom to justify the United States' colonial governance of Cuba, the Philippines, and Puerto Rico after taking them from Spain:

> The sovereign tendencies of our race are organization and government. We govern so well that we govern ourselves. . . . In America it wove out of segregated settlements that complex and wonderful organization called the American Republic. Everywhere it builds. Everywhere it governs. Everywhere it administers order and law. Everywhere it is the spirit of regulated liberty. Everywhere it obeys that Voice not to be denied which bids us strive and rest not, makes us our brothers' keeper and appoints us *steward under God of the civilization of the world.*[61]

What grows pale in this kind of idolatrous nationalism is any sense of the transcendent, universal wisdom of God, which sets a limit to our self-appropriation of God's messianic functions, while the sense of a universal spiritual destiny under God grows ever stronger. What is forgotten in this kind of nationalism is the humility of Abraham Lincoln's "almost" in his sense of Americans as "the almost chosen people," while all emphasis falls on being divinely "chosen."[62]

These are issues that no theology dare forget. Part of Reinhold Niebuhr's service to American society as its preeminent theologian in the past
generation was that he did not allow us to forget these limits, even when
he supported the United States government's policies and sometimes also
its polemics:

> The communists are dangerous not because they are godless but be-
> cause they have a god (the historical dialectic) who, or which, sanctifies
> their aspiration and their power as identical with the ultimate purposes
> of life. We on the other hand, as all "God-fearing" men of all ages, are
> never safe against the temptation of claiming God too simply as the
> sanctifier of whatever we most fervently desire. Even the most "Chris-
> tian" civilization and even the most pious church must be reminded that
> the true God can be known only where there is some awareness of a
> contradiction between divine and human purposes, even on the highest
> level of human aspirations.[63]

### Russian Slavophilism

Russian spirituality has had its own messianic tendencies (ironically
appropriated even by its Communists), so that when Pedro Ramet wanted
to illustrate religious nationalism he could find nothing better than Fy-
odor Dostoevsky's affirmation that the Russian people are "the only God-
Bearing people in the whole world, slated to revive and save the world."[64]
How close Dostoevsky's Slavophil version of religious idealism could
come to the universal relationality we are seeking to understand is evident
in the address he gave honoring the great Russian author Pushkin, who
remained celebrated even during the Communist period:

> Yes, the vocation of the Russian man . . . is doubtless universal-European
> and even ecumenical. To become a true Russian, entirely Russian, means
> (perhaps only in the last issue, please emphasize this) to be brother of
> every man, to become an "All-man," if you wish. . . . To become then
> truly Russian means to provide the solution of European contradictions
> . . . to receive with brotherly love all brothers into his Russian soul, and
> perhaps even finally to be able to utter the word of universal great har-
> mony, of final brotherly concord between nations, according to Christ's
> commandments.[65]

To think that "the word of universal great harmony" is to come
through the spirit of any one people, it must be pointed out, is exactly the
kind of national messianism that requires limitation and transformation
within the universal relationality of God. The Russian soul, like the
American or any other soul, may be panentheistically in God but may not
be identified with God. Indeed, the idolatry of such identification, as

perhaps the Muslims teach us best, is one of the most grievous forms of the sin that continues to beset us all.

The last overprocurator of the Holy Synod, Pobedonostsev, who served from 1881 to 1905 under appointment of the Russian czar, was perhaps more realistic but not therefore theologically more correct. He contrasted the Slav communal spirit and mystic attachment to relics and icons with the more Western forms of individualism and rationalism: "The more we consider the distinctive ethnical features of religion the more firmly we are convinced how unattainable is an union of creeds. . . . The essential elements are so involved with the psychical nature of the race, with the principles of their moral philosophy, that it is futile to separate one from the other."[66] It was the uniquely communal form of Russian faith, in Pobedonostsev's judgment, that allowed for the kind of union of state and church that Peter the Great had imposed two centuries before. Pobedonostsev seems to have forgotten that the Western-oriented Peter had found the model for his church-state relations in the Scandinavian Lutheran states. It was also this religio-national state, led by those like Pobedonostsev, that demonically instigated the widespread massacres of Jews in the government-promoted pogroms of 1881, 1903, and 1905.

There is no intention to approximate the more universal aspirations of Slavophilism with the more crass forms of nationalism typified by Pobedonostsev, which were carried in a hidden way even in the Communist Soviet state and may now receive more overt expression since its dissolution. Dimitry Pospielovsky summarizes the essential ideas of Slavophilism that continue to live in Russia in ways that may yet prove beneficial:

1. the philosophical concept of *sobornost*, i.e., the idea of a free interplay between the individual human being and society when both are sublimated by a common hierarchy of spiritual values;
2. an organic Weltanschauung, partly inherited from the German romantics: rejection of revolutionary disruptions of the historical development of societies and acceptance of only evolutionary or "organic" progress, emanating from within the society and its evolving institutions.[67]

To work out what it means to be a free person in loving and just internal/organic relations in societies increasingly open to the universal, as we have attempted in our previous two chapters, is at the heart of the universal relationality of peace. And from the perspective developed in this chapter, it is possible to affirm slavophilism as a Russian prejudice, in Gadamer's positive sense, that may be fused with a more universal horizon not restricted to a unique Russian soul.

What must be guarded against is any return to the idolatrous kind of slavophilism in the form of Russian religiopolitical nationalism described by Salo Baron:

> In the writings of such Slavophils as Kireevski, Khomiakov, Samarin, the brothers Constantine and Ivan Aksakov and Danilevski, or of such sympathizers as Dostoevski, Russia's old imperial drive received an un-matched religious and humanitarian rationale. . . . They thus ascribed to their nation a messianic role which invested Russia's imperial expansion with qualities redemptive of mankind at large.[68]

Pospielovsky is convinced that apart from a few extremist "National Bolsheviks" there is no national messianism in the neo-Slavophile movement in contemporary Russia.[69] Perhaps seventy years of Communist Bolshevik rule was enough to break the caesaro-papist link in Russian spirituality and prepare them to move into genuinely ecumenical and universal forms of human relationality. The participation of the Russian Orthodox Church in the World Council of Churches and the Conference of European Churches for the past three decades points in this direction and enhances this possibility.

May we similarly hope to transform the prejudice of American civil religion? Russell Richey's and Donald Jones's distinction between civil religion as "folk religion" and as the "transcendent universal religion of the nation" is important in conceiving an answer to this question. The first is simply what "emerges out of the ethos and history of the society and inevitably becomes an idolatrous faith competing with particularistic religions rooted in a reality and traditions transcending the common life of a people." The second is more normative and even "prophetic," as the "understanding of the American experience in the light of ultimate and universal reality."[70] The second is also closer to the original Puritan intention that played so dynamic a role in engendering American civil religion. A biographer of Cromwell points out that a nationalism "decided not by blood but by faith . . . is a nationalism which runs easily and naturally into internationalism," Salo Baron notes. This is especially true when the faith is in a transcendent and universal God. American civil religion as the transcendent universal religion of the nation may merit Baron's judgment that "from its inception American nationalism, even more pronouncedly than that of Cromwell, bordered on internationalism."[71]

This internationalism, however, may function as it often has in the past, either to cloak an essentially idolatrous messianic view of America as "the renovator of the world" (Jonathan Edwards) or to express the more universally relational perspective that Robert Bellah expresses:

> If America can have any meaning and value in the future, it is only a relative value, only as *part of a greater encompassing whole*. It is in this

sense that I would interpret Charles Long when he says of the American experience that "there is no center" or "there are many centers."[72]

It is only when our nationalisms can accept their place as relative "parts of a greater encompassing whole" that religio-national messianisms, whether of Germany, Russia, or the United States, can make a contribution from their potentially idolatrous universal concerns toward realizing the genuinely universal relationality of God's peace. We shall not make that contribution, however, if we come to the "enlightened" view that there is no center and affirm the spiritually debilitating relativism that has been correlated since the Enlightenment with the absolute sovereignty of nation-states. We must rather affirm many centers in the universal relationality of the God who is the Center that empowers, limits, judges, renews, and finally brings peace to and between the various centers of all of our societies.

## Understanding the Sectarian
## Limits of the World's Religions

Understanding the relation of particular religions to an emerging global culture has been increasingly discussed by theologians since the end of Euro-America's second thirty years war. Arend Van Leeuwen a generation ago interpreted "the meeting of the faiths of East and West" from both cultural and religious standpoints. His major cultural conclusion was that the high economic standard of living almost universally sought after "requires a social transformation; a society organized on a technocratic pattern." He understood such a technocratic pattern to be the "product of Western Christian civilization, brought about through the complexities of history in which a whole range of factors, such as the rise of democracy, modern capitalism, the technological revolution, a high valuation of labour and socialist and liberal movements, have been at work."[73]

Since the presumably universal value of a high standard of living depends on a pattern that may be learned only from Western culture, Van Leeuwen's major religious conclusion was that the Christian church might develop a "truly ecumenical theology" out of only its own resources:

> The Christian Church has to do for our age what at a turning-point in world history Augustine did for his own and for succeeding generations: namely, to interpret past and present, discerning the signs of the times in the prophetic light of the dawning Day of the Lord. This the Church can only do—as Augustine did in his own day—with the intellectual and philosophical equipment which the twentieth century affords and with

the historical and scientific knowledge now placed at her disposal. That means that the best theological approach to history must inevitably be a "Christian philosophy of history" which is "contemporary" in the sense of being highly provisional and relative. . . .

A sound theology of history is no merely theoretical business, something "all right for theologians." It has an extremely practical relevance and urgency, above all to two of the most thorny problems facing this and future generations: the struggle for world peace and the struggle for world-wide prosperity—two things which belong inseparably together.[74]

A generation later the concern for world peace remains strong but now is seen to be more inseparably joined with justice than with prosperity; or, more fully expressed, world peace may only be joined with the degree of prosperity that may become genuinely worldwide because attained and maintained by just relations with all humanity and the whole of creation. The *oikoumene* has now properly become the whole inhabited earth and not just the extension of European Christendom as it still was a generation ago. Thus Van Leeuwen's conclusion that any philosophy of history must be provisional and relative holds even more strongly, but for that reason it must not finally be understood as only a *Christian* philosophy of history.

The concrete faiths of East and West, as well as North and South, cannot really meet in peace if our Christian horizon, while remaining Christian, does not fuse with the horizons of other faiths in a way that will not allow the resulting philosophy of history to be named simply and only as Christian. As our understanding of the universal relationality of God becomes more comprehensive, so may our praxis be better directed to what Van Leeuwen designated as "the struggle for world peace." World religions and the communities that embody them will better contribute to world peace when they realize that they are all sects on a world scale.

The sectarian nature of all religious institutions may be better understood as we discern their analogy with the secular salvations offered humanity by idolatrous political sects at the climax of Euro-America's second thirty years war. Ernest Koenker's conclusion after studying Nazism and Communism was that the essential question faced by humanity then, and perhaps always, is, "In what do you participate?"[75] Both of these political sects presented themselves as sociopolitical communities that could heal alienated persons and create social peace. Egoistic motives, identified as Western and/or decadent, would be transformed into a national-socialist or a universal-socialist community of comrades. Koenker notes how the various articulations of Nazi and Communist morality carried the virtues of "social responsibility, productive work, family unity, and devotion to nation"—all of which, he comments, are not far from Judeo-Christian (or, we might add, most other kinds of) morality.[76]

Insight into secular sectarianism may also be gained from reflection on two of its earlier Euro-American forms: the Jacobin cult of reason that was intended to unite France spiritually and politically but ended in a reign of terror, and the cult of Abraham Lincoln that reveres his having saved the Union from American injustices and hostilities. Ralph Gabriel describes and analyzes the Lincoln Memorial in Washington, D.C., in these religious terms:

> It is a Greek temple. Within it is a graven image. John Chester French's figure is a romanticized Lincoln. Three devices enhance the religious atmosphere: on the walls in bronze are the words of the hero; a light falls from the ceiling upon his forehead; and above the brooding figure is an inscription. It reads: "In this temple as in the heart of the people *for whom he saved the Union* the memory of Abraham Lincoln is enshrined forever."[77]

Few Americans who have visited this shrine, to judge from my experience, have gone away without feeling this participatory emotion in the national community that Lincoln saved. If Lincoln had not successfully stopped the dissolution of the United States in the mid-nineteenth century, it would not have become the predominant superpower—for good *and* for ill—of the mid-twentieth century. Koenker names these experiences of Nazis, Communists, Frenchmen, and Americans rightly; they are both secular and saving—at least in Whitehead's sense of peace resulting from the transfer of self-control to "coordinations wider than personality."

The crucial question is whether these coordinations are wide enough? And the religious, as well as the realistic, answer must be no! To participate, even to participate religiously, in nation or class is not enough. We must realize our participation in the universal relationality of God through more explicitly religious experience if we are to know a more complete salvation and struggle toward a more universal peace. But if our religions are to become truly saving in the secular realm, we must recognize their sectarian character in the religious realm.

Conor Cruise O'Brien calls the most dangerous contemporary forms of secular salvation "holy nationalism" and holds that "the management of holy nationalism is the greatest problem in peacekeeping." But he fears that any adequate answer to this problem "may be too much to hope for":

> Ideally those responsible for international affairs ought to be able to understand and moderate the holy nationalism of their own country and to discern, even when disguised, the operations and limits of holy nationalism in rival countries as well as in third-party countries.[78]

In my judgment, it is exactly at the ideal point of discerning, understanding, and moderating holy nationalisms that world religions may make a creative contribution to universal peace—but only if they recognize their sectarian limits. It is only as we strengthen our worshipful sense of participation in that which *both* comprehends and transcends our participation in family, tribe, nation, race, and class that we shall enable the praxis of peace at the margins of these real but limited communities. Religion, however, must add itself to this list of limited communities if we are to enable the praxis of peace also to move beyond the limits of religious sectarianisms.

### Discerning the Sectarian Character of World Religions

All of our world's religions are sects. Christians may better discern this truth by noting the correlation of religious sectarianism with nationalism in our own tradition from beginning to end. Salo Baron noted that "Monophysitism, for instance, served as a convenient cloak for Egyptian as well as Armenian nationalism, which refused to be submerged in 'the sea of Romanism.' "[79] Hussitism later became a major vehicle for Czech nationalism, as did Lutheranism, and especially Lutheran pietism, for German nationalism. Though Lutheran orthodoxy after the first thirty years war had resignedly taught the German people to accept the *Kleinstaaterei* (system of small states) of regional rulers and the associated *Landeskirchen* (regional churches), Lutheran pietism radically challenged and changed such orthodox resignation: "Pietism salvaged German religious feeling," as Baron comments, "from its threatening petrification under overweening state control, but also set the pattern for the national enthusiasm and irrationalism that was to color so deeply all German nationalist thinking in the nineteenth century."[80]

Reflection on these brief examples helps us discern the dialectical truth our world now so desperately needs: On the one hand, concrete sectarianism/nationalism resists imposed universals, even if they participate in a genuinely spiritual universal—the sea of Romanism, historically in the form of the Holy Roman Empire. Egyptians, Armenians, Czechs, and Germans, among others, would have none of it. But that resistance may tragically be extended even to more adequately ecumenical forms of the universal relationality of God. Post–Vatican II Roman Catholicism is not the Holy Roman Empire; yet many still refuse to "come home," as the Vatican sometimes puts it. The deeply motivated religious spirit seeks a concrete universal and will not settle for a universal that does not enable her/his free participation. On the other hand, because sectarians concretely participate—sometimes with too unbridled an enthusiasm—in their genuine communities, their attempts to create a more inclusive community border on the idolatrous.

We are led by these reflections again to the conclusion that the transcendent universals of religious experience and the immanent universals of reason may, and I think must, be united in the Holy Spirit. The Holy Spirit is the universal Spirit that *comprehends and transcends* our religious sectarianisms and political nationalisms, enabling our participation through our concrete communities in a genuinely universal community, thus making peace. From the standpoint of universal peace in the Holy Spirit, all of the world's religions are sectarian. No matter how closely one or another religion may approximate the church type at a national level, we all belong to sects at a world level.

Consider the distinctions between church and sect as Ernst Troeltsch defined them for European Christianity:

> The Church is that type of organization which is overwhelmingly conservative, which to a certain extent accepts the secular order, and dominates the masses; in principle, therefore, it is universal, i.e. it desires to cover the whole of humanity. The sects, on the other hand, are comparatively small groups; they aspire after personal inward perfection, and they aim at a direct personal fellowship between the members of each group. From the very beginning, therefore, they are forced to organize themselves in small groups, and to renounce the idea of dominating the world.[81]

None of the world religions, no matter how large or evangelical, may any longer desire to cover the whole of humanity once they know what that really means; and to the degree that they desire to contribute to world peace, they must renounce the idea of dominating the world. These two moves already put them in the category of sects. Troeltsch's other criteria of personal fellowship, perfection, and organization into small groups also analogically characterize the world religions from a universal perspective, for they each and all create a distinctive ethos (though not perfection) within a discernible *sangha*, *umma*, or *koinonia* (though not small).

If we learn to discern and participate as sectarians in the concrete universals of our religions, what may we contribute to the universal relationality of God's peace and the moderation of the holy nationalisms that threaten it? I am convinced that contribution will come more in the concrete form of religious communities than in the abstractions of their teachings—though there is often, and should be always, a close correlation between the two. This means for Christianity, making clear to its faithful that their churches' openness to many nationalisms arises primarily from its social essence rather than its ethnic history, and that the church's social essence, grounded in sacramental participation in the Trinitarian God even within the contextual relationality of a national church, is lured toward universalism by God's universal Spirit. Ecclesial communities that understand their social essence sacramentally must also pro-phetically proclaim that any contextual sectarianism ceases to be holy when any of its margins are closed to just and loving relations and thus closed off from the universal relationality of God.

The church's communal essence grounded in sacramental participation in the universal God requires that the biblical promise of the land, which has played so tragic a role in the political hardening of Euro-American religious nationalisms, be relativized within the whole biblical message. A biblical perspective such as that of Georges Florovsky, the noted Russian Orthodox émigré theologian, helps do so:

> The whole phraseology of Scripture is highly instructive: the Covenant, the Kingdom, the Church, "a holy Nation, a peculiar People." The abstract term "Christianity" is obviously of a late date. From the very beginning Christianity was socially minded. The whole fabric of Chris-tian existence is social and corporate. All Christian sacraments are in-trinsically "social sacraments," i.e., sacraments of incorporation. . . . To build up the Church of Christ means, therefore, to build up a new society and, by implication, to rebuild human society on a new basis.[82]

This profoundly orthodox theology only requires that the sectarian perspective of God's universal relationality be emphasized in ways that are still strange to most Eastern Orthodox or to the orthodox of any other church. Christian communities must now recognize that they are sacra-mentally to incorporate their members into the universal human commu-nity, which they cannot and do not fully incorporate or represent—neither in their Russian, nor Roman, nor American, nor even ecumenical forms. The churches must become emphatic that they can only incorpo-rate and enculturate their faithful into a sect that requires loving and just intersection with other sects if the full meaning of their sacramental life in the universal relationality of God is to be realized. The theologians of the other world religions must be challenged and invited to enter this dia-logue analogously, lest the multicolored universality of God's peace be reduced in our monological reflections to what Hegel derisively called the "night in which all cows are black."

## Toward a Sectarian Religious Understanding of Universal Peace

The intersection of the teachings on peace of the world religions may contribute to recognizing and perhaps even transforming the sectarian-isms and holy nationalisms that threaten world peace. John Ferguson found two decades ago that much had been written on peace from the standpoint of Christianity, and some in relation to Judaism, but not "very much explicitly on the subject in relation to other religions."[83] Attention to the wider interreligious dimensions of peace has grown since then, however, so that there is a growing theological resource available.[84] As late as 1987 Rashmi-Sudha Puri of Punjab University could write of even so auspicious an example as Mahatma Gandhi, "curiously enough, not much work on Gandhi's concern for peace and abhorrence of war seems to have been done."[85] Fortunately, Puri herself has now remedied that lack.

What can be learned for the universal relationality of peace from studying the world's religions? The primal teachings of their founders carried in their classic/canonical texts provide the first and richest learnings: Thich Minh Chau of the Vietnamese Buddhist Sangha says that "all Buddhists remember the following teachings of our Lord Buddha, Gatha Number Five, in the Dhammapada:

> Hatred cannot put an end to hatred,
> In this world this never happens.
> Only non-hatred can bring hatred to an end,
> This is an eternal law."[86]

Even if all Buddhists do not yet or always remember it, those of us for whom Gautama is not, or not yet, "Lord Buddha" would do well to learn this teaching as we intersect and interact with those for whom he is.

Sivaya Subramuniyaswami was asked, "What are the scriptural roots of nonviolence in Hinduism?" His citations from the Vedas, Upanishads, Agamas, Tirumarai, Dharma Shastras, Yoga Sutras, and other sources include:

"Let your aim be one and single. Let your hearts be joined in one—The mind at rest in unison—At peace with all, so may you be." *Rig Veda*: X.191.4. "One should never do that to another which one regards as injurious to one's own self. This, in brief, is the rule of dharma. Yielding to desire and acting differently, one becomes guilty of adharma." *Mahabharata*: XVIII.113.8.[87]

Christians may also find that acting differently than the teaching of the *Mahabharata* makes one guilty not only of *adharma* but of refusing to follow their own Christ's teaching.[88] Even, and perhaps especially, because of this significant similarity, Christians may learn something from Hindus about how to bring our minds to "rest in unison" so as to experience peace with all and thus be the better able to follow this universal golden rule.

John Ferguson wrote of Islam that "the essential view of the Qur'an is of a single worldwide community: one God, one mankind, one law, one ruler. 'If there were two gods, the universe would be ruined' (Qur'an 21,23)."[89] Wasim Siddiqui concretizes this teaching as a devout Muslim:

God-awareness grows into an obedience to the Will of God which, in turn, fosters the creation of inner peace. This peace grows as the individual recognizes the oneness and omnipotence of God and realizes that God's justice is the basis for achieving social equilibrium and cooperation. Thus, in Islam, world peace may be attained through the evolution of the passions and desires of individual consciousness into an inner harmony of obedience to God's will.[90]

When interaction with Muslim neighbors, near or far, contributes to our world becoming unified in peace and justice through obedience to the will of God, perhaps we should all become Muslims—at least on this point.

We forgo any attempt to recover all of the relevant teachings found in the classical scriptures of the world religions to revert to our primary and concrete concern of how these teachings are actualized in praxis. The history of Islam especially requires and enables a refocusing on what we have called the sectarian form of this praxis because it has failed, after making the most resolute effort, to establish the worldwide theocratic community its faith requires. Islam's territorial expansion was halted long since at Tours and Vienna in the West and India in the East. The fact that these struggles continue in India, as we have seen, as well as in sub-Saharan Africa, just now most notably in Nigeria and the Sudan, makes this focusing on sectarian praxis the more urgent.

For orthodox Islam, the world remains divided between the *dar-al-Islam*, the territory of Islam, and *dar-al-harb*, the territory of war, in ways that are all too similar to the divisions the rest of us know:

> The first [*dar-al-Islam*] comprised Muslims, with full citizenship, and members of other religious faiths, who were allowed partial rights and granted toleration, provided that they acceded to Muslim rule and paid their taxes. The second was the realm of infidels or unbelievers. Between these two territories a state of war exists. There may be periods during which the *jihad* is in suspense, but they are temporary only, and theoretically should not last more than ten years. In practice, however, most Muslims accept the suspension of the *jihad* as normalcy, and Ibn Khaldun saw it as the passage from militarism to civilization.[91]

Those concerned for peace in our world must be grateful for whatever proportion of Muslims agree with Ibn Khaldun that military *jihad* must be suspended for the sake of civilization. Should we therefore also hope that the militant faith of Muslims like Wasim Siddiqui, with its strong commitment to God's will for peace with justice, also be suspended? It must be obvious by now that this question is only rhetorical. The answer is clearly no! What we should, however, learn to emphasize with Muslim brothers and sisters is the distinctions they make between the four different types of *jihad*: that of the heart, the tongue, the hands, and the sword.

The *jihad* of the heart, and not only for Muslims, is one's own personal struggle against evil—a large part of which are the hatreds and hostilities that lead to war. The second of the tongue is the resolute effort to communicate one's faith in religious congregations and public squares—an important part of which is articulating what establishes justice and makes for peace. The third, *jihad* of the hands, requires the hands-on praxis of opposing social evil—largely by creating the familial, educational, economic, and political structures that are essential to human welfare. The active praxis of these three forms of *jihad* while renouncing the *jihad* of the sword is clearly analogous to the differentiation between cultural and political forms of religio-nationalism we have interpreted and urged heretofore for Christians and Jews.

Muslim community—the *dar-al-Islam*—is crucial for the creation of the Muslim ethos and ethic. We all must learn analogously to create by the mutual *jihad* of our hands, as we exercise our interreligious *jihads* of heart and tongue, the kind of domestic and international political structures that enable and protect religiocultural communities, whose sectarian margins may remain open to interreligious justice because they are no longer externally threatened by religiopolitical idolatries. That is to say, we must enable and sustain contextually relational communities who have the freedom to respond to God's universally relational grace, so that they may understand themselves within the universal relationality of God.

### The Inadequate Answer of Eclectic Religious Communities

This need not mean spinning off new and eclectic religious communities focused on universal relationality. Islam has a history of such spin-offs. Guru Nanak founded Sikhism in the Punjab five hundred years ago to try to reconcile the Hindus and Muslims who were fighting one another then. They have continued to fight intermittently ever since. Like Muhammad almost a millennium before him, Nanak tried to create a united brotherhood under one God whose "True Name" lay behind the names of Allah, Rama, Siva, etc. But persecution from both sides led the Sikhs finally to take military measures to protect themselves. By the time of their tenth Guru Gobind Singh their devotional writing tragically "concentrated on the Sword and on God as the Sword":

> Thou art the Subduer of countries, the Destroyer of the armies of the wicked, in the battlefield Thou greatly adorned the brave. . . .
> Hail, hail to the Creator of the world, the Saviour of creation, my Cherisher, hail to Thee, O Sword.[92]

What began as a reconciling community existing between conflicting communities became one of the most militant—in the sense of military—

religious communities in the world. Indeed, it was a militant Sikh, chosen to be one of the prime minister's guards because of his military prowess, who assassinated Shrimati Indira Gandhi.

Four centuries after Guru Nanak, the Bab (Mirza Ali Muhammad) in Iran, and Baha'ullah (Mirza Husayn 'Ali) after the Bab was executed, attempted universally to address shah and czar, queen and pope to bring an end to conflict and wars. The Bab was received by some as the "Gate" and Baha'ullah as the "Promised One" who would bring in the new era of peace and freedom. The Baha'is who joined in this faith have sought ever since to create a theocentric religion appropriate to a united world. They seek religiously to unite the truths that have come to humanity through Abraham, Krishna, Moses, Buddha, Christ, and Muhammad. But the result, at least in Iran where it originated and where it is now the largest religious minority, has been unending conflict and persecution. A contemporary Baha'i reflects the violence they have suffered:

> Baha'is are not strangers to violence. The persecutions of the Baha'i faith in Iran, a Moslem nation, began as soon as the religion itself was born in 1844. . . . In the early years of the Faith over 20,000 members were martyred. . . . Persecution of Baha'is continues intermittently to the present day. Baha'i holy places have been seized and in many cases destroyed. Elected officials of the Faith have been kidnapped and executed. . . . Again in Iran, Baha'is are officially considered non-persons and are deprived of their human rights.[93]

Despite this history of ongoing persecution, Baha'is, unlike their Sikh predecessors, have continued to reject all violence as they affirm the sanctity of all life. Their international governing body, calling itself the "Universal House of Justice," continues to issue, from its world center on Mt. Carmel in Israel, hopeful statements like that of 1985 on "The Promise of World Peace":

> The Great Peace towards which the people of good will throughout the centuries have inclined their hearts . . . is now at long last within the reach of nations. For the first time . . . it is possible for everyone to view the entire planet. World peace is not only possible but inevitable. It is the next stage in the evolution of the planet . . . "the planetization of mankind."[94]

This good witness to the universal relationality of peace, whose ultimate influence cannot yet be measured, has thus far reaped little more than conflict and persecution. Their suffering, of course, is to be lamented and protested, but it is also to be learned from.

What is to be learned? We finite human beings must finally learn that we cannot create ontologically universal structures or even social structures that represent the universal. Christendom was and is no such struc-

ture. Dar-al-Islam also was and is not. The Sikhs have given up their
original hope to become such a structure, and the Baha'is should realize
they have no realistic hope of becoming such. When the Universal House
of Justice, or the World Council of Churches, or the Vatican, or the
Ecumenical Patriarch, or whoever even suggests that they have this
power, the consequence is at least ridicule and at worst conflict.

The same lesson must also be learned in Asia, even though their religions are often considered less aggressive in their claims to universality.
Jürgen Moltmann is nevertheless justified in noting that, "The emperor
of China was probably the last *priest-emperor* in the world."[95] The Confu-
cian-inspired attempt to unite universal religion with politics remained in
China until 1911. Though its universality took a more rational form, its
concrete praxis was no less imperial and dangerous. The imperial Confucian court taught that peace, prosperity, and harmony might be attained
and maintained only if heaven and earth were properly related through
the emperor. Julia Ching puts it: "According to the Confucian conception, the political ruler was regarded as bearer of Heaven's Mandate, Son
of Heaven, and father and teacher to the people."[96] This exorbitant claim
was idolatrous because the ruler of the Middle Kingdom claimed to be
the center of order for the whole natural and human world.

The failure of this "natural political religion" (Moltmann) to approximate universal peace led to its overthrow in our century, first by the
Western-inspired movement of Sun Yat-sen and then by the Marxist-
inspired movement of Mao Tse-tung. Their modern ideas of historical
progress—meaning largely industrial progress—transformed the Confucian emperors' strategy of natural harmony into one of industrial and
commercial development. Moltmann makes the theological distinction
involved in this transition clear: "The beyond in heaven above us is replaced by the historical future before us. The fluid equilibrium of Yin and
Yang is replaced by the contradictions of history which lead to the class
struggle."[97] But Julia Ching sees better the religiopolitical similarity in
this discontinuity:

> Like the Confucian *Tao* of old and replacing it, Dialectical Materialism
> is now taught and revered as infallible doctrine, the norm for all philos-
> ophy, logic, history, and even "eschatology." In place of the "philoso-
> pher-king" myth, we have now the reality of a Party Chairman, the
> political ruler as well as the guardian and exponent of the new ideology,
> and father and mother of the people. The goal of Chinese society is
> a New Socialism—a universal vision with strong resonances of the
> Confucian ideal society, formulated as a world "belonging to all"
> (ta-t'ung).[98]

Ching's criticism of Maoism does not reflect any preference for the
way in which Confucianism continues to be used in some other Asian

states, for example, Singapore, South Korea, and Taiwan, to justify paternalistic, authoritarian governments. She finds both the ancient and modern claims to universality equally ridiculous. Such claims are as fallacious in the East as in the West, because they are equally dangerous to the peace of universal relationality, which lives only by honestly critical and creative dialogue at recognized contextual boundaries, so that justice may be sought by all for all.

### Religious Examples of Universal Relationality

The Buddhist *Sarvodaya* movement in Sri Lanka provides a far more positive example of an Asian religious community that has penetrated the ideological rigidity of its own society to recognize their relational reality:

> It is common knowledge that there is a disturbed situation in Sri Lanka today where legalised structural violence prevails and extra-legal violent methods are used as well to resolve conflicts. Some call it an "ethnic problem." Some others call it a "terrorist problem." Yet others call it a "militant struggle for liberation." There are still other groups trying to identify it with a more simplistic description, calling it a kind of war between the Sinhala Buddhist majority and the Tamil Hindu minority. Whatever it is, there is violence and counter-violence which has already taken a toll of several thousand lives, most of them innocent and powerless people who could not comprehend what was going on around them.[99]

Though Buddhists are a 70 percent majority in Sri Lanka, the name of this Buddhist organization—*Sarvodaya*—literally means the "awakening of *all*." This could be another idolatrous religious claim to represent the universal all, but it is not:

> The Sarvodaya Movement has succeeded in breaking social and political barriers by bringing the temple, kovil, mosque, and the church together and making them all centres for the promotion of common spiritual values. In this way unity in diversity becomes a living reality. . . . Perhaps the steadfastness with which most Sinhalese, Tamil, and Muslim communities stand together peacefully in most parts of the country despite irresponsible rabble rousing by the media and demagogues is due to the silent work done by these simple grassroots communities influenced by Sarvodaya thought and action.[100]

Despite threats from extremists in periods of violent conflict as in July 1983, the Sarvodaya Movement opened the first refugee camps for the Tamils, which could not have been possible were it not for the relational and dialogical approach they had been practicing for the quarter of a century prior to such a tragedy. This is the kind of praxis of relational

universalism that brings peace to the world and, to my mind, expresses
the universal relationality of God—though a Buddhist would never conceive or speak of it in those terms.

The terms more native to Buddhism are "inner universalism," the focal
concept of a peace proposal "Toward a New Globalism" made by the
Japanese Buddhist movement Soka Gakkai International in January 1989.
It was presented as a Buddhist concept and method—to contrast with the
"external universalism" of communism and the "transcendental universalism" of liberal democracy—"for searching the inner self to find a universal value within it."[101] Such contrasts notwithstanding, the Soka Gakkai's
interpretation of the inner self has significant Western parallels in the
psychology of Carl Jung, as may be recognized when they write: "The
common karma of groups of people is continuously engraved in the collective consciousness of the respective peoples and countries since the
time of their ancestors." A similar presupposition underlies the hermeneutic of Gadamer, which we have relied upon so heavily for interpreting
the possibility of universal relationality.

The Buddhist tradition of the Soka Gakkai, however, interprets inner
universalism as the key to changing our common karma through "*bodhisattva* practice":

> Good will and benevolent conduct, represented by nonviolence and
> dialogue, are not only engraved in the individual's *alaya*-consciousness
> but are integrated into the common karma of the people and country,
> influencing to some degree the consciousness of other living beings and
> all humanity. In this way, the *bodhisattva* practice based on compassion
> effects the individual and the nation, thus helping to make manifest the
> universal wisdom that is inherent in humanity.[102]

These are concepts so clearly analogous to those we have been developing
that they need no transformation into the more theistic form of dialectical
panentheism to contribute to the universal relationality of peace that
many Buddhists and Christians seek.

The dialogue between inner universalism and universal relationality,
however, may continue around issues of human corporate alienation:
Cannot the dialectic between collective injustice and the possibility of a
more universal struggle for peace remain clearer if we limit the attribu-
tion of universality strictly to the consequent nature of God in whom we
participate, rather than attributing it to our own ambiguous and finite
inner selves? Are not the limits and the ambiguity of our selves even the
more dangerous because they have the universal dimension of collective
memory, which lies at the base of so much continuing ethnic conflict? I
continue to think so, while recognizing the contribution that the Soka
Gakkai make toward actualizing a more universal peace.[103]

Since their founding in 1930, the Soka Gakkai have consistently rejected war and all other forms of violence on the basis of Nichiren's interpretation of Buddhism. They have adopted as a major goal "the elimination of nuclear weapons and the realization of a warless world by upholding the spirit of the United Nations Charter and cooperating with the U.N. effort to maintain world peace."[104] Their praxis has involved organizing antiwar and antinuclear programs in their native Japan and other countries, collecting ten million signatures calling for abolition of nuclear weapons, raising funds for Asian and African refugees, and publishing antiwar books.

Whether arising out of inner universalism or the universal relationality of God, this is a praxis of the universal relationality of peace that must be affirmed by all who love peace. We may agree with the Soka Gakkai that "the world awaits a movement that will manifest the spirit of nonviolence and the compassion of Buddhism,"[105] even as we dialogically ask them and all others to consider the sectarian character and limits of the way they and we move toward universal peace.

Even the magnificent legacy of Mahatma Gandhi must be challenged to such reconsideration. Rashmi-Sudha Puri, near the conclusion of her study of Gandhi's life and teaching, declared that he "had no doubt whatsoever that nationalism, instead of being narrow or exclusive, is a vital prerequisite for internationalism."[106] But the Indian nationalism he espoused was more contradictory of his religious conviction that "perfect peace comes when mind and heart are pure" than Gandhi realized as he devoted himself to:

> purifying the heart and elevating the mind of his countrymen with the contagion of his tireless pursuit of truth—concretized in nonviolence, fearlessness, sense of responsibility and duty, and a loving concern for his fellow beings.[107]

After thirty-two years devoted to leading the Congress Party to practice nonviolence in the struggle for independence, Gandhi endured the anguish of his party, after it took over the leadership of a newly independent India, deciding to continue and even strengthen its military forces. And if he had lived long enough, he also would have witnessed their jubilation, as I did in 1974, in successfully creating a nuclear bomb, something he had so adamantly opposed while he lived. The point is that India's Hindu heart was not yet as pure as Gandhi had hoped and that not even sectarianism and/or nationalism may simply provide a prerequisite for international peace.

Until more of us collectively approximate the personal purity of Gandhi, we had better remain more dialectical than he did about the possibility of any of our religions overcoming the narrowness of their associated holy nationalisms. And we therefore may only dialectically support whatever contributions our religions make to the universality of peace with a prophetic awareness of the sectarian limitations of their and our purity and truth—virtues that Gandhi had achieved to a degree that most of us may still only pray for.

## A Dialectical and Dialogical Praxis of Universal Peace

How may a dialectical and dialogical praxis of peace in any sense improve upon so magnificent a peace praxis as Gandhi's? The answer to so difficult a question may begin with a dialogue with Hans Küng, who a generation after Gandhi has provided one of the most astute contemporary theological discussions of our global responsibility for peace.[108] We share both of the affirmations made by Küng:

> The key concept for our strategy for the future must be: human responsibility for this planet, a planetary responsibility.
> There can be no peace among the nations without peace among the religions. In short, there can be no world peace without religious peace.[109]

Our problem with his theological analysis—analogous to our problem with Gandhi's nationalism—begins with the nondialectical way Küng posits our God-relation as the basis for "the absoluteness and universality of ethical obligations." Despite his anthropological insight that an "unconditional claim, a 'categorical' ought, cannot be derived from the finite conditions of human existence, from human urgencies and needs," he asserts theologically that for "at least the prophetic religions—Judaism, Christianity and Islam," God is "the one unconditional in all that is conditioned that can provide a basis for the absoluteness and universality of ethical demands."[110]

Leaving aside his implicit recognition that no absolute ethical demand may be established for the nonprophetic religions in this way—which should be enough to give pause to any theologian who recognizes the importance of religious relations to world peace—this affirmation of an unconditional basis for our peace ethic is also problematic for Christians who recognize the relational relativity of the God who was ontologically immanent in Jesus and remains so in the universal relational immanence of the Holy Spirit. There is no absolute relation with the transcendent Absolute that provides some kind of pure religious basis for the global ethics we need. Our relation with the relational God is mediated through our total experience in the cultures we have co-created with God. Our religions may transcend our cultures in their focus on our God-relation, but none is pure enough to transcend the narrowness introduced by their social histories.

We, nevertheless, may and must share Küng's sense of urgency:

> The one world in which we live has a chance of survival only if there is no longer any room for spheres of differing, contradictory, and even antagonistic ethics. The one world needs one basic ethic. This one world society certainly does not need a unitary religion and a unitary ideology, but it does need some norms, values, ideals, and goals to bring it together and be binding upon it.[111]

We do urgently need a growing global consensus on the ethical issues of human and ecological peace with justice. But the dilemma that Küng recognizes for modern democracies—that they require a moral consensus which they may not prescribe by law[112]—holds at least as clearly for religions. A Roman Catholic theologian who has struggled as valiantly as Küng for the possibility of dissidence in his church must recognize that not even a religious appeal to a transcendent principle will bind social consensus. Yet he dismisses Habermas too easily and, by implication, much of the perspective we have been developing: "Those who want to dispense with a transcendent principle have to follow a long path of horizontal communication with the possibility that in the end they have just been going round in a circle."[113]

To "go around in a circle"—to follow his metaphor imaginatively for a moment—is important socially if one is to communicate the globe around; and it is suggestive theologically if we are to understand our human participation in the circuminsession of the relational God, whom Christians worship sacramentally in the symbol of the Trinity. To understand the circle and accept its associated long path of human communication within the universal relationality of God, however, does not intend to dispense with a transcendent principle, but only to dispense with understanding "It" as a nonrelational Absolute. That is, God is better understood as interpersonally relational and thus contextually relative in a way that grounds social consensus dialogically while allowing for free participation by representatives of various traditional and critical perspectives.[114]

Hans Küng already knows the objection "that religions are by no means agreed among themselves, and that their statements are different, indeed contradictory, not only about the Absolute, but also about human ethics."[115] But he has studied world religions enough to be able to articulate some significant ethical consensus, which he summarizes in "six decisive perspectives," two of which are especially important for our discussion:

> a) . . . human well being and dignity as the basic principle and goal of human ethics is brought out with unconditional authority. . . .

> b) they [the religions] can offer convincing motives for action on the basis of . . . the living embodiment of a new attitude to life and a new lifestyle . . . with reference to a compelling, specific model for such a lifestyle: to follow Buddha, Jesus Christ, Con-futse, Lao-tse, or the prophet Muhammad.[116]

These two perspectives are especially decisive for universal peace because they express an interreligious commitment to human dignity that is known in, and mediated through, religious relationality.

To articulate a globally responsible ethic religiously on the basis of a careful study of world religions and personal participation in inter-religious dialogue, as Küng has, is a singular contribution to world peace. Indeed, Küng is himself a living example of his maxim that the "capacity for dialogue is ultimately a virtue of capacity for peace."[117] But in my judgment, neither he, nor Gandhi, nor anyone else, may have had, or hope to have, so nondialectical a relation with God as to provide the universal and absolute ethic that may bind a global consensus. We are all too finite and perhaps too sinful for that, and our religiocultures are too narrow and perhaps too alienated to make it possible.

Such consensus as we human beings achieve arises only from an ongoing process of dialogical interaction. Our participation in the ontological Whole that God is creating becomes actual only through the praxis of peace with justice that begins in the center and extends to the margins of our concrete communities. Both of the examples of peace praxis we have presented—the Soka Gakkai in Japan and the Sarvodaya Movement in Sri Lanka—acted from the center of their Buddhist identity and moved toward dialogue with contrasting perspectives—as the Soka Gakkai attempted in their program "Toward a New Globalism," and to patterns of active cooperation—as the Sarvodayas achieved in Sri Lanka.

There is, of course, the danger that beginning from the contextual center of religious identity will lead to such hardening of that center as to make difficult, if not impossible, dialogical interaction at its margins. The Muslim Brothers, who now seem to many in the West so dangerous to peace, were begun in 1928 by an Egyptian elementary school teacher as a movement for reforming the individual and social morality of their own society. Hasan al-Banna taught them at the beginning:

> You are not a benevolent society, nor a political party, nor a local organization having limited purposes. Rather, you are a new soul in the heart of this nation to give it life by means of the Qur'an. . . . When asked what it is for which you call, reply that it is Islam, the message of Muhammad, the religion that contains within it government, and has as one of its obligations freedom. If you are told that you are political, answer that Islam admits no such distinction. If you are accused of being revolutionaries, say, "We are voices for right and for peace in

which we dearly believe, and of which we are proud. If you rise against us or stand in the path of our message, then we are permitted by God to defend ourselves against your injustice.[118]

By 1945 at the end of the second European thirty years war, the Muslim Brothers had become a major political force in Egypt, with considerable influence in a number of other Muslim countries. Professor Albert Hourani comments that "the teachings of the Brothers seemed to offer a principle of united action in terms of which the struggle against the British and against corruption could be carried on in unity and trust."[119] But by 1964 some of their leaders had set themselves against any and all continuing Western leadership of the world. Sayid Qutb, executed two years later by Nasir's (Gamal Nasser's) regime, wrote in 1964:

> The leadership of western man in the human world is coming to an end, not because western civilization is materially bankrupt or has lost its economic or military strength, but because the western order has played its part, and no longer possesses that stock of "values" which gave it its predominance. . . . The scientific revolution has finished its role, as have "nationalism" and the territorially limited communities which grew up in its age. . . . The turn of Islam has come.[120]

It is tragic that our world still provides so few dialogical opportunities for difficult interreligious discussions of such possibly dangerous but potentially creative affirmations. Western Christians and Jews might well find more consensus with Muslim perspectives on the scientific revolution, nationalism, and territorially limited communities than Muslim Brothers could anticipate, or at least enough to work together in peace toward peace. Such an ethos might enable honest discussion of the dangers, as well as the possibilities, of the Brothers' anachronistic "aim at creating a universal Muslim society, in which there were no distinctions of race, and one which was worldwide."[121] That is, Muslims might very well make a contribution to universal peace by their spiritual power to overcome the tribal distinctions of race, which have been so pernicious in Euro-American societies, but only if they understand their struggle for universality in a religiocultural, not a religiopolitical, framework. No dialogue may be sufficient to achieve consensus on this crucial point, but resolutely to attempt it is the dialectical and dialogical way of the praxis of peace.

### African-American Struggles for Peace with Justice

Islam's spiritual power to overcome racism was dramatically manifested in the life of Malcolm X during the mid-century struggle for black liberation in the United States. Islam empowered Malcolm X, just as Christianity empowered Martin Luther King Jr., to exercise the kind of leadership in the black struggle that increasingly moved toward universal relationality. Elijah Muhammad's Black Muslim adaptation of Islam started Malcolm's transformation in the Norfolk Prison Colony in Massachusetts. Even after he had broken with Elijah Muhammad, he continued to testify:

> When I was a foul vicious convict, so evil that other convicts had called me Satan, this man had rescued me. He was the man who trained me, who had treated me as if I were his own flesh and blood. He was the man who had given me wings.[122]

Malcolm X had found the kind of genuine community that transformed his human core. And he dedicated himself to bringing similar transformation through participation in that kind of community to his black people in North America.

His disenchantment with the disparity between Elijah Muhammad's life and his teaching finally led him beyond the Black Muslim's rhetoric of hate, rooted in fury over the dehumanization of their people, to a more universally relational rhetoric. After his further transformation during his personal *Hajj* to Mecca, he wrote: "I'm for truth, no matter who tells it. I'm for justice, no matter who it is for or against. I'm a human being first and foremost, and as such I'm for whoever and whatever benefits humanity as a whole."[123] He characterized that Muslim experience of his *Hajj* to Mecca in terms that express how much his sense of community had been enlarged:

> And I know once and for all that the Black Africans look upon America's 22 million blacks as long lost brothers! They love us! They study our struggle for freedom! They were so happy to hear how we are awakening from our long sleep—after so-called "Christian" white America had taught us to be ashamed of our African brothers and homeland![124]

And finally he could see a way even to relate at the margins of his black community to white Americans:

> In our mutual sincerity we might be able to show a road to the salvation of America's very soul. It can only be salvaged if human rights and dignity, in full, are extended to black men. Only such real, meaningful actions as those which are sincerely motivated from a deep sense of humanism and moral responsibility can get at the basic causes that produce the racial explosions in America today. Otherwise the racial explosions are only going to grow worse.[125]

Malcolm X's position had become very similar to that of Martin Luther King Jr. as he sought to synthesize the Black Power movement for liberation that had emerged within his movement with his own understanding of reconciliation and social integration. As he struggled with the issues of "chaos or community," Martin Luther King Jr. wrote near the end of his ministry for peace and justice:

> There is no theoretical or sociological divorce between liberation and integration. In our kind of society liberation cannot come without integration and integration cannot come without liberation. I speak here of integration in both the ethical and the political senses. On the one hand, integration is true intergroup, interpersonal living. On the other hand, it is the mutual sharing of power. I cannot see how the Negro will be totally liberated from the crushing weight of poor education, squalid housing, and economic strangulation until he is integrated, with power, into every level of American life.[126]

The continuing difference in the growing similarity between Malcolm and Martin at the tragically foreshortened end of their careers was only that Martin remained more focused on the margins of his community for the sake of reconciliation, while Malcolm remained more focused on the dignity and freedom of the African-American persons in the center of his community. But they now both were concerned for both as they sought justice for the black community and reconciliation with the white community.

Paul Lehmann, after reviewing the life and thought of both the Muslim Malcolm X and the Christian Martin Luther King Jr., expressed succinctly the growing convergence in their strategy, if not theology: "The unfolding dynamics of the movement in which they were caught up carried Martin Luther King, Jr., from passive resistance to nonviolent protest to militant non-violence, as almost concurrently Malcolm X was carried from hatred and violence to separatism to nonviolent militancy."[127] Professor Lehmann also provided one of the most adequate theological expressions of the universally relational meaning of the movement for which Martin and Malcolm literally lived and died:

> Indeed, the human meaning of black reality and black revolutionary experience and aspiration was precisely not the amalgamation of the races but the justice and freedom that made room for a reconciliation through which the light of the Creator's own joy in the creation shone. In that light, difference has been purged of its destructive operation as an occasion of preference and power. It has indeed been restored to its original design, according to which difference is, in truth, a thing of beauty and a joy forever.[128]

The dialogical and dialectical relation of the creative and tragic lives of Martin Luther King Jr. and Malcolm X thus provide crucial insight into the dialectical and dialogical praxis of peace, which by God's universal grace may occur at the margins of the communities whose spiritual centers provide meaning and sustenance for our lives.

*Peace Praxis during the Cold War*

Much of my peace praxis for a quarter century was at the margin of East and West that ran through Euro-America during the cold war.[129] There were many opportunities for common effort across Churchill's bitter metaphor of the iron curtain, which many other Americans thought an insuperable barrier to any universal peace praxis. In the midst of this effort in 1980, I expressed my emerging sense of universally relational peace as I contemplated the wall that ran through the heart of Germany for almost thirty years: "Representatives of Christ's churches should make no great adventure out of crossing the world's walls, just because they are still there. Nor should Christians take themselves too seriously for crossing the walls Christ already has overcome. The penetration of walls must increasingly become a commonplace for Christians."[130] Further reflection on such experience during the past quarter century has led to this articulation of a theology of the universal relationality of peace.

One of the major avenues for peace praxis at this East-West margin from 1961 to 1990 was the Christian Peace Conference, founded by Professor Josef Hromádka after he returned to the Comenius Theological Faculty in Prague, after serving for ten years on the faculty of Princeton Theological Seminary in the United States. Because it was based in Eastern Europe, many of its participants had to accommodate in various ways to their Communist governments. To many more tribal Christians here, my Eastern colleagues were more Communist than Christian—if they were Christian at all.[131] This situation was exacerbated after Professor Hromádka's resignation as the president of the C.P.C., because of the Warsaw Pact invasion of Czechoslovakia in 1968, and the succession to that office of Metropolitan Nikodim of Leningrad and then Bishop Karoly Toth of Budapest. To work for peace at that margin became increasingly difficult thereafter, as financial support from American churches declined and the secretariat for our American group was removed from the National Council of Churches.

To continue so marginal a peace praxis required a clearly dialectical sense of its ambiguities. While struggling with this issue, I was invited in September 1975 to address several hundred members of the Continuation Committee of the Christian Peace Conference at Siofok, Hungary, on "The Calling of Christians to Cooperate for Peace and Justice." The three major speakers obviously had been chosen from the East, West, and South, or the so-called first, second, and third worlds, so I accepted the responsibility of speaking contextually as a North American Christian. Before I was finished there was "consternation and indignation in the meeting," as Dr. Toth had warned there would be in an earlier letter.

Indeed, there were some who urged Metropolitan Nikodim that evening to exclude me from further participation in the Christian Peace Conference. It was characteristic of his leadership, however, to refuse so tribal a suggestion.

What was said that was so difficult for those who had to accommodate to dictatorial Communist governments? Principally two things: The first arose from a citation of Martin Luther King Jr.'s April 1967 speech against the American war in Vietnam: "Even when pressed by the demands of inner truth, men do not readily assume the task of opposing their government's policy. . . . Nor does the human spirit move without great difficulty against all the apathy of conformist thought within one's own bosom and in the surrounding world." Recognizing that reality in our American struggle, I extended it analogously to Christian colleagues in the East:

> Is it really required of my Russian colleagues that they only praise their society when we all know that nothing like perfect liberation or justice has been achieved there? . . . Will the churches in socialist societies contribute to the discussion of so difficult and so crucial an issue? Can you make your own prophetic critique of what appears to some of us to be excessive, yes sinful, claims to exclusive power and special privilege of some of your new ruling and bureaucratic classes?[132]

The second issue related to the Christian-Marxist dialogue then being practiced in Europe. I found it analogous in some ways to the successful struggle in America to remove President Richard Nixon from office after Watergate, which demonstrated to us again how crucial are the freedoms of speech, assembly, and press to attain or maintain democracy and justice. Given this American experience of social struggle, I addressed the refusal of most of them to risk entering such dialogue because they held that it really was only "practical cooperation" not "theoretical dialogue" that was important:

> I may have misunderstood [I said], but this always sounded to me like it meant cooperation without genuine communication, a kind of political accommodation without the freedom or trust to try to help clarify for each other the shape of that human future which a common praxis was supposedly seeking to create.

I dare to cite my own dialogical experience only to show that it was possible despite great difficulties even in the midst of the cold war.[133] Some of that dialogue, of course, had to be more careful than my public address in Siofok. Metropolitan Nikodim's response to me was personal and off the record after that public meeting: "You may be correct in principle," he said, "but you must not think that you as a North American know better than your brothers and sisters in the Soviet Union when the proper time has come for the kind of dialogue and communication you are advocating." He, of course, was right; but *glasnost* and *perestroika* did come a decade later, and the peace process on this East-West margin now may go on much more publicly and perhaps with increasing fruit.

It was, of course, not only the Soviet government that made the dialogical praxis of peace difficult during the cold war. The U.S. government often did all that it could to hamper and undermine it. The most egregious example of many was its attempt to stop participation of North American church leaders in the conference that the Russian Orthodox Church hosted in Moscow May 10–14, 1982. The typically long title of the conference articulated its genuinely serious purpose: "The World Conference of Religious Workers for Saving the Sacred Gift of Life from Nuclear Catastrophe." At that point in our national history, the government of President Ronald Reagan did not want church leaders or anyone else working against its massive nuclear arms program. So the Department of State, members of Congress, and, at least in the instance of Billy Graham, Vice President George Bush did what they could—unsuccessfully—to dissuade those invited from participating. Participants from three other Western countries also told us in Moscow of approaches from their United States' embassies seeking to dissuade their attendance in Moscow.

The conference was successful in articulating the growing moral consensus of the world's religions in opposing nuclear arms as a threat to the sanctity of human life. But it was difficult to learn anything of this religious consensus on so crucial an issue through the national news media in the United States, which changed the entire focus in their reporting to the human rights issues related to the freedom of religion in the Soviet Union, largely on the basis of press releases from the United States' embassy in Moscow. Thus the political agenda of their government was temporarily and partially successful in blocking the peace agenda of American religious leaders, even though it could not entirely inhibit their dialogical and dialectical peace praxis across what were then very hostile political margins. Nevertheless, the religious teaching against nuclear arms continues to gain ever greater consensus in the world, as political margins are drawn and redrawn, and various governments come and go.

*Peace Praxis in the*
*Universally Relational Spirit of God*

No grandiose claim for any particular peace praxis as being the historical cause of any good consequence, however, is possible or intended. The problems are always too complex and the myriad interacting factors too organically related to make any such claim credible. More than that, the effort to sustain the religious spirit in faithful praxis is often more under-mined than helped when acclaimed for success. So a theology of peace, when it is informed by the universal relationality of God, finally attributes all real success in the actualization of peace to God's Holy Spirit. That is, to that dimension of God's relational being that receives the whole world into God's consequent nature, so that through forgiveness and new possi-bility our world may increasingly and finally become reconciled in peace.

When the Jewish-American ethicist Philip Hallie first read of the Christian French village of Le Chambon, he was in the midst of an objec-tive study of cruelty, reading an anthology of documents from the Holo-caust. He reports that "about halfway down the third page of the account of this village, I was annoyed by a strange sensation. . . . I reached up to my cheek to wipe away a bit of dust, and I felt tears upon my finger-tips."[134] He was at first chagrined by this intrusion of emotion, as indicat-ing that he had ceased objectively learning about cruelty to become one more of its victims. That night, however, as he reviewed his day, he found himself weeping once more; so he returned to his office in the middle of the night to re-read the account of Pastors Andre Trocmé and Edouard Theis leading Christian villagers at great risk for four years in a quiet struggle against the Nazis and their Vichy government to save thousands of Jews during the concluding phase of Europe's second thirty years war.

"And to my surprise," he writes, "again the spear, again the tears, again the frantic, painful pleasure that spills into the mind when a deep, deep need is being satisfied, or when a deep wound is starting to heal."[135] This is the way the Holy Spirit multiplies and magnifies the praxis of peace, no matter how seemingly insignificant or unsuccessful. For Augustine was correct, there is finally no one who in the depths of his or her heart does not wish to have peace. And peace is, as Whitehead discerned, the trans-fer of interest to coordinates wider than our personality. Whenever and wherever we see those coordinates of love and justice actualized, whether Jewish and American, French and Christian, Sri Lankan and Buddhist, or Egyptian and Muslim, the Holy Spirit begins to heal our human wounds and satisfy what Hallie accurately names our deep, deep need for peace.

But even so powerful an existential experience may only be a begin-ning. It is completed as we enter into the praxis of peace to create our own expressions of Le Chambon. Most such acts will be little noticed, and when they are they may often be at first opposed. Hallie's reflections are also helpful here:

> But acts of conscience are not important news, especially while a war is going on. Only actions directly related to the national self-interest re-ceive a measure of fame then. . . . This is also why the armed resistance produced heroes like General de Gaulle himself, and the passionately beloved coordinator of the armed French Resistance, Jean Moulin.

There are no such nationally known names in the story of Le Chambon. When France was liberated, there were no triumphal marches for Andre Trocmé and his villagers through the streets of Paris or Marseilles. And this was as it should have been: they had not contributed directly to saving the life of the French nation. They were not so much French patriots as they were conscientious human beings.[136]

The universally relational God enables our being French or any other kind of patriots if only we become, above all, conscientious human beings in a universally relational praxis of peace—both in the center of whatever is our village and at its margins, as we build the ethos of a planetary culture for our emerging global village. Perhaps there will yet come a day in God's universal providence when villagers like those in Le Chambon in whatever obscure villages found at the world's margins will be recognized as having done as much or more to save the real life of whatever is their nation than any more tribal patriot in their political center.

As great as is this eschatological hope, our faith does not rest in it but in the Holy Spirit of our universally relational God who calls us to, and sustains us in, the praxis of a universally relational peace.

# Notes

## Introduction

1. Eunice Tietjens, "A Plaint of Complexity," *Body and Raiment* (New York: Alfred A. Knopf, 1919).

2. I have articulated some of these dimensions of my understanding of Christian faith in *A Christology of Peace* (Louisville, Ky.: Westminster/John Knox Press, 1989). The issues addressed there were ecumenically Christian but did not yet address the cross-cultural and interreligious problematic that requires the more theocentric focus of this discussion.

3. These are almost the words of Hans-Georg Gadamer. Cf. his *Truth and Method*, 2d rev. ed., tr. Joel Weinsheimer and Donald G. Marshall (New York: Crossroad, 1989), xxiv. Gadamer's hermeneutical concerns, however, do not have the scope of our discussion because they remain limited to the European "historical tradition to which we all belong" (xxv). He wrote, however, in a way with which I basically agree:

> A new critical consciousness must now accompany all responsible philosophizing which takes the habits of thought and language built up in the individual in his communication with his environment and places them before the forum of the historical tradition to which we all belong.

4. Ibid., xxxvi–vii. I consider Gadamer's phrase misleading because Gadamer's work refers almost entirely to the Western cultural traditions and thus is not really universal.

Gadamer also makes a misleading claim for Hegel; "Hegel's philosophy represents the last mighty attempt to grasp philosophy and science as a unity." I owe this reference to George Lucas, Jr., who found it in *Philosophical Hermeneutics*, tr. David E. Linge (Berkeley and Los Angeles: University of

231

California Press, 1976), 110. Gadamer obviously does not know of White-head's later mighty attempt, which has proven so fruitful for many process philosophers and theologians—as I hope this book also will demonstrate. All claims to universality, however, are misleading because no finite person can fully reach it.

5. Alfred North Whitehead, *Process and Reality*, corrected ed., ed. David Ray Griffin and Donald W. Sherburne (New York: Free Press, 1978), 39.

6. Ibid., 39–40.

7. Though I have not derived this way of phrasing this concept directly from any other author, its closeness to the Whiteheadian tradition of process philosophy and theology may be seen in articles published in a recent edition of *Process Studies* devoted to "dialogical method," in which Leslie Muray wrote of "The Process-Relational Vision" and David Wheeler of "Process-Relational Christian Soteriology," *Process Studies* 18, no. 2 (Summer 1989): 83–94 and 102–13.

The concept of "relationality" is becoming widely used, however, far beyond the Whiteheadian process circle. Cf. Leonard Swidler, *After the Absolute* (Minneapolis: Fortress Press, 1990), 6–7:

> Where immutability, simplicity, and monologue had largely character-ized our Western understanding of reality in an earlier day, in the past 150 years mutuality, relationality, and dialogue have come to be under-stood as constitutive elements of the very structure of human reality.
> . . . Though not all critical Western thinkers conceive of reality as pro-cess, they do, however, think of it at least as constituted in mutuality and relationality.

8. The illuminating discussion of this point in Daniel Day Williams, *The Spirit and the Forms of Love* (New York: Harper & Row, 1968), has been a blessing to my mind and spirit for decades.

9. The best analysis of this problem that I know is in Charles Harts-horne, *The Divine Relativity: A Social Conception of God* (New Haven, Conn.: Yale University Press, 1948).

10. The influence of one of my teachers, Paul Tillich, is obvious. For one of his many discussions of ultimate concern, see his *Systematic Theology* (Chi-cago: University of Chicago Press, 1963), 3:130.

11. Thomas J. J. Altizer, *Genesis and Apocalypse* (Louisville, Ky.: Westmin-ster/John Knox Press, 1990), cf. especially 13–15. Another learning happily discovered while reading Altizer is that my method of dialogical hermeneutics is not the only method hard to read.

12. Ibid., 14.

13. Ibid., 15.

14. Ibid.

15. Ibid., 35, emphasis added.

16. Ibid., 57, emphasis added.

Chapter 1
The Spatiotemporal Relationality of Creation

1. Cf. especially Plato's *Protagoras* 320 and *Timaeus*.

2. Cf. Samuel Terrien's "Introduction" to his exegesis of Job in *The Inter-preter's Bible*, 3:897–902 especially.

3. Perhaps no recent historian or phenomenologist of religion has been more influential in reestablishing the cosmological function of religion than Mircea Eliade; see especially his *Sacred and Profane*, tr. W. R. Trask (New York: Harcourt, Brace & Co., 1959). I have also found the discussion of Charles Long, Eliade's student and colleague, helpful; see especially chapter 3 on "Archaism and Hermeneutics" in his *Significations* (Philadelphia: Fortress Press, 1986).

4. I am indebted here to the methodological reflections of J. G. Platvoet of the Netherlands, who was my colleague lecturing on African traditional religion in the University of Zimbabwe, where I had the privilege for six months as a visiting professor to lecture on the philosophy of religion.

5. See Jean-Paul Sartre, *Being and Nothingness* (New York: Philosophical Library, 1956), and for a more graphic expression, his novel *Nausea* (New York: New Directions, 1959).

6. Lord Russell's conclusion at the end of his lecture on "Why I Am Not a Christian" is worthy of remembrance:

> We want to stand upon our own feet and look fair and square at the world—its good facts, its bad facts, its beauties and its ugliness; see the world as it is and be not afraid of it. Conquer the world by intelligence and not merely by being slavishly subdued by the terror that comes from it. The whole conception of God is a conception . . . quite un-worthy of free men.
>
> *Why I Am Not a Christian and Other Essays*
> (New York: Simon & Schuster, 1957), 23

7. Cf. Hunter Lewis's interpretation of Einstein's perspective as "neo-Buddhist" in *A Question of Values* (New York: Harper & Row, 1990), 146–53.

8. I was struck by the disbelieving laughter of some Africans at the thought that there actually are some people who do not believe in God. Perhaps Immanuel Kant's analysis of "The Sense of the Beautiful and of the Sublime," whatever one thinks of his judgments about the national character of various Europeans, illuminates this African response:

> Finally a vain and carefree man is at all times without a strong sense of the sublime; his religion is without emotion, but is mostly a matter of fashion which he attends to with grace though remaining cold. This is the practical *indifferentism* (toward which the French national spirit seems most inclined); from such indifferentism to impious mockery is

only a step; it means, if one considers the inner value, little more than a complete rejection [of religion].
   *The Philosophy of Kant* (New York: Modern Library, 1949), 12–13

9. It is, of course, true that many Buddhists reject the whole notion of creation as Christians understand it in the traditional doctrine of *creatio ex nihilo*, but I don't think this negates the essential point of the cosmological function of religion. One might compare Langdon Gilkey's too confident assertion of this doctrine in his early neo-orthodox study of creation, *Maker of Heaven and Earth* (Garden City, N.Y.: Doubleday & Co., 1959), esp. chapter 3, with Harvey Cox's comment inspired by interaction with Buddhists: "Jesus exemplified in his life something Buddhist teachers constantly emphasize— that reality is always different from even our best ways of talking and thinking about it" (*Many Mansions: A Christian's Encounter with Other Faiths* [Boston: Beacon Press, 1988], 88). That is, Buddhists seek in their own way what might be termed a nonconceptual orientation to the cosmos.

10. Langdon Gilkey, *Naming the Whirlwind* (Indianapolis: Bobbs-Merrill, 1969), 91–92. His analysis of the breakdown of neo-orthodox theology, pages 92–106, is very persuasive.

11. Thomas Altizer, *Radical Theology and the Death of God* (Indianapolis: Bobbs-Merrill, 1966), 102.

12. Gerhard von Rad, *Old Testament Theology*, tr. D. M. G. Stalker (New York: Harper & Brothers, 1962), 136. Von Rad points especially to passages like Isaiah 44:24, 28, which clearly interrelate cosmic creation and historical redemption:

> Thus says the LORD, your Redeemer,
>    who formed you from the womb:
> "I am the LORD, who made all things,
>    who stretched out the heavens alone,
>    who spread out the earth . . . ;
> who says of Cyrus, 'He is my shepherd,
>    and he shall fulfil all my purpose';
> saying of Jerusalem, 'She shall be built,'
>    and of the temple, 'Your foundation shall be laid.' "

13. Ibid., 152.
14. Cf. Psalm 74:12–13:

> Yet God my King is from of old,
>    working salvation in the midst of the earth.
> Thou didst divide the sea by thy might;
>    thou didst break the heads of the dragons on the waters.

15. Abraham Joshua Heschel, *God in Search of Man: A Philosophy of Judaism* (New York: Meridian Books, 1955), 16.
16. Ibid., 16–17.
17. Ibid., 209.
18. Ibid., 210–11.

19. Byron L. Haines and Frank L. Cooley, eds., *Christians and Muslims Together* (Philadelphia: Geneva Press, 1987), 106–7.

20. John Bowlby, *Charles Darwin: A New Life* (New York: W. W. Norton & Co., 1990), 400.

21. Ibid., 398.

22. The creative struggle to establish this conclusion in the scientific, philosophical, and theological thought of Pierre Teilhard de Chardin is classical. See his *Vision of the Past*, tr. J. M. Cohen (New York: Harper & Row, 1966), and *The Phenomenon of Man*, tr. Bernard Wall, intro. Julian Huxley, (New York: Harper & Brothers, 1959).

23. The widely influential work of Thomas Kuhn seems definitive on the point that science always works with a theoretical paradigm dependent on a worldview. See his *The Structure of Scientific Revolutions* (Chicago: University of Chicago Press, 1962).

24. For an instructive analysis of what is at issue here in North American culture, both in its schools and courts, see David S. Caudill, "Law and Worldview: Problems in the Creation-Science Controversy," *Journal of Law and Religion* 3, no. 1 (1985): 1–46.

25. Langdon Gilkey, *Religion and the Scientific Future* (New York: Harper & Row, 1970), 57.

26. J. Bronowski, *Science and Human Values*, rev. ed. (New York: Harper & Row, 1965), 15–16. I am grateful to Prof. Evan Hazard, who while "visiting scientist-in-residence" at Garrett-Evangelical Theological Seminary, reminded me of the value of Bronowski's work in responding to an earlier draft of this chapter.

27. See Robert M. Grant, *The Early Christian Doctrine of God* (Charlottesville, Va.: University of Virginia Press, 1966), especially chap. 1 on "God the Father" and appendix II on "The Impassibility of God."

28. Langdon Gilkey looks upon this development critically but evaluates it more positively than I. Nevertheless, his description is similar:

> Insofar as the Christian God was really ultimate and his power and sovereignty truly universal, it was necessary that Christian modes of reflective speech express a maximum of transcendence, universality, and permanence. . . . Christian language about God employed the philosophical concepts of Stoicism, middle Platonism, neo-Platonism, and then Aristotelianism in order to express the transcendence of God as the source and ruler of all things, and the activity of God in the world.
>
> *Religion and the Scientific Future*, 110

29. Darwin remarked that he studied Paley's *Evidences of Christianity* and *Natural Theology* "in a thorough manner" while at Cambridge and found then that their logic gave him "as much delight as did Euclid." Cited in Bowlby, *Charles Darwin*, 104.

30. Cf. the discussion in Charles P. Henderson, Jr., *God and Science: The Death and Rebirth of Theism* (Atlanta: John Knox Press, 1986), chap. 3.

31. Charles Darwin, *The Origin of Species* (New York: Collier and Son, 1909), 505–6; quoted in Henderson, *God and Science*, 58.

32. Henderson quotes from Darwin's long correspondence with his friend and colleague, Asa Gray (*God and Science*, 59):

I am conscious that I am in an utterly hopeless muddle. I cannot think that the world, as we see it, is the result of chance; and yet I cannot look at each separate thing as the result of Design. I am in thick mud; the Orthodox would say in fetid abominable mud. I believe I am in much the same frame of mind as an old gorilla would be in if set to learn the first book of Euclid . . . yet I cannot keep out of the question.

33. Cf. John Baillie, *The Belief in Progress* (New York: Charles Scribner's Sons, 1951). In reviewing it while writing, I have been surprised at how formative its influence has remained.

34. The works of Douglas John Hall, especially in *Lighten Our Darkness: An Indigenous Theology of the Cross* (Philadelphia: Westminster Press, 1976) and *The Steward: A Biblical Symbol Come of Age* (New York: Friendship Press, 1982), provide important analysis of this view of North America.

35. Paul Tillich, *Systematic Theology* (Chicago: University of Chicago Press, 1957), vol. 2.

36. This judgment, of course, is not undisputed, especially among European scholars hermeneutically dependent upon their own tradition rooted in Descartes, Leibniz, Kant, Hegel, Husserl, and Heidegger. Cf. the excellent discussion in George R. Lucas, Jr., *The Rehabilitation of Whitehead: An Analytic and Historical Assessment of Process Philosophy* (Albany, N.Y.: State University of New York Press, 1989).

37. Alfred North Whitehead, *Process and Reality*, corrected ed. (New York: Free Press, 1978), xii.

38. Michael Welker provides a convenient summary of this development in his essay, "Alfred North Whitehead's Basic Philosophical Problem: The Development of a Relativistic Cosmology," *Process Studies* 16, no. 1 (Spring 1987): 1–25.

39. A. N. Whitehead, *Religion in the Making* (New York: Macmillan Co., 1926), 16 and 59.

40. Whitehead, *Process and Reality*, 14.

41. Ibid., 15.

42. Whitehead wrote: " 'Creativity,' 'many,' 'one' are the ultimate notions involved in the meaning of the synonymous terms 'thing,' 'being,' 'entity.' These three notions complete the category of the Ultimate and are presupposed in all the more special categories" (Ibid., 21).

43. Ibid. for all quoted phrases in this paragraph.

44. Reto Luzius Fetz, "Creativity: A New Transcendental?" in *Whitehead's Metaphysics of Creativity*, ed. Friedrich Rapp and Reiner Wiehl (Albany, N.Y.: State University of New York Press, 1990), 189–208.

45. When seen in this way, Whitehead's notion seems less offensive to traditional theology. Cf. *Process and Reality*, 31.

46. Thomas Aquinas *Summa Theologiae* 1.45.1, 8, cited in Fetz, "Creativity," 199.

47. Whitehead, *Process and Reality*, 223.

48. Ibid., 222.

49. Carl F. H. Henry, "The Stunted God of Process Theology," in *Process Theology*, ed. Ronald Nash (Grand Rapids: Baker Book House, 1987), 375.

50. A. N. Whitehead, *Science and the Modern World* (New York: New American Library, 1925), 173. The whole of chap. 11 simply bears the title "God."

51. Ibid., 174.

52. Whitehead, *Process and Reality*, 343.

53. Whitehead, *Science and the Modern World*, 178.

54. Ibid., 179; also for the quotations earlier in this paragraph.

55. Whitehead, *Process and Reality*, 345.

56. Ibid.

57. Ibid., 342.

58. Cf. the analysis of Fetz in *Whitehead's Metaphysics of Creativity*, ed. Rapp and Wiehl, 196.

59. Whitehead, *Process and Reality*, 345.

60. Donald Bloesch, "Process Theology and Reformed Theology," in *Process Theology*, ed. Nash, 41.

61. James Mannoia, "Is God an Exception to Whitehead's Metaphysics?" ibid., 270. The internal quotation is from L. Eslick, "God in the Metaphysics of Whitehead," *New Themes in Christian Philosophy*, ed. R. M. McInerny (Notre Dame, Ind.: University of Notre Dame Press, 1968), 80.

62. Charles Hartshorne, *The Divine Relativity* (New Haven, Conn.: Yale University Press, 1948), 89.

63. Marjorie Suchocki, *God—Christ—Church* (New York: Crossroad, 1988), 37.

64. Mannoia, "Is God an Exception . . . ?" in *Process Theology*, ed. Nash, 263.

65. Ibid., 272.

66. Whitehead, *Process and Reality*, 346.

67. Suchocki, *God—Christ—Church*, 63.

68. Errol E. Harris, *Formal, Transcendental, and Dialectical Thinking: Logic and Reality* (Albany, N.Y.: State University of New York Press, 1987), 143.

## Chapter 2
## The Cross-Cultural Relationality of Meaning

1. A very useful resource for tracing the history of this discussion in Western culture from Plotinus through contemporary philosophers is Ian Ramsey, ed., *Words about God* (London: SCM Press, 1971). An excellent recent discussion is Sallie McFague's *Metaphorical Theology: Models of God in Religious Language* (Philadelphia: Fortress Press, 1982).

2. This is a fascinating text because after affirming the *deus absconditus*, this text, nevertheless, addresses the "God of Israel" as "Savior." Here the tension between the negation of "idolatrous" claims to know God directly

and universally and the affirmation of the possibility of our knowing the true and mysterious God in our finite history is clearly expressed.

3. Augustine *On the Trinity* 5.9, quoted in Ramsey, *Words about God*, 1.

4. Aquinas *Quaestiones Disputatae de Potentia Dei* 7, 5, 14, quoted in Ramsey, *Words about God*, 1.

5. "Dialectical" here, as in the last chapter, means the kind of thinking and logic appropriate to a structure of elements in relation, but for the special focus of this chapter, it also means the dialogical form of communication appropriate to an open system. Cf. Errol E. Harris, *Formal, Transcendental, and Dialectical Thinking* (Albany, N.Y.: State University of New York Press, 1987), chap. 8.

6. David Hume, *An Enquiry concerning Human Understanding* (1748).

7. A. J. Ayer, *Language, Truth, and Logic* (London: Dover Publications, 1950), provides his later, more careful articulation of this perspective.

8. Elie Wiesel, "Recalling Swallowed-Up Worlds," *The Christian Century*, May 27, 1981, 611; cited in John Piippo, *Metaphor and Theology: A Multidisciplinary Approach* (unpublished Ph.D. diss., Garrett-Evangelical Theological Seminary and Northwestern University, 1986), 308.

9. A. N. Whitehead, *Process and Reality*, corrected ed. (New York: Free Press, 1978), xiv.

10. Ibid., 42; emphasis added.

11. Kosuke Koyama, *Mount Fuji and Mount Sinai* (London: SCM Press, 1984, and Maryknoll, N.Y.: Orbis Books, 1985), ix–x.

12. The quoted phrases are from F. S. C. Northrop, *The Meeting of East and West* (New York: Macmillan Co., 1946), 421.

13. Kosuke Koyama, *Three Mile an Hour God* (London: SCM Press, 1979, and Maryknoll, N.Y.: Orbis Books, 1980), 61.

14. Quoted in ibid., 59–60.

15. Hans-Georg Gadamer in the "Afterword" of his *Truth and Method*, 2d rev. ed. (New York: Crossroad, 1989), 570.

16. Ibid., 571.

17. Ibid., 290.

18. Ibid., 293.

19. Ibid., 302.

20. Ibid., 304; all of the briefer citations in this paragraph are taken from 302–4.

21. "The fundamental prejudice of the Enlightenment is the prejudice against prejudice itself, which denies tradition its power." Ibid., 270.

22. Ibid., 306–7.

23. Reinhold Niebuhr, *The Nature and Destiny of Man* (New York: Charles Scribner's Sons, 1941, 1943, and 1949), 2:4.

24. Gadamer, *Truth and Method*, 199.

25. Ibid., 203, emphasis added. Gadamer refers to Ranke's *Weltgeschichte* and Gerhard Masur's *Rankes Begriff der Weltgeschichte*.

26. Ibid., 209. Gadamer's reference is to Ranke, *Weltgeschichte*, 9, part 1, p. 270f.; and to Hinrich's *Ranke und die Geschichtstheologie der Goethezeit*, 239f.

27. Cited from Ranke, *Weltgeschichte*, 9, parts 2, 5, 7, in ibid., 210. The phrases quoted from Ranke are assigned by him directly to the "Deity," but Gadamer shows how they were then analogously related to the historian.

28. Gadamer, *Truth and Method*, 258.

29. Ibid., 305.

30. John Mbiti, *Concepts of God in Africa* (London: SPCK, and New York: Praeger, 1970), 327–36.

31. Ibid., xiv.

32. Ibid., 8. Mbiti does specifically deny, however, that pantheism may be found in any African religion (17).

33. Ibid., 15.

34. Ibid., 91–92.

35. Ibid., 92, 115.

36. Ibid., 117–27.

37. Ibid., 161, 171.

38. Ibid., 264.

39. Zulu Sofola, "The Theatre in the Search for African Authenticity," in *African Theology en Route* (Maryknoll, N.Y.: Orbis Books, 1979), 127.

40. Engelbert Mveng, "Black African Art as Cosmic Liturgy and Religious Language," ibid., 141.

41. Cited in Northrop, *Meeting of East and West*, 314.

42. Ibid., 315. Kuang-Sae Lee's response to Northrop confirms and supports his analysis from an Asian viewpoint, though he disagrees with Northrop's solutions. See his "A Critique of the Scope and Method of the Northropian Philosophical Anthropology and the Projection of a Hope for a Meeting of East and West," *Journal of Chinese Philosophy* 2 (1984): 255–74.

43. Northrop, *Meeting of East and West*, 318.

44. Ibid., 320.

45. A good introduction to these concepts may be found in John Clark Archer, revised by Carl E. Purinton, *Faiths Men Live By*, 2d ed. (New York: Ronald Press, 1958), 86–97, 125–29. Archer as a historian, however, sees far more difference between Confucius and Lao-tse than the philosopher Northrop, though Archer does see the Taoist Mo-ti, whom he calls perhaps "the most religious Chinese thinker of all time," as mediating between Lao-tse and Confucius in teaching "universal love (*jen*)" and that *jen* is "a quality of nature in itself." Cf. 130 and 134–135.

46. Northrop, *Meeting of East and West*, 331. Gadamer's critique of modern Western aesthetic philosophy is similar to Northrop's, though the similarity is obscured because Gadamer reverses the terms. When a pure work of art is abstracted from its original religious or social context that gave it significance, Gadamer terms it "aesthetic differentiation." But he objects to this aesthetic kind of consciousness that differentiates aesthetic experience "from all the elements of content that induce us to take up a moral or religious stance towards it." Gadamer, like Northrop, wants a hermeneutic of aesthetics that relates it to the universal continuum. Gadamer, *Truth and Method*, 85.

47. William James, *The Varieties of Religious Experience* (New York: Modern Library, 1902), 376.

48. Ibid., 377, n. 2.

49. Thomas M. King, *Teilhard's Mysticism of Knowing* (New York: Seabury Press, 1981), 92–93.

50. Ibid., 91.

51. Pierre Teilhard de Chardin, *Letters to Leontine Zanta*, tr. Bernard Wall (New York: Harper & Row, 1969), 104–5, cited in ibid., 91.

52. Northrop, *Meeting of East and West*, 343–44.

53. Kim Sung-dong, *Mandala*, tr. Ahn Jung-hyo (Seoul: Dongsuh Munhaksa, 1990), 126.

54. Ibid., 78, 81.

55. Ibid., 125.

56. Cf. E. A. Burtt's review, "The Meeting of East and West," *The Philosophical Review* 56 (1947): 75.

57. Stuart M. Brown, Jr., "The Meeting of East and West," ibid., 81.

58. Laurence J. Rosan, "Desirelessness and the Good," *Philosophy East and West* (April 1955): 57.

59. Cf. J. P. McKinney, "Comment and Discussion: Can East Meet West?" 3–4 (October 1953): 257–67.

60. Cf. Peter Munz, "Basic Intuitions of East and West," *Philosophy East and West* (April 1955), esp. 52.

61. Ibid., 53.

62. Ibid., 56.

63. J. P. McKinney makes this point in his response to Northrop's analysis, "Comment and Discussion: Can East Meet West?"

64. Kuang-Sae Lee, "A Critique of the Scope," 258. The internal citations are from Kant's *Critique of Practical Reason*.

65. Preface to the second edition of the *Critique of Pure Reason*.

66. Kant, *First Critique*, tr. Kemp Smith (New York: Macmillan Co., 1929), 632, quoted in George Lucas, *The Rehabilitation of Whitehead* (Albany, N.Y.: State University of New York Press, 1989), 84. Cf. Gadamer's interpretation of Kant on this point in *Truth and Method*, 50–51: "As beautiful, nature finds a language that brings to us an intelligible idea of what mankind is to be."

67. Whitehead, *Process and Reality*, part II, chap. 8.

68. Ibid., 49–50.

69. Ibid., 50, 51.

70. Ibid., 342–43.

71. Northrop's closeness to Whitehead's thought is not very surprising because Northrop had been (with Charles Hartshorne, Gregory Vlastos, and Paul Weiss) one of Whitehead's best students at Harvard. For the Northrop reference, see n. 52 above.

72. Whitehead, *Process and Reality*, 344.

73. Ibid., 343.

74. These phrases are quoted from chapter 7 of the *Tao-Te Ching* by Kuang-Sae Lee, "A Critique of the Scope," 259.

75. Errol Harris's more philosophical way of articulating this insight concerning loving action within the whole provides unusual conceptual clarity, in his *Formal, Transcendental, and Dialectical Thinking*, 244–45:

Practical activity is the outward expression in action of the mind's awareness of its world, of the condition in that world of its conscious self, and of its relation to other things and other selves. . . . The immanence in the individual mind of the principle of wholeness generates, from this consciousness of self and others, a conception of a more adequate and complete realization of that universal principle—in other words, of a better state of the self and its world. The universal nisus toward wholeness is thus, in the self, the nisus toward self-fulfillment. . . . As human personality is the latest phase in the developing scale of natural forms, the subjectivity of values may be acknowledged without denying their equally objective significance. In fact, since objectivity has turned out to be systematically integrated wholeness, if that also proves to be the hallmark of value, its criteria will be just as objective and universal in their validity as are standards of truth.

76. Sang Il Kim, *Han and World Philosophy* (Seoul: Hinang Publishing Co., 1989). I am indebted to Hwa Young Chong for calling my attention to this work and for her translation.

77. Teilhard, *Writings in Times of War*, tr. Rene Hague (New York: Harper & Row, 1968), 205, 124; cited in King, *Teilhard's Mysticism of Knowing*, 5.

78. Teilhard, *The Phenomenon of Man*, tr. Bernard Wall (New York: Harper & Brothers, 1959), 266; cited in ibid., 6.

79. These citations are culled by Thomas King from Teilhard's essay on "Cosmic Life." See King, *Teilhard's Mysticism of Knowing*, 9.

80. Teilhard, *The Heart of the Matter*, tr. Rene Hague (New York: Harcourt Brace Jovanovich, 1979), 24; cited in King, *Teilhard's Mysticism of Knowing*, 8. Teilhard's rejection of a "pantheism of fusion" is entirely analogous to Sang Il Kim's criticism of Taoism's and Buddhism's integration of the one and the many into the same by making them middle.

81. King, *Teilhard's Mysticism of Knowing*, 149, n. 1, cf. 14.

82. Teilhard, *The Phenomenon of Man*, 271, cited in ibid., 25.

83. Teilhard, *The Future of Man*, tr. Norman Denny (New York: Harper & Row, 1964), 45; cited in King, *Teilhard's Mysticism of Knowing*, 44.

84. Ibid., 32, emphasis added.

85. E. A. Burtt, "The Meeting of East and West," 75–76. Cf. Robert C. Smith, "Aesthetic/Theoretic Polarity in Northrop's Aesthetic Continuum," *Journal of Aesthetic Education*, January 1977, 28–29.

## Chapter 3
## The Interreligious Relationality of Redemption

1. Reinhold Niebuhr, however, attributed this aphorism to another source: "I still think the 'London Times Literary Supplement' was substan-

tially correct when it wrote some years ago: 'The doctrine of original sin is the only empirically verifiable doctrine of the Christian faith.' " *Man's Nature and His Communities* (New York: Charles Scribner's Sons, 1965), 24.

2. Reinhold Niebuhr also obviously knew this. His, magnum opus on *The Nature and Destiny of Man* (New York: Charles Scribner's Sons, 1941, 1943, 1949) is an extended illustration of his sophistication on this issue as it relates to other thinkers. And his last book reveals his own critical self-awareness as he gradually changed "from a purely Protestant viewpoint to an increasing sympathy for the two other great traditions of Western culture, Jewish and Catholic." *Man's Nature and His Communities*, 15.

3. Mark Kline Taylor, *Remembering Esperanza: A Cultural Political Theology for North American Praxis* (Maryknoll, N.Y.: Orbis Books, 1990), 31–32.

4. Paul Tillich, "Informal Report on Lecture Trip to Japan—Summer 1960," 15, cited in George Rupp, *Christologies and Cultures* (The Hague: Mouton, 1974), 232n.

5. Paul Tillich, *The Future of Religions* (New York: Harper & Row, 1966), 91.

6. Raimundo Panikkar, "Faith and Belief: A Multireligious Experience," *Anglican Theological Review* 53 (1971): 220; cited in Leonard Swidler, *After the Absolute* (Philadelphia: Fortress Press, 1990), 52.

7. Interpreted from personal experience of the author as a member and participant in the World Methodist Council meeting.

8. This is Whitehead's phrase for the conception of an empirical fact as an object with a simple location in space and time construed by inductive logic, as developed by Galileo, Descartes, Newton, and Bacon in the seventeenth century, which still dominates the common sense of the Western world. See Alfred North Whitehead, *Science and the Modern World* (New York: Macmillan Co., 1925), chap. 3.

9. Alfred North Whitehead, *Process and Reality*, corrected ed. (New York: Free Press, 1978), 7.

10. Tillich wrote in *The Future of Religions*, 86:

> My approach is dynamic-typological. There is no progressive development which goes on and on, but there are elements in the experience of the Holy which are always there, if the Holy is experienced. These elements, if they are predominant in one religion, create a particular religious type.

11. Ibid., 94. I see Tillich's approach as a necessary corrective to Wilfred Cantwell Smith's claim that the history of religion is the one true basis for theology. His definition of the historian of religion as "that scholar whose aspiration is to apprehend, and to render intellectually apprehensible the truth about God; the transcendently true," is in danger of ending with those transcendent abstractions which strip religion of its dynamic redemptive power. See his "Theology and the World's Religious History," in *Toward a Universal Theology of Religion*, ed. Leonard Swidler (Maryknoll, N.Y.: Orbis Books, 1987), 67.

12. Arend Theodoor van Leeuwen, *Christianity in World History*, tr. H. H. Hoskins (New York: Charles Scribner's Sons, 1966), esp. 165–73.

13. David Ray Griffin and Huston Smith, *Primordial Truth and Postmodern Theology* (Albany, N.Y.: State University of New York Press, 1989), xi–xiii.

14. George Rupp, *Christologies and Cultures*, in which he develops a typology of religious worldviews based on Hegel's philosophy.

15. Ibid., 3.

16. Ibid., 6.

17. For insight into the relation of Hegel and Whitehead, see the work of George R. Lucas, *The Rehabilitation of Whitehead* (Albany, N.Y.: SUNY Press, 1989), chap. 6, "Whitehead, Hegel, and the Philosophy of Nature"; or, more extensively, the volume he edited, *Hegel and Whitehead: Contemporary Perspectives on Systematic Philosophy* (Albany, N.Y.: SUNY Press, 1986).

18. Rupp, *Christologies and Cultures*, 86.

19. Hegel, *The Phenomenology of Mind*, tr. John B. Baillie (New York: Harper Torchbook, 1967), 80; cited in Rupp, *Christologies and Cultures*, 102.

20. Cf. Rupp, *Christologies and Cultures*, 136–37.

21. Hegel, *The Philosophy of History*, trans. J. Sibree (New York: Dover Publications, 1956), 18; cited in Rupp, *Christologies and Cultures*, 88–89. The translation cited is Rupp's own.

22. George Rupp indicates this possibility by using the typological categories derived from the European tradition via Hegel to interpret Theravada and Mahayana Buddhism, *Christologies and Cultures*, 239–49.

23. The Greek word *kairos* means fulfilled time or the qualitatively right time when something new may happen. Cf. Paul Tillich's discussion in "The Decline and Validity of the Idea of Progress" in *The Future of Religions*, 64–79; among many other considerations, he points to "the increasing awareness, even among conservative theologians, that our attitude toward the non-Christian religions has to be one of dialogue" (70).

24. From the ancient baptismal formula cited by Paul in Gal. 3:28, NRSV.

25. These are Winston L. King's words, as he commends the work of the Japanese Buddhist Keiji Nishitani in coming westward to meet us, in the foreword to *Religion and Nothingness*, tr. and ed. Jan van Bragt (Berkeley and Los Angeles: University of California Press, 1990), vii.

26. Cox has written in his recent book on the issue, "I believe that the most nettlesome dilemma hindering interreligious dialogue is the very ancient one of how to balance the universal and the particular." *Many Mansions: A Christian's Encounter with Other Faiths* (Boston: Beacon Press, 1988), 2.

27. Ibid., 5.

28. Ibid., 18.

29. David Tracy, *Plurality and Ambiguity* (New York: Harper & Row, 1987), 90.

30. David Tracy, *The Analogical Imagination* (New York: Crossroad, 1981), 51.

31. Ibid., 55f.

32. Ibid., 57.

33. Kenneth Seeskin, *Jewish Philosophy in a Secular Age* (Albany, N.Y.: SUNY Press, 1990), chap. 9, "Universality and Particularity."

34. Ibid., 221.

35. Michael Wyschogrod, "Judaism and Evangelical Christianity," in *Christianity through Non-Christian Eyes*, ed. Paul J. Griffiths (Maryknoll, N.Y.: Orbis Books, 1990), 58–59.

36. Ibid., 64.

37. Cited in Richard Henry Drummond, *Toward a New Age in Christian Theology* (Maryknoll, N.Y.: Orbis Books, 1985), 4.

38. Cf. Isa. 53:11, NRSV:

> Out of his anguish he shall see light;
> he shall find satisfaction through his knowledge.
> The righteous one, my servant, shall make many righteous,
> and he shall bear their iniquities.

39. Cf. John 1:1–14; Eph. 1:9–10; Col. 1:15–20.

40. Drummond, *Toward a New Age*, 14.

41. James E. Will, *A Christology of Peace* (Louisville, Ky.: Westminster/ John Knox Press, 1989), 82.

42. George Lindbeck, *The Nature of Doctrine* (Philadelphia: Westminster Press, 1984), 54–55.

43. S. Mark Heim articulates these issues from a somewhat more conservative theological perspective in his recent book, *Is Christ the Only Way? Christian Faith in a Pluralistic World* (Valley Forge, Pa.: Judson Press, 1985).

44. Cited in Martin Buber, *Moses: The Revelation and the Covenant* (New York: Harper & Brothers, Harper Torchbooks, 1958), 9.

45. Ibid., 9–10. Buber, of course, goes on to find in the God of Moses those qualities and activities that create a holy people of justice and loyalty, just as Christians have found them in Jesus, who is interpreted especially in the Gospel of Matthew with the paradigm of Moses.

46. Cf. Sura 4:5: "And who has a better religion than he who resigns himself to God, who does what is good, and follows the faith of Abraham in all sincerity? And God took Abraham for his friend."

47. Cf. my essay on "The Politics of Religion in the Middle East Peace Process," *American-Arab Affairs* 30 (Fall 1989): 77–80. Harvey Cox tells the whole story of this conflictual history in his *Many Mansions*, chap. 2.

48. Gamal Badr, "The Middle East Peace Process: An Islamic Perspective," *American-Arab Affairs* 30 (Fall 1989): 82.

49. Seyyed Hossein Nasr, "The Islamic View of Christianity," in *Christianity through Non-Christian Eyes*, ed. Griffiths, 133.

50. Cf. Sura 4:116: "God truly will not forgive the joining other gods with Himself. Other sins He will forgive to whom He will; but he who joins gods with God has erred with far-gone error." See also v. 51.

51. Jamal Badawi, "The Earth and Humanity: A Muslim View," in *Three Faiths, One God: A Jewish, Christian, Muslim Encounter*, ed. John Hick and

Edmund Meltzer (Albany, N.Y.: State University of New York Press, 1989), 95.

52. Cf. the discussion of Nasr, "The Islamic View of Christianity," 131.

53. Ibid., 130. Cf. Sura 4:127–29:

And if a wife fear ill usage or aversion on the part of her husband, then shall it be no fault in them if they can agree with mutual agreement, for agreement is best. "Men's souls are prone to avarice; but if ye act kindly and fear God, then, verily, your actions are not unnoticed by God." . . . But if they separate, God can compensate both out of His abundance; for God is Vast, Wise.

54. Badawi, "The Earth and Humanity," 95.

55. Cf. Rosemary Radford Ruether, *Faith and Fratricide* (New York: Seabury Press, 1974), and my *Christology of Peace*, 27–28, esp. the whole of chap. 2 on "The Jewishness of Jesus and the Struggle for Peace."

56. Nasr, "The Islamic View of Christianity," 130. This appears to me to be the clear teaching of Sura 17, "The Night Journey."

57. John Hick, "Trinity and Incarnation in the Light of Religious Pluralism," in *Three Faiths, One God*, 197–210.

58. Swami Nikhilananda, *The Upanishads* (New York: Harper & Brothers, 1949), 94. It is of more than anecdotal interest that Bertrand Russell remembered that Whitehead used a similar metaphor to distinguish his thought from Russell's Cartesian form of empiricism: "You think the world is what it looks like in fine weather at noon day, I think it is like what it seems like in the early morning when one first wakes from deep sleep." *Portraits from Memory*, 41, cited in "The Pardshaw Dialogues," *Process Studies* 16, no. 2 (Summer 1987): 98.

59. Raimundo Panikkar, "The Invisible Harmony: A Universal Theory of Religion or a Cosmic Confidence in Reality?" in *Toward a Universal Theology of Religion*, ed. Leonard Swidler (Maryknoll, N.Y.: Orbis Books, 1987), 118–53.

60. Ibid., 122.

61. Ibid., 132.

62. Ibid., 127.

63. *Bhagavad-Gita* 2:24–25.

64. Nikhilananda, *Upanishads*, 48.

65. Ibid., 48–49, emphasis added.

66. Cox, *Many Mansions*, 58.

67. *Bhagavad-Gita* 18:66.

68. Ibid., 9:27.

69. Cf. ibid., 2:71, "The man who casts off all desires and walks without desire, with no thought of a Mine and of an I, comes unto peace"; and 3:19, "Therefore fulfill ever without attachment the work that thou hast to do; for the man that does his work without attachment wins to the supreme."

70. Mohandas Gandhi, "The Story of My Experiments with Truth," in *Christianity through Non-Christian Eyes*, ed. Griffiths, 225.

71. Ibid., 224.

72. Swami Vivekananda, "Christ the Messenger," in ibid., 214.

73. M. M. Thomas, *The Acknowledged Christ of the Indian Renaissance* (Bangalore: Christian Institute for the Study of Religion and Society, 1970), 335.

74. Ibid., 22, 29.

75. Ibid., 19.

76. Ibid., 27.

77. Harold Coward, ed., *Hindu-Christian Dialogue: Perspectives and Encounters* (Maryknoll, N.Y.: Orbis Books, 1989), 37–39.

78. Ibid., 166–67.

79. Ibid., 172.

80. Cf. the wonderful and terrible depiction of Krishna in the *Bhagavad-Gita*, 11:5–46.

81. The word *Upanishad* derives from a Sanskrit root that means "to sit," according to Nicol Macnicol in his "Introduction" to *Hindu Scriptures* (London: J. M. Dent & Sons, 1938), xvii.

82. Cited by Walpola Rahula in *What the Buddha Taught* (New York: Grove Press, 1959), 11.

83. Ibid., 3.

84. Cited in ibid., 25–26.

85. Cited from the Buddha in ibid., 37.

86. Gunapal Dharmasiri, "A Buddhist Critique of the Christian Concept of God," *Christianity through Non-Christian Eyes*, ed. Griffiths, 155.

87. Ibid., 160.

88. Ibid., 161.

89. Ibid., 159.

90. Masao Abe, "Kenotic God and Dynamic Sunyata," in *The Emptying God*, ed. John C. Cobb and C. Ives (Maryknoll, N.Y.: Orbis Books, 1990), 4.

91. Abe currently is the central participant in the Purdue Interfaith Project of the Department of Philosophy of Purdue University and an associated "Interfaith Dialogue Series" carried out from 1991 to 1993.

92. Cf. Winston King's foreword to Nishitani's *Religion and Nothingness*, vii–xxii.

93. Ibid., xii–xiii.

94. Ibid., xxiv. From the preface of Kitaro Nishida's *Intelligibility and the Philosophy of Nothingness* (Honolulu: East-West Center Press, 1958), cited in the "Translator's Introduction" by Jan van Bragt.

95. See John A. Hutchinson, *Paths of Faith* (New York: McGraw-Hill, 1991), 144.

96. Cited in Rahula, *What the Buddha Taught*, 40n. Dr. Rahula takes the position that there is a more direct development than many others think from the ancient texts treasured by Theravada (Hinayana) Buddhism to the views developed in Mahayana Buddhism, with the thought of Nagarjuna being the bridge.

97. Nishitani, *Religion and Nothingness*, 281.

98. Ibid., 46.

99. Ibid., 48.

100. Ibid., 13–15.

101. Abe, "Kenotic God and Dynamic Sunyata," 45.

102. Nishitani, *Religion and Nothingness*, 14.

103. Cf. ibid., 77–90. Much else of what Nishitani has to say about modern culture, such as the ambivalent role of technology in it, is also of great interest.

104. Ibid., 69.

105. Ibid., 215.

106. Ibid., 280.

107. Ibid., 282.

108. Ibid., 70.

109. Ibid., 40, 60, and 90.

110. Cf. ibid., 74, where he speaks of "the supremely unreal heart and mind of the shadowy man . . . [that] originate from moment to moment as things completely temporary . . . and at the same time and on every occasion, in their very temporality they stand ecstatically outside of time." This seems to be an Asian existentialist way of expressing what Whitehead means by the concrescence of the occasional self.

111. Nishitani repeats a long passage from an eighteenth-century Buddhist sermon of Takusui to raise doubt "regarding the subject in you that hears all sounds." Ibid., 20–21. I find this an Asian analogue to the Whiteheadian argument that the self is constituted by its prehensions.

112. Ibid., 109.

113. Ibid., 136.

114. Ibid., 139.

115. A. N. Whitehead, *Adventures of Ideas* (Chicago: Free Press, 1933), 168–69.

116. Whitehead wrote in this regard, ibid., 169: "But their general concept of the Deity stopped all further generalizations. They made no effort to conceive the world in terms of the metaphysical categories by means of which they interpreted God."

117. Nishitani, *Religion and Nothingness*, 149, for the words in the introductory clause, and 150 for the longer quotation. Cf. 159.

118. Nishitani would be on firmer ground, however, in claiming that Zen Buddhism articulated this insight far earlier than any Western thinker. He twice cites (164 and 196) a maxim from Dogen (1200–1253), the pioneer of Zen Buddhism, that articulates in remarkable parallel the contrast that Whitehead saw between Kant's transcendental idealism and his own philosophy. Dogen said: "To practice and confirm all things by conveying oneself to them, is illusion; for all things to advance forward and practice and confirm the self, is enlightenment." Whitehead's contrast of his thought with Kant's is found in *Process and Reality*, 88: "*The Critique of Pure Reason* describes the process by which subjective data pass into the appearance of an objective

world. The philosophy of organism seeks to describe how objective data pass
into subjective satisfaction."

119. Nishitani, *Religion and Nothingness*, 164.

120. Ibid., 283.

121. Ibid., 146.

122. Ibid., 123.

123. Ibid., 201.

124. Ibid., 203.

125. John Cobb, "On the Deepening of Buddhism," in *The Emptying God*, 93.

126. Nishitani, *Religion and Nothingness*, 249.

127. Cf. ibid., 235.

128. Ibid., 239. Cf. also 264 where he claims that "the field of circumin-sessional interpenetration" yields "harmony" between the self and the other.

129. Abe, "Kenotic God and Dynamic Sunyata," in *The Emptying God*, ed. Cobb and Ives, 10.

130. Ibid., 14.

131. Ibid., 16.

132. Ibid., 18.

133. Ibid., 29.

134. Ibid., 28 and 33.

135. Ibid., 39–40.

136. Ibid., 41.

137. Ibid., 44 and 56.

138. Cf. Cobb, "On the Deepening of Buddhism," in *The Emptying God*, ed. Cobb and Ives, 98.

139. Cf. Catherine Keller, "Scoop up the Water and the Moon in Your Hands: On Feminist Theology and Dynamic Self-Emptying," in *The Emptying God*, ed. Cobb and Ives, 108–9.

140. I have written about this heretofore in *A Christology of Peace*, 60:

> The theology that emerges from being grounded in and participating in
> Christ's Holy Spirit is finally a trinitarian Christology, which under-
> stands the total event of Jesus' life, death, and resurrection as an event
> in the trinitarian being of God. The relation that Jesus had sustained
> with his *Abba* during life, and through death, was now experienced and
> conceived as the ground for his disciples' participation in the eternal
> process of God's salvation of the whole creation. As such, it is also the
> ground of hope for the Christian's continued participation in the dialec-
> tic that brings us both personal peace and requires us to struggle for
> social peace in full recognition of the demonic forces that distort even
> our lives and society. For God is in this struggle, and the whole of it is
> in God, where it is being transformed through gracious forgiveness into
> new possibility. In such dialectical panentheism we may "rest" both
> conceptually and existentially, for it is the power of the Holy Spirit that
> gives us both life and peace.

141. Cf. Kenneth Cragg, *The Call of the Minaret* (London: Oxford University Press, 1956), 47. I owe this formulation and reference to the work of my student, Wafiq Wahba.

142. This more relational perspective is not unknown in Islam, especially in the experience and thought of the Sufis. Cf. Abdoldjavad Falaturi, "How Can a Muslim Experience God, Given Islam's Radical Monotheism?" in *We Believe in One God* (New York: Seabury Press, 1979), 79–82. Here too I am indebted to Mr. Wahba.

143. Cf. Reinhold Niebuhr's comments about the Gandhian use of "soul force" in *The Nature and Destiny of Man* (New York: Charles Scribner's Sons, 1949), 2:261.

144. Cf. Jürgen Moltmann, "God Is Unselfish Love," in *The Emptying God*, ed. Cobb and Ives, 120–21.

145. Cf. David Tracy, "Kenosis, Sunyata, and Trinity: A Dialogue with Masao Abe," in ibid., 150–52.

146. Abe, "A Rejoinder," in ibid., 165.

147. Ibid., 172.

148. Ibid., 179–83.

149. Nishitani, *Religion and Nothingness*, 197.

## Chapter 4
## The Contextual Relationality of Justice

1. Stanley Hauerwas devotes an entire chapter of *After Christendom* (Nashville: Abingdon Press, 1991), 45–68, to this argument. At the very end, he disclaims any intention to dissuade anyone from working for justice. If so, he might do better to alter his journalistic style toward more dialectical balance throughout his discussion.

2. Ibid., 53–54.

3. The words are Lesslie Newbigin's in *Foolishness to Greeks: The Gospel in Western Culture* (Grand Rapids: Wm. B. Eerdmans Publishing Co., 1986), which Hauerwas cites to make their common point, ibid., 66. Newbigin goes on:

> Since the pursuit of happiness is endless, the demands upon the state are without limit. If for modern Western people, nature has taken the place of God as the ultimate reality with which we have to deal, the nation-state has taken the place of God as the source to which we look for happiness, health, and welfare (76).

4. Hauerwas, *After Christendom*, 37.

5. Keiji Nishitani, *Religion and Nothingness*, tr. and ed. Jan van Bragt (Berkeley and Los Angeles: University of California Press, 1990), 203. Though this is a fitting response to undue claims for the church, as a repudiation of the Judeo-Christian experience and idea of covenant relation, it is too polemical, as I said in the previous chapter.

6. David Toole in Hauerwas, *After Christendom*, 153–61 (the quotations

are from pp. 158 and 160). All teachers continue to learn from their students, which belies Professor Hauerwas's claim that "I tell my students that my first object is to help them think just like me" (98). Fortunately, he corrects himself on this point in his own note (180).

7. Ibid., 160.

8. Leonardo Boff, *Jesus Christ Liberator*, tr. Patrick Hughes, (Maryknoll, N.Y.: Orbis Books, 1978), 230.

9. Jeffrey Carlson, "The Syncretic Self: A Way to Hope," *The Council of Societies for the Study of Religion Bulletin* 20, no. 4 (November 1991): 81.

10. Umberto Eco's provocative way of stating the danger of false infinitizing is, "You can hang the pendulum from a brothel; any point becomes 'the' fixed point of the universe." George Lucas, to whom I owe this reference, says it comes from *Foucault's Pendulum*.

11. Cf. Hauerwas, *After Christendom*, chap. 4. A statement that all Euro-American Christians would do well to ponder is on 93–94:

> That the church has difficulty being a disciplined community, or even cannot conceive what it would mean to be a disciplined community is not surprising given the church's social position in developed economies. The church exists in a buyer's or consumer's market, so any suggestion that in order to be a member of a church you must be transformed by opening your life to certain kinds of discipline is almost impossible to maintain.

12. M. Douglas Meeks, *God the Economist: The Doctrine of God and Political Economy* (Philadelphia: Fortress Press, 1989), 37.

13. John Rawls, *A Theory of Justice* (Cambridge, Mass.: Harvard University Press, 1971).

14. Allan Bloom, "Justice: John Rawls vs. the Tradition of Political Philosophy," in idem, *Giants and Dwarfs: Essays 1960–1990* (New York: Simon & Schuster, Touchstone Books, 1990), 315; emphasis added.

15. Cf. ibid., 344:

> Rawls' "original position" is based on a misunderstanding of the state-of-nature teachings of Hobbes, Locke, and Rousseau. His "Kantian interpretation" is based on a misunderstanding of Kant's moral teaching. His "Aristotelian principle" is based on a misunderstanding of Aristotle's teaching about happiness. And these three misunderstandings constitute the core of the book.

16. Ibid.

17. Robert Benne bases much of *The Ethic of Democratic Capitalism* (Philadelphia: Fortress Press, 1981) on agreement with Rawls's theory. See especially chap. 4. The citation is from 49.

18. Rawls, *A Theory of Justice*, 17–21.

19. Ibid., 136.

20. Ibid., 60.

21. Ibid., 83.

22. Ibid., 250-51.

23. Bloom, "Justice," in *Giants and Dwarfs*, 321. Prof. Bloom's answer to the question is no because he is convinced that Rawls does not adequately understand the moral problems posed by either nature or history.

24. Rawls, *A Theory of Justice*, 543.

25. Ibid., 542.

26. Bloom, "Justice," in *Giants and Dwarfs*, 325–26, emphasis added.

27. George F. Will, syndicated column, April 22, 1990, cited in Hauerwas, *After Christendom*, 30.

28. Cf. Kant, *Groundwork for the Metaphysics of Morals*, tr. H. J. Paton, (New York: Harper Torchbook, 1964), 89: "Act as if the maxim of your action were to become through your will a universal law of nature."

29. Ibid., 61.

30. Ronald M. Green, *Religion and Moral Reason* (New York: Oxford University Press, 1988), 11–12.

31. Mark C. Taylor, "The Politics of Theo-ry," *Journal of the American Academy of Religion* 59, no. 1 (Spring 1991): 1–37.

32. Ibid., 32.

33. Ibid., 34.

34. Ronald Green's discussion of Kierkegaard's notion of the "teleological suspension of the ethical" in his interpretation of the biblical story of Abraham's temptation to sacrifice Isaac (Genesis 22) has great insight on this issue. Cf. Green, *Religion and Moral Reason*, 84–129.

35. Boff, *Jesus Christ Liberator*, 219–20.

36. Boff put the paragraph quoted under the heading "The Presence of Christ in Anonymous Christians," ibid., 219.

37. Stephen Toulmin, *Reason in Ethics* (Cambridge: Cambridge University Press, 1960), 133.

38. Cf. ibid., 195–97. I have reformulated Toulmin's argument, which he presents under the theme "Ethical Theories as Rhetoric." My concern is that accepting Bentham's utilitarian principle as the only or basic form of ethical rationality would be to substitute the formal logic of an aggregate of externally related units for the dialectical logic that is the only adequate form of reason for internally related, interactive communities.

39. Cf. ibid., 171, where Toulmin concludes: "It is in the nature of ethics that changes in the moral code should have as their goal a self-developing 'open' society—a society in which individuals are free, and encouraged, to make their own moral decisions—rather than the tribal, tyrannical, and collectivist 'closed society.' "

40. Gadamer, *Reason in the Age of Science*, tr. Frederick G. Lawrence (Cambridge, Mass.: MIT Press, 1981), 49.

41. Matthew Foster, *Gadamer and Practical Philosophy* (Atlanta: Scholars Press, 1991), 77.

42. Ibid., 4.

43. Cf. ibid., 287, where Foster is reflecting on the Mosaic discourse in Deut. 30:6 and 11–14: "Moses intends to reveal a new possibility in human

existence, predicated on the concrete condition of living in covenant with God. . . . But the path of our inquiry suggests added reasons for thinking that this possibility is unconditional—that it is received beyond that historical community and across the centuries." I also have supported in chap. 3 the universalizability of the Judeo-Christian covenant, though I think there are important reasons to prefer the word "universal" to Foster's use of "unconditional."

44. Ibid., 6.

45. Marcus G. Raskin, *The Common Good: Its Politics, Policies, and Philosophy* (New York: Routledge & Kegan Paul, 1986), 38. Raskin relates the same issue to U.S. society, when he points out that the Federal Reserve System that governs the U.S. economy "is a banker's club using the federal government's legitimating power" (179).

46. Jürgen Habermas, "A Review of Gadamer's Truth and Method," cited in Foster, *Gadamer and Practical Philosophy*, 124.

47. Habermas understands the "ideal speech situation" to be achieved only through the unconstrained and unrestricted discussion of equal and rational individuals free from any external pressure.

48. David Tracy, "Theology, Critical Social Theory, and the Public Realm," unpublished paper dated September 15, 1988, 1. I have followed Prof. Tracy's reflections in this entire paragraph.

49. Jürgen Habermas, *The Philosophical Discourse of Modernity*, tr. Frederick Lawrence (Cambridge, Mass.: MIT Press, 1987).

50. Ibid., 40.

51. Cf. Paul Lakeland, "Habermas and the Theologians Again," *Religious Studies Review* 15, no. 2 (April 1989): 104–9.

52. Foster, *Gadamer and Practical Philosophy*, 15.

53. Ibid., 116.

54. Cf. Gadamer's "Hermeneutics and Social Science," in *Cultural Hermeneutics* 2 (1975): 315; cited in ibid., 142.

55. Cf. Foster, *Gadamer and Practical Philosophy*, 176–77.

56. Jürgen Habermas, *Autonomy and Solidarity*, ed. Peter Dews (New York: Verso, 1986), 206.

57. Hans-Georg Gadamer, *Truth and Method*, 2d rev. ed., tr. Joel Weinsheimer and Donald G. Marshall (New York: Crossroad, 1989), 458.

58. Foster, *Gadamer and Practical Philosophy*, 284.

59. Toulmin, *Reason in Ethics*, 152.

60. Ibid., 153; the emphasis is from Toulmin.

61. Gadamer, *Truth and Method*, xxiii.

62. Foster, *Gadamer and Practical Philosophy*, 242. Foster also suspects that Gadamer was influenced by the negative example of Heidegger's venture into cultural politics in his ill-fated support for National Socialism in the early 1930s. Despite (and perhaps also because of) Heidegger's philosophical erudition, he lacked the political sophistication to understand that the means he supported to break the political influence of the church and the stifling traditions of the university were not compatible with his intention. Ibid., 271–74.

63. Clifford Geertz, *The Interpretation of Cultures* (New York: Basic Books, 1973), 141.

64. Ibid., 5.

65. Max Weber, *The Protestant Ethic and the Spirit of Capitalism*, tr. Talcott Parsons (London: George Allen & Unwin, 1930), 48.

66. Geertz, *Interpretation of Cultures*, 126.

67. Weber, *Protestant Ethic*, 24.

68. Ibid., 79–80.

69. Ibid., 112–13.

70. Ibid., 172.

71. Ibid., 282, n. 108.

72. Ibid., 181, emphasis added. Weber is responding to Baxter's *Saints' Everlasting Rest* with an irony appropriate to the fact that those now "born into this mechanism" have little possibility of celebrating any kind of "sabbath rest" in the biblical sense.

73. These descriptive phrases characterizing Ellul's thought are from John Wilkinson's "Translator's Introduction" to Ellul's *The Technological Society* (New York: Vintage Books, 1964), xii–xiii.

74. Ibid., 51.

75. Ibid., 319.

76. Weber, *Protestant Ethic*, 105.

77. Philip Slater, *The Pursuit of Loneliness* (Boston: Beacon Press, 1970), 7: "Technological change, mobility, and the individualistic ethos combine to rupture the bonds that tie each individual to a family, a community, a kinship network, a geographical location. . . . An enormous technology seems to have set itself the task of making it unnecessary for one human being ever to ask anything of another in the course of going about his daily business."

78. Robert L. Heilbroner, *An Inquiry into the Human Prospect* (New York: W. W. Norton & Co., 1974), 22.

79. Karl Marx, *Capital* (New York: International Publishers, 1967), 1:372 n. 3. I owe this reference to Colin Grant, "The Promise and Perils of Praxis," *Cross Currents* 40, no. 1 (Spring 1990): 64–86.

80. The young Marx was the author of *Toward the Critique of Hegel's Philosophy of Law*, *The Holy Family*, *The German Ideology*, and *The Economic-Philosophical Manuscripts of 1844*. It is especially the last that articulates the theme of alienation. These works, unfortunately, were almost unknown even to Marxists until after World War II when they finally were published in Western Europe.

81. Adam Schaff, *Marxismus und das menschliche Individuum* (Vienna, Frankfurt, Zurich: Europa Verlag, 1956), 9, my translation. For a more complete discussion of the work of Professor Schaff and other Marxists within the context of the Christian-Marxist dialogue of the 1960s, see my "The Uses of Philosophical Theology in the Christian-Marxist Dialogue," *Union Seminary Quarterly Review* 26, no. 1 (Fall 1970): 19–42.

82. Milan Machovec, *The Meaning of Human Life*, tr. O. Prochazka, a manuscript written during the early 1960s that remained unpublished in that

turbulent period, which culminated with Prof. Machovec losing his faculty position in Charles University from 1970 to 1990. Prof. Machovec became rather well known in the West through his later publication of *Jesus für Atheisten*, translated and published as *A Marxist Looks at Jesus* (Philadelphia: Fortress Press, 1976).

83. Colin Grant, "The Promise and Perils of Praxis," 78.

84. Albert Jonsen and Stephen Toulmin, *The Abuse of Casuistry: A History of Moral Reasoning* (Berkeley and Los Angeles: University of California, 1988).

85. Aristotle *Rhetoric* 2.12–17.

86. Jonsen and Toulmin, *Abuse of Casuistry*, 146–51.

87. Ibid., 181–94. See especially the high evaluation given to the careful work of the casuist on this economic issue, on 194:

> Although fostered by social circumstances, these new doctrines about the morality of economics were not merely a passive reflection of those circumstances. The casuists did not concede their novel points merely at the insistence of imperious rulers, avaricious prelates, or greedy bankers; they sought, in the midst of the economic pressures, to bring to light the morally relevant circumstances that would permit meaningful moral discriminations. The cases they considered were genuine manifestations of new social, cultural, and economic conditions; the moral arguments they worked out to deal with these cases were honest efforts to direct the consciences of rulers, prelates, and bankers.

88. Philip Turner, "Review of *The Abuse of Casuistry*," *Religious Studies Review* 17, no. 4 (October 1991): 304.

89. Ibid., 338–39.

90. Ellul, *The Technological Society*, 281.

91. Agnes Cunningham, Donald Miller, and James E. Will, "Toward an Ecumenical Theology for Grounding Human Rights," *Soundings* 67, no. 2 (Summer 1984): 235. This essay was originally a study produced in the Faith and Order Commission of the National Council of the Churches of Christ in the U.S.A., based in part on theological work done by the Roman Catholic Pontifical Commission on Justice and Peace, the Lutheran World Federation, and the World Alliance of Reformed Churches.

92. Heilbroner, *An Inquiry into the Human Prospect*, 140.

93. Raskin, *The Common Good*, 333.

94. Ibid., 19.

95. Günter Krusche, "The Political Efficacy of the Church's Responsibility for Peace in the German Democratic Republic," in *The Moral Rejection of Nuclear Deterrence*, ed. James E. Will (New York: Friendship Press, 1985), 165. The interior quotations used by Gen. Supt. Krusche of the Berlin-Brandenburg church are from documents of the church.

96. Cf. my editorializing on this response: "Must Walls Continue to Divide?" *The Christian Century* 106, no. 39 (December 20–27, 1989): 1191–92; also printed in *Occasional Papers on Religion in Eastern Europe* 10, no. 2 (March 1990): 34–40.

97. Robert McAfee Brown, *Theology in a New Key* (Philadelphia: Westminster Press, 1974), 71.

98. José Míguez-Bonino, *Doing Theology in a Revolutionary Situation* (Philadelphia: Fortress Press, 1975), 88–89.

99. The most relevant texts from Whitehead on this point are *Science and the Modern World* (New York: Macmillan Co., 1925), *Religion in the Making* (New York: Macmillan Co., 1926), and *Process and Reality* (New York: Macmillan Co., 1929).

100. Here Whitehead's most relevant work is *Adventures of Ideas* (New York: Macmillan Co., 1933). Though it has only one direct reference to Marx, that is a very telling one:

> The learned economists are unanimous in telling us that *Das Kapital* does not express a sound scientific doctrine. . . . The success of the book—for it is still with us as a power—can then only be accounted for by the magnitude of the evil ushered in by the first phase of the industrial revolution. The early liberal faith that by the decree of benevolent Providence, individualistic competition and industrial activity would necessarily work together for human happiness had broken down as soon as it was tried. . . . But no one now holds that . . . mere individualistic competition . . . will produce a satisfying society (35).

101. Ibid., 66.

102. Whitehead himself characterized his ethos as Victorian: "I am exactly an ordinary example of the general tone of the Victorian Englishman," in *Essays in Science and Philosophy* (New York: Philosophical Library, 1948), 88.

103. Randall Morris, *Process Philosophy and Political Ideology* (Albany, N.Y.: State University of New York Press, 1991), analyzes Whitehead's social location in a way that illumines his contextual ideology. For a critical review of Morris, see George Lucas's review in *Journal of the History of Philosophy* 31, no. 3 (July 1993): 147–49.

104. Whitehead, *Adventures of Ideas*, 43.

105. Morris, *Process Philosophy and Political Ideology*, 214.

106. Ibid., 221.

107. Franklin Gamwell, "A Discussion of John B. Cobb, Jr., 'The Political Implications of Whitehead's Philosophy,' " in *Process Philosophy and Social Thought*, ed. John Cobb, Jr., and W. Widick Schroeder (Chicago: Center for the Scientific Study of Religion, 1981), 37.

108. James E. Will, "Dialectical Panentheism: Towards Relating Liberation and Process Theologies," in *Process Philosophy and Social Thought*, ed. Cobb and Schroeder, 249–50.

109. Christopher Dawson, *The Making of Europe* (London: Sheed & Ward, 1932; New York: New American Library, 1952), 25.

110. Ibid., 40.

111. Cited in ibid., 40.

112. Ibid., 191; emphasis added.

113. G. W. F. Hegel, *The Philosophy of Right*, tr. T. M. Knox (1821; London: Oxford University Press, 1952), 217–18 (par. 347).

114. Dante Germino, *Machiavelli to Marx: Modern Western Political Thought* (Chicago: University of Chicago Press, 1972), 8.

115. Ibid., 10. Cf. the similar judgment of Christopher Dawson at the conclusion of *The Making of Europe*, 243: "We no longer have the same confidence in the inborn superiority of Western civilization and its right to dominate the world."

116. Jane Kramer, *Unsettling Europe* (New York: Random House, 1980), xvi.

117. These statistics are gleaned from a manuscript in preparation by Prof. Jung Young Lee, "Marginality: Towards a Multi-Cultural Theology from an Asian-American Perspective," as yet unpublished.

118. Ibid., 91 of chap. 2. What Professor Lee takes to be the majority point of view is quoted from Everett V. Stonequist, *The Marginal Man* (New York: Russell & Russell, 1961), 8.

119. Henry J. Young, *Hope in Process* (Minneapolis: Fortress Press, 1990), 83.

120. Michael Harrington, *The Other America: Poverty in the United States* (New York: Macmillan & Co., 1962; Baltimore: Penguin Books, 1963).

121. Ibid., 24.

122. Robert Thobaben, Donna Schlagheck, and Charles Funderbusk, *Issues in American Political Life* (New York: Prentice Hall, 1991), 37.

123. Ibid., 39.

124. Barbara Ward, *The Rich Nations and the Poor Nations* (New York: W. W. Norton & Co., 1962), 60.

125. Ibid., 115.

126. Alexis de Tocqueville, *Democracy in America*, ed. and abr. Richard Heffner (New York: New American Library, 1956; original published in 1835 and 1840), 26.

127. Ibid., 219–20.

128. Cf. Robert Lekachman, *Economists at Bay* (New York: McGraw-Hill, 1976), 266: "Shorn of morality and history, economics is reduced to techniques, no doubt useful and lucrative for economists and their clients, but as guides to social policy no better than the ruminations of accountants."

129. Rajah B. Manikam, ed., *Christianity and the Asian Revolution* (New York: Friendship Press, 1956), 4–5.

130. Yap Kim Hao, *Doing Theology in a Pluralistic World* (Singapore: Singapore Methodist Book Room, 1990), 147.

131. Jong-Sun Noh, *Religion and Just Revolution: Third World Perspective* (Seoul: Voice Publishing House, 1987), 153.

132. Cf. Suh Nam-Dong, "Towards a Theology of Han," in *Minjung Theology: People as Subjects of History*, ed. Commission on Theological Concerns of the Christian Conference of Asia (Maryknoll, N.Y.: Orbis Books, 1981, 1983), 58: "*Han* is the underlying feeling of Korean people. On the one hand, it is a dominant feeling of defeat, resignation, and nothingness. . . . On the other

hand, *han* is the tenacity for life of oppressed spirits; it is a tendency for social revolution."

133. The Kuang Lim Methodist Church of Seoul is the largest Methodist congregation in the world, with 60,000 members when I visited it in 1991.

134. All three of these documents are now published in *Kairos: Three Prophetic Challenges to the Church*, ed. Robert McAfee Brown (Grand Rapids: Wm. B. Eerdmans Publishing Co., 1990).

135. Ibid., 53.

136. Ibid., 57.

137. The South African authors of their *Kairos* document put this point in their own way, ibid., 62, n. 17: "The individual Christian, therefore, is both a member of the Church and a member of society, and, on both accounts, Christians should be involved in doing what is right and just. The same is no doubt true of people who adhere to other religious faiths."

138. Ibid., 78.

139. Ibid., 126–33.

140. Ibid., 138.

141. Cf. Pope John XXIII's influential encyclical *Pacem in Terris*.

142. M. Douglas Meeks, *God the Economist*, 40.

143. Black intellectuals often provide more salient expression of this point than their white confreres in North American society. Cf. bell hooks and Cornel West, *Breaking Bread: Insurgent Black Intellectual Life* (Boston: South End Press, 1991), 144: "An intelligentsia without institutionalized critical consciousness is blind, and critical consciousness severed from collective insurgency is empty. The central task of postmodern black intellectuals is to stimulate, hasten, and enable alternative perceptions and practices by dislodging prevailing discourses and powers."

## Chapter 5
## The Interpersonal Relationality of Love

1. Daniel Day Williams, *The Spirit and the Forms of Love* (New York: Harper & Row, 1968), vii.

2. Sigmund Freud, *Civilization and Its Discontents*, tr. James Strachey (New York: W. W. Norton & Co., 1961), 56–57.

3. Alfred North Whitehead, *Adventures of Ideas* (New York: Macmillan Co., 1933), 15–16.

4. Williams, *The Spirit and the Forms of Love*, 138.

5. Sigmund Freud, *Introductory Lectures on Psychoanalysis*, tr. Joan Riviere (London: George Allen & Unwin, 1922), 12.

6. Sigmund Freud, *New Introductory Lectures on Psychoanalysis*, tr. W. J. H. Sprott (New York: W. W. Norton & Co., 1933), 248.

7. Cf. Ernst Kris's "Introduction" to the volume of Freud's letters published under the title *The Origins of Psychoanalysis*, ed. Marie Bonaparte, Anna Freud, and Ernst Kris (New York: Basic Books, 1954), 22: "Bruecke's physiology, firmly based on ideas taken from the world of physics and having the

measurability of all phenomena as its ideal, was the point of departure from which psychoanalytic theory was built up."

8. Freud, *New Introductory Lectures*, 131.

9. Ibid., 133.

10. Sigmund Freud, *A General Introduction to Psychoanalysis*, tr. J. Riviere (Garden City, N.Y.: Garden City Publishing Co., 1938), 289.

11. Ibid., 274.

12. Sigmund Freud, *Beyond the Pleasure Principle*, tr. C. J. M. Hubback (London: Hogarth Press, 1948), 1, emphasis added.

13. Ibid., 79.

14. Freud, *Civilization and Its Discontents*, 85.

15. Ibid., 44–47. Cf. 102.

16. Maurice Friedman, *Contemporary Psychology* (Pittsburgh: Duquesne University Press, 1984), 40.

17. Freud, *New Introductory Lectures on Psychoanalysis*, 104.

18. Patricia Goldman-Rakic, "Working Memory and the Mind," *Scientific American*, September 1992, 111. The whole of this "special issue" is devoted to the report and interpretation of contemporary research on the relations of brain and mind.

19. These measurements and the computer metaphor come from Gerald Fishbach's introductory essay "Mind and Brain" in ibid., 50–51.

20. Antonio and Hanna Damasio, "Brain and Language," ibid., 95. Cf. Patricia Goldman-Rakic's similar hope in ibid., 117:

> At present theories describing the fundamental causes of schizophrenia are inadequate, much as knowledge of the functioning of the working memory system remains frustratingly sketchy. Fortunately, neurobiological research has been advancing at a breathless pace in the past few years. Such research should lead to a greater understanding.

Cf. the very similar hope expressed by Geoffrey Hinton in "How Neural Networks Learn from Experience," ibid., 151:

> Although investigators have devised some powerful learning algorithms that are of great practical value, we still do not know which representations and learning procedures are actually used by the brain. But sooner or later computational studies of learning in artificial neural networks will converge on the methods discovered by evolution. When that happens, a lot of diverse empirical data about the brain will suddenly make sense, and many new applications of artificial neural networks will become feasible.

21. Ibid., 89.

22. F. Crick and C. Koch, "The Problem of Consciousness," ibid., 153.

23. Ibid.

24. Ibid., 54.

25. Ibid., 61. Cf. for confirmation C. Trevarthen, "Brain Sciences and the Human Spirit," *Zygon*, June 1986. I owe this reference, as well as other good counsel, to James Ashbrook.

26. Semir Zeki, "The Visual Image in Mind and Brain," *Scientific American*, September 1992, 69.

27. Ibid., 76.

28. James Ashbrook, *The Brain and Belief* (Bristol, Ind.: Wyndham Hall Press, 1988), 144.

29. James Ashbrook, *The Human Mind and the Mind of God* (Lanham, Md.: University Press of America, 1984), xviii.

30. Ibid., 287.

31. Ashbrook, *The Brain and Belief*, 121.

32. Ashbrook, *The Human Mind and the Mind of God*, 334. Yet in his later work when he is concerned to interpret his position that "brain" and "mind" are interchangeable and equivalent terms, he affirms a "radical monism" in *The Brain and Belief*, 118.

> In contrast to a dualism or even a sophisticated interactionism, I assume a radical monism. This emergent view of higher cortical activity—the activity of *human* animals—neither negates biochemical processes by an exclusive attention to the supposedly transcendent nor reduces that vivid personal experience of a sense of self, a sense of humor, and a sense of deity at the interface with sensory input to the supposedly biochemical.

33. Alfred North Whitehead, *Process and Reality*, corrected ed., ed. David Ray Griffin and Donald W. Sherburne (New York: Free Press, 1978), 4.

34. Carl G. Vaught, *The Quest for Wholeness* (Albany, N.Y.: SUNY Press, 1982), 9.

35. Ibid., 3–4.

36. Cf. Albert C. Knudson, *The Philosophy of Personalism* (Nashville: Abingdon-Cokesbury Press, 1927), 62:

> This form of personalism had its chief sources in Leibnitz (1646–1716), Berkeley (1685–1753), Kant (1724–1804), and Lotze (1815–1881). Roughly speaking, it owes its spiritual individualism and activism to Leibnitz, its immaterialism to Berkeley, its epistemology and ethical conception of personality to Kant, and its first general and distinctive formulation to Lotze. It was Lotze who took the personalistic elements contributed by his predecessors and wove them into a new type of theism.

C. C. J. Webb said much the same for England as Knudson had for North America in *A Study of Religious Thought in England from 1850* (London: Oxford University Press, 1933), 124–25:

> If the British absolute idealism against which the "personal idealists" were protesting had behind it the great German thinkers who succeeded Kant, and especially Hegel, so the personal idealists themselves at any rate derived encouragement in their protest from the writings of a German critic of Hegel who, when Personal Idealism appeared, had not long passed away, Hermann Lotze.

37. Hermann Lotze, *Metaphysics*, tr. Bernard Bosanquet (Oxford: Clarendon Press, 1867), 1:216.

38. Ibid., 2:165.

39. Ibid., 2:174.

40. Ibid., 1:229.

41. Hermann Lotze, *Microcosmus: An Essay Concerning Man and His Relation to the World*, tr. Elizabeth Hamilton and E. E. Constance Jones (Edinburgh: T. & T. Clark, 1899), 1:647.

42. G. T. Ladd in the "Editor's Preface" for Hermann Lotze, *Outlines of Psychology*, tr. G. T. Ladd (Boston: Ginn & Co., 1886), vi.

43. Lotze, *Metaphysics*, 2:170.

44. Lotze, *Outlines of Psychology*, 9.

45. Lotze, *Metaphysics*, 2:316.

46. The philosophical theology now ably articulated at Boston University by Robert Neville, dean of its school of theology, is far closer to the ontological anthropology we seek to elucidate in this chapter. Cf. his *The High Road Around Modernism* (Albany, N.Y.: SUNY Press, 1992).

47. Borden Parker Bowne, *Metaphysics* (New York: Harper & Brothers, 1882), 100. Albert Knudson spells out this idea more completely in a paragraph in *The Philosophy of Personalism* (Nashville: Abingdon-Cokesbury Press, 1927), 237–38:

> It is in personality that individuality finds its only adequate realization. It is personality alone that has the characteristics necessary to a basal unity. It is in personal agency that we have the source of the idea of causality and its only self-consistent embodiment. It is the reality of personality that constitutes the foil to the phenomenality of matter, space, and time and renders it intelligible. From every point of view it is thus evident that in personality we have the crown of the personalistic system, the keystone of its arch, the masterlight of all our metaphysical seeing.

48. Borden Parker Bowne, *Personalism* (Boston and New York: Houghton Mifflin Co., 1908), 53. Cf. Edgar Sheffield Brightman, *Nature and Values* (Nashville: Abingdon-Cokesbury Press, 1945), 50–51; and Peter Anthony Bertocci, *Introduction to the Philosophy of Religion* (Englewood Cliffs, N.J.: Prentice-Hall, 1951), 59–60, for essentially the same Cartesian position.

49. Bowne, *Metaphysics*, 98.

50. Edgar S. Brightman, *Is God a Person?* (New York: Association Press, 1932), 53–54. Cf. Peter A. Bertocci, *The Empirical Argument for God in Late British Thought* (Cambridge, Mass.: Harvard University Press, 1938), 204.

51. Edgar S. Brightman, "Some Definitions for Personalists," reprinted from *The Personalist*, no date or pagination in the reprint. Cf. also his *Nature and Values*, 38.

52. Bertocci, *The Empirical Argument for God*, 203.

53. Edgar S. Brightman, *Persons and Values*, University Lecture of Boston University (Boston: Boston University Press, 1952), 24. Prof. Brightman said

this in the first instance about this lecture, but the lecture intended to characterize the history of personalist thought as developed in Boston University.

54. Edgar S. Brightman, *Personality and Religion* (Nashville: Abingdon-Cokesbury Press, 1934), 35.

55. Alfred North Whitehead, *Process and Reality*, 45.

56. Ibid., 160.

57. Immanuel Kant, John Locke, David Hume, Hermann Lotze, and Borden Parker Bowne could also be named here with Descartes.

58. Ibid., 170.

59. Ibid., 177.

60. Ibid., 221.

61. Ibid., 222.

62. Ibid., 224.

63. Cf. Whitehead's discussion, ibid., 234.

64. Ibid., 237.

65. Ibid., 267.

66. Ibid., 273.

67. Lotze, *Microcosmos*, 1:367.

68. Ibid., 2:66.

69. Brian J. Martine, *Individuals and Individuality* (Albany, N.Y.: SUNY Press, 1984), xi.

70. Albert C. Knudson, *Basic Issues in Christian Thought* (Nashville: Abingdon-Cokesbury Press, 1950), 45. He first published this passage, however, in *Present Tendencies in Religious Thought* in 1924.

71. Albert C. Knudson, *The Validity of Religious Experience* (Nashville: Abingdon-Cokesbury Press, 1937), 16–17.

72. Brightman, *Nature and Values*, 55.

73. Martine, *Individuals and Individuality*, 12.

74. Ibid., 68.

75. Cf. Carl G. Vaught, *The Quest for Wholeness*, 67.

76. Martine, *Individuals and Individuality*, 85.

77. Vaught, *The Quest for Wholeness*, 184.

78. Martin Buber, *I and Thou*, tr. Ronald Gregor Smith (Edinburgh: T. & T. Clark, 1937), 3–6.

79. Ibid., 7. The context here is the possibility of both kinds of relation with a tree. Buber found it possible to have I-Thou relations not only with human beings but also with nature and with intelligible forms (6).

80. Jean-Paul Sartre, *Being and Nothingness*, tr. Hazel E. Barnes (New York: Philosophical Library, 1956), 255. The earlier phrase is from 253.

81. Friedman, *Contemporary Psychology*, 100–102. Binswanger's case study was published in *Existence: A New Dimension in Psychiatry and Psychology*, ed. Rollo May, Ernest Angel, Henri F. Ellenberger (New York: Basic Books, 1958).

82. Harry Stack Sullivan, *The Interpersonal Theory of Psychiatry*, ed. H. S. Perry and M. F. Gowel (New York: W. W. Norton & Co., 1953), 103.

83. Ibid., 32.

84. Cf. Clara Thompson, "Sullivan and Psychoanalysis," in *The Contributions of Harry Stack Sullivan*, ed. Patrick Mullahy (New York: Hermitage Press, 1952), 108.

85. Philip Wagner in ibid., 156.

86. Gardner Murphy and Elizabeth Cattell, "Sullivan and Field Theory," ibid., 170.

87. Friedman, *Contemporary Psychology*, 23.

88. Ibid., 108.

89. Whitehead, *Process and Reality*, xiii, emphasis added.

90. Cf. ibid., 91: "This epoch is characterized by electronic and protonic actual entities, and by yet more ultimate actual entities which can be discerned in the quanta of energy. . . . Also each electron is a society of electronic occasions, and each proton is a society of protonic occasions."

91. Ibid., 98.

92. Ibid., 105–6.

93. Ibid., 109.

94. Ibid., 104.

95. Ibid., 96.

96. Reto Luzius Fetz, "In Critique of Whitehead," tr. James W. Felt, *Process Studies* 20, no. 1 (Spring 1991): 6.

97. Ibid., 7. Whitehead also was aware that personal unity is a reality that requires adequate philosophical explanation. Cf. his *Adventures of Ideas*, 186:

> Yet personal unity is an inescapable fact. The Platonic and Christian doctrine of the Soul, the Epicurean doctrine of a Concilium of subtle atoms, the Cartesian doctrine of Thinking Substance, the Humanitarian doctrine of the Rights of man, the general Common Sense of civilized mankind—these doctrines between them dominate the whole span of Western thought. Evidently there is a fact to be accounted for. Any philosophy must provide some doctrine of personal identity. In some sense there is a unity in the life of each man, from birth to death.

Yet his primary concern and metaphysical focus was to articulate the general continuity between human experience and the structure of the universe. Thus he failed adequately to articulate the individuation of the personal self. Cf. ibid., 225:

> The truth is that the brain is continuous with the body, and the body is continuous with the rest of the natural world. Human experience is an act of self-origination including the whole of nature, limited to the perspective of a focal region, located within the body, but not necessarily persisting in any fixed coordination with a definite part of the brain.

98. Ian G. Barbour, *Issues in Science and Religion* (New York: Harper & Row, 1966), 347, quoted in Frank G. Kirkpatrick, *Community* (Washington, D.C.: Georgetown University Press, 1986), 116.

99. Edward Pols, *Meditation on a Prisoner: Towards Understanding Action*

*and Mind* (Carbondale, Ill.: Southern Illinois University Press, 1975), 65, quoted in Kirkpatrick, *Community*, 130.

100. One might compare here the similar modification that process theologian John Cobb, Jr., suggested in his *A Christian Natural Theology* (Philadelphia: Westminster Press, 1965), 83:

> In opposition to Whitehead's view, I suggest that the soul may occupy a considerable region of the brain including both empty space and the regions occupied by many societies. This proposal assumes that it is possible for the region that constitutes the standpoint of one occasion to include the regions that constitute the standpoints of other occasions.

The obvious difference is that he extends the locus of the person only to larger regions of its brain.

101. Reto Fetz, "In Critique of Whitehead," 3.

102. Our reflection has benefited from Frank Kirkpatrick's *Community: A Trinity of Models*, especially at the points of his discussion of the thought of Barbour and Pols. His conclusion after reviewing Pols's modification of Whitehead's thought is instructive: "On the basis of this notion of the unity of the agent, Pols can make the kind of claims about agents which Whitehead could not make and which need to be made if we are to justify the ongoing endurance of persons who enter into relations with others in community" (130-31).

103. Jürgen Moltmann, *The Trinity and the Kingdom: The Doctrine of God*, tr. Margaret Kohl (New York: Harper & Row, 1981), 139.

104. Eberhard Jüngel, *The Doctrine of the Trinity: God's Being Is in Becoming*, tr. Horton Harris (Grand Rapids: Wm. B. Eerdmans Publishing Co., 1976), 100–101, n. 152, emphasis in original, quoted in John J. O'Donnell, *Trinity and Temporality* (New York: Oxford University Press, 1983), 88.

105. Gregory of Nyssa, Basil the Great, and Gregory of Nazianzus are so designated because they shared a common geographical region in Asia Minor (modern Turkey).

106. Cf. the discussion of the Cappadocian theologians in J. N. D. Kelly, *Early Christian Doctrines* (New York: Harper & Brothers, 1960), 258–69.

107. "The Definition of Chalcedon," *Documents of the Christian Church*, ed. Henry Bettenson (London: Oxford University Press, 1947), 73.

108. Gregory of Nazianzus *Epist. 101*, quoted in Leonardo Boff, *Jesus Christ Liberator* (Maryknoll, N.Y.: Orbis Books, 1978), 186.

109. I have developed this point more extensively in my *Christology of Peace* (Louisville, Ky.: Westminster/John Knox Press, 1989), in the section on "The Unity of Christ as the Logos of Creation," 82–95.

110. Alfred North Whitehead, *Adventures of Ideas* (Chicago: Free Press, 1933); the earlier quotations are from 167–69, while the longer citation is entirely from 169. Despite his criticism of the theological tradition, Whitehead urged that leaders of religious thought should concentrate upon the historical origins of their tradition because "in so far as such an appeal to

tradition can be made with complete honesty, without any shadow of evasion, there is an enormous gain in popular effectiveness" (171).

111. John Cobb, Jr., *Christ in a Pluralistic Age* (Philadelphia: Westminster Press, 1975), 257, 260.

112. That Whitehead developed his idea of God's primordial nature *first* was underscored by the reaction of Henry Nelson Wieman, one of Whitehead's early admirers. Wieman followed and made much use of Whitehead's earlier metaphysics in his theological work at the University of Chicago but reacted vigorously against the further development of God's consequent nature: "Whitehead's system could not stand without the primordial nature. It enters into the essential structure. The consequent nature, on the other hand, is added on like dome and spire." *American Philosophies of Religion* (Chicago: Willett, Clark & Co., 1936), 237. Cf. C. Robert Mesle's two essays on the relation of Wieman to Whitehead, "Sharing a Vague Vision: Wieman's Early Critique of Whitehead" and "Added On Like Dome and Spire: Wieman's Later Critique of Whitehead," *Process Studies* 20, no. 1 (Spring 1991): 23–53.

113. Whitehead's summary statement of his dipolar understanding of God may be found in the concluding section of *Process and Reality*, 345:

> Thus, analogously to all actual entities, the nature of God is dipolar. He has a primordial nature and a consequent nature. The consequent nature of God is conscious; and it is the realization of the actual world in the unity of his nature, and through the transformation of his wisdom. The primordial nature is conceptual, the consequent nature is the weaving of God's physical feelings upon his primordial concepts.

114. Schubert Ogden, *The Point of Christology* (New York: Harper & Row, 1982), 131, emphasis added.

115. Schubert Ogden, "On the Trinity," *Theology* 83 (March 1980): 102; cited in O'Donnell, *Trinity and Temporality*, 86.

116. Henry Nelson Wieman, *Religious Inquiry* (Boston: Beacon Press, 1968), 41–42; cited by Mesle, 50. Mesle, however, disagrees with Wieman at this point, even though he usually takes him as a mentor: "Clearly these attacks are wholly inappropriate for the process vision of God as the supremely related social being."

I differ from Mesle, my friend and former student, from whom I have learned much about Wieman, because, though he is right in characterizing the Whiteheadian vision of God as "supremely related," God is nevertheless not adequately conceived as a "social being."

117. Joseph A. Bracken, *The Triune Symbol: Persons, Process, and Community* (Lanham, Md.: University Press of America, 1985), 23.

118. Ibid., 24.

119. Ibid., 25, author's emphasis.

120. Ibid., 26.

121. Jürgen Moltmann, *The Trinity and the Kingdom of God*, 175.

122. Ibid., 150; the first emphasis is the author's, but the second is added.

123. Ibid., 175.

124. Ibid., 178.

125. Ibid., 190. The emphasis on "time" is the author's; the other two emphases are added.

126. Robert C. Neville, *A Theology Primer* (Albany, N.Y.: State University of New York Press, 1991), 44.

127. Cobb, *Christ in a Pluralistic Age*, 75.

128. Whitehead, *Process and Reality*, 343.

129. Moltmann, *The Trinity and the Kingdom*, 166.

130. Ibid., 167.

131. This point is analogous to Robert Neville's critique and revision of process theology in his concept of the Logos. He rejects defining the Logos only in Whiteheadian terms of abstract form, to understand the Logos as "determinate." Cf. his *Theology Primer*, 45:

> Although some theologians have identified the Logos with form, more than that is involved in being determinate. There are, in fact, four elements that must be talked about in grasping something as determinate: form, components to be formed, their actual mixture, and value as the cause of their mixture. Hence there are four elements to the Logos. . . . The Logos is thus the character of God expressed in each determinate thing by virtue of its determinateness, and it consists in the implications of form, components, actuality, and value.

Neville's revision, however, is related to his interpretation of *creatio ex nihilo* rather than our concern to interpret the Trinity as a paradigm for the interpersonal relationality of love.

132. Ibid., 168.

133. Cf. Ex. 20:12.

134. Buber, *I and Thou*, 75.

135. Vaught, *The Quest for Wholeness*, 1.

136. Ibid., 93.

137. Williams, *The Spirit and the Forms of Love*, 209.

## Chapter 6
## The Universal Relationality of Peace

1. Augustine *The City of God* 19.12; emphasis added.

2. Cf. Gerald J. Larson, "The Rope of Violence and the Snake of Peace: Conflict and Harmony in Classical India," in *Celebrating Peace*, ed. Leroy S. Rouner (Notre Dame, Ind.: University of Notre Dame Press, 1990), 138–39.

3. Khambo Lama Kh. Gaadan in his opening address to the fourth International Seminar on Buddhism and Leadership for Peace, in *Buddhism and Nonviolent Global Problem-Solving*, ed. Glenn D. Paige and Sarah Gilliatt (Honolulu: University of Hawaii Press, 1991), 7.

4. Cf. Jer. 8:11.

5. Three hundred thousand Hindu pilgrims were in the city of Ayodhya

on December 7, 1992, when Hindu militants destroyed the Babri Masjid mosque, which a Mogul general had built in 1528. Many Hindus believe that the god Rama was born 900,000 years ago on the place where the mosque stood, and that Muslims destroyed the Hindu temple that had stood on that spot before the mosque was built. A previous attempt to destroy the mosque in 1990 cost 1,000 lives in the riots that followed the Hindus' storming of it.

6. Alfred North Whitehead, *Adventures of Ideas* (Chicago: Free Press, 1933), 285–86.

7. John Ferguson, *War and Peace in the World's Religions* (Oxford: Oxford University Press, 1978), 17.

8. Larson, "The Rope of Violence and the Snake of Peace," in *Celebrating Peace*, ed. Rouner, 136–37.

9. Alfred North Whitehead, *Process and Reality*, corrected ed., ed. David Griffin and Donald Sherburne (New York: Free Press, 1978), 208.

10. Ibid., 338. I owe my attention being called to these passages in this context to Larson, "The Rope of Violence and the Snake of Peace," in *Celebrating Peace*, ed. Rouner, 137–38.

11. Rashmi-Sudha Puri, *Gandhi on War and Peace* (New York: Praeger Publishers, 1987), 200; cf. the entire section on "True Internationalism," 198–202.

12. Pedro Ramet has provided a thoughtful analysis of why religion is a constitutive element in the identity of most nationality groups in the volume he has edited, *Religion and Nationalism in Soviet and East European Politics* (Durham, N.C.: Duke University Press, 1984), 149:

> First, it is the historical core of the culture that shaped the evolution of primitive tribes into politically conscious nations. Second, it is a badge of group identity, distinguishing "us" from "them." . . . Third, religious groups always have been in the forefront of the development of national languages, national literature, and the dissemination of literature in the national tongue through the printing press. Fourth, being more highly educated, more respected, and more politically conscious, the clergy naturally stepped into leadership roles and does so even today.

13. John Ferguson, *War and Peace in the World's Religions*, 28.

14. Roland E. Miller, "The Context of Hindu-Christian Dialogue in Kerala," in *Hindu-Christian Dialogue*, ed. Harold Coward (Maryknoll, N.Y.: Orbis Books, 1989), 50–51.

15. Ibid., 51.

16. In the Papal Bulls of 1493 and 1506.

17. Cited in ibid., 53, from Gaspar Correa in Rémy, *Goa, Rome of the Orient*, tr. L. C. Sheppard (Arthur Baker, 1957), 34.

18. Salo Baron, *Modern Nationalism and Religion* (New York: Harper & Brothers, 1947), 146.

19. Ibid., 214, emphasis added.

20. Ibid.

21. Conor Cruise O'Brien, *God Land: Reflections on Religion and Nationalism* (Cambridge, Mass.: Harvard University Press, 1988), 2–3.

22. Gen. 13:14–15, KJV: "Lift up now thine eyes, and look from the place where thou art northward, and southward, and eastward, and westward: for all the land which thou seest, to thee will I give it, and to thy seed forever." Cf. the repetitions of this promise to Abraham in Gen. 15:18; 17:8; 26:1–5; 28:1–5; 35:11–12; and Ex. 6:4.

23. Baruch Spinoza, *Tractatus Theologico-Politicus*, chap. 19, cited by O'Brien, *God Land*, 49.

24. Spinoza, *Tractatus*, chap. 3, cited in ibid., 48–49.

25. Cf. Baron's discussion of the "Zionist Renascence," *Modern Nationalism and Religion*, 227ff.

26. O'Brien, *God Land*, 50.

27. Ibid.

28. Helmut Gollwitzer, *Reich Gottes und Sozialismus bei Karl Barth* (Munich: Chr. Kaiser Verlag, 1972), 9. Gollwitzer's interpretation of Barth's socialism is disputed by more conservative Barthians, but the fact that Gollwitzer was Barth's personal choice to succeed to his chair of theology in the University of Basel is perhaps a sufficient indication from Barth of the adequacy of Gollwitzer's understanding of his position.

29. Cited in Baron, *Modern Nationalism and Religion*, 202.

30. Pedro Ramet, "Religion and Nationalism in Yugoslavia," in *Religion and Nationalism in Soviet and East European Politics*, ed. Ramet, 166.

31. Baron, *Modern Nationalism and Religion*, 16, emphasis added.

32. Baron quotes and seems to be influenced on this point by a Croat nationalist leader, Kukulievich, who declared in 1848: "Byzantium and Rome succeeded in separating the Serbs and the Croats, but the fraternal tie which unites them is so strong that henceforth nothing in the world will be able to sever it." Ibid., 188. But there is precious little evidence since 1848 that their linguistic unity provides a sufficient basis for their "fraternal tie."

33. Ibid., 111.

34. Cited in ibid., 102.

35. Ramet, ed., *Religion and Nationalism*, Introduction, 19.

36. Cited in Baron, *Modern Nationalism and Religion*, 20.

37. Spas T. Raikin, "Nationalism and the Bulgarian Orthodox Church," *Religion and Nationalism in Soviet and East European Politics*, ed. Ramet, 187.

38. Cited in ibid., 198.

39. Cf. Trond Gilberg, "Religion and Nationalism in Romania," ibid., esp. 181.

40. Vincent C. Chrypinski, "Church and Nationality in Postwar Poland," ibid., 137.

41. Cf. my article, "Promise and Peril in Poland," *The Christian Century* 98, no. 3 (January 28, 1981): 73–77; or my essay "Poland," *Three Worlds of Christian-Marxist Encounters*, ed. Nicholas Piediscalzi and Robert Thobaben (Philadelphia: Fortress Press, 1985), 81–98.

42. Leslie Laszlo, "Religion and Nationality in Hungary," ibid., 146.

43. Nancy Lubin, "Nancy Lubin Examines the Complexities of Central Asia," *United States Institute of Peace Journal* 6, no. 4 (August 1993): 4–5.

44. Salo Baron, *Modern Nationalism and Religion*, 82–83, summarizes the teaching of Alfred Rosenberg, whom Hitler appointed in 1934 to supervise the total system of Nazi ideological education: The Christian doctrine of love always runs counter to the essential Teutonic sense of honor, and its offshoot in the modern humanitarian idea is an "abstract wishful phantom." "Conversely the history of the religion of blood is the great world narration of the rise and decline of peoples, their heroes and thinkers, their inventors and artists." Everything of value in human history has derived from the four Aryan races of Indians, Persians, Greco-Romans, and Teutons. Now that this "myth of blood" is being given free reign, it would create the "truly German church" and the "uniform German national culture."

Baron's response: "It was with such high-sounding 'mystical' rubbish that the minds of German youth were turned from Christian ethics to the worship of an apotheosized 'race' and the glorification of war."

Our further response now must be that we shall end the apotheosis of any political form of religio-nationalism, for the sake of co-creating the reliogiocultural basis for our emerging universal human community.

45. Paul Tillich, *The Protestant Era*, tr. James Luther Adams (Chicago: University of Chicago Press, 1948), 59.

46. These are terms that Tillich used to describe his "personal feeling" in lectures that he delivered at the Deutsche Hochschule für Politik in Berlin in 1951 and published in *Political Expectation* (New York: Harper & Row, 1971), 180.

47. Tillich, *The Protestant Era*, 60.

48. This is a part of Mircea Eliade's remarks at the memorial service held for Tillich at the University of Chicago. Eliade's remarks were published as "Paul Tillich and the History of Religions," in *The Future of Religions*, ed. Jerald C. Brauer (New York: Harper & Row, 1966), 31–32.

49. Ibid., 88; Tillich's lecture is entitled "The Significance of the History of Religions for the Systematic Theologian."

50. Ibid., 93.

51. Emmanuel Hirsch, *Deutschlands Schicksal* (Göttingen: Vandenhoeck & Ruprecht, 1920), 153–54, tr. and cited by Jack Forstman, *Christian Faith in Dark Times* (Louisville, Ky.: Westminster/John Knox Press, 1992), 70.

52. Wilhelm and Marion Pauck, *Paul Tillich: His Life and Thought* (New York: Harper & Row, 1976), 1:153.

53. Adolf Hitler, *Mein Kampf*, tr. Ralph Mannheim (Boston: Houghton-Mifflin Co., 1943), 42; cited in Ernest B. Koenker, *Secular Salvations* (Philadelphia: Fortress Press, 1965), 154.

54. Ibid., 157.

55. O'Brien, *God Land*, 65.

56. Winthrop Hudson, ed., *Nationalism and Religion in America* (New York: Harper & Row, 1970), xi.

57. Cited in ibid., xxviii.

58. Cited in Garry Wills, *Under God: Religion and American Politics* (New York: Simon & Schuster, 1990), 207, emphasis added.

59. Cited in ibid., 208, from Cotton Mather's *Magnalia Christi Americana*, emphasis added.

60. Included in *Sourcebook of American Methodism*, ed. Frederick A. Norwood (Nashville: Abingdon Press, 1982), 504–5.

61. Albert J. Beveridge, "For the Greater Republic, Not for Imperialism," included in Hudson, *Nationalism and Religion in America*, 117, emphasis added.

62. Cf. William J. Wolf, *The Almost Chosen People: A Study of the Religion of Abraham Lincoln* (Garden City, N.Y.: Doubleday & Co., 1959).

63. Reinhold Niebuhr, *The Irony of American History* (New York: Charles Scribner's Sons, 1952), 173.

64. Cited in Ramet, *Religion and Nationalism*, 7.

65. Cited in Baron, *Modern Nationalism and Religion*, 209, from Dostoevsky, "Speech on Pushkin," *Pages from the Journal of an Author* (Boston, 1916).

66. Cited in ibid., 182.

67. Dimitry Pospielovsky, "The Neo-Slavophile Trend and Its Relation to the Contemporary Religious Revival in the USSR," in *Religion and Nationalism*, ed. Ramet, 45.

68. Baron, *Modern Nationalism and Religion*, 195.

69. Pospielovsky, "The Neo-Slavophile Trend," 56–57.

70. Russell Richey and Donald Jones, eds., *American Civil Religion* (New York: Harper & Row, 1974), 15–16; the last sentence is their quotation from Robert Bellah.

71. Baron, *Modern Nationalism and Religion*, 128–29.

72. Robert Bellah, "American Civil Religion in the 1970s," in *American Civil Religion*, ed. Richey and Jones, 270, emphasis added.

73. Arend Theodeor van Leeuwen, *Christianity in World History: The Meeting of the Faiths of East and West*, tr. H. H. Hoskins (New York: Charles Scribner's Sons, 1966), 436.

74. Ibid., 232.

75. Koenker, *Secular Salvations*, 162–67.

76. Ibid., 34–35.

77. Ralph Henry Gabriel, *The Course of American Democratic Thought: An Intellectual History since 1851* (New York: Ronald Press, 1940), 412; cited in ibid., 72, emphasis added.

78. O'Brien, *God Land*, 80.

79. Baron, *Modern Nationalism and Religion*, 10.

80. Ibid., 131.

81. Ernst Troeltsch, *The Social Teaching of the Christian Churches*, tr. Olive Wyon (New York: Macmillan Co., 1931), 1:331.

82. Georges Florovsky, *Christianity and Culture* (Belmont, Mass.: Nordland, 1974), 131; cited by Alan Scarfe, "National Consciousness and Christianity in Eastern Europe," in *Religion and Nationalism*, ed. Ramet, 31.

83. John Ferguson, *War and Peace in the World's Religions*, ix.

84. I found 1505 entries under relevant headings in the holdings of the Northwestern University libraries, including the library of Garrett-Evangelical Theological Seminary.

Several of the best resources that have come to my attention are published by the Center for Global Nonviolence Planning Project of the Spark M. Matsunaga Institute for Peace of the University of Hawaii.

85. Puri, "Preface" to *Gandhi on War and Peace*, ix.

86. Thich Minh Chau, "Five Principles for a New Global Moral Order," in *Buddhism and Nonviolent Global Problem-Solving*, ed. Paige and Gilliatt, 87.

87. Gurudeva Sivaya Subramuniyaswami, "Hindu," *Nonviolence in Hawaii's Spiritual Traditions*, ed. Glenn Paige and Sarah Gilliatt (Honolulu: University of Hawaii, 1991), 60–61.

88. I have developed the Christian perspective on peace at length in *A Christology of Peace* (Louisville, Ky.: Westminster/John Knox Press, 1989).

89. Ferguson, *War and Peace in the World's Religions*, 130.

90. Wasim Siddiqui, "Islamic," in *Nonviolence in Hawaii's Spiritual Traditions*, ed. Paige and Gilliatt, 69–70.

91. Ferguson, *War and Peace in the World's Religions*, 130–31.

92. Cited in ibid., 143.

93. Tony Pelle, "Baha'i," in *Nonviolence in Hawaii's Spiritual Traditions*, ed. Paige and Gilliatt, 13.

94. Cited in ibid., 23.

95. Jürgen Moltmann, *Creating a Just Future: The Politics of Peace and the Ethics of Creation in a Threatened World* (London: SCM Press, and Philadelphia: Trinity Press International, 1989), 91.

96. Julia Ching, *Confucianism and Christianity* (New York: Kodansha International, 1977), 188.

97. Moltmann, *Creating a Just Future*, 97.

98. Ching, *Confucianism and Christianity*, 207.

99. A. T. Ariyaratne, "Nonviolent Buddhist Problem-Solving in Sri Lanka," in *Buddhism and Nonviolent Global Problem-Solving*, ed. Paige and Gilliatt, 61.

100. Ibid., 69–70.

101. Yoichi Kawada, "The Importance of the Buddhist Concept of Karma for World Peace," in *Buddhism and Nonviolent Global Problem-Solving*, ed. Paige and Gilliatt, 97.

102. Ibid., 101–2.

103. What religiously sensitive person could fail to appreciate the profound wisdom they draw from their Lotus Sutra? Consider what Yoichi Shikano writes in "Disarmament Efforts from the Standpoint of Mahayana Buddhism," in *Buddhism and Nonviolent Global Problem-Solving*, ed. Paige and Gilliatt, 111–12:

> It reveals the supreme law that pervades the universe and human existence. The eternal life is what can be called the "greater (universal) self" or "non-self (selflessness)" in contrast to the "lesser (individual) self." On the basis of the "greater self," the *bodhisattvas* of the Lotus Sutra,

truly and freely displaying creative vitality of life and prompted by the passion of joy, go forth in high spirits to wage a spiritual campaign to reform from the roots the actual society which is filled with suffering. In this way Buddhism essentially directs itself to create infinite value in life and society, based on the life condition of the "greater self," the true self.

104. Ibid., 113.

105. Ibid., 117.

106. Puri, *Gandhi on War and Peace*, 198.

107. Ibid., 220.

108. Hans Küng, *Global Responsibility*, tr. John Bowden (London: SCM Press, 1991).

109. Ibid., 29 and 76.

110. Ibid., 51–53.

111. Ibid., xvi.

112. Ibid., 27.

113. Ibid., 43.

114. I think the dialogue in the Parliament of World Religions as it met in Chicago in the summer of 1993 to revise and finally to accept the "global ethic" that Küng originally drafted confirms this point.

115. Ibid., 54.

116. Ibid., 56, 59.

117. Ibid., 104.

118. Quoted in R. Mitchell, *The Society of the Muslim Brothers* (London, 1969), 30, from which it is cited by Albert Hourani, *A History of the Arab Peoples* (Cambridge, Mass.: Harvard University Press, 1991), 348.

119. Ibid., 398.

120. Sayyid Qutb, *Ma'alim fi'l-tariq* [*Signposts on the Path*] (Cairo, 1964), 4–5; cited in English translation in ibid., 445–46.

121. Ibid., 446.

122. Malcolm X, *The Autobiography of Malcolm X*, with the assistance of Alex Haley (New York: Grove Press, 1964), 298; cited in Paul Lehmann, *The Transfiguration of Politics* (New York: Harper & Row, 1975), 203.

123. Ibid., Malcolm X, 366, Lehmann, 200.

124. Ibid., Malcolm X, 361–62, Lehmann, 204.

125. Ibid., Malcolm X, 376–77, Lehmann, 205.

126. Martin Luther King Jr., *Where Do We Go from Here: Chaos or Community?* (New York: Harper & Row, 1967; New York: Bantam Books, 1968), 71.

127. Ibid., 197.

128. Ibid., 204.

129. I have reported and interpreted this praxis in many publications. Some of the major ones are *Must Walls Divide?* (New York: Friendship Press, 1981); "Church and State in the Struggle for Human Rights in Poland," *The Journal of Law and Religion* 2, no. 1 (1984): 153–76; and *The Moral Rejection of Nuclear Deterrence* (New York: Friendship Press, 1985).

130. Will, *Must Walls Divide?* 32.

131. There was realistic basis for this suspicion; it should have been understood, however, more largely from the standpoint of a difference in context. When Karoly Toth's *Reorientation to Peace* (Bangalore: Indian SPCK, 1985), which consists of his reports and addresses to the Christian Peace Conference, is read, one finds some good theological reflection on the theology of peace in its relation to many issues around the whole world but nothing directed to the issues in Eastern Europe or the Soviet Union.

When he addressed, for instance, "Human Rights and International Tensions" in a meeting of the C.P.C. in Sofia, Bulgaria, in 1974, where I also was present, he referred to situations in Chile, Vietnam, and Israel but not then or ever publicly to situations in Eastern Europe. Cf. 102–6.

The situation was quite different, however, in the working committee of the Churches Human Rights Programme for Implementation of the Helsinki Final Act, which was also chaired by a church leader from Eastern Europe, Frau OKR Christa Lewek of the Federation of Evangelical Churches in the German Democratic Republic. As an alternate member from the National Council of the Churches of Christ in the U.S.A., which created this program with the Canadian Council of Churches and the Conference of European Churches from 1980 to 1985, I participated in almost all of its meetings and know that it dealt with many issues in both East and West.

132. Needless to say, this address was never published by the Christian Peace Conference under the difficult conditions of the mid-1970s. I am quoting from my manuscript.

133. Lest it be thought that this was the only such occasion, let me give one more example. The following is a paragraph from a letter sent to the Christian Peace Conference in Prague and the Department of External Church Relations of the Russian Orthodox Church in Moscow on June 13, 1980. Christians Associated for Relations with Eastern Europe (CAREE), of which I was then president, wrote to oppose the Soviet invasion of Afghanistan:

> We owe one another the truth in love, that we may all be guided and corrected thereby. In this spirit and context, we must strongly deplore the intervention by the Soviet Union in Afghanistan, especially in its present military form, and, as Christians committed to justice and peace, oppose it. Intervention by one country in the affairs of another, even if initiated for socially desirable reasons, cannot be condoned. Superpower intervention contains especially grave dangers, as it becomes a politically destructive force far beyond the violated borders. Interference by one country in another country's autonomy and sovereignty, whether by military, political or economic means, is a violation of respect for the integrity of the other, on which peace is built.

When I came to Moscow with a group of students six months later, the welcoming speech of Metropolitan Juvenally, chairman of the Department of External Church Relations, who undoubtedly had been required to discuss the letter with the Soviet government, included the probably mandatory sentence: "We sometimes have some difficulty with Professor Will." Otherwise, he continued to welcome me and others across these terrible margins as a brother.

134. Philip P. Hallie, *Lest Innocent Blood Be Shed: The Story of the Village of Le Chambon and How Goodness Happened There* (New York: Harper & Row, 1980), 2–3.

135. Ibid., 4.

136. Ibid., 10.

# Index

274

Printed in March 2021
by Rotomail Italia S.p.A., Vignate (MI) - Italy

Printed in March 2021
by Rotomail Italia S.p.A., Vignate (MI) - Italy